The Americans: 1976

The Americans: 1976

An Inquiry into Fundamental Concepts of Man
Underlying Various U.S. Institutions

Critical Choices for Americans

Volume II

Edited by

Irving Kristol

and

Paul Weaver

Lexington Books
D.C. Heath and Company
Lexington, Massachusetts
Toronto   London

Library of Congress Cataloging in Publication Data

Main entry under title:
The Americans, 1976.

(Critical choices for Americans; v. 2)
"A report to the Commission on Critical Choices."
Includes index.
1. United States—Social policy—Addresses, essays, lectures. 2. United States—Social conditions—Addresses, essays, lectures. 3. National characteristics, American—Addresses, essays, lectures. I. Kristol, Irving. II. Weaver, Paul, 1942-   III. Commission on Critical Choices for Americans. IV. Series.
HN65.A683   309.1'73'0925   75-44719
ISBN 0-669-00145-4

Foreword

The Commission on Critical Choices for Americans, a nationally representative, bipartisan group of 42 prominent Americans, was brought together on a voluntary basis by Nelson A. Rockefeller. After assuming the Vice Presidency of the United States, Mr. Rockefeller, the chairman of the Commission, became an ex officio member. The Commission's assignment was to develop information and insights which would bring about a better understanding of the problems confronting America. The Commission sought to identify the critical choices that must be made if these problems are to be met.

The Commission on Critical Choices grew out of a New York State study of the Role of a Modern State in a Changing World. This was initiated by Mr. Rockefeller, who was then Governor of New York, to review the major changes taking place in Federal-State relationships. It became evident, however, that the problems confronting New York State went beyond State boundaries and had national and international implications.

In bringing the Commission on Critical Choices together, Mr. Rockefeller said:

As we approach the 200th Anniversary of the founding of our Nation, it has become clear that institutions and values which have accounted for our astounding progress during the past two centuries are straining to cope with the massive problems of the current era. The increase in the tempo of change, and the vastness and complexity of the wholly new situations which are evolving with accelerated change, create a widespread sense that our political and social system has serious inadequacies.

We can no longer continue to operate on the basis of reacting to crises, counting on crash programs and the expenditure of huge sums of money to solve our problems. We have got to understand and project present trends, to take command of the forces that are emerging, to extend our freedom and wellbeing as citizens and the future of other nations and peoples in the world.

Because of the complexity and interdependence of issues facing America and the world today, the Commission has organized its work into six panels, which emphasize the interrelationships of critical choices rather than treating each one in isolation.

The six panels are:

Panel I: Energy and Its Relationship to Ecology, Economics and World Stability;

Panel II: Food, Health, World Population and Quality of Life;

Panel III: Raw Materials, Industrial Development, Capital Formation, Employment and World Trade;

Panel IV: International Trade and Monetary Systems, Inflation and the Relationships Among Differing Economic Systems;

Panel V: Change, National Security and Peace

Panel VI: Quality of Life of Individuals and Communities in the U.S.A.

The Commission assigned, in these areas, more than 100 authorities to prepare expert studies in their fields of special competence. The Commission's work has been financed by The Third Century Corporation, a New York not-for-profit organization. The corporation has received contributions from individuals and foundations to advance the Commission's activities. The Commission is grateful to the Vincent Astor Foundation particularly for its contributions to the work of our Panel VI, "Quality of Life of Individuals and Communities in the U.S.A."

The Commission is determined to make available to the public these background studies and the reports of those panels which have completed their deliberations. The background studies are the work of the authors and do not necessarily represent the views of the Commission or its members.

This volume is one of the series of volumes the Commission will publish in the belief that it will contribute to the basic thought and foresight America will need in the future.

WILLIAM J. RONAN
Acting Chairman
Commission on Critical Choices
for Americans

Members of the Commission

THE HONORABLE JOHN RHODES
  Minority Leader
  United States House of Representatives

Acting Chairman

WILLIAM J. RONAN
  Chairman, Port Authority of New York
  and New Jersey

Members

IVAN ALLAN, JR.
  Former Mayor of Atlanta, Georgia

MARTIN ANDERSON
  Senior Fellow, Hoover Institution of War,
  Revolution and Peace, Stanford University

ROBERT O. ANDERSON
  Chairman, Atlantic Richfield Company

MRS. W. VINCENT ASTOR
  Philanthropist and Author

WILLIAM O. BAKER
  President, Bell Telephone Laboratories, Inc.

DANIEL J. BOORSTIN
  Senior Historian, Smithsonian Institution

NORMAN ERNEST BORLAUG
  Agronomist; Nobel Peace Prize, 1970

ERNEST L. BOYER
  Chancellor, State University of New York

GUIDO CALABRESI
  John Thomas Smith Professor of Law,
  Yale University

LEO CHERNE
Executive Director, Research Institute
of America, Inc.

JOHN S. FOSTER, JR.
Vice President for Energy Research
and Development, TRW, Inc.

LUTHER H. FOSTER
President, Tuskegee Institute

NANCY HANKS
Chairman, National Endowment for the Arts

BELTON KLEBERG JOHNSON
Texas Rancher and Businessman

CLARENCE B. JONES
Former Editor and Publisher,
The New York Amsterdam News

JOSEPH LANE KIRKLAND
Secretary-Treasurer, AFL-CIO

JOHN H. KNOWLES, M.D.
President, Rockefeller Foundation

DAVID S. LANDES
Leroy B. Williams Professor of History
and Political Science, Harvard University

MARY WELLS LAWRENCE
Chairman and Chief Executive Officer,
Wells, Rich, Greene, Inc.

SOL M. LINOWITZ
Senior Partner of Coudert Brothers

EDWARD J. LOGUE
Former President and Chief Executive Officer,
New York State Urban Development Corporation

EDWARD TELLER
   Senior Research Fellow, Hoover Institution
   on War, Revolution and Peace.
   Stanford University

ARTHUR K. WATSON*
   Former Ambassador to France

MARINA VON NEUMANN WHITMAN
   Distinguished Public Service Professor
   of Economics, University of Pittsburgh

CARROLL L. WILSON
   Professor, Alfred P. Sloan
   School of Management,
   Massachusetts Institute of Technology

GEORGE D. WOODS
   Former President, World Bank

Members of the Commission served on the panels. In addition, others assisted
the panels.

BERNARD BERELSON
Senior Fellow
President Emeritus
The Population Council

C. FRED BERGSTEN
Senior Fellow
The Brookings Institution

ORVILLE G. BRIM, JR.
President
Foundation for Child Development

LESTER BROWN
President
Worldwatch Institute

LLOYD A. FREE
President
Institute for International Social Research

*Deceased

J. GEORGE HARRAR
Former President
Rockefeller Foundation

WALTER LEVY
Economic Consultant

PETER G. PETERSON
Chairman of the Board
Lehman Brothers

ELSPETH ROSTOW
Dean, Division of General and Comparative Studies
University of Texas

WALTER W. ROSTOW
Professor of Economics and History
University of Texas

SYLVESTER L. WEAVER
Communications Consultant

JOHN G. WINGER
Vice President
Energy Economics Division
Chase Manhattan Bank

Preface

Over the past decade, it has become clear to many Americans that the institutions and values which have accounted for our astounding progress as a nation are straining to cope with the problems of today. Many Americans feel that our institutions are no longer up to the task that must be done.

When the Commission on Critical Choices for Americans began its work, it decided to initiate a study of the ideas of human nature that are implicit in our institutions and our way of life. It was clear that as a nation, we did not have as sensitive and aware, and as good an understanding as we should have, regarding the basic philosophy reflected in our political and social institutions in the rapidly changing and increasingly complex world we now live in.

Panel VI of the Commission—charged with the study of "The Quality of Life of Individuals and Communities in the U.S.A."—decided to commission a major work of scholarship in this regard. The Panel asked Irving Kristol and Paul Weaver to select fifteen prominent Americans to analyze the ideas and values of human nature inherent in United States institutions—and also to select the institutions. Their thought-provoking essays on our founding and way of life offer a new perspective on America—a warmer understanding of our country as it grew up, and new ideas about an America of tomorrow.

W.J.R.

Contents

Introduction

Irving Kristol and **Paul Weaver**

No view of human nature is entirely false—else men would not hold it for long. But none is entirely true, either—else the philosophical question of "the nature of human nature" would have yielded a scientific answer and would have been settled beyond all argument. And these two propositions, once accepted, themselves add up to a third conception of human nature—as capable of knowing itself, but never finally; as capable of shaping itself, but never ultimately; as capable of being shaped, but never totally. This is a view that is congenial to the Judeo-Christian tradition, but quite uncongenial to various modern ideologies, whether of the right or of the left, which insist that man is either fully the master of his fate or completely a slave to it.

Any particular conception of human nature is an exercise in self-definition. As such it has implications extending to every aspect of life, from the relationship between men and women to the way society should be governed. It is only to be expected, given what is at stake, that such efforts at self-definition should assume many forms. In a sense, the history of political philosophy is the record of a competitive struggle among such various self-definitions. Each philosophy reflects the circumstances out of which it emerges—but each also shapes those circumstances through its intellectual cogency and moral power.

In an age when textbooks routinely "place" political thinkers in their social-economic-political (and even psychoanalytic) context, we today are readily inclined to take account of the circumstantial background of ideas. It is a peculiar feature of the modern mind, however, that it is always inclined to underestimate the power of the ideas themselves and to see them as little more than "superstructures" based on a firmer and more material reality. Yet it is ideas that form men's minds, inflame their imaginations, soften or harden their hearts, and end up recreating the world which in the first instance gave birth to them.

No one has pointed to the active power of ideas with more perspicacity and eloquence than Alexis de Tocqueville when, in 1852, he looked back to ask what caused the great French Revolution:

Was it all the politicians, princes, ministers and great lords of the eighteenth century? They do not need our blessing or our curses, but only our pity, for they almost always did otherwise than they intended, and in the end arrived at a result they detested. The great shapers of this formidable revolution were every one of them men who did not take the smallest part in public affairs: they were, as everyone knows, authors. It was political theory, and often that theory at its most abstract, which put into our fathers' hands the germs of those new ideas which have since suddenly blossomed into political institutions and civil laws unknown to their forebears.

And we must note that what political theory did here with such brilliance, is continually done everywhere, although more secretly and slowly. Among all civilised peoples, the study of politics creates, or at least gives shape to, general ideas; and from those general ideas are formed the problems in the midst of which politicians must struggle, and also the laws which they imagine they create. Political theories form a sort of intellectual atmosphere breathed by both governors and governed in society, and both unwittingly derive from it the principles of their action.

Other thoughtful students of history have, at different times and in their own ways, made much the same point. John Adams, for example, declared that "the real American revolution" antedated the Declaration of Independence, and consisted of a "radical change in the principles, opinions, sentiments and affections of the people." And John Maynard Keynes, in the midst of the Great Depression of the 1930s, penned lines that have become memorable:

... The ideas of economists and political philosophers, both when they are right and when they are wrong, are more powerful than is commonly understood. Indeed the world is ruled by little else. Practical men, who believe themselves to be quite exempt from any intellectual influences, are usually the slave of some defunct economist. Madmen in authority, who hear voices in the air, are distilling their frenzy from some academic scribbler of a few years back. I am sure that the power of vested interests is vastly exaggerated compared with the gradual encroachment of ideas.

Nor do these ideas have to be clean and precise. They may emerge, especially at the beginning, as moods or vague presentiments that find rational articulation only later. This is what both Confucius and Plato had in mind when they independently declared that a change in the mode of music forebode a change in the constitution of the political and social order. Can anyone doubt, in retrospect, that the rise of rock music in the 1950s foreshadowed the youthful discontents of the 1960s? A dionysiac music, celebrating the liberation of impulse and passion, is not easily assimilated to a bourgeois way of life whose fundamental principle is individual self-government sustained by individual self-discipline and self-control. And, eventually, various aggressive philosophies of "liberation" did appear to give theoretical sanction and significance to this new effort at human self-definition.

When any way of life, and the economic-social-political order associated with that way of life, has been in existence for a long time, the particular assumptions about human nature on which it is based become so familiar as to be invisible. Thus, that way of life which we may call liberal democracy, and which has been dominant in the West for the past two hundred years, has established a set of rules for self-government and the good life. These rules are then regarded as having a life and vitality of their own, are studied in the abstract, and are often applied in the abstract. Imperceptibly, we are led to believe that it is the rules that are the very substance of the regime—and we are then taken aback when the rules of a liberal democratic order, applied to different peoples in different circumstances, seem not to possess the viability we expected. What we forget is that rules do not work unless there is a prior willingness to abide by the rules.

In other words: the rules only work when the kinds of people to whom they apply want to see them work. A free market economy will not survive unless people are willing to respect the law of contract; if everyone tries to cheat, and if all contracts have to be enforced by the courts and the police, the system will collapse. Liberal capitalism, then, assumes a high level of personal integrity and mutual trust, yet one would never learn this by reading our economics textbooks, which simply take these human qualities for granted. And to achieve this degree of personal integrity and human trust, you need human beings who conceive of themselves in a certain way, who define themselves in a certain way—in short, who incarnate a particular idea of "human nature," of what it is "natural" and "right" for human beings to be and do. It is obvious—one has only to look at the United States and Japan—that more than one idea of human nature is capable of producing those personal traits that are consistent with a liberal capitalist economy. It is equally obvious (or ought to be) that not all ideas of human nature are endowed with this capability.

As with economics, so with politics. Our students of civics and American government have, by now, a routinely technological interest in the mechanisms of our political system. They study how it works, and pay little attention to why it works. They certainly pay very little attention to the basic assumptions about human nature made by the Founding Fathers—assumptions on which our institutions were established, assumptions which both define and delimit the aspirations of the American polity. Without an examination of such assumptions, all sorts of important questions never even get asked. Why, for instance, should a minority of 49 percent quickly accept the election of a president by a 51 percent majority? It's an interesting question, and exploring it will lead to some important reflections as to *what kinds* of people, constituting *what kind* of political community, will permit themselves to submit to such non-self-evident laws of political arithmetic. That not all peoples are of this kind, and that not all political communities are so constituted, are facts which even a cursory acquaintance with history and current events will establish. Still, it is astonishing how many Americans, in their ethnocentricity, are able to close their eyes to these facts and their implications. We are eager to "make the world safe for democracy" without considering, as Martin Diamond so aptly puts it, how one goes about "making democracy safe for the world."

Or take another, largely unnoticed, tiny aspect of the American democratic system. When a representative is elected to Congress, whom does he represent? Is his constituency those who voted for him, or does it also include those who voted against him? In the United States, the answer is clearly the latter—but the reasons behind this answer are rarely explored, though they are certainly not obvious. Any such exploration would soon find itself enmeshed in the larger question of why our two-party system is so relatively non-ideological, and would then have to inquire further as to what kind of people Americans are, or think themselves to be, and how much significance is attached to politics as against the pleasures and obligations of private life in a liberal community. The ancient Greeks, for whom politics was noble as contrasted with the "idiocy" of private life, would find our theory of representation both incomprehensible and reprehensible. Marxists today, for the most part, would agree with the ancient Greeks as against modern liberals. In the end, what is at issue is a conception of the nature of man, a theory of human fulfillment and frustration, a notion of where "true" human happiness is to be discovered. If one genuinely believes that politics is all-important, one cannot ultimately accept the rather easy-going American theory of representation.

Thus, from this point of view, one of the most interesting developments in the two great liberal democracies of Britain and the United States, over recent decades, has been the growing predominance of professional sports over the amateur variety. That seems far removed from political philosophy or even political reality. But if politics is eventually shaped by the human nature it must cope with, then it does indeed make a difference if you believe in sportsmanship and "fair play" on the one hand, or if on the other hand, you believe with the late Vince Lombardi that "winning isn't everything, it's the only thing." President Nixon was a known admirer of Mr. Lombardi—a poster bearing the Lombardi maxim hung in the headquarters of his Reelection Committee—and it is not far-fetched to speculate on how this may have affected his conception of what was proper and legitimate behavior in politics.

Though prevailing ideas and assumptions about human nature have profound political consequences, and silently shape much of government policy, it does not follow that statesmen ought to be scholarly students of the subject. It is as undesirable for statesmen to be professional psychologists as it is for professional philosophers to be kings. The reason, quite simply, is that statesmen are concerned with reality, and no theory is a sure and comprehensive guide to reality, which is always larger than the sum of all theories. Indeed, a statesman who is overly impressed with theory is in grave danger of thinking himself both wiser and more powerful than, in fact, he is. He can then become "the man of system" about whom Adam Smith, in his *Theory of Moral Sentiments*, wrote so shrewdly:

The man of system . . . seems to imagine that he can arrange the different members of a great society with as much ease as the hand arranges the different pieces upon a chessboard. He does not consider that the pieces upon the chessboard have no other principle of motion besides that which the hand impresses upon them, but that, in the great chessboard of human society, every single piece has a principle of motion of its own, altogether different from that which the legislature might choose to impress upon it.

In American society today, as it breeds ever larger numbers of professionals, experts, and technicians, "men of system" are becoming more numerous and more influential than before. Such people are more likely to populate the academy and government bureaucracies than the political arena proper, but this actually gives them more power rather than less, since they are in entrenched positions which are protected from "mere" political interference—i.e., from any process of political learning that might cause them to modify their ideas. These are the conscientious and learned people who "know" what the American public "really" wants—whether it be in city planning, automobile design, medical care, or even in modes of child-rearing. They aren't always entirely wrong, of course; but they are never entirely right either.

The existence of these people, in such enormous numbers, in these important positions, is a relatively new problem for the American statesman, and potentially a very serious one. Traditionally statesmen have relied upon their common-sense understanding of "their" people, on their historical sense of what was generally right and proper for this kind of political community, and on their intuition as to the source of grievance and its appropriate remedy. In Michael Oakeshott's phrase, their skill has been that of continually "tending to the arrangement of society"—a kind of gardener's skill that it is impossible to express or describe in any rigorous, theoretical fashion. The successful statesman is someone who has a "green thumb" in matters political, and this is altogether different from having a scientific understanding of horticulture. Today, however, the statesman more and more resembles an experienced gardener who is exposed to—is deluged with—a barrage of conflicting horticultural advice. There is no surer way to make him lose his nerve and thereby wreck the garden.

The problem, then, is not to provide the statesman with a "correct" theory of human nature on which he can base his policies—there is no such "correct" theory—but rather to protect him from overexposure to the bewildering variety of doctrinaire theories propounded by our latter-day "men of system." Under the circumstances that now prevail, alas, such protection is quite impossible. Among these circumstances is the ever-increasing involvement of government in almost every aspect of the citizen's life. Legislation against crime, against poverty, against unemployment, legislation for education, for transportation, for conservation, for mental health services—all these will and must be based on preconceptions about American human nature. A "welfare state" has to be rooted in an idea as to what constitutes a citizen's well-being, and a democratic welfare state has also to be alert to the citizen's own conception of his well-being (or ill-being). So as government expands, ideas of human nature naturally proliferate and impinge directly upon the statesman's activities.

That being the case, the only possible protection for the statesman is a more acute and self-conscious awareness of his predicament. When innocence is gone—when, as we say, the times are "out of joint"—the only cure for rampant "sophistication" is a larger and more skeptical sophistication. In a sense, that is the justification for this collection of essays about "human nature." It is not merely to show the statesman—and the citizen, too, for in a democracy we are all "statesmen," to a degree—that he has been operating all along with implicit beliefs about human nature, that he has, as it were, been speaking prose all his life. Rather, the purpose is to make us all aware that we have more theories of human nature than we know what to do with, and that we have a tendency to slide from one to the other in an unthinking way, or to hold incompatible beliefs without facing up to that fact. The sad truth of the matter is that we haven't been talking prose all of our lives; much of the time we have been talking gibberish.

For example, as Daniel P. Moynihan suggests in his essay, American thinking about social policy seems torn between two contradictory ideas of man in society. On the one hand, we have long insisted on the moral autonomy of people to choose and live as they like; in fact, the historic ambition of social reform has been to bolster that autonomy. On the other hand, our social reformers have often spoken of the beneficiaries of social policy as "stimulus-response" mechanisms—as machines, in effect, utterly devoid of any human characteristic. They are not entirely wrong, of course: There is a sense in which everyone responds reflexively to stimuli of various sorts. And yet there is always a danger that, by viewing citizens in this way, and by treating them accordingly, we will end by reducing rather than strengthening their ability to attain moral autonomy.

Something similar, Thomas Sowell suggests, has happened with the idea of "economic man." Since economic transactions play such a large role in modern life, it is inevitable that we are all today more frequently cast in the role of "economic man" than were our forebears. It is also inevitable that a social science should have emerged—the science of economics—which analyzes our relations to one another *as if* we were nothing but economic men and women. This science does indeed give us a deeper understanding of our economic activities, but its influence can be perverse if our political leaders and opinion leaders take the useful fiction of economic man as a surrogate for the real flesh-and-blood citizen and human being. They have in fact done so—to a degree that has provoked a notable rebelliousness among young people, who quickly perceive that this fiction is demeaning if proposed as a complete conception of human nature. And these young people, in turn, then conclude that it is immoral to "think economically" at all, even about economic matters. Surely our current confusion about ecology, the environment, and economic growth—a confusion in which abstract ideas obstinately collide with one another—has its ultimate source in the fact that certain partial conceptions of human nature claim sovereignty over the whole.

Though statesmen usually rely on their common sense, rather than on any set of theories propounded by political philosophers or social scientists, it is important to remember that common sense, in addition to being a not too common virtue, has its own genesis in the realm of ideas. What we ordinarily call "common sense" is the residue of yesteryear's theories—about human nature, the social order, international relations—after these theories have been tested and refined by experience: It is rare in a liberal democracy for a statesman to hold beliefs after they have been demonstrated to be inadequate to current circumstances—such fanaticism goes against the grain of democratic politics, since it makes the statesman an opponent of public opinion rather than its spokesman. On the other hand, in periods of flux and tumult, the consensus which constitutes "public opinion" is shattered and fragmented. The statesman, then, discovers that "common sense" has become an aspiration rather than a reality. He finds himself speaking out of both sides of his mouth and carrying water on both shoulders. This, in turn, creates a cynical distrust of politics itself among the citizenry.

Something of this sort, it is clear, has been happening in the United States during the past fifteen years. There is no traditional value, no venerable cliché, that has not been challenged or inverted. For the most part, this "transvaluation of values" has been the work of a new generation moving in massive numbers into American society during the 1960s. There is nothing unusual in that: Generational conflict in a democracy is almost always more acute and more important than class conflict. What is new is the scope and depth of the conflict.

In the field of mental health, for instance, Robert Coles' essay shows how, after many decades of development and debate, the psychiatric community is increasingly uncertain that there is even such a thing as "mental health," however hard it may be to define. One now hears it commonly said that people in our mental institutions are not really sick, but that society cruelly defines them as sick. In the area of ideology, Peter Berger argues that the issues which historically divided left and right have been muddled, in some instances to the point where what was "left" a century ago has now become "right," and vice versa—leaving all of us in a state of utter confusion. In recent years this chaos has come to encompass, as Sheila Rothman illustrates, the one non-political institution which is the ultimate source of social stability: the family. When people are no longer certain what a family is or should be—and, by extension, what it means to be a man, woman, or child—their uncertainty infects every other institution and every other accepted value.

And how does a democratic statesman cope with such a state of affairs? His natural instinct will be to temporize, to equivocate, to conciliate, to "fudge," all in the desperate hope that time will finally produce that consensus without which he cannot govern. His instinct will tell him that, in a society so evidently suffering the agonies of transition, patience is the supreme political virtue. This instinct is surely right. The trouble is that it is precisely when society is experiencing such travail that it most desperately feels the need of, and most importunately demands, "leadership." So he will have to sponsor all sorts of "reforms" which he may not himself have much faith in, which in many cases may be more symbolic than real, and which frequently have no real bearing on the deeper sources of discontent—and which, since they rarely "cure" anything, may even have the effect of aggravating an already inflamed condition. Then, in his heart of hearts, he can only pray that the body politic is basically healthy enough to survive both its maladies and his ministrations.

Will it then do him (and us) any good also to peruse a volume such as this one, which tries—through a discussion of the different conceptions of human nature which underlie our prevailing dissensus—to offer a larger and longer perspective? It just might. Such a perspective itself provides a kind of knowledge, and knowledge is power, if only the power to endure. It is also a useful antidote for pseudo-knowledge—for doctrinaire theories and passionate myths, all so sincerely held as to be (temporarily at least) invulnerable to the disproof of experience. To understand our confusion is to achieve a minor but crucial triumph over that confusion. Even to understand our confusion *as* confusion, rather than as something else, is no negligible achievement. It is to be hoped that these essays do accomplish this latter task, at least.

This volume was prepared as a report *to* the Commission on Critical Choices. Neither the writers nor the choices of subjects were suggested by the Commission; they are entirely the responsibility of the editors. Neither the editors nor any member of the Commission can be assumed to be in agreement with any of the essays that compose it. And since the writers are only too obviously in some disagreement among themselves, neither the editors nor any member of the Commission could possibly be in agreement with all of them.

I

The American Idea of Man: The View from the Founding

Martin Diamond

Americans tend to take for granted the system of representative democracy with which they have lived for upwards of two centuries. Since that system has worked so well for so long, this is perhaps an understandable instinct. But in the course of regarding the system as somehow natural and automatic, many Americans often succumb to the temptation to conclude that any set of "values," any pattern of behavior, any sort of person is as much "at home" in America as any other.

That is not how the Founding Fathers saw it. The system of popular government they designed presupposed a distinctive view of human nature and was intended to encourage the emergence of certain kinds of men. For, as they understood the matter, a system of liberal democracy such as that in the United States could not and would not persist under any and all conditions. In this essay, Martin Diamond describes the Founders' idea of man and what it implied to them about the nature of American democracy.

The philosophical question of what human nature is, and the implication of any particular answer for political life, are very important matters indeed. But they are also—and fortunately—matters that only infrequently need fully and explicitly to be raised in practical politics. This is because the question of human nature comes only at the end of a long chain of reasoning that always has its origin in the immediately practical questions that constitute politics. Those who are curious to know the nature of political things, and who love that knowledge for its own sake, must pursue that whole line of reasoning eagerly and as thoroughly

1

as possible. But it is only seldom necessary that those who must act in politics need press the inquiry to the very last philosophical premise. Indeed, it violates the nature of political practice to force philosophy too violently upon it; the realm of the practical has its own dignity, its own peculiar kind of chasteness. Ordinarily, then, in dealing with practical affairs, the sensible approach is to philosophize grudgingly, and only when a political issue itself compels a philosophic inquiry. But what is most interesting about our present political situation in the United States is that we are apparently in the grip of just such a compelling necessity now.

Before considering precisely how we are now thus compelled, let us first sketch the steps by means of which, in general, the philosophic question of human nature may be found to lie at the bottom of practical political issues.

Politics always begins with the agitation of the practical question: What should we do? What should we do about garbage collection, about local law enforcement, about taxes, about inflation, about détente, about our fundamental laws and institutions? But whenever we ask what to do about any particular problem, large or small, we are, of course, asking what it is *best for us* to do in the circumstances. It is in judging what is "best for us" to do that the roots of politics inevitably reach down to the philosophic issues. For in order to judge what is best for us at any given moment, we need some notion of who we are and want enduringly to be. That is, apart from a very few problems in which the dictates of sheer survival obliterate all other considerations, the political question of what it is best to do about any immediate problem raises necessarily the question of what is good for us in general and in the long run. This is because we always want to deal with the immediate problem in such a way as to wind up with our permanent character still intact or improved. Thus practical politics always points, however vaguely, to the question: What kind of a people or country do we wish fundamentally and enduringly to be?

But the implications go deeper still. The question about what kind of country *we* want to be summons forth the question of what is good for human beings *in general*. Countries, like individuals, in choosing among all the possibilities presented by the welter of human desires and needs, have to have some general standard of human excellence in the light of which, with varying degrees of awareness, they form themselves in particular. Each country is that particular way of being human which results from that country's decision most to achieve, in its particular circumstances, what is best for human beings as such. That is what Aristotle meant, in a famous passage, when he taught that any political community worthy of the name is constituted by its partnership or sharing in some particular view of what is "good and bad" for human beings.

There is one final step to be taken. Any conclusion about what is "good or bad" for human beings must ultimately depend upon a view of what it means to be human, that is, on an idea of what are the human needs and their order of dignity, on what are the human capacities, possibilities, and limits—in short, on an idea of man. In principle, then, any political problem points citizens and politicians to the questions of their country's enduring good, of the human good as such, and, ultimately, to some idea of what conforms to or completes our "human nature."

As was already noted, citizens and politicians do not ordinarily need to make fully philosophic inquiries into such matters. They already have their country "in their bones"; its political-moral presuppositions belong to them by a kind of birthright. Indeed, that is just about what it means to be a country—a community, a commonality, a having-together of certain political-moral ideas in the bones. And citizens and politicians, without plumbing those ideas to their depths, can ordinarily proceed to deal with practical problems simply with common sense and prudence. It is therefore almost always unnecessary to intrude the philosophic issues upon the practical political urgencies. But only *almost* always; sometimes it becomes precisely a practical necessity to raise the deeper questions. This is when the common political-moral ideas have been shaken and uprooted, when citizens and politicians have lost confidence in the foundation upon which their common sense and prudence rest, when the idea of man that has inspirited their fundamental laws has lost its silent persuasiveness.

Is this not how things now stand with us? The old root American ideas have been challenged on nearly every front and cast into doubt by the most powerful contemporary intellectual currents. It is not possible in this essay to discuss the newer ideas that have disordered those traditional American political-moral presuppositions; it suffices only to be reminded of the force and direction of the intellectual onslaught upon them. Perhaps it may all be brought to mind with a single image in which that onslaught often expresses itself—namely, of the American constitutional foundation as belonging to a superseded historical era and thus as dangerously antiquated and obsolete. The typical journalistic cartoons on the "antiquated Electoral College" or the "moribund Congress" are only obvious examples of the denigrating rhetoric of the critics of the constitutional foundation. Whatever the contemporary intellectual basis—Marxist, Freudian, historicist, existentialist, behavioralist—the image tends to be the same: the American constitutional framework as obsoletely inadequate to contemporary needs, as the product of a bygone era, and as resting upon untenable "old hat" theoretical ideas. All this has produced something like a failure of nerve in American public opinion, a causing of citizens and politicians to falter and to be unable to act confidently with the knowledge of their country and its presuppositions that they have "in their bones."

It is by no means the case that average Americans have simply abandoned their traditional beliefs. The contemporary intellectual currents, precisely in being intellectual, have not reached down with full disordering vigor into the stratum of mass public opinion. There remains in that mass a reservoir of affection for the constitutional order and a comfortable capacity to act within it. Nor have most politicians been led to disaffection—though even in this stratum of American politics there is a nervous or resentful sense that somehow the old ideas have been rendered dubious. It is only the closer one comes to the contemporary realms of intellect—the academy, the intelligentsia, the media— that the likelier it is that the root American political-moral ideas have lost their force or are even the primary target of derision and attack.

It is the clash of these elements in American politics now—the clash of aggressively critical intellectuals, of politicians who follow the critical fashions and other politicians who resist them, of mass opinion, ill at ease, or, in any event, feeling unled by men and women who share their deepest convictions— that has begun to change the character of American politics. Ordinary policy disputes become exacerbated, issues seem to deepen as they are being dealt with, and differences are no longer constrained by broad underlying agreement. Every argument that takes place at the surface has now a dangerous unsteadiness that compels something like a philosophic inquiry into the disordered foundation.

However other countries ought to proceed when compelled to reconsider their theoretical roots, we Americans have a route marked for us by ancient habit, namely, to look for our theoretical roots in our historical origins. That is, we habitually and rightly turn back to the thought of the Founding Fathers.

One good reason for the habit is the fact that the American political order has remained remarkably the same as that founded in 1787. The thought that shaped the original republic therefore may be presumed still to speak to our present condition. Contrary to the familiar harping on the degree to which we are supposed to have been transformed from tiny rustic origins, the fact is that the American political order was "born modern" and is today more nearly unchanged from its original character than is the case in any other major country. In 1787, monarchs ruled post-feudal societies in most of Europe; Catherine the Great ruled in Russia and a Manchu emperor in China. Such rulers, and the statesmen of those societies, would now find their countries incomprehensible. In comparison, an American founder like James Madison would be almost at ease in modern America. The point to be emphasized is not the degree of change, but the remarkable political continuity. The Constitution of 1787 is still the fundamental document of the American polity still the source of its basic institutions and powers, and still the matrix within which are shaped its politics and opinions.

But this political continuity would not alone justify the turning back to the founding. What further justifies that, and also explains the persistently retrospective cast of American political thought, is the fact that the principles of our political order were most vividly evident in the moment of our founding. The founding of politics is the greatest and most comprehensive of political acts. The deepest political questions are then "writ large" and are then most likely to have been dealt with consciously and fully. This was extraordinarily the case in the American founding when the enduring themes of American life were set forth deliberately and copiously. Few great political communities have been formed in a single deliberate act; fewer still leave behind instructive records of such precision and completeness as ours; and perhaps no other was ever the handiwork of men who combined statesmanship with such thoughtful consideration of the deepest political questions.

Indeed, the American founding is peculiarly instructive when compared with other great, modern, founded political orders. One learns pitifully little from the Russian or Chinese foundings about the projected structures of Russian and Chinese government and politics, for the obvious reason that there was not long intended to be any. The Marxist idea of the "withering away of the state" made serious Communist reflection on government and politics unnecessary. Thus, one goes back to the Russian Revolution to learn about the original principles and aspirations, perhaps as a standard against which to understand and measure the present "deviation," but surely not as a way to see "writ large" the principles of contemporary Russian practice. Similarly, although fascism like communism rested upon philosophic presuppositions, the Fascist principle of dictator-rule rendered serious reflection on government and politics relatively unnecessary in Fascist foundings. The revolutionary founding of the first French republic, too, would have been uninstructive regarding that republic's politics, had it long survived. This is because Jacobinism did not regard democracy as sufficiently problematic to require profound thought as to the structuring of its subsequent government and politics.

And this is the clue to the peculiarly instructive character of the American founding. The American founding belonged to the classic tradition of great foundings at least in this: The American founders understood politics as a perennially problematic enterprise. Specifically, they knew themselves to be establishing a democratic political order, and thought that a desperately difficult task. Their awareness of the problematic character of democracy compelled them to reflect deeply upon political things so as to be able to devise a government and politics that would render the American democracy free, decent, and competent. That is what makes the American founding so rich a source of instruction regarding the relationship in general of theory to practical institutions and politics and, of course, regarding the precise nature of that relationship in the American democratic case in particular.

Perhaps the most influential, and very likely the most widely read scholarly statement on the political ideas of the American founders, is the first chapter of Richard Hofstadter's *The American Political Tradition.*[1] In the spirit of Charles Beard, Hofstadter admires the founders' republican decency and "realism," but, at the same time, severely rebukes that "realism" because it antiquatedly restricts the moral possibilities of American democracy. The founders, he claims, "did not believe in man," and had "a distrust of man [which] was first and foremost a distrust of the common man and democratic rule"; consequently, they aimed at "cribbing and confining the popular spirit." Hofstadter's analysis of the founding does not merely make an interpretive claim as to how the "philosophy of the Constitution" should best be understood; most American disputation has been of that sort, a kind of "quarrel among the heirs" as to the precise meaning of the political heritage. Rather, Hofstadter challenges the worth of the heritage itself; his criticism goes to the very root of the matter—the founders' idea of man. Hofstadter's chapter opens with a critical characterization of that idea as Calvinist in its sense of evil and Hobbesian in its view of man as selfish and contentious, and the chapter closes with a long final paragraph that strongly condemns that idea of man. It is a condemnation that is implicit in many of the contemporary rejections of the American political-moral presuppositions and rewards careful examination.

Hofstadter writes: "From a humanistic standpoint there is a serious dilemma in the philosophy of the Fathers, which derives from their conception of man." The dilemma is this: Although the founders were not full-blooded Hobbesians, they had not advanced sufficiently beyond Hobbes to be satisfactory "from a humanistic standpoint." The founders had advanced beyond Hobbes in that, while they accepted his view of man as murderously self-interested, "they were in no mood to follow Hobbes to his conclusion," namely, to that unlimited and absolute political power—the Leviathan State—Hobbes deemed necessary to restrain natural, anarchic man. Rather, despite their Hobbesian view of man, they nonetheless "wanted him to be free—free, in essence, to contend, to be engaged in an umpired strife. . . ." But such freedom, while no doubt better than Hobbesian absolutism, is still unsatisfactory from a "humanistic standpoint" because it does not put an end to "the Hobbesian war of each against all." Indeed, the founders did not even have such an intention; they wanted "merely to stabilize it and make it less murderous." The crucial defect of the American founding, then, is this:

They had no hope and they offered none for any ultimate organic change in the way men conduct themselves. The result was that while they thought self-interest the most dangerous and unbrookable quality of man, they necessarily underwrote it in trying to control it.

And, Hofstadter continues, things have worked out exactly as the founders intended; the American political system has provided just the sort of "stable and acceptable medium" for "grasping and contending interests" that the founders had in mind.

Such a political system, and the ideas which shape and inspirit it, cannot apparently be recommended to the "humanistic standpoint." Especially the chief idea, the idea of an unchanging human nature characterized by rapacious self-interestedness, is humanistically indefensible:

No man who is as well abreast of modern science as the Fathers were of eighteenth-century science believes any longer in unchanging human nature.

Modern humanistic thinkers who seek for a means by which society may transcend eternal conflict and rigid adherence to property rights as its integrating principles can expect no answer in the philosophy of balanced government as it was set down by the Constitution-makers of 1787.

Hofstadter seems always to have been too sensible and moderate a man to act fully on the implications of this criticism of the American political system and in his later work moderated the view which in the early work received such wide dissemination. But the harsh implications are there. "Modern humanistic thinkers" must turn away from the American idea of man and the political system based on it; those who want society to "transcend eternal conflict" must look elsewhere if they are to achieve their humanistic goals.

It must instantly be acknowledged, indeed insisted upon, that Hofstadter's characterization of the founders' idea of man does indeed have a leg to stand on.[a] Their idea of man unquestionably bore a kinship with that of Hobbes, for like Hobbes they, too, were practitioners of what was called the "new science of politics." But to understand the American founders more precisely, one must see not only wherein they agreed with Hobbes, but also what was distinctive in their view. To understand that, it is necessary to appreciate anew what the "new science of politics" was all about.

The eruption of modern political philosophy in the sixteenth through eighteenth centuries, in the context of which the American founding must be understood, must itself be understood in contrast with the tradition of classical political thought from which it so radically departed.[b] The departure consisted, precisely, in a profound difference regarding human nature and its potentialities. The ancients saw man as reaching nearly to the divine and took their bearings from the highest possibilities of human nature. While the ancients had no illusions about the capacity of *most* men, they thought that every resource of the political art should be employed to draw out and up the potential of *the exceptional few*. Indeed, this orientation to the excellence of the few was implicit in the way the ancients understood the very idea of "nature." Moderns think of the natural as what exists uniformly everywhere. The ancients thought of the natural as the completed or perfected state of a given species. This was a state achieved in relatively rare instances, perhaps, but still it was only in those instances that the *nature* of the species was fully actualized and revealed.

Thus, the ancients' very idea of human nature led classical thinkers to make the preeminent political task the bringing toward completeness or perfection of the relatively few who were "naturally" capable of fulfilling their humanness. The classical idea of human nature is, as it were, aristocratic: All men are human but some are more so, and that is the crucial political fact. The modern idea of

[a]Notice must also simultaneously be given of a demurral to Hofstadter's claim that seeking to "transcend eternal conflict" is the hallmark of humanism.

[b]Acknowledgment is gladly made of my indebtedness here to the late Professor Leo Strauss, whose instructive account of the battle of the books, ancient and modern, has done so much to restore the meaning of the modern enterprise.

human nature is democratic: No difference among us can reach so far as to alter our naturally equal humanness, and *that* is the crucial fact.

The classical effort to nurture the human excellence of the few explains the extraordinarily difficult and "idealistic" demands that the classical teaching placed before humanity, demands that modern thought came to find ineffectual and excessive. It helps explain laws that aim primarily at moral excellence; censorship of art and speech deemed to threaten that excellence; the premium placed on education to mould character, on civic piety, on honor and reputation; the restraints on private economic conduct and commerce; and the insistence on keeping the political community small so as to provide the milieu in which such "social controls" would be feasible. These strenuous measures were necessitated by the height to which it was intended to raise human nature in the few capable of such elevation. A strenuous politics and a demanding political art were needed if men were to be raised so high against the powerful downward pulls of the baser and easier pleasures which exert their charms on all men.

Against all this, the "new science of politics" arrayed itself. The ancient teaching, it was charged, had been ineffective and excessive—that is, "utopian." Despite two millennia of such elevated teachings, man's estate had still not been relieved; greed and vainglory ruled under the guise of virtue or piety. The religious tyrannies and wars of the sixteenth and seventeenth centuries had climaxed two millennia of the failure of the traditional political science.

What is more, the whole rigamarole had been unnecessary. It was in fact possible, the new science argued, to achieve, not the delusive heights at which the ancients aimed, but solid human decencies, by far more efficacious and, at the same time, far less excessive means. This great new claim rested upon a new and aggressively more "realistic" idea of human nature. Ancient and medieval thought and practice were said to have failed disastrously by clinging to illusions regarding how men *ought* to be. Instead, the new science would take man as he actually *is*, would accept as primary in his nature the self-interestedness and passion displayed by all men everywhere and, precisely on that basis, would work out decent political solutions. This meant, as against ancient and medieval exhortation and compulsion of man to virtue, a lowering of the aims and expectations of politics. And it meant the achievement of these more modest aims by a shrewd, but perhaps coarse, reliance upon those natural human passions and interests.

Ironically, what followed from this new and rather debunking view of human nature was a new and conquering case for democracy. For this view of man is debunking primarily regarding the pretensions of the few; in important respects, the new science of politics had a higher opinion than ancient thought had of the capacities of most men. This became especially evident in the American founding, as we shall see when we examine James Madison on those "qualities in human nature which justify a certain portion of esteem and confidence."

Until the early modern era, political thought quite unanimously had held that in political communities, ruling over which was the noblest of arts, the naturally ablest few ought to rule over the less able many. The great tradition was that of the "mixed regime," a balancing of the various classes so as to avoid the corrupt rule of any single claimant. But the crucial principle remained: An idea of man in which the best were separated by a gulf of inequality from the great mass of deficient and imperfect humanity. And this claim of inequality now came steadily under attack. The pretensions of the few to rule on the basis of superior wisdom and virtue were leveled by a succession of powerful arguments. Since "a degree of depravity" was now argued to inhere even in the so-called best of men, no one was wholly free of dominating interest and passion. From this it followed that none was sufficiently superior to be entitled to rule. And superiority in wisdom and virtue, when admitted to exist, came nonetheless to be seen as secondary to the important political respects in which mankind were equal— namely, the equal desire of all for life, liberty, and the pursuit of happiness.

From this barrage against the claims of inequality came, first, the demand that government, whatever its form, rest upon the voluntary consent of equals to be governed, and subsequently, the argument for the democratic form of government itself. But it was a sober argument for democracy, derived from a sober idea of man and the propensities of his nature.

It was in the American founding that this argument for democracy burst forth fully. The aim of the American founders was, I believe, to "make democracy safe for the world."[c] Traditional political thought had held popular government to be indefensible; the rule of the many unwise meant either the folly and ineptitude of democracy or the tyranny of the majority. That had been for two thousand years the perspective of all thinking men regarding any purely popular system of government. But the American founders believed themselves in a position to rescue this form of government "from the opprobrium under which it has so long labored," so that it could at last "be recommended to the esteem and adoption of mankind."[2] The Founding Fathers believed that for the first time in human history it was going to be possible to found a polity exclusively upon the popular principle (that is, without recourse to or admixture with any of the other basic forms of government), but one so resting upon an arrangement of passions and interests, and so moderated and structured, as to make it a free, stable, vigorous, and hence intellectually defensible, popular regime. In short: Democracy made safe for the world.

Now a democracy derived, so to speak, from the natural equality in depravity (or at least mediocrity) of all mankind is obviously a democracy itself in need of moderation if it is to rise above its source somehow, and be made into a decent and stable political order. And the means for achieving this moderation, also

[c]I borrow this phrase from Professor G.W. Pierson; it seems also to have been used earlier by Walter Lippmann.

obviously, would have to be drawn from that same human nature, the universal fallibility of which had justified democracy in the first place. The scheme for thus moderating democracy is nowhere stated more thoughtfully, nor more chillingly, than by James Madison in *Federalist* 51, the most comprehensive of all the essays.

Madison is discussing the separation of powers and is showing how, under the proposed Constitution, the "gradual concentration of the several powers" into one dominant branch will be prevented. His solution leads him to a general statement of the deepest strategy that underlies the Constitution, a strategy based on the modern idea of human nature. "The great security against a gradual concentration," Madison tells us, consists in giving to the members of each branch "the necessary constitutional means and personal motives to resist encroachments of the others. . . . Ambition must be made to counteract ambition. The interest of the man must be connected with the constitutional rights of the place."

This using of one person's passion or interest to check another's passion or interest all sounds perfectly sensible, indeed commonplace, to present-day Americans who have lived in freedom and comfort for nearly 200 years within the moral horizon of the system Madison did so much to devise. But Madison was writing at a time when the new science of politics was still unhackneyed, and he knew that there was something shocking in this new view of man upon which his scheme rests. He thus pauses to apologize, as it were, for his recommendations and to justify them as necessary. "It may be a reflection on human nature that such devices should be necessary to control the abuses of government. But what is government itself but the greatest of all reflections on human nature?" "Experience" of what human nature is like, Madison concludes, "has taught mankind the necessity" of the kinds of precautionary devices the Constitution embodies. His scheme thus justified, he now states its principle in a bold and comprehensive form. "This policy of supplying, by opposite and rival interests, the defect of better motives, might be traced through the whole system of human affairs, private as well as public."

Restated plainly, Madison is saying something like the following. Human nature is such that there just are not enough "better motives" to go around, not enough citizens and politicians who will be animated by motives that rise above self-interestedness and the gratification of their own passions so as to get the work of government and society done. Therefore, we will have to "supply that defect," that is, make up for the insufficiency of better motives by a shrewdly arranged system of opposite and rival interests. This policy has worked remarkably well and, in my judgment, remains indispensable to our political well-being. But the policy has not only its useful results; it has also its costs in our private and public lives.

In the private realm, the policy accepts as useful, and even encourages, what had hitherto always been censured and constrained, namely, the aggressive pursuit by all of immediate personal interest. In the public realm, the policy likewise condones and even encourages hitherto reprobated passions like self-serving ambition. The "personal motives" that the classical teaching had sought to subdue so as to enhance in some their "better motives," the modern teaching emancipates and employs because of a despair that those better motives exist in human nature in sufficient quantity or at all. Now these better motives, being also a part of human nature, can never be entirely extinguished in their effect; thus, as Tocqueville wryly observed, sometimes even "in the United States, as elsehwere, one sees people carried away by the disinterested, spontaneous impulses natural to man."[3] But the question is whether the reliance upon "personal motives," by the modern teaching and in American practice, does not adversely affect also the operation of those "better motives" which the classical teaching had understood needed strenuous support.

We may look to James Madison's *Federalist* 10 for an answer. Here Madison shows how, at the level of individuals in the private realm, the "system of opposite and rival interests" helps solve what is, perhaps, the gravest problem of democracy—the tendency of majorities to become violently factious and use their power disastrously or impose their power tyrannically. What Madison was trying to do can be understood in contrast with Karl Marx. For example, Madison might well have agreed with Marx that all history had hitherto been a history of class struggle. But Marx thought that history was now reaching its dialectical climax and that with the victory of the final majority, the proletariat, the truly human society would be ushered in. Madison had no such millennial hopes. He believed that the "class struggle" was rooted in the human condition; circumstances could mute or intensify the struggle but could not eradicate it. Moreover, he believed that the perennially possible class struggle had been the actual cause of the demise of all earlier democracies. Indeed, it was its peculiar vulnerability to class struggle that had earned democracy the "opprobrium under which it has so long labored." Earlier democracies, he charged, had "been spectacles of turbulence and contention . . . as short in their lives as they have been violent in their deaths." The great task, therefore, was to find a democratic way to deal with the propensity of majorities to constitute themselves into a class and to engage in fatal factiousness.

In Madison's way of dealing with the problem, we will find answers to the question of whether the unleashing of "personal motives" is at the cost of the flourishing of the "better motives." Madison first contemplates and then rejects the possibilities of "curing the mischiefs of faction" by removing its causes; this cannot be done because "the latent causes of faction are . . . sown in the nature of man." That is, as Hofstadter and so many complain, Madison offers no hope of "any organic change in the way men conduct themselves." But while Madison rejects as utopian the hopes of "theoretic politicians," and of others who expect the eradication of factionalism by means of a change in human nature, he nonetheless claims to have found a new practical solution to the problem, one realistically derived from that same human nature that causes the problem in the first place.

Madison reminds us that, while the latent causes of faction exist everywhere because they are "sown in the nature of man," they are "brought into different degrees of activity according to the different circumstances of civil society." That is, "circumstances" such as the size of the political community, the kind of economy fostered, the structures and processes of government, the beliefs citizens are encouraged to hold, all affect the operation of the "latent causes of faction." Thus, which causes will be most at work, and how they will work, and therefore what the actual pattern of factionalism will be, depend upon the peculiar circumstances of each society. These circumstances are, of course, precisely what founders deal with. But in order to decide how to create or manipulate the "circumstances," founders must know what kind of factions they want to avoid and, since some factionalism is inevitable, what kind they are willing to accept or encourage, and how to do the avoiding and the encouraging. In short, democratic founders need a science of faction.

Accordingly, Madison sets forth a typology of factions which have "divided mankind" and caused them " to vex and oppress each other." Those factional causes that must be most diminished in their effect are divided into the threefold scheme that informs the entire essay, namely, into opinions, passions, and interests. Madison deals first with man's natural inclination to opining: his "zeal for different opinions concerning religion, concerning government, and many other points, as well of speculation as of practice." Such opinions are not merely the rationalization of prior interest or passion; rather these opinions are the autonomous product of the sheer human need to opine about human matters. This is an exercise of a high human faculty and such opining, it should be noted, deals with elevated matters. But, unfortunately, such opining has the devastating effect, especially in democracies, of inflaming mankind with mutual and ruinous animosity over matters of religious belief and political philosophy. Hence the natural human tendency to such elevated opining must somehow be muted and moderated if American democracy is to avoid the fate of all earlier popular governments.

Madison next turns to the causes of faction which derive directly from the human passions: from "an attachment to different leaders ambitiously contending for preeminence and power; or to persons of other descriptions whose fortunes have been interesting to the human passions." These are not the factional angers or affections that inevitably build up around a pre-existing interest or opinion; Madison means here the factions that have their origin directly in the passions themselves. He seems to mean that humans have a natural political readiness to love and hate, a spiritedness that is evoked by or reaches out to exceptional leaders. The attachments based on such loves and hates are by no means simply contemptible, and indeed can have something exciting and elevating about them. But out of such "attachments," factions are generated which torment society and hence must somehow be avoided. Madison is in effect saying: No Caesars or Cromwells, or other extraordinarily "interesting" figures, thank you. What is wanted are men of lesser but safer political ambition and religious attraction. The thrust of the American political order must be somehow to diminish the availability of leaders of such outstanding appeal and/or to diminish the readiness of ordinary Americans to respond to them.

The bold and novel requirement, thus, of Madison's teaching and of the American political order, is to mute and moderate these age-old kinds of political behavior that derive from the fundamental sources of faction, namely, disputation about political and religious matters, and passionate attachment to the cause of brilliant and ambitious leaders and "to persons of other descriptions."

But in addition to the disastrous political behavior deriving from opinion and passion, there is also the political behavior that derives from still another fundamental source of faction, namely, economic interest. Indeed "the most common and durable source of factions has been the various and unequal distribution of property." Madison is far from seeking to diminish the efficacy of this cause, as he is of the other two causes of faction. On the contrary, his intention is precisely the opposite: He wishes to magnify the efficacy of this cause, because therein lies the new cure for the "mischiefs of faction." If Americans will divide themselves according to their narrow and particularized economic interests, they will avoid the fatally turbulent factionalism that opinion and passion generate. In contrast, the relatively tranquil kind of factions derived from economic interests make possible a decent democracy.

Madison does not, of course, have in mind economic-based faction in general. He makes an important distinction between two kinds of economic faction, one resulting from the "unequal distribution of property," and one resulting from its *various* distribution. Faction based on property inequality, like faction based on opinion and passion, also leads to fatal factionalism, specifically, to the perennial struggle of the many poor with the few rich, under grandly conflicting ideas of justice. The American polity looks to replace this fatal, older kind of economics-based struggle by making predominant a new kind of economic faction derived from the "various . . . distribution of property," on the basis of which can arise a tranquil, modern *politics of interest groups*, as distinct from a politics of class struggle. This is the meaning and intention of Madison's famous "multiplicity of interests" and of democratic government based upon the "coalitions of a majority" that rise out of that multiplicity.

But whence derives the "multiplicity" which makes it all possible? It is uniquely the product of a modern commercial society. For millennia, the mass of men have been poor in but a handful of ways, toilers little differentiated in their class poverty by the ways they eked out their existences. The rich likewise have been so in but a handful of ways that little differentiated their common oligarchic impulses and interests. Only the modern commercial spirit and a complex modern economy supply the faction-differentiating division of labor and the great economic diversity which can turn the attention of all away from the faction—compacting issues that rise from opinion, passion, and class—to the moderating pursuit of individual economic happiness.[4] In such a commercial society, there will not be a simple division into the poor and the rich but a fragmentation of men into many different, particular economic activities, around which there will grow different, particular economic interests as well as economic and social groupings. Men will then tend to think in terms of their various immediate economic interests as members of an "interest group," rather than of a class or sect. They will form political opinions around their interests, and jockey for group and party advantage on the basis of them. From this will arise a new kind of politics, as Madison prophetically understood, one differing greatly from the spirit and character of the politics of the pre-modern era. "The regulation of these various and interfering interests forms the principal task of modern legislation and involves the spirit of party and faction in the necessary and ordinary operations of government."

Such a view, of course, accepts a society in which "personal motives" come to the fore; it "emancipates acquisitiveness" to a degree never contemplated by traditional political thought and it accepts the "costs" of such an emancipation. In defense of this policy, Madison argued that when a great mass of men turn to visions of political philosophy or to opinionated piety, or follow some impassioning or "charismatic" leader, they torment each other and destroy their society. The example the eighteenth century feared was the religious zealotry that helped cause the religious despotisms and religious wars so fresh to the minds of the founders. Has the twentieth century with its ideological despotisms and wars and demagogic leaders made the prospect of opinionated piety or mass ideology less frightful or repulsive? The durable decency of the American polity during this century of horrors is testimony to Madison's prudence. Must we not agree with that prudence if only on negative grounds, that is, in terms of the evils he sought to avoid, because the same evils threaten to descend upon us?

But to agree regarding the danger and the Madisonian defense, and to opt for the many positive excellences of the Madisonian polity, is to accept what the defense entails. We may not pick and choose among the parts of a closely interwoven political order, but must see and accept its essential principles. The sketch given above, of Madison's solution to the problem of faction, has disclosed one such fundamental principle. Rather than welcome the operation of opinion, passion, and class—those high, but dangerously volatile sources of faction—the founders accepted the necessity to moderate and dampen them. The way that had to be done was to unleash the ordinary "personal motives" that the long tradition of political thought had shunned. This unleashing gives to American life certain ineradicable distinctive features and was the substratum on which the American political system was intended to rest. It is the cost of

Madison's policy. It is this substratum or cost that offends and angers so many critics of the American political system, who find it "vulgar." But it is only at such a cost that the excellences of the system can be enjoyed.

It would be a melancholy defense of the American political order which rested only at the level of this "substratum." But we all "know in our bones" that there is much more to America than merely the deterrence of tyranny and folly by the "system of opposite and rival interests." Passing reference has already been made to certain positive American excellences. While not forgetting the force of gravity exerted by the base, we may now begin in contemplation the cheerful ascent toward those excellences.

The founders' orientation toward those excellences derives from their idea of human nature. Classical thought, it will be remembered, had an exalted view of what human nature could achieve in a few; and, as could be expected from the perspective of such rare excellence, the qualities of the many tended to seem low. Modern thought, contrarily, tends to deny in human nature any such exalted possibilities; but, perhaps precisely because of the denial, modern thought tends to a more respectful appreciation of the possibilities of average men and women. Such at least was the case with the American founders. Far from taking a merely cynical view of man, the founders frequently claimed that their achievement of a successful democratic republic would "vindicate human nature."

To understand how these very realistic men meant this, it will help to recall the earlier discussion of Professor Hofstadter's view that the founders had simply opted for a Hobbesianism made "less murderous." It was acknowledged that the founders partially shared Hobbes' dim view of man, but it was claimed that they also significantly parted company with him. This is the clear, and all but explicit, meaning of an important statement made by Madison at the end of *Federalist* 55.

As there is a degree of depravity in mankind which requires a certain degree of circumspection and distrust, so there are other qualities in human nature which justify a certain portion of esteem and confidence. Republican government presupposes the existence of these qualities in a higher degree than any other form. Were the pictures which have been drawn by the political jealousy of some among us faithful likenesses of the human character, the inference would be that there is not sufficient virtue among men for self-government; and that nothing less than the chains of despotism can restrain them from destroying and devouring one another.

We have paid ample attention to Madison's "circumspection and distrust" due to the "degree of depravity" in mankind; it is rewarding now to see how his view of man also encompasses "sufficient virtue ... for self-government." To understand him, we must recognize the context of his remarks. By "the political

jealousy of some among us," he is referring to the anti-Federalist opponents of
the Constitution. He is twitting them for a contradiction into which their too
jealous love of republican liberty had betrayed them. Loving liberty and fearing
its loss too jealously, they portray all men as certain to abuse any power
entrusted to them under the strong new government. Such a view of the "human
character," Madison points out, would legitimate a Hobbesian monarchy, not
the republicanism they professed.

Madison's prudent love of liberty saves him from his opponents' contradiction because, equally with the liberty they excessively defend, he is also
concerned with the strength, the "energy and stability," of government; indeed,
he believed that energetic and stable government was the pre-condition of
political freedom. And he has a warrant for his dual concern in a view of human
nature more subtle and compound than that of his opponents. While they see
only "depravity" and deny, in effect, that men have "sufficient virtue" to
govern themselves, Madison pays attention also to certain "other qualities in
human nature." These are estimable qualities which permit democratic "confidence" that elected representatives will not habitually betray their public trust.
(Their fidelity, as *Federalist* 57 reminds, is also secured by the taking of various
"effectual precautions.") "Republican government," Madison firmly claims,
"presupposes the existence of these qualities in a higher degree than any other
form." But this ringing statement must be understood first in a narrow way.
Madison means that, while other forms of government, like monarchy, aristocracy, and a mixed regime, can rely on dynastic or class interests and traditions to
hold magistrates somewhat to their trust, democratic representatives can have no
such built-in restrictions; in the nature of the case, democracy *has* to rely on the
natural decency which human nature happily supplies. But even thus narrowly
understood, one can see in Madison's statement something of the lifelong pride
he took in republican self-government. He gloried in his country (see the long
eloquent ending of *Federalist* 14) that it would be the first to achieve a truly
successful democratic republic, and thus permit the flourishing of these "other
qualities." And he could not wholly conceal, in the ending of *Federalist* 10, his
pride in helping to make such a republic possible by his own elaboration of the
"new science of politics."

This happier other side of Madison's compound view of human nature is even
more evident in another statement, similar to the one we have been examining
from *Federalist* 55, that he made to the Virginia convention that ratified the
Constitution. While again rebuking the too jealous anti-Federalists for presuming
that representatives will "do everything mischievous that they can," he assures
his opponents that he does not "place unlimited confidence in representatives,"
nor presume that they will have the "most exalted integrity and sublime virtue."

But I go on this great republican principle, that the people will have virtue and
intelligence to select men of virtue and wisdom. Is there no virtue among us? If

there be not, we are in a wretched situation. No theoretical checks, no form of government, can render us secure. To suppose any form of government will secure liberty or happiness without any virtue in the people, is a chimerical idea. If there be sufficient virtue and intelligence in the community, it will be exercised in the selection of these men; so that we do not depend on their virtue, or put confidence in our rulers, but in the people who are to choose them.[5]

Warm praise of the "republican principle" that this is, it must not be understood as opening the rhetorical floodgates on "democratic virtue," as populists have later understood that phrase. It will be seen to be sober praise. By virtue, Madison does not mean the ancient idea of ethical excellence, or the more recent idea of original goodness, but rather something like "public-spirited-ness" or concern for the general good; he used the word in the sense given to it by the "new science of politics" and especially by the influential Montesquieu.[6] By intelligence, he likely meant not reasoning power, as in "intelligence quotient," but rather "mutual conveyance of information . . . news, tidings," an eighteenth-century usage still familiar in phrases like "intelligence-gathering agency." In short, the people would have enough sense and information to know who were the men deserving of election.[7] This meaning of intelligence brings out a careful distinction Madison preserved between the generality of men, who have only virtue and such intelligence, and the superior men who ought to be chosen as representatives because they have virtue and *wisdom*. His statement, then, must not be read as fulsome praise of democracy uttered by a Whitman or Sandburg or by some modern ideologist of democracy. But it is praise nonetheless, and praise that rests upon Madison's view of the decencies, which together with "depravity" make up human nature. Thus, we see within Madison's very idea of man a prospect of excellences that go far above the harsh element of raw interest involved in the "policy of opposite and rival interests."

Even in the very commercial interests that are so important to Madison, one can see the ground for some of those positive excellences. But only a careful distinction brings that to light—a distinction between greed or avarice on the one hand and acquisitiveness on the other. The commercial society unleashes acquisitiveness; but this is by no means the same thing as to give vent to the avarice or covetousness which all philosophies and religious creeds have condemned. Both modern acquisitiveness and traditional avarice have perhaps the same root, namely, the desire, even an inordinate desire, for bodily and material things. But in age-old avarice the emphasis is on the passion of *having*, whereas in modern acquisitiveness, the emphasis is on the *getting*. Avarice is a passion centered on the things themselves, a narrow clutching to one's self of money or things. The passion of avarice has no built-in need for any limitation of itself, no need for moderation or for the cultivation of any virtues as instrumental to the satisfaction of the passion. But acquisitiveness teaches moderation to the desiring from which it derives, because to acquire is not primarily to have, but to get and to earn and, moreover, to earn justly, at least to the extent that the acquisition must be the fruit of one's own exertions or qualities. This requires the acquisitive man to cultivate certain excellences, minimal ones perhaps but excellences nonetheless, as the means to achieve his ends. He wants enlargement and increase, and these require of him at least a venturesomeness, hard work, and the ability to still his passion so as to allow time for the ripening of his acquisitive plans and measures. In short, acquisitive man, unlike avaricious man, is likely to have what we call the bourgeois virtues.

It is in this context that we must understand Hamilton's observation that a commercial society nurtures "the assiduous merchant, the laborious husbandman, the active mechanic, and the industrious manufacturer." Avarice has no such salutary effects. And it is not only excellences like assiduity, labor, activity, and industry that a commercial society nurtures. "Honesty is the best policy" is not acceptable prudence to the avaricious man, but it is almost natural law to the "assiduous merchant." Acquisitiveness may not be the highest motive for honesty, but if it produces something like honesty in great numbers, is that not a prodigious accomplishment? Similarly, "it takes money to make money," a familiar maxim to acquisitiveness, bears at least a relation to the ancient virtue of liberality; but the avaricious man simply cannot let loose his money to the extent that the commercial principle makes common practice. Scrooge was surely not less successful as a merchant after he acquired the liberal spirit of Christmas; indeed, the old Scrooge belonged to the old world of avarice, while the new Scrooge would be more at home in a modern commercial society. Finally, the acquisitive man is plunged by his passion into the give and take of society and must thus learn to accommodate himself to the interests of others. In this he is at least pointed toward something like justice. But the avaricious man is drawn by his passion wholly within the confines of his own narrow soul.

When Madison's "policy of opposite and rival interests" is understood in the light of this distinction between avarice and acquisitiveness, we can begin to see the ground for some of the excellences we all know to be characteristic of American life. We can then avoid thinking, as many have, that the vice of avarice peculiarly flourishes in America. On the contrary, we can claim that avarice here is peculiarly blunted by the supervening force of acquisitiveness and its attendant qualities. No one understood this more profoundly than Montesquieu who argued that "frugality, economy, moderation, labor, prudence, tranquility, order, and rule" are qualities that arise naturally in a "democracy founded on commerce."[8] These may be put down as merely "bourgeois virtues," but they are virtues or human excellences nonetheless, and never more attractive than now when they seem to be in less abundant supply. And they are among the "estimable" qualities which are as important in the founders' idea of man as are the harsher qualities that the American political system unblinkingly builds upon.

Tocqueville, who learned from Montesquieu, also teaches republican virtue in the same spirit, but still more broadly and hopefully, and with him we may see a higher level to which the quality of American life reaches. The foundation, Tocqueville understands as does Montesquieu, is an acquisitive commercial order in which self-interest must be allowed to flourish; Tocqueville coolly accepts that it cannot be suppressed or transcended. Whatever might have been possible in earlier aristocratic ages, when men had perhaps been able to sacrifice self-interest for the "beauty of virtue," this is now impossible. In the modern age of equality, "private interest will more than ever become the chief if not the only driving force behind all behavior." But this is no cause for despair; if there is no hope of transcending private interest, still much depends on how "each man will interpret his private interest."[9] What is necessary is that men learn to follow the "principle of self-interest properly understood." The Americans, Tocqueville says, have "universally accepted" that principle and have made it the root of all their actions. The Americans

enjoy explaining almost every act of their lives on the principle of self-interest properly understood. It gives them pleasure to point out how an enlightened self-love continually leads them to help one another and disposes them freely to give part of their time and wealth for the good of the state.

Oddly, and in a manner reminiscent of Madison in *Federalist* 51, Tocqueville interrupts his presentation at this point as if wishing to draw a veil over the harsh foundation of this "principle." But he forces himself, as it were, to a full statement of its implications.

Self-interest properly understood is not at all a sublime doctrine. . . . It does not attempt to reach great aims, but it does . . . achieve all it sets out to do. Being within the scope of everybody's understanding, everyone grasps it and has no trouble bearing it in mind. It is wonderfully agreeable to human weaknesses, and so easily wins great sway. It has no difficulty in keeping its power, for it turns private interest against itself and uses the same goad which excites them to direct the passions.

The doctrine of self-interest properly understood does not inspire great sacrifices, but every day it prompts some small ones; by itself it cannot make a man virtuous, but its discipline shapes a lot of orderly, temperate, moderate, careful, and self-controlled citizens. If it does not lead the will directly to virtue, it establishes habits which unconsciously turn it that way.

Tocqueville makes clear how remarkably these "habits" that lead to "virtue" are the common stuff of American political life. By virtue Tocqueville, in the tradition of Montesquieu and *The Federalist*, means "public-spiritedness," that is, a positive and lively concern for the common well-being. Thus not only does "self-interest properly understood" cause Americans to acquire certain valuable personal qualities, and not only does it lead them regularly to help one another in joint private endeavors, it also "disposes them freely to give part of their time and wealth for the good of the state." This is a "habit" that comes very close to being "virtue" itself for Tocqueville. From this habit of voluntarily serving the state there results, according to Tocqueville, the extraordinary extent to which Americans actually govern themselves. This imposing fact has been obscured in recent years because observers have brought to the question a utopian expectation which degraded the reality. Tocqueville, by making realistic comparisons and taking his bearings from the nature of things, was able to appreciate the astonishing degree in America of self-governing and self-directing activity in all spheres of life. In fact, he warns his readers that, while they could very well conceive all other aspects of America,

the political activity prevailing in the United States is something one could never understand unless one had seen it. No sooner do you set foot on American soil than you find yourself in a sort of tumult; a confused clamor rises on every side, and a thousand voices are heard at once, each expressing some social requirements.[10]

This tumult, this clamor, is the sound of men and women governing themselves. And in presupposing and summoning forth the capacity of a people to govern themselves, the American political order advances far beyond mere self-interest, toward that full self-governance which is the very idea of virtue.

It will have been noted that Tocqueville's account of the "principle of self-interest properly understood," and of the heights to which it can extend, is exactly in the spirit of Madison's understanding of the compound nature of man, a nature in which self-interest is primary but in which there are also "other qualities." The entire ascent we have been tracing, from raw self-interest and acquisitiveness through enlightened self-interest to "habits" of virtue and to republican self-governance, has a firm foundation in Madison's idea of man. Had he viewed a human being as merely "an atom of self-interest,"[11] as Hofstadter and many believe he did, then there would be no such ascent, Madison's enthusiastic republicanism would be unintelligible, and his scheme would have no entitlement to the decencies he obviously counted on. Unquestionably, Madison placed his primary reliance on the "new science of politics" and the way it grasped firmly the nettle of human selfishness. But he emphasized that man was also, albeit secondarily, a "social being"; and this sociality was one of those "favorable attributes of the human character," all of which were "valuable, as auxiliaries,"[12] to the devices that guarded against the darker side of man's nature. They were indispensable auxiliaries, indispensable attributes of human nature, which, when permitted to flourish, generated the positive excellences we are considering.

As a statesman-theorist, Madison never had the necessity to explore to its philosophic limits this question of man's sociality. But he had to presuppose it; his republican scheme depended upon the existence in human nature of such sociality and of the moral and political decencies that could be derived from it. Many of the great modern thinkers wrestled with the same problem, as, for example, Rousseau on "compassion," Hume on "sentiment," and Smith on "sympathy." They had to. The manifest facts of human history simply cannot be accounted for without some such idea; and republican government, which requires reasonably faithful representatives and reasonably civic-minded citizens, simply cannot be expected unless some such qualities have a footing in human nature. But Madison, like these great moderns, while presupposing human sociality, still accepted that the selfish qualities were primary in human nature and had the superior force. The problem, then, was precisely how can human sociality, how can these "valuable auxiliary attributes," be brought to the fore?

In a way, this question sums up the problem of republican government: how to nurture the estimable "other qualities" which republican government peculiarly presupposes. One could give a sketch of the American political system entirely from this perspective. But it suffices here to have seen how Madison's idea of man comprehended qualities that accommodate and account for the positive excellences in American political life that we have been considering.

We may briefly note two further related aspects of American life which are, in a way, at the peak of the "ascent." First, American democracy as understood by its founders made only a modest claim. It never denied the unequal existence of the human excellences; it only denied the claim of excellence to rule *as of right.* As in the distinction Madison candidly made between the "intelligence" of the people and the requisite "wisdom" of their representatives, the American political order presupposed an inequality of virtues and abilities rooted in human nature. The original American democratic idea, then, deferred to a relatively high idea of virtue, while denying its claim to rule *save by popular choice.*

Indeed, not only was the idea of unequal excellence acknowledged, it was the proud claim of American democracy to be the political system in which merit, incarnated in Jefferson's "natural aristocracy," was likeliest to be rewarded with office, in contrast with the "artificial aristocracy" that flourished corruptly in other systems. Nothing is more dangerous in modern America than those subverting conceptions of human nature or of justice that deny that there are men and women who deserve deference, or deny to democracy its aspiration to be that system which best defers to the truly deserving.

Finally, one should also note gratefully that the American political order, with its heterogeneous and fluctuating majorities and with its principle of liberty, supplies a not inhospitable home to those minds that wish to pursue the love of learning. This is at a respectable distance indeed from its foundation in a "policy of opposite and rival interests."

The American founders had a subtle and compound idea of man. They saw in human nature dominant elements of passion and interest, but also a widespread "capacity of mankind for self-government." Based on this compound view of man, they framed a political order which sought to take account of both sides of human nature. This order has its foundation in the willing use of human passion and interest, but it has also certain enduring excellences necessary to its fulfillment. Preserving that foundation and, at the same time, nurturing the appropriate excellences is the task of enlightened American citizenship and statesmanship. It is easy to fail: easy to indulge a preference for liberty that exults only in the free play of the passions and interests and easy to make utopian demands for universal excellences which ignore the limiting requisites of the American political system.

It is harder than ever to grasp the compound political-moral demands of the American idea of man because of the contemporary intellectual onslaught upon it. That onslaught makes it now a matter of great practical urgency to reflect as deeply as we can on the subtleties of the political system derived from the compound American idea of man. And not only urgent. It is intellectually exciting and morally rewarding to find again in the American idea of man the way "to attain that form of greatness and of happiness which is proper to ourselves,"[13] and even enclaves of other greatnesses as well.

Notes

1. Richard Hofstadter, *The American Political Tradition* (New York: Vintage Books, 1956).

2. *Federalist* 10. See Clinton Rossiter, ed., *The Federalist Papers* (New York: Mentor Books, 1961), p. 81.

3. "Alexis de Tocqueville," *Democracy in America*, eds. J. P. Mayer and Max Lerner, trans. George Lawrence (New York: Harper & Row, 1966), p. 498.

4. *Cf.* Hamilton in *Federalist* 12 on how the "prosperity of commerce" entices and activates "human avarice and enterprise." But this leads to a result which Hamilton regards with satisfaction. "The assiduous merchant, the laborious husbandman, the active mechanic, and the industrious manufacturer—all orders of men look forward with eager expectation and growing alacrity to this pleasing reward of their toils."

5. June 20, 1788. Elliot's *Debates on the Adoption of the Federal Constitution.* I am indebted to my wife, Professor Ann Stuart Diamond, for urging upon me the importance of this passage.

6. *Cf. Federalist* 57 on the need for rulers who have the "most virtue to pursue . . . the common good of the society."

7. The quotation is from the *Oxford English Dictionary; cf.* Dr. Johnson's *A Dictionary of the English Language*: "commerce of information . . . mutual communication . . . commerce of acquaintance."

8. *The Spirit of the Laws*, V, 6.

9. All references in this section are to Tocqueville, *Democracy in America*, pp. 497-99.

10. Tocqueville, *Democracy in America*, p. 223.

11. Hofstadter, *The American Political Tradition*, p. 3.

12. Speech to the Virginia Constitutional Convention, December 2, 1829. In G. Hunt, ed., *The Writings of James Madison* (New York: G. Putnam's Sons, 1900), IX, 360-361.

13. Tocqueville, *Democracy in America*, p. 679.

Social Policy: From the Utilitarian Ethic to the Therapeutic Ethic

Daniel P. Moynihan

According to Daniel P. Moynihan, social policy in America today is torn between two conflicting sets of assumptions about man. On the one hand, there stand the traditional ideas that make up what Moynihan calls the "utilitarian ethic," which assumes that man is a reasoning and responsible creature, and that social policy should entail incentives and deterrences to which the citizen might respond. This ethic was overwhelmingly dominant in the nineteenth century and remains strong today. But since the Great Depression, it has increasingly given way to a new "therapeutic ethic" that arose out of Freudianism and modern social science. The therapeutic ethic envisions man as a creature of circumstance: When conditions are good, he is calm and peaceful; when they are bad, he is frustrated and becomes aggressive. "Therapeutic" social policy thus requires a far greater degree of government intervention in order to "restructure" man's environment.

Neither assumption, Moynihan suggests, is empirically proved, and neither is a sufficient guide to policy-making. But much of the confusion, conflict, and ineffectiveness which attend current social policies derive from the incompatibility of the two assumptions in a polity in which both are widely and sometimes simultaneously held—but in which this incompatibility is not perceived.

The American bicentennial will mark the anniversary also of the publication of the *Wealth of Nations*, a coincidence not without a certain serendipity. The Declaration of Independence, asserting all men to be created equal, in the same voice and in those very words declared them equal to competing one with

25

the other.[a] A new dimension was given to the ancient *bellum omnium contra omnes* that Wordsworth evoked as

> The good old rule
> ... the simple plan
> That they should take, who have the power,
> And they should keep who can.

Smith's object was the "wealth of nations"—the collective well-being, not simply the well-being of the strong. But he perceived—asserted—that this collective well-being was most likely to be achieved by giving ample scope to individual energies in pursuit of individual self-interest, which he did not see as devoid of moral worth, either in and of itself, or in its larger consequences. His market system, in Lionel Robbins' view, was "merely an engine of response" to such energies and interests. But he did not assume the free market would satisfy all human needs. His "third duty" of the sovereign was to erect and maintain "public institutions which it can never be to the interest of any individual, or small number of individuals, to erect and maintain." Subsequent generations have tinkered with the market engine more than Smith might have desired, and have expanded the list of institutions under the patronage of the sovereign more than he possibly would have held prudent, but American society today is still recognizably shaped along the principles Smith proposed, and which he would have found already well established in the young republic.

For the longest time this version of a good society—"The Great Society," Smith actually called it—was encouraged and abetted by the public philosophers and statesmen identified as Utilitarians. British in the main, they were nowhere so well received as in the United States, where their Victorian compound of economic efficiency with moral purpose proved immensely attractive. Theirs was an idea of man somewhat removed, now, from the rude and barbarous highlands; an idea, we are forced to conclude, much conditioned by the comparatively peaceful, and incomparably prosperous experience of the nineteenth century British. Man remained acquisitive and aggressive, as of yore, *but man was also proved reasonable.* There is a mixture of meaning in this term: that man is both capable of reasoning and also *disposed* to reasoning, such that sensible outcomes are more likely than not when, on the one hand, men are rewarded for being reasonable, and when, on the other hand, they find that failure to be reasonable in this manner is costly, and needlessly so.

In and around these ideas there developed a distinctive civic culture: individualistic but cooperative; demanding, at times even punishing, but optimistic. Wealth accumulated; men did not noticeably decay. Youth, in the ideal, was trained to competition but also, simultaneously, to rectitude; to the deferral of gratification, but also to the creation of capital and its sensible utilization. Again

---

[a] I am indebted to David Denoon for this insight.

in the ideal, this combination minimized the need of the state either to energize the population or to discipline it, the two primal objects of social policy, when there has been anything such, in ages past and ages since.

Social policy, in such a setting, defined itself fairly readily. The state should intervene in social arrangements mainly to restore or maintain the equilibrium of a largely self-regulating system: to intervene so as to attain a minimum of intervention. Only the ideologue will associate this with a ritual avoidance of government action. Thus it was a *Liberal* British government which in 1911 introduced unemployment insurance to the modern world. Faced with the charge that unemployment benefits might be used for drink, Winston Churchill, then president of the Board of Trade, replied that a man who had earned his benefits might consume them as he would, it being no business of government to tell him how. It *was* the business of government, however, to ensure that he might have such benefits. A worker on his own could not necessarily or always find work in an industrial society. But on his own he could choose to stay sober, and if he did not he would be on his own with the consequences. If not on his own, then, well, dependent on private charity which did indeed flourish at this time, much as did drunkenness.

Social insurance was a characteristic utilitarian social policy. In the United States, workman's compensation laws were widely enacted before World War I. Safety and health legislation was typical—much of it oriented to the work place. Pure food laws were characteristic. Anti-monopoly legislation was perhaps quintessential, along with anti-trade union court orders. The individual and the market were to be left as free as conscience and common sense would allow. There were limits to such freedom. Thus at one point The State of Virginia wished to sterilize mental defectives: no small interference with individual liberty. Doubtless, said Justice Holmes, but "Three generations of imbeciles are enough." Tempered in this—reasonable—manner, the Utilitarian approach to social policy had great attractions; and these persist. On balance it is probably still the majority belief of Americans.

It would seem no longer to be the dominant belief of the elites who set the style and considerably influence the agenda of social policy. This is in part due to the failures of utilitarianism. It became too much the property of a property-owning class which used utilitarian arguments to oppose perfectly utilitarian proposals—in the United States, measures such as Social Security and Unemployment Insurance—and ended by casting doubt on the authenticity of the whole position. This kind of rigidity may be part of the life cycle of any such set of ideas. (In this connection it is useful to recall that well into the Great Depression itself, the *labor movement* also opposed unemployment insurance: Such was the grip of doctrine.) The depression was a staggering blow to the notion that the theory worked. The two world wars thoroughly shook the idea of progress and reasonableness. Thus confidence in the system was weakened by failure, a sequence Marxists had seemingly forecast, just as they had asserted that, inasmuch as individual ends are socially determined, the utilitarian calculus was *not* the formula for progress it had been held to be. In a different perspective, Schumpeter held that the system would be destroyed by its own success, that the time would come when its singular efficiency in enhancing the wealth of nations would no longer seem either singular or, even, desirable.

Just as importantly, however, the decline of utilitarian belief among elites was associated with the rise of Freudian psychology, and with it a very different idea of man. Utilitarianism may have been relatively indifferent to Christianity as a religion, but it had no doubts about the utility of traditional Christian morality. It merely sought a different, more "rational" justification for all those "thou-shalt-not's." But Freudianism "explained" religious tradition in terms that suggested that any such rational justification was impossible. The "truth" of such rules was questioned to the point where belief in them became itself something of an intellectual achievement. Further, and perhaps even more devastating, the utility of such rules was questioned, for Freudian doctrine quite undermined the basic utilitarian notion that man was reasonable. Capable of reasoning, to be sure. But reasonable? No. To the contrary, man was depicted as a creature of unreason, his most important motivations inaccessible to conscious-ness, or at best dimly so. It required two generations for Freudian theory to be translated into prescription for social practice, but when at length this did take place, it could be seen that a huge divergence had occurred. It may be more useful to state that it can *now* be seen, for the divergence was not much noted at the time. Still, it took place and it left us with a new view of human nature, which wholly challenged the preceding one, without quite displacing it. The consequences for social policy have been pervasive and, in the main, unhelpful.

Now the first object of social policy is social peace, which is to say the establishment of rules of conduct which are sufficiently accepted and observed so as to make it possible for man to *be* social, and *not* to be isolated in a Hobbesian state of nature. The old utilitarian and the new Freudian doctrines diverged fundamentally at this point, and with this divergence much confusion commenced. We have seen that these ideas were formulated in the eighteenth and nineteenth century respectively. But as each took time to come into general usage they may, for the purpose of an essay, be described as the nineteenth century school and the twentieth century school.

The nineteenth century school set great store by rules which gave rise to the prospect of reward or punishment. Arrangements were future-oriented. It was the *prospect* of good or bad consequences which shaped behavior, because man—being reasonable—would choose pleasurable consequences over disagree-able ones.

The psychological paradigm of the twentieth century school was fundamen-tally at odds with this earlier one. It asserted that behavior is fundamentally shaped by *past* events and not by future ones. It stated that human behavior is *not* reasonable, as the utilitarians understood that term "Understandable," yes, but not "reasonable." The utilitarian ethic, which so much depended on the belief that behavior freed of restraint would seek an optimal level, was simply undermined. Behavior came to be seen as much less predictable, far more problematic. If anything useful was to influence behavior in the masses, it would almost by definition have to be the work of persons of special understanding. Philip Rieff has called this "the therapeutic ethic."

For the purposes of social policy, a crucial distinction between these two schools of belief lies in their time perspective. The utilitarian ethic, as stated, is future-oriented. Behavior is seen as controlled by events yet to come. The prospect of gain or loss, punishment or reward, results in certain kinds of conduct. The therapeutic ethic, in contrast, is past-oriented. Behavior is seen as significantly controlled by events that have already occurred. The basic paradigm of the therapeutic ethic is that of the formation in childhood of psychological characteristics which carry a heavy predictive load. The Freudian formulation "anatomy is destiny" gives a feel for the determinist nature of the doctrine. If one thinks of the present as the past for purposes of the future, the implications which the different perspectives have for social policy becomes more distinct. At what point in *time* does society intervene in order to bring about desired behavior? Now? Or sometimes from now? If one desires good behavior in a child, does one *give* him a candy bar or *promise him one?*

In the Freudian view, the basic mechanism seen to be at work is the frustration-aggression syndrome—the assertion that in the individual the one leads to the other, and always to the other. As a fully-articulated social theory, applying to groups as well as to individuals, the hypothesis made its definitive appearance with the publication in 1939 of John Dollard's *Frustration and Aggression*, a product of the Institute of Human Relations of Yale University.[1] Three points are to be noted about this work by Dollard, very possibly the most distinguished American social scientist of that period, and his not less gifted associates. First, the work did not purport to account for *all* forms of aggression, although this quickly became the "vulgar" interpretation. To the contrary, Dollard and his associates would have cheerfully agreed that all manner of aggression can arise from nothing more or less than the utilitarian perception that something was to be gained by acting in such a manner.[b] Second, they claimed to present what was "still" only an "hypothesis." Nothing more. They had illustrative material, but were not prepared to assert that they had proof. Third, the work, while assertive of its limitations, was *not* limited in its ambitions (and far less in its ultimate influence). The authors write:

In no sense can it [*Frustration and Aggression*] claim to be a complete systematization of human behavior, either of the individual or the group. But it does endeavor to place within a common discourse such diverse phenomena as

[b]This thought was confirmed by Dollard in a personal conversation in 1975. I would wish to acknowledge a profound debt to this great innovator and humanist.

strikes and suicides, race prejudice and reformism, sibling jealousy and lynching, satirical humor and criminality, street fights and the reading of detective stories, wife-beating and war.

A number of writers were seen as having anticipated the hypothesis. William James had spoken of the terrible tension in man, "the most ruthlessly ferocious of beasts," and yet a "gregarious" animal also. The Marxian doctrines of class struggle and of the nature of the state were seen to depend "to some extent, again by implication" on the frustration-aggression principle. But Freud was their master, specifically the early Freud who "regarded the tendency to seek pleasure and avoid pain as the basic mechanism of all mental functioning." (The later doctrine of the death wish is noted, but stated to be outside the scope of their volume.) Freud held that "Frustration occurred whenever pleasure-seeking or pain-avoiding was blocked; aggression was the 'primordial reaction' to this state of affairs. . . ." It was normally directed outward: it *could* be turned inward.

All of this was not so much a rejection of the utilitarian calculus, which also saw man as governed by pleasure-seeking and pain-avoidance, as it was a fundamentally new view of the *mode* of governance over these motives. There was no longer a "calculus" at work—but, rather, impulse. The new model of behavior was simple enough. Behavior begins with *instigation*, "some antecedent condition of which the predicted response is the consequence." In the authors' illustration, the bell of an ice-cream vendor rings on the street and "James, aged four" runs toward his mother, tugging her skirt and declaring his desires. A *goal-response* is "that reaction which reduces the strength of the instigation to a degree at which it no longer has as much of a tendency to produce the predicted behavior sequence." Goal responses have a *reinforcing effect* "that induces the learning of the acts preceding them." Such sequences, however, can be interfered with, blocked. "Such an inteference with the occurrence of an instigated goal-response at its proper time in the behavior sequence is called a frustration." It is always followed by aggression, "*an act whose goal-response is injury to an organism* (or organism-surrogate)." When a frustrating condition occurs to several individuals simultaneously, a social response occurs, as against a merely individual response. That is to say, group aggression occurs. "Acts of physical violence," fantasies of "getting even," and generalized destructive or remonstrative outbursts" are all "clearly forms of aggression. . . ." The greater the interference with the goal-response, the greater the aggression.

Although, as noted, the hypothesis is illustrated in terms of a child seeking to persuade his mother to buy ice cream, the authors turn quickly enough to adult behavior, and not infrequently behavior of a vicious and violent kind. Dollard, in his great work on race relations, *Caste and Class in a Southern Town*, had formulated the general principle of frustration and aggression from the early writings of Freud and "applied it to a Southern Community in the United

States." It was a profoundly empathic, even passionate work, but his hatred of oppression did not prevent an illusionless depiction of the self-destructive behavior of the oppressed. In a similar mode of even-handed assessment, *Frustration and Aggression* cited research that associated the rise and fall of violence, and of political fortunes, with quite external economic conditions. Thus, in the Southern United States:

Low indices, or bad economic conditions, should represent a greater interference with customary goal-responses than do high indices or good business conditions. The annual numbers of lynchings and property crimes with violence were taken as measures of aggression. As one index of the severity of interference with economic actions, the annual per acre value of cotton was computed for fourteen Southern states for the years 1882 to 1930. The correlation between this index and the number of lynchings in these same fourteen years was =.67; i.e., the number of lynchings (aggression) increased when the amount of interference increased.

As with the powerless, so with the powerful. "That politicians as well as Negroes may be the target of displaced aggression is indicated by two studies which suggest that there is a greater tendency for rural districts to vote the incumbents out of office following years of poor rainfall than of good." Indeed, true political motive can become markedly elusive in such analysis. "Lasswell reports the case of a political reformer, part of whose zeal, the investigator believed, could be traced back definitely to basic hatreds against his father and brother."

Crime in Britain came to their attention. A British researcher writing in 1925 on *Social Aspects of the Business Cycle* had found that property crimes with use of violence had a similar correlation of minus 0.44 with economic indices. As stock prices had gone down, robbery had gone up. Political extremism and violence in other countries came in for considerable speculation, although little research was at hand. The thesis that the rise of the Nazis was a consequence of the harshness of the Versailles Treaty was duly noted; communism and fascism were dealt with in terms of frustration and aggression—whence the book drifted off into a discussion of the Ashanti.

The book lived on. It may prove to have been the formative political study of the mid-century, for it gave to political discourse its newest, most powerful argument, an argument now so pervasive as to be almost unnoticed. In a period of four months[c] between settling on the subject of the present essay and finally writing it, I kept watch on the newspapers and periodicals of a number of countries. The frustration-aggression argument was repeatedly encountered, and almost always (to anticipate a later point) in connection with a claim for activist social policies.

Dollard and his associates illustrated their hypothesis with topical material

---

[c]March-June, 1974.

concerning race relations in the United States, criminal behavior in Great Britain, and political extremism in other countries. Thirty-five years later the same subjects were still much in the news, only in the interval public debate, which the researchers had seen as illustrating the concept, had ended up by adopting it.

In the United States racial violence continued as a subject of intense public concern. Dollard had discussed the frustrations which had led to white aggression. Now rather the opposite was to be explained—black aggression—the explanations were almost invariably cast in the frustration-aggression mode. The report of the National Advisory Commission on Civil Disorders (1968) was a quintessential statement of this view, a point of interest not least because the members were chosen almost at random in the course of a frantic day in the White House in mid-1967 that was to conclude with a presidential speech announcing the establishment of the body. Whatever else it was, the Commission was representative of the opinion of public figures of the time, and its clearest model of social behavior was that of Dollard and his associates. The report catalogued a huge list of conditions frustrating American minorities and stated that unless a massive effort was undertaken by government to change these conditions, aggression would continue and would mount. Judgments will differ as to how much or how little the federal government did in fact respond to this warning and this challenge. (It will be recalled that the legislative "bill" presented by the Commission was so formidable that the president who had established it would not formally receive its report.) But there can be little doubt that in the judgment of the Commission members the government response was wholly inadequate. In a follow-up report *One Year Later* (1969) this was so stated. Vast violence was seen to be at hand. Although at this very point violence, in the form of large-scale civil disorders, all but ceased, the Commission supporters—products of a strong belief system—were no more shaken by this than were the nineteenth century religious groups which had set dates for the end of the world.

A very few years later, a publicist who had been much associated with the thesis of the Commission report sought to explain the abrupt end to violence by asserting that the Commission had in fact offered two possibilities for social policy: To do a great deal, or to *do nothing*. He wrote, "In actuality, the Commission predicted that doing nothing more for the cities and their disadvantaged residents would lead to a period of relative calm, if only because no new hopes would be raised to be frustrated." He did not, however, reject the basic model of behavior implicit in the Report: ". . . the Commission also predicted that such a course of inaction . . . in the long run would lead to more violence than before. . . ."

Who is to say? For all anyone knows, mass violence could be permanently at an end, or it could resume with unparalleled force in the morning. Our concern here is with the ideas of man that are employed in the formulation and advocacy of social policy. Here, with respect to this American issue, the frustration-aggression mode is by every appearance pervasive and generally unchallenged.

Thus in the spring of 1974, a governor of the Federal Reserve System, appointed by a Republican president, spoke out in strong protest against a critic of Federal Reserve monetary policies, in this instance a professor of the University of Chicago, who proposed that the central bank raise its discount rates. The central banker stated that if this were done there would be massive unemployment, riots in the streets, and possibly even a change in the American form of government. Nor would this be the least of it. He guessed that if such policies were followed, by the time the professor returned from his summer in Vermont he would find the "cities burned down and the University of Chicago along with them."

Meanwhile, in Britain, crime and other forms of deviant behavior remained an issue of public debate, as it had been when Dollard wrote, but increasingly were being explained and "justified" in terms of the Dollard hypothesis. Not inappropriately, the leader of the British Liberal party deplored this tendency in a letter to the *Times* (London).

The . . . most vicious aspect of our world is the growing custom of blackmailing the government or anyone else you dislike by attacking a third party. Violence in a free society is always contemptible but violence and force, whether by kidnapping, indiscriminate destruction aimed at a third party or, on a less serious level, by strikes aimed at the public, is a new horror in the long list of evil ingenuity. Yet some of the press and television with their thirst for sensation often pander to this peculiarly repulsive vice by building up the perpetrators as heroes. Further, perfectly decent people are coming to believe that they will get no attention unless they indulge in a demonstration or a strike. And, also, they are often right.

If I think Scotland should have self-government or if I don't like the decision of a court of law, I should seize a small child and take off its ears, fingers and nose one by one until I got my way. I should then at least get an interview on TV. No doubt, too, I should receive sympathetic support from those who attribute it all to the wickedness of the capitalist system or to the intolerable provocation of the [Tory] Monday Club. If anyone interfered they would be castigated by some of the press for irresponsible conduct.

Simultaneously, the threat of Fascist movements was abroad—or was seen to be—as much as in Dollard's time. Only weeks before the British Liberal deplored individual violence, the central body of the Indian Congress Party deplored collective violence. If it did so in less convincing terms, it nonetheless deployed the Dollard hypothesis. As summarized in the *Statesman* (Calcutta):

The Right reaction and vested interests, it [The Central Committee] said, had resorted to "naked and systematic violence" because in free elections, the common people had repeatedly frustrated their attempts to capture power. "Frustration in the camp of reaction has increased because of repeated reaffirmations of the people's support to the programmes "[of] the Congress. . . ." According to the committee, the vested interests found the Congress an obstacle and "hence the verdict of the ballot box is being sought to be thwarted by extra-parliamentary and Fascist methods of coercion and duress."

It is to be expected that a proposition as universal as that which Freud, and then Dollard, set forth should manifest itself in international terms, and this has been very much the case. The foreign aid programs begun by the United States following World War II, and similar programs adopted by other countries and by various international organizations, have characteristically been propounded in terms of frustration and aggression. As may be characteristic of a settled and affluent society, the prospect of aggression arising from individuals and groups and nations either absolutely poor or "relatively deprived" has been much in the minds of American statesmen in the postwar period. It led, almost immediately, to a very considerable program of foreign aid, which endures to this day. In the rhetoric of the program, humanitarian concerns are usually accorded a certain priority, but the *threat* of poverty, absolute or relative, is never far from the center of the argument. In 1949, in an address at Colgate University on the Marshall Plan, Harlan Cleveland spoke of "the revolution of rising expectations," which became the master concept providing an enduring rationale to what might otherwise have proved a fleeting impulse. A quarter century later the president of the United States, justifying the most recent foreign aid proposal, assured the Congress in these terms: "It is clear that in the modern world, peace and poverty cannot easily endure side by side. In the long term, we must have peace without privation, or we may not have a durable peace at all."

In 1975, to sum up at the summit, the president of the World Bank officially endorsed this view of human nature in his annual report. The Indian Congress Party showed some ingenuity in explaining that democracy made *capitalists* violent, that is to say a privileged class. The president of the World Bank employed the hypothesis for the much more common purpose of explaining *mass* violence. More accurately, for predicting it. Yet more accurately, for threatening it, it having become commonplace to propose that unless some social program or other was adopted, frustration, then violence, would ensue. The president of the World Bank wanted more loans to more developing countries which are becoming more urbanized, and which, in the specific context of the President's statement, many children die of malnutrition:

Now what do these figures imply?

They make it certain that the cities of the developing world are going to find it incredibly difficult to provide employment, and minimally decent living conditions, for the hundreds of millions of new entrants into urban economies which are already severely strained.

An even more ominous implication is what the penalties for failure may be. Historically, violence and civil upheaval are more common in cities than in the countryside. Frustrations that fester among the urban poor are readily exploited by political extremists. If cities do not begin to deal more constructively with poverty, poverty may well begin to deal more destructively with cities.

There is an idea of man at work here which arises from something other than man's experience. Twentieth century history does *not* record the war of the poor against the rich. Without significant exception, the major wars of this century, as of the last, and of the ones before that, have been wars either of the rich against the rich, or the rich against the poor. (Indeed, the later model—"imperialist" war—was supposed to be the characteristic form of modern violence.) Nor is there, so far, any instance of a postwar country having "gone Communist" because its rising expectations of material well-being were frustrated. Yet the assertion that this would happen has been a central theme of American foreign policy for three decades. In 1965, for example, President Johnson explicitly told leaders of the Senate that unless massive amounts of emergency food relief were sent to India, the subcontinent world would "go Communist," presumedly as an act of psychological aggression against the affluent West. He was almost certainly wrong, but he believed what he said, and was believed.[d]

The frustration-aggression argument seemingly grows stronger as poor nations acquire aggressive resources. The *New York Times*, in an editorial noting with "dismay" the diversion of resources which enabled India to explode a nuclear device a few weeks after the president had proposed the 1974 aid program, nonetheless thought this very fact an additional grounds for going ahead with an aid program: "Countries are more likely to cooperate with the international systems upon which we depend if they are achieving their development goals than if they are failing to do so."

Again, there is an idea of man at work here. An Indian journalist, writing from the United States at the time of the above-mentioned editorial, was confident that aid donors would not cut off or curtail their assistance to India in the aftermath of its "going nuclear." He estimated that the humanitarian grounds for aid might diminish: To the extent that aid had been given out of pity, he said, it would decrease. But what would not decrease was aid based on the perception of the threat of aggression arising from frustrated aspiration: "The international community today accepts the fact that unless the gap between the rich nations and the poor and within a country between the rich and poor is narrowed there is a domestic and international threat to peace and stability."

The object of this review of randomly encountered evidence is modest: It is merely to suggest that the idea of man implicit in the frustration and aggression hypothesis has taken hold, is widely believed, and perhaps even more widely deployed in the advocacy of social policy. A page from Dollard's own work may be relevant here. In the tentative and measured way that characterized their argument throughout, they had illustrated the hypothesis that criminality derives either from "higher-than-average frustration, lower-than-average anticipation of punishment, or both."

---

[d]On the other hand, I would suspect that a good deal of *elite* attraction to Soviet or Chinese Communism in the Third World is a form of aggression against the United States arising out of frustrated attempts to develop in the American manner.

This conclusion, once it has been arrived at, seems to sink almost to the level of a truism; but its validity has not always been so obvious. It must be remembered that a few decades ago the most widely accepted view of crime held that it was a mark of congenital degeneracy.

Just so with their central hypothesis: It was quite rare a generation or so back; it is commonplace today. In the minds of many, an old idea of man has been supplanted by a new idea.

Consider the assertion that poverty and distress lead to social conflagration. They may well do. But this was not always thought to be the case. No earlier paradigm of behavior leads routinely to this conclusion. A hoary charge of British politics is that the capitalist classes desire there to be a "pool of unemployed" because it "maintains labor discipline." Now the charge may or may not be true; for our purposes the important point is that it was believed to be true. This is to say that persons sympathetic to the British working man accepted as reasonable the idea that the frustration inherent in unemployment would *lower* aggressiveness, not raise it. This conviction may be encountered in the United States as well. In the spring of 1975 an article in the *New York Times Magazine* entitled "Recession is Capitalism as Usual" carried the subhead "A radical economist argues that our present system requires periodic slumps to restore profits and discipline labor." I would offer the impression that whereas in Britain the doctrine is most often encountered in relatively unsophisticated surroundings, in the United States the hold of the "frustration-aggression" doctrine on elites tends to make the earlier view rather a no-nonsense utilitarian view, one that is special indeed and a sign of almost super sophistication. In the succession described by Midge Decter, the "radical economist" of the *Times Magazine* is the offspring of two liberal economists: elites within elites. How very different from the view of a contemporary American newspaper columnist who writes: "Franklin Roosevelt was probably a great man, . . . but essentially he worked through the 30's to make America safe for corporations. The whole welfare apparatus of the New Deal served to head off a revolution, and protect the property of the rich." A similar transition has occurred in the depiction of international affairs. Where it was once asserted and believed that colonialist countries kept others submissive by keeping them poor, it is now asserted that the rich provide aid only to ward off "worldwide class war."

For all this divergence of emphasis, and genuine clash of interpretation, it is not at all clear that a utilitarian outlook is necessarily incompatible with Freudian insight. Nor do psychologists seem disposed to insist that the evidence points in one direction or another—or, more precisely, that there are these opposed directions. Some of the evidence Dollard cited would no longer be accepted. Crime is at best weakly correlated with the business cycle. (But then they did not cite a *strong* correlation.) Political scientists searching for the causes of urban unrest in the 1960s find, if anything, that protest flourishes in relatively open political systems, as against closed ones.[2] But as a basic psychological mechanism, the hypothesis seems secure. So, equally, does the utilitarian hypothesis continue to command the regard of persons concerned with decent and reasonably effective government. The difficulties arise from the translation of an hypothesis into an ethic in such ways that *interests* commence to distort perceptions.

It happens that each school of thought—no accident, perhaps—appeared at about the time a new social class, which found distinct advantages in the selective use of the new learning, was also appearing. The nineteenth century school appeared at a time of a general movement toward lesser government regulation and intervention, and was put to use justifying this movement. The twentieth century school appeared at a time of a general movement toward greater intervention, and was correspondingly employed. An ethic was constructed out of materials that were ethically neutral, or at least not imperative. To cite a utilitarian example, Sidney and Beatrice Webb, good Socialists at the time, were nonetheless disdainful of Lloyd George's reforms of the period 1908-11. Their views of the motivations of British workmen seem scarcely removed from those of the most primate of mill owners. Beatrice Webb writes in her autobiography:

To us, the compulsory insurance with automatically distributed money, allowances during illness or worklessness, with free choice of doctor under the panel system, would not and could not prevent the occurrence of sickness or unemployment. Indeed, the fact that sick and unemployed persons were entitled to money incomes without any corresponding obligation to get well and keep well, or to seek and keep employment, seemed to us likely to encourage malingering and a disinclination to work for their livelihood.

It is fair to assume that this was a common understanding, for the time, of what made people tick. It is simply that the Webbs—and the "mill owners" alike!— translated this understanding into an ethic. This ethic held that men must be driven: to socialism, or sobriety, or whatever, but driven by iron necessity. In the process utilitarianism acquired a reputation for an unfeeling callousness toward the unorganized and the weak. To repeat, this was not immanent in doctrine; it was a selective use of doctrine to serve class interests.

Something similar occurred with the translation of Freudian doctrine into an ethic. Utilitarian thought was not automatically inclined to oppose government intervention, and neither was Freudian thought disposed to favor it. Freudians have been in ways the most apolitical of theorists. Certainly they are not compulsively committed to big government. (Indeed, Freudian doctrine can be thought close to fundamentalist religion in this regard, holding the world to be rather a hopeless place and concentrating on the salvation of the individual.) But here again a class interest appeared that could be served by selective use of Freudian doctrine, in this instance the hypothesis of frustration and aggression.

Frustration and aggression itself makes explicit how wide a range of policy conclusions might be drawn from its hypothesis. Recall the assertion that criminality may originate not only in frustration, but in a "lower-than-average anticipation of punishment." This *could* be made into an argument for restoring public executions. (Indeed some research indicates that each execution prevents eight to twenty murders; a student of Gordon Tullock estimates at least two.[3]) It would be wrong to say that the case for intimidating the would-be criminal is never made, but it is now made defensively, at least by persons who would wish to appear well intentioned. The policy implications of the view of crime which Dollard set forth are almost invariably directed toward intimidating society rather than the criminal.

Similarly, Dollard cites the view that the harshness of the Versailles treaty led to German extremism, but he also offers the judgment of himself and his colleagues that the frustration-aggression hypothesis would suggest that the aggressiveness of Nazi Germany resulted in part from "the conciliatory attitude of the English upper classes which has diminished the anticipation of punishment. . . ." This is scarcely a soft view of the world. But it is simply a fact that wherever the Freudian hypothesis would lead with equal cogency to a hard or a soft policy conclusion—public hangings or the abolition of capital punishment— it is almost always soft option that prevails.

Typically, such implications are drawn by persons of a professional, *therapeutic* class that has been growing apace for several generations now, whose economic and social interests reside heavily in the expansion of government activity. In a passage from *Tortilla Flat* (1935), John Steinbeck nicely caught the intersection of the old and the new view of things in which it is the *poor* child who preaches contentment and the professional—specifically, the *doctor*—who becomes outraged (having been frustrated in his expectations!) at this cheerfulness.

At about this time in California it became the stylish thing for school nurses to visit the classes and to catechize the children on intimate details of their home life. In the first grade, Alfredo was called into the principal's office, for it was thought that he looked thin.

The visiting nurse, trained in child psychology, said kindly, "Freddie, do you get enough to eat?"

"Sure," said Alfredo.

"Well, now. Tell me what you have for breakfast."

"Tortillas and beans," said Alfredo.

The nurse nodded her head dismally to the principal.

"What do you have when you go home for lunch?"

"I don't go home."

"Don't you eat at noon?"

"Sure. I bring some beans wrapped up in a tortilla."

Actual alarm showed in the nurse's eyes, but she controlled herself. "At night what do you have to eat?"

"Tortillas and beans."

Her psychology deserted her. "Do you mean to stand there and tell me you eat nothing but tortillas and beans?"

Alfredo was astonished. "Jesus Christ," he said, "what more do you want?"

In due course the school doctor listened to the nurse's horrified report. One day he drove up to Teresina's house to look into the matter. . . .

The doctor stayed two hours, for his scientific interest was piqued. He went away shaking his head.

He shook his head incredulously while he made his report. "I gave them every test I know of," he said, "teeth, skin, blood, skeleton, eyes, co-ordination. Gentlemen, they are living on what constitutes a slow poison, and they have from birth. Gentlemen, I tell you I have never seen healthier children in my life!" His emotion overcame him. "The little beasts," he cried. "I never saw such teeth in my life. I never saw such teeth."[4]

In its own way the doctor's view is as callous as that of any root-hog-or-die fundamentalist. The children are content, but he would have them otherwise. He has, if you will, a class interest in their being otherwise. Just how long any American community was going to be satisfied with tortillas and beans for a diet is questionable, but there is no doubt that by this time—the 1930s—American elites were acquiring a view of the individual and society radically at odds with those of their parents. Dollard writes (in 1939): "Even [sic] college students have been instructed systematically through courses in the social sciences that 'society' is really responsible for many of the problems confronting individuals." An essential detail. The new doctrine—which so often in practice took the form of asserting a general community interest in "the forgotten man" and made a case for sympathy with persons lower in the social order—had its first impact much higher in that social order. It was taught to college students in an age when, to a considerable extent, that still meant the likes of Yale men.

Dollard and his colleagues wrote in a time that truly *was* one of transition. An "old" America was still intact.

Americans advertise themselves as "masters of their fate." Concretely this means that Americans tend to blame only themselves for their frustrations and that they incline to be self-aggressive when they fail. To place responsibility in this fashion is the essence of what is sometimes called "the pioneer tradition" in American life. It is part of the individualism of the business man to proclaim not only that he does not require aid from the government, but that such aid, if and when it is forced upon him, will hinder his own efforts to be successful. Men who fail, therefore, frequently turn the aggression they experience upon themselves and mumble that "things would have been different if I had been able to. . . ." The dominant Protestant religion, as Max Weber has shown in somewhat exaggerated fashion, helps to foster this general feeling that it is the duty of the individual to seek virtue, to avoid evil, and to be held culpable if he deviates from the path of righteousness.

Guilt, as ever, is the coinage of exchange here. Who is responsible? What is to be done? An older generation had thought the individual to be captain of his fate, master of his soul, and when all did not go well, that individual was likely to turn his aggression inward, on himself. A newer generation learned otherwise. Or, rather, an elite of that generation—those exposed to the new teachings, just as it had been a similar elite which learned utilitarian individualism six or seven generations earlier.

(Although an elite class interest can be seen at work when a group adopts a theory of human behavior which sets great store in the kinds of services which that group is uniquely qualified to provide—i.e., to sell—one senses something less reassuring in the more recent applications of the frustration-aggression theory. Without evidence—what would *be* the evidence for or against such a proposition?—let me state a personal conviction that some American elites have more and more turned to the frustration-aggression thesis as a means of *denying* aggression. In particular "old American" elites, finding themselves so much assailed at home and abroad, take refuge in the thought that their assailants are motivated by hidden factors for which neither they—nor their evidently intended victims—can rightly be held accountable. In other words it is not really aggression that is showing, but merely frustration, a less frightening phenomenon. This is of course something very like infantilism, and may be trusted to put an end to that elite in fairly short order. It will not be the first ruling class undone by its own decencies, and the inability to perceive the indecencies of others.)

For the longest while older persons did not readily pick up the new ideas. Less educated persons did not. Not all college students did. In rough political terms, Democrats did and Republicans did not (after a time, Democrats who had not intended to become Republican, while a reverse migration commenced toward the Democratic party). Easterners did, Southerners and Midwesterners did not. This is only to restate the commonplace impressions of recent politics. Careful surveys are certainly in order before any final pronouncement is possible.

But none need doubt that only part of the nation changed its mind. The assumption that it is the responsibility of the individual to look after himself shattered in some groups, but remained intact in others. There was a partial break with the past, resulting in a fissure running raggedly along generational, cultural, class, and regional lines. This is already evident enough from survey data: Low income respondents are decisively less "permissive," more "old-fashioned."

So are older persons. In the 1972 election, as an instance, a New England senator, of considerable seniority and great respect, was defeated by a younger man from the opposing party, after having first beat back a challenge from a similar young man within her own party. By most accounts the most damaging event to her reelection campaign came when the charge was raised that she had done nothing to relieve unemployment in the state. The senator replied that this was not in fact a problem, that there were plenty of jobs available for men willing to work. Her challenger expressed disbelief that anyone in the present age could think so ill of humanity and so well of society. His political instinct was sound.

Successful politicians adapt. Any of our recent three American presidents was capable of thinking as the senator did, but none has been so imprudent as to say as much. President Ford possibly excepted. Presidents preside as over a society torn by deep religious antagonism and at most send coded signals of support to either side. In the case of Lyndon B. Johnson, the contending views were part of his own intellectual and emotional make up. He could follow a frustration and aggression argument when applied to foreign affairs. Indians must be fed, else they would become explosive and radical. He brought the Secretary of Health, Education and Welfare with him to meet with South Vietnamese generals in planning their struggle against communism. But when much the same analysis was employed in shaping his war on poverty at home, he was first baffled, then frustrated, then—he, too!—not inconsiderably aggressive.

The president was proud of his antipoverty legislation. It was, as he said when first apprised of the planning begun in the Kennedy days, *his* kind of program. Yet in short order he found himself dismayed by what he had evidently wrought. I have argued in *Maximum Feasible Misunderstanding* (1969) that the source of this great falling out was the surprise, even consternation, in the Bureau of the Budget and the White House at the way the OEO Community Action Programs seemed to be turning out. Nothing has more confirmed this view, to my mind at all events, than the unanimity with which those associated with the program took offense at what I wrote, finding it incomprehensible and presumptively malicious.

The Community Action Programs, although in time they became quite varied in nature and won considerable support, were originally conceived in terms of the "opportunity theory of delinquency" set forth by Cloward and Ohlin in their study *Delinquency and Opportunity* (1960). This theory was directly derived from the frustration-aggression model of human behavior. Youth, finding opportunity blocked, became delinquent. To prevent delinquency, opportunity structures must be changed through community action, which would inspire self-confidence and reduce aggression.

President Johnson left the White House asserting that "kooks and sociologists" had ruined his poverty program. Looking back it is quite clear that as between the Office of Economic Opportunity, the Budget, and the White House there was indeed great disparity as to what each thought the other was doing. My study was directed almost solely to this bureaucratic process, and had nothing to say concerning the desirability or undesirability of the Community Action Programs as such. But my account would have been better understood if I had stated more clearly that the frustration-aggression model of behavior implicit in the theoretical antecedents of these OEO programs was simply not familiar, in that formulation, to persons schooled in the utilitarian model.

President Johnson could react to threats abroad arising, as he thought, from frustration, but instinct told him not to go about encouraging such behavior at home. "Once you have paid him the danegeld," Kipling had written, "You never get rid of the Dane."

To have been involved in social policy over the past two decades is to have encountered this dichotomy—between groups, within groups, and even within individuals—repeatedly; but at no point so vividly as at the end of the 1960s.

In the winter of 1968-69, I was appointed to the new position of Assistant to the President for Urban Affairs. The post was established because of the rise of violence in cities—group violence as in riots, individual violence as in crime. This violence, though limited, even contained by most standards, was widely—and for widely different reasons—seen as exceptionally ominous and threatening.[e] (Certainly it threatened the liberal political tradition. If mass violence were not brought to an end, and individual violence not curbed, some kind of decisive illiberal response was likely.) For the widest range of reasons it was necessary for mass violence to cease and for individual violence to moderate. To a degree, this task fell to me, and, to a degree, I was able to carry it out. My approach was not especially systematic, but if it had to be characterized, the term "utilitarian" would probably make the best fit. Which is to say that keeping the peace would

---

[e]An example of this perception may be seen in this excerpt from a question and answer period which the Prime Minister of Canada held at Queen's University, Kingston, on November 8, 1968, at the height of the mood which I describe:

On NATO for instance, I happen to believe that in a very real sense civilization and culture in North America are more menaced, more strongly menaced, more strongly threatened, by internal disorders than by external pressure.

I feel very strongly that disorder in the great cities of the United States of America, problems created by urbanization, problems created by racial strife, problems created by the unrest in many sectors of the society—not only the young and the trade unions but also the new elites in the North American society. I believe these troubles may quite seriously lead to large rebellions and large disturbances of civil order and of social stability in North America.

And I believe that if in the next half a dozen years or so there were to be great riots and beginnings of civil war in the United States of America, I am quite certain they would overflow the borders and they would perhaps link up with the underprivileged Mexican and the underprivileged Canadian—it might be the peon south of the American border but in Canada it might be the Indian, it might be the Metis, it might be a lot of underprivileged in Canada. I don't think it would be the separatists but that is another argument. I personally happen to believe that these sources of disturbance, these are areas which we should fear and seek to correct with as great urgency as perhaps anything that is happening in Europe.

And for this reason I am very concerned that the Canadian Government through its own policies, and through any influence it might have on its friends and allies in and out of NATO, that we get people to understand this, that in a very real sense we are not so much threatened by the ideologies of Communism or of Fascism or by even I would say we are not so much threatened by atomic bombs and ICBM's, as we are by the large sectors of the world—two-thirds of the world's population that goes to bed hungry every night and large fractions of our own society which do not find fulfillment in this society.

And this is the background of these reviews in which we are embarked. I am not predicting what the outcome will be but I am saying that in my scale of values I am perhaps less worried now about what might happen over the Berlin Wall than what might happen in Chicago, New York, and perhaps in our own great cities in Canada.

be rewarded and breaking the peace would be punished—this principle to apply not coincidentally but deliberately and most importantly to the matter of keeping the rhetorical peace. A number of new social programs, such as revenue sharing for cities and the Family Assistance Plan—a guaranteed income—were proposed; no old program was discontinued; some, such as food stamps, were greatly expanded. But the main signal was that mass violence would not be rewarded and must end. It ended.

I should not wish to be misunderstood here. *I* did not end it. There wasn't that much government *could* do to end it. But in the main, given the disorderliness of government, the limits of my own ability, and the ill-defined nature of such brief authority as I had, government followed about the course I had hoped for and in a fairly concise sequence mass violence stopped, while individual violence—crime—began at least to level off. I did not expect this to be an agreeable task, but neither did I expect to be anathematized as I was in so many settings for the role that had been thrust upon me.

The president of an Ivy League university pronounced himself profoundly anxious and distressed that the care of such matters should have fallen into such hands. He could scarce disguise his conviction—hope?—that violence would only grow worse in the aftermath of my ministrations. A man of conscience, he spoke out. A man of strict conformist views, he said what was being said in his circle—to wit, that there would be more violence not less because of approaches to the problem then being taken in Washington. Frustrated at not being heeded, he, too, became aggressive, if only rhetorically—a technique the upper-class students of the period had rather perfected.

How very far from the moral sentiments of that most utilitarian president of Princeton, who in his inaugural address as president of the United States in 1913 declared that "the firm basis of government is justice, not pity. . . ." Or for that matter, how very distant from the president of Harvard who, in 1927, delivered a most severe judgment on alleged anarchistic violence of that era. Yet it was no less fitting that an Ivy League president should be permissive about communal violence two generations later. To risk a larger assertion than can perhaps be proved, there is every appearance of class interest at stake in all these pronouncements. To a surprising degree, it would appear that the same "people" are involved, and much the same urge to predominate. But where the earlier mastery was based on control of property, the more recent seems to be based on control of government.

It may be speculated that in a post-industrial society the importance of property recedes and that of government advances. What persists is the "New World" equivalent of a "Tory will to power," hence the changing rhetoric of elite education and the institutions that are manned by it. Such assertions are, to repeat, perilously speculative, yet that is the purpose of this essay. We recall the way in which a "new" class, which is to say persons with a new economic function, chose selectively from the doctrine to laissez-faire just those aspects of doctrine that best suited their interests. In the process they imparted to the doctrine an association with class interests which continues to this time.

In just this way a yet newer, government-oriented class is selective in lessons learned from Dollard and, again, this class bias begins to make its impression. A representative of this viewpoint, for example, may say that a slum dweller is driven to violence by bad housing, or a college student by bad foreign policies, but may never say that a policeman is driven to brutality by feelings of relative deprivation brought about by a narrowing differential between his terms of employment and those of garbage men. In the course of the informal newspaper survey carried out for this essay, a *New York Times* article appeared reporting the early difficulties of the Community Action Programs of the Office of Economic Opportunity. One "incensed" Democratic governor had complained that OEO was providing money to groups for "beating up on local officials." The trouble had not gone away, the journalist wrote.

Politics is always close to the operations of the agency, and huge Democratic strongholds like Chicago, under the tight rein of Mayor Richard J. Daley, made certain that the community action funds in their areas were funneled with their approval to those they recognized as "indigenous leaders."

Often in such cases the representatives of the poor on a community action board were handpicked toadies of political machines.[5]

Now "toadies" would seem a strong word for use in a news story. But the middle-class OEO ideologists of the period were free in the use of such epithets against their working-class opponents, and middle-class journalists joined in. Just as laissez-faire assertions became more extreme as time passed, so have those of the newer school. The most persuasive explanation is that a class interest is served here, the post-industrial surplus of functionaries who, in the manner of industrialists who earlier turned to advertising, induce demand for their own products. The advent of the frustration-aggression hypothesis has facilitated—it may even have precipitated—a structural change in the demands that may be made on society. It is the largest accession yet to the armamentarium of those whose interests or inclination tends toward increasing the social activities of the state. The therapeutic ethic implies an "understanding" which is intrinsically linked to "compassion," and the government is seen as a possible engine of organized compassion.

To repeat, one final time: Such a tendency is not logically implicit in the frustration-aggression hypothesis, it is merely that the hypothesis is easily brought to bear for this purpose—as was utilitarianism for earlier purposes. In essence, it vastly facilitates the perception and interpretation of threat. In particular, when collective or aggregated misbehavior is observed or anticipated, it is comparatively easy, given this model of behavior, to assert that society is to blame and that the individuals or their groups are not morally responsible for their actions. As the psychological paradigm changes, there is a huge shift of responsibility. Society becomes guilty until proven innocent. Society in the abstract, that is. Such charges need never be taken too personally, and hence not overmuch resisted. Blaming society avoids the political cost of blaming specific individuals or groups. And, no matter how bad things get in the aftermath of anticipatory efforts to prevent their doing so, it may always be contended, and always is contended, that things would have been worse without such effort. If things get better, the effort succeeded.

More. There is a tendency of social policy formulated in this mode almost to *anticipate* failure, as a hedge against the prospect of running out of things to do. The words of the publicist commenting on the Kerner Commission are revealing. The Commission, he wrote, had in fact predicted that "doing nothing more for the cities and the disadvantaged residents would lead to a period of relative calm, *if only because no new hopes would be raised to be frustrated.*" (My italics.) Note the implied expectation. Even if something *were* done it wouldn't work, because hopes would be raised to a degree that would involve *some* frustration. Society is put on permanent notice: More must be done; more will always be insufficient.

This mode attained its highest form in New York City in the 1960s, and did not much change when the city verged on bankruptcy in the mid-1970s. Without noticeable exception, the city authorities made public the view that if municipal services of various kinds were to be cut back, "social insurrection" would follow. (This was the term of one of the Mayor's closest financial advisers. In private conversations, this belief was, if anything, stated with greater conviction.) Again, a curiously persisting class interest was to be perceived: The specific of the city's financial crisis was the need to raise money to pay interest on tax-free municipal bonds, a form of paper hardly much held among the proletariat. But there was absolutely no contrition about the extravagance that had brought the city to its desperate state: an extravagance in which the educated classes of the service-dispensing sort had got their share and more. More importantly, for our purposes, no one suggested that hard times might make for quiet times. Such a "model" of social behavior served no class interest—recall that it was bondholders as well as welfare recipients who were in jeopardy, the former perhaps the more so—nor did it make any independent claim on social policy by virtue of superior credibility.

It is the nature of social innovations—in a socially innovative society—mostly to fail. Most new businesses fail. Most new products fail. On one point in his researches that produced the electric light bulb, Thomas A. Edison is said to have noted that at least he had by then discovered eighty-seven varieties of filament that would *not* work. But some things do succeed, and that is what the process is all about. It is another thing, however, to ascribe failure to intention. An example may be taken from a letter sent in 1974 to *The New Republic* by an authority on housing at the University of California at Berkeley. Public housing was once a major interest of liberal social policy, and since the New Deal various housing programs have absorbed vast sums, at no point more than in recent years. But evidently to little advantage.

Public housing has been a massive failure, to be sure. But the reasons this program failed—which are well known—are not inherent in a program to create decent housing for poor people. We can design better programs, if we really want to provide the poor with decent homes and suitable living environments (which I'm not at all sure is the nation's goal, congressional pronouncements notwith-standing). But that will require along the order of $25 billion annually; more government intervention, not less (to control costs of land and mortgage funds, end housing discrimination, enforce housing codes, control rents and profits, establish meaningful tenant rights); and an end to the old public housing notion of creating special, stigmatizing compounds for the poor. The new infatuation with housing allowances . . . represents an unwillingness to face these realities.[6]

Twenty-five billion dollars is about what the Gross Nation Product of the United States *was* when the public housing programs began. Four prosperous decades later, it will barely suffice for a housing program—though in these intervening decades the housing of all Americans (including poor Americans) has much improved. Note particularly the concluding disdainful reference to the proposal to give cash payments to poor families to obtain housing in the market along with those not poor. That which does not increase the activities of government evidently does not serve the interests of this new class, any more than that which did increase the activities of government served the interests of the old one.

The emergence of this new class has been widely remarked. It is, at base, a technological phenomenon. A post-industrial society needs progressively fewer farmers, fewer factory workers, fewer clerks, fewer technicians, proportionate to the available work force; whilst simultaneously it educates an ever larger proportion of its youth at possibly declining, in the event not rising, levels of competence. Work has to be found, and in the main it is government work, or work paid for by governments, or subsidized (as through tax exemptions) by government.

This has every appearance of an international phenomenon, rather as was industrialization. In the United States the development has been pronounced for some while. During the Kennedy years, one of the factors influencing economic policy was the fact that such an extraordinary proportion of new jobs then being created were in government. The case for the New Economics was, in part, that the alternative was something conservatives would like even less, a continuation of this trend. The economic expansion associated with the Vietnam War interrupted this pattern, but evidently it has resumed following a pattern of "wedding cake federalism" (in contradiction to Morton Grodzin's "marble cake federalism"). This is to say, a four-tiered government employment profile surmounted by a bounteous president and first lady. First, a rather small federal establishment, stepping down and outwards to state government, local govern-ment, and then a large base of educators and others doing what Brigette Berger has called "people work."

In the most recent *Occupational Outlook Handbook* the Bureau of Labor Statistics estimates that through 1985 two-thirds of job openings will be to replace workers who die or retire. "New" jobs will be heavily concentrated in government—state and local government employment will rise 50 percent—following the wedding cake profile. In considerable measure these will be jobs for this new class and its political allies, created in response to a rhetoric of rising need for government intervention and government service.

Signs of discontent with the aggressiveness of this class began to appear in the 1970s. The 1972 election is probably best seen as such a reaction. The Democratic platform of that year called for an uninhibited expansion of government services. Given the composition of the delegates to the nominating convention of that year, it would be difficult to distinguish the pattern of politics involved from a late nineteenth century Republican convention calling for total tariffs and unlimited Civil War pensions.

The consequence of these tendencies is to be seen most graphically in the small towns where much of America continues to live. Increasingly this has become a world of public affluence and private squalor. Anyone living off the public sector lives well. The professors in the local teachers college-turned-state university branch go abroad for the summer. The state troopers fly to their fishing vacations. The school teachers have good houses and pensions. The men in the Agricultural and Soil Conservation Service have only the worry that their log of "telephonic communications" not show such a decline as to lead to thoughts of closing down the office. In the meantime, the small farms close down; the filling station attendants live week to week; the grocers die off; the "bench workers" in the local mills worry about tariffs and mergers. Any building associated with government is painted and trim; the others tend to sag. When they sag far enough, the case is made for a regional development program, financed with a mixture of federal and state funds.

In an address given in 1975 to the Liberal Party of New York, Senator Edmund S. Muskie of Maine expressed some of this feeling:

Four decades ago, we . . . discovered the possibilities of government action to better the lives of Americans. People were excited by the possibilities, and they prospered as a result.

But something has happened since then—and it's basically happened to us.

People still are discontented. They still want change, and it is still our responsibility to help them make change a reality.

Yet when the average citizen turns to us for help, what does he find?

Consider, for example, the 1972 National Platform of the Democratic Party.

If you wanted to read it, it would take a while. It runs about fifty pages, or nearly 15,000 words, and it reads like the catalogue of virtually every problem that we liberals think bothers the American people.

The Platform speaks knowledgeably about the Railway Labor Act, capital gains, taxes, funding for ethnic studies, the Equal Employment Opportunity Commission, the new towns program, bilingual education, community-based rehabilitation facilities, the Food for Peace Program, the Protocol on Chemical Warfare, and literally hundreds of other aspects of our incredibly complex national government.

It was a wonderfully comprehensive and esoteric document. It showed that we knew all about government, and knew just what government programs needed change.

Yet the results of the election showed that the 1972 platform was irrelevant, for all practical purposes.

For in promising so much for so many, it was meaningless. Nowhere in there was there any statement of what those hundreds of changes would cost. How much, for example, would the new towns program cost? Would we need higher taxes to pay for it? How many people really would be helped?

Or, what about capital gains tax reform? Would it soak just the rich? What about retired couples, supplementing their social security check with a blue-chip stock dividend? Would they be soaked, as well?

I read my mail, I talk with voters in the towns of Maine, and I listen. I find everywhere people who can't cite from the Federal Register but know what's wrong anyway.

They work hard, but they are not so sure anymore that 14 hour days in a lobster boat or the monotony of an assembly line are worth the effort. . . .

They sense that things are getting worse, not better. . . .

And most important, they don't believe that government really cares about them. All they need is one encounter with some government bureaucrat to confirm that. In Maine, for example, it now takes a full year to process a social security disability claim.

The people I hear in Maine, plainly, are demoralized and alienated. People everywhere are demoralized.

This is a class interest at work, corresponding to the postwar emergence of the "military-industrial complex" which, institutionalized in the Joint Chiefs of Staff, has made threat analysis a way of life in Washington. (Doubtless a Council of Social Advisors or any of a dozen similar proposed arrangements would serve the same purpose for this yet newer complex.) It is, moreover, a dynamic class—still up for bids, and and being bid for. Democrats, with their New Deal legacy, have a margin of advantage for its loyalty. A 1974 Gallup poll found only one college student in seven who would describe himself as a Republican. But 49 percent of the collegians called themselves Independents. Republicans such as Nelson Rockefeller in New York have prospered while increasing public expenditure, and it is certainly arguable from the budget data that the Republican national success in 1972 was at the very least accompanied by a great increase in such expenditure. In five years, 1969-1974, the national Republican administration increased the federal budget by half, and with a war winding down, not up. This makes all the more impressive the charge repeatedly made during the period that social expenditure was being reduced, when in fact it was increasing in an unprecedented amount. In the first five years of that Republican administration, spending exceeded revenues by $120 billion. There has been a deficit in roughly four years out of five since World War II.

Inflation may yet break the spell of the new ethic, much as depression discredited the old. Everything rises during inflationary period save generosity and a sense of abundance, or so historians suggest. Yet it is legitimate to suggest that these ideas of man that have contributed to inflation—or whatever—have an autonomy of their own, and are capable of revision and modification through further observations "reasonably propounded." The utilitarian ethic was, in its time, a new idea and into the time of John XXIII the Roman Catholic Church was arguing with it, challenging for instance the "liberal" doctrine that the market place alone might settle the wages of a workman. Others similarly charged utilitarianism with overemphasizing the rationality of man, and of slighting the affective and emotional in man's nature. The disappearance of "community" became a common theme in this literature. So, in turn, does the analysis of Freud and his followers invite critique. At the risk of depicting a process altogether more mannerly and cumulative than is ever the case, such a critique ought to proceed less in the manner of correcting error than in that of refining truth.

For great truths have been revealed. We are capable of understanding ourselves so much more in the aftermath of that great teacher, and of his followers such as Dollard. Consider the following passage by an author of utilitarian bent, touching on the most devastating of all the phenomena associated with the therapeutic ethic—that nothing ever seems to get better.

The transformation of the bourgeois citizen into the bourgeois consumer has dissolved that liberal-individualist framework which held the utopian impulses of modern society under control.

One used to be encouraged to control one's appetites—now one is encouraged to satisfy them without delay. The inference is that one has a right to satisfy one's appetites without delay—and when this "right" is frustrated, as it always is in some way or other, an irritated populace turns to the state to do something about it. All this is but another way of saying that twentieth-century capitalism itself, in its heedless emphasis on economic growth and ever-increasing prosperity, incites ever more unreasonable expectations, in comparison with which the actuality of the real world appears ever more drab and disconcerting. It doesn't matter what economic growth is actually achieved, or what improvements are effected—they are all less than satisfying. Ours is a world of promises, promises—and in such a world everyone, to some degree or another, automatically feels deprived.

The authors of *Frustration and Aggression* are not able to save us from this condition, but clearly enough anticipated it. They wrote:

Whether or not a so-called higher standard of living leads to the gratification or the frustration of the additional instigated goal-responses to which it gives rise is an issue that must be raised but that cannot be answered satisfactorily.

This is work of enduring quality, and altogether unpolitical. The difficulty of the new doctrine, as with the old, lies in the uses to which it is put. If man was once seen as too autonomous, the therapeutic ethic depicts him as too dependent. If the tendency was once to exaggerate rationality, it is now the opposite—to exaggerate the irrational. In the sequence of threat and response, the possibility of charity is denied. In the quest for compassionate policy, it is made to seem that society responds only from fear. Society becomes distributive, but not sharing. Society becomes distracted as political violence, or politically interpreted violence, commands attention first here, then there, in a mindless and meaningless competition. Most seriously, a preoccupation with the past, and the present-that-will-become-the-past has a morbific effect on social policy, a kind of seizure of sin that denies the possibility of redemption. And through all this, there is the peculiarly disturbing spectacle of elites exploiting a legitimate egalitarian tradition.

A reaction has set it—as in the growing criticism of the "services strategy" in dealing with problems of poverty and social disorganization. Let it be hoped that it is not reactionary. For it could be. A far more moderate correction is in order. Man is neither autonomous nor autonomic. Man is merely social. It is curious how often we end where Aristotle began.

Notes

1. Reprinted by permission of the Yale University Press from *Frustration and Aggression* by John Dollard, Leonard W. Doob, Neal E. Miller, O.H. Mowrer, Robert R. Sears *in collaboration with* Clellan S. Ford, Carl Iver Hovland, Richard T. Sollenberger. Copyright 1939, Yale University Press.

2. See Peter K. Eisinger, "The Conditions of Protest Behavior in American Cities," *American Political Science Review* 67, 1 (March 1973): 11-28.

3. Gordon Tullock, "Does Punishment Deter Crime," *The Public Interest*, no. 36 (Summer 1974): 103-11.

4. John Steinbeck, *Tortilla Flat* (New York: Bantam Books, 1965), pp. 106-07.

5. Copyright 1974 by The New York Times Company. Reprinted by permission.

6. Reprinted by permission of *The New Republic.* Copyright 1974, The New Republic, Inc.

"Rights" v. "Needs": American Attitudes Toward Women, Children, and the Family

Sheila M. Rothman

For a long time, according to Sheila Rothman, women, children, and indeed men were thought to find their identities—and personal fulfillment—principally through their participation in that age-old institution, the family. Selfhood was achieved as a result of fulfilling one's obligation to assume a role in a cooperative family situation.

Today, such notions have long since been superseded by an idea of selfhood that puts the identity of each individual in a differential relationship to that of every other. Self, that is, is now increasingly understood as something a person fulfills outside the arena of the family, that indeed may be attainable only in opposition to the family. Sheila Rothman described this evolution of American attitudes and social roles, and analyzes its implications for American culture and social policy.

Perhaps the most simple and dramatic indicator of the dimension of the change that has transformed American attitudes and policies toward women, children, and the family is the initial suspicion and wariness that greets any attempt to place these three subjects into one framework. During the nineteenth century and for most of the twentieth, such a linkage seemed obvious and sensible. Social practice assumed that the welfare of women and children were inevitably tied to the family, that the best interest of women coincided with the best interest of children, that the solidarity of the family was a prerequisite for the cohesion and social order of society.

Now, however, each of these assumptions is strongly contested. We can no longer presume that what benefits women also benefits their children, that the internal stability of the family necessarily promotes the common weal. Put most succinctly, where our predecessors saw only harmony and interdependence, we perceive competing claims and conflict of interest. An analysis of the dimensions and causes of this revolutionary change clarifies both the dilemmas and the possibilities confronting contemporary policy.

Republican Order

The consensus reached in the first decades of the new republic on the ideal roles of women, children, and the family persisted through most of the nineteenth century. It was a coherent and consistent scheme, bringing together views on personhood and social order, and giving clear direction to public policy. Its fundamental assumption was that the good order of society depended finally on the good order of the family, its ability to instill discipline and regularity in its members. Success in this mission augured well for the safety of the republic. Failure jeopardized the experiment that was democracy.

One element promoting this perspective was a new faith in the malleability of the child. The darker, eighteenth century Calvinist views of innate depravity gave way to a more optimistic and environmental outlook—one which made the child eminently trainable, fully receptive to parental control. Another element was the definition of woman as mother, a being whose ultimate satisfactions came from the care of her children. She stood as a sensitive, indeed delicate creature, and although biologically and intellectually not the equal of her husband, she embodied and could transmit the finer virtues. At the core of the family, then, was a ready pupil and an able teacher.

The crucial consideration setting the tasks for the family was a pervasive fear, especially acute in the Jacksonian period, that unless this institution dedicated itself to a cult of obedience, the cohesion of society was in danger. As these first republicans saw it, the ideas and practices that had worked to preserve order in the colonial period had become ineffective. In that earlier day, fixity of place in a geographical sense, and fixity of station in an occupational sense, had insured social stability. In highly insular and localistic settlements, where children followed quite literally in their fathers' footsteps, all community institutions, from the church to the school to the family, worked together to promote harmony.

By the opening decades of the nineteenth century, however, the idea of hierarchy was outmoded and the reality of movement was incontestable. Migration to the west and to burgeoning eastern cities, and an unprecedented amount of social mobility had destroyed the insularity and static character of the community. That one church on the village green which had united citizens was now splintered into a number of competing sects, few of which could command strong allegiances. The schools themselves only seemed dedicated to promoting more mobility. Where in all this flux were points of stability? What forces would operate to insure the cohesiveness of the community? The answer came down to the family. Only it could counter public disorder through private training. As the favorite metaphor of the period expressed it: The family had to gird its members in armor to withstand the chaos and corruptions at loose in society.

The full weight of this charge appeared in the spate of child-rearing books first published in the 1830s. Their authors, laymen assuming a function that heretofore had been performed by ministerial sermons, endowed their tracts with a grand significance. They were, by their own light, confronting "the alarming features of this age," warding off "the fearful crisis," in essence, safeguarding the future of the republic. And the advice they offered reflected still more starkly their concern for social order. "The first, the second, and the third requisite in family government," insisted one typical volume, "is obedience. This must be secured." Cheerful submission, obedience through love, was most desirable—"secure this great end by gentle means," parents were told. "But if that fails, do not hesitate to use the rod."

The woman-mother was to devote herself completely to this end. "The efficient government of a judicious mother," these guidebooks agreed, kept children from deception and disobedience. "The mother of Washington is entitled to the nation's gratitude," learned the readers of Jacob Abbott's *The Mother at Home*. "She taught her boy the principles of obedience." Occasionally, the father's firm intervention might be necessary to buttress maternal authority. But the task of child-rearing belonged finally to the woman, and she was not to transfer it to anyone else.

The enormousness of this responsibility sharply defined a woman's life choices. Celibacy was both morally and socially unacceptable; the single woman deprived herself of ultimate satisfactions and endangered the well-being of society. Once married, the woman was to concede and submit to her husband's authority. Reason and nature seemingly demanded it; and the child who witnessed a bitter division of authority within the family might not respect authority outside it. Indeed, the goal of a well-ordered family was so pervasive that designers of model plans for cottage architecture instructed women to make their homes so comfortable and attractive that husbands would not be tempted to stray from the fireside and enter a saloon. The woman's duty was really twofold: to train the child to obedient citizenship and to make sure that the man-child did not deviate from it.

With the need for family solidarity so intense, divorce was an unacceptable solution to unhappy marriages. "If your marriage has been an unfortunate one," wrote Lydia Child in the widely read *Mother's Book*, "I do not know what to say. If patience, humility and love cannot win him to a sense of duty, the only thing you can do, is to redouble your vigilance for the good of your children."

Divorce was a legal possibility, but it carried such strong social disapproval that few public spokesmen would sanction it. If the family could not stay together, there seemed little hope for the larger society.

This outlook also precluded women from entering the work force. No advice book to young wives so much as broached the subject, let alone debated its pros and cons. Lower class women, it was recognized, might have to work to meet the needs of family subsistence. But these women were urged to take jobs as domestics. They would then come under the good government and moral influences of a family, bringing the values back to their own households. Any other form of denial of motherhood also violated public norms. Contraception was morally repugnant. The occasional pamphlet that set out to defend the practice and supply the limited and crude information on techniques that existed, was banned. In fact, such tracts as Robert Owen's *Moral Physiology* devoted almost all its attention to philosophical and social arguments in defense of contraception, leaving for the last page or two its advice to practice coitus interruptus. And, of course, abortion stood as an act worse than murder, the "Great Crime," the "Crowning Sin." There was almost the character of treason about it.

The cult of obedience also helped to inspire and to justify a new departure in the ways that Americans responded to dependent and delinquent children. Beginning in the 1820s, almshouses, orphan asylums, and reformatories became central to charity and corrections, places of first resort when lower class families could not or did not function well. At the heart of the movement was the belief that well-ordered institutions could perform the essential task of child care, that is, instill discipline and regularity. The children at the New York House of Refuge, according to the managers of this early reformatory, would "be made tractable and obedient ... [through] a vigorous course of moral and corporal discipline." After all, "the most benevolent and humane method for the management of children is, to require prompt and implicit obedience."

Orphan asylums were just as committed to these methods. The directors of the Boston Asylum and Farm School assured its benefactors that destitute and vagrant children "have been received within the walls of a Christian asylum, where they have listened to good counsel, and acquired habits of *order, industry*, and *usefulness.*" Sharing fully the ideology that linked personal discipline to the welfare of the republic, they concluded: "We know not how anyone interested in the preservation of order or stability of government, can withhold his sympathy."

These principles also defined social attitudes toward child education and labor. Both the school and factory were to discipline their charges. As Horace Mann, one of the founders of the common school movement, argued when advocating the use of public tax monies for education: "Those who refuse to train up children in the way they should go, are training up incendiaries and madmen to destroy property and life, and to invade and pollute the sanctuaries of society." So too, defenders of child labor boasted of the regularity that factories instilled. Thus while some states did pass protective legislation, generally setting a ten-hour limit to children's work hours, and more occasionally insisting on three months of school attendance, they did not forbid child labor. Since order and obedience were the goals, the factory and the school were almost interchangeable.

The Cult of Affection

In the opening decades of the twentieth century, beginning in the Progressive era and continuing through the World War II period, new definitions of childhood, womanhood, and the family altered in fundamental ways private behavior and public policy. A cult of affection replaced a cult of obedience. Or as one contemporary student of this change put it: "The family bond is no longer coercion but persuasion." Now parent-child and husband-wife relationships were to be highly emotive, to the point of monopolizing energy and attention. And those who spread this message were certain that such private intensity would enhance public order. Confidently and successfully, they helped to revise a wide range of policies, from the laws of divorce and contraception to the procedures for poor relief and juvenile corrections.

Although one finds in the literature of these years an extraordinary variety of opinion, nevertheless something of a consensus can be identified and its implications traced. The notion that a harmony of interests bound women, children, the family, and the polity together still predominated, but the ways for achieving and maintaining this harmony had changed.

It was psychologists, not moralists, who established the new conception of childhood. First the doctrines of G. Stanley Hall, later those of behaviorist John Watson, and later still those of Sigmund Freud, altered traditional definitions. The differences among these theories were not as important as their common message: Parents had to attune themselves very finely to the child's changing needs. The child, these schools agreed, was a creature who moved through a series of separate and distinct stages, and parents had to react skillfully and sensitively to each stage. They all offered a new criterion for success—wholesome personality development—and insisted that the growing child not only demanded attention, but affection as well. Whereas the earlier focus on obedience had given a static quality to childhood and asked for one kind of parental reaction, the new views made the child active, and insisted upon a large repertory of parental responses. The key word, repeated again and again in the child-rearing literature, was *individualization*—not common molds but particular ones, not one strategy but a multiplicity, not uniformity but diversity.

Sociologist Ernest Groves effectively summarized the components of this new perspective. Parents, he insisted, needed even more insight than skill. They should not "fall into household dogmatism or the routine of habit." Rather, they had to respond in special ways "as the child passes through the progressive stages of his development. At no point can the interpretation of problems become fixed, for wholesome parenthood can never be static. The child changes, and the parent must meet him differently." Parental reactions to the child certainly had to be "deeply emotional," but affection must never rob the child of his individuality; he was not to be 'smothered in love'." The value of parental attachments had to come "from its quality, not its quantity."

Appropriately, one finds for the first time in the Progressive period a concern that the child be "wanted" and a concomitant fear that the "unwanted child" would become a social problem. Given the high level of dedication necessary for successful child-rearing, a parent truly would have to want the child to do the job well. The unwanted child, deprived of emotional satisfactions, his special needs ignored, and his particular problems neglected, was bound to become a troublemaker—at best someone unable to work or marry, at worst, a delinquent.

The new concerns for affection and individuality also prompted a reconceptualization of the position of woman, a change in her role from mother to wife. This shift reflected first the popular elevation of the ideal of romantic love—the family was to be a highly emotive setting not only for children but husbands and wives as well. "Marriage," declared critic and writer Ludwig Lewisohn, "should be held to be created by love, and sustained by love . . . that precise blending of passion and spiritual harmony and solid friendship without which . . . the close association of a man and a woman is as disgusting as it is degrading." A woman was to be able to choose her husband freely, without economic duress, and to stand beside him as companion, not as servant. Should the initial choice prove a poor one, should husband and wife be "obviously unhappy in each other's presence," they had to be free "to change partners in love."

Implicit in these judgments was a definition of the woman as an individual, one who had every right to exercise freedom of choice before and during marriage. "The very stress of individuality that accompanies modern culture," declared Groves, "tends to elevate . . . the desire for an intense, trustworthy, and reciprocating comradeship." But the expectation was that the satisfaction of the woman's particular needs would take place within a family setting, *that the role of wife fulfilled, not negated, her individuality.*

This conclusion represented a new sensitivity to the sexuality of womanhood. The impact of Freudian ideas cannot be exaggerated here—indeed, these doctrines first affected husband-wife relationships and only much later parent-child ones. From the vantage point of the 1970s, the recognition in the 1920s and 1930s of woman as a sexual creature does not seem so much liberating as confining, one more mode of denying woman personhood. But in the context of the time, when the only role accorded woman was that of mother, the shift to wife was expansive. Public images of the woman, as they appeared, for example, in advertisements, placed her in glamorous poses next to a man, rather than in maternal ones, in the nursery next to a child. The 1920s appropriately witnessed the growth of the cosmetic industry, and the proliferation of beauty parlors. Perhaps no statistic better exemplifies the degree and character of the change than to note that in 1931, for the first time, the *Ladies' Home Journal* carried more advertisements devoted to cosmetics than to food.

The role of wife expanded, albeit within limits, other options available to women. According to the popular rhetoric, a career was an insurance policy, guaranteeing that women would make the right marriage choices. Their ability to earn a living freed them from the need to marry quickly; and work skills enabled them to escape more easily from a bad marriage. A career also made a woman into a better wife-companion; she could more effectively communicate with her husband about his concerns. So too, enlarged educational opportunities increased women's individual satisfactions and at the same time better equipped them to be friends to their husbands. A few critics, it is true, did recognize the ambiguities and tensions implicit in this view, that the idea of individuality did not fit neatly with a concept of woman as wife-companion. But the rhetoric establishing the new norms for the most part ignored these potential points of conflict. They focused enthusiastically on the fact that the woman could leave the kitchen and the nursery for the bedroom and the study, not on the fact that she was still to remain very much at home.

Progressive conceptions of social order also promoted these new definitions. Rather than perceive the highly private and emotional character of the nuclear family as threatening a broader social cohesion, Progressives insisted that the insular quality of the nuclear family would further the common weal. Crucial to this outlook was the belief that social mobility and property mobility, opportunities to climb the ladder of success and to consume the products of an industrial organization, would insure stability. Whereas Jacksonians viewed mobility as a centrifugal force, Progressives saw it as centripetal; the nightmare of the fathers had become the glory of the sons. When men of talent could rise in the hierarchy, those at the bottom would not challenge the acquisitions of those on top. Even more important, a high standard of living would bind everyone to the system. It became the task of the family to train these men on the move, to raise individuals to pursue their personal satisfactions, confident that the end result would serve the general welfare.

These propositions certainly did provoke dissent. Thorstein Veblen, for one, condemned the new ethos of consumption; and there were those who worried that self-encapsulated families would only breed a generation of self-seeking and finally selfish individuals. And in retrospect it does seem puzzling that at the very moment when American industry and government entered its most bureaucratic phase, the language of individualism grew most popular. But these objections and incongruities did not weaken the power of the rhetoric. The more typical response was to celebrate the department store as the monument to America's blessings, the cathedral at whose altar all citizens would unite, and to celebrate the family as the institution which would prepare its members for maximum self-development and achievement.

One notable effect of the new norms was to revolutionize attitudes toward divorce. The romantic ideal meant, in the words of one Progressive, that "the forcible maintenance of a loveless union is unethical and involves sacrifices too great to be compensated for by any utilities which marriage otherwise might conserve." Others used even stronger language, comparing a loveless marriage to a form of prostitution. The children's stake in liberalized codes seemed equally clear: Affection between parent and child depended upon affection between the parents themselves. Divorce thus became a legitimate option. No longer did family counselors stand with Lydia Child, despair at the bad marriage, and advise mothers to suffer for the sake of their children.

To be sure, legal changes were slower to take effect. Many states in the period 1900-1930 revised their divorce laws to expand the grounds allowable for divorce. But the codes remained generally stringent, inviting either subterfuge on the part of the couple, or a trip to a state like Nevada or Idaho which permitted quick and easy divorce. Still, the number of divorces rose dramatically (from 0.38 per 1,000 of the population in 1880 to 1.55 by 1925)—and so did the number of pronouncements that defended the practice as in the best interests of the family.

No less dramatic was the change in popular views on contraception. The ideal of affection legitimated a procedure heretofore regarded as dreadful. Birth control, Margaret Sanger repeated time and again, promoted marital affection. Husbands and wives had to be free to enjoy sexual expressions of affection without the fear of conception. Citing Freud as her authority, Sanger insisted that abstinence produced "deep disturbances," that coitus interruptus caused nervous disorders, that female frigidity was the result of fears of pregnancy, and that sexual repression generally hindered woman's self-fulfillment. Birth control, she promised, would produce happiness, even ecstasy, unleash the "feminine spirit," the "absolute inner urge of womanhood."

The new commitment to the emotional needs of children provided another justification. It was Sanger who popularized the slogan: "Every child a wanted child," who insisted that "no child can be what it should be, physically, mentally, or spiritually, if it is conceived and carried by a mother to whom the embraces of her husband are repugnant." Or, as one of her disciples, Caroline Robinson, phrased it: "If there is a cause to think that the child will *not* 'bring its love with it when it comes', then that is an adequate reason not only for justifying, but requiring contraception." The unloved child, Robinson concluded, is a "potential wrongdoer," its life "takes its swing toward crime." Since birth control would ostensibly improve the genetic composition of the population and elevate the lot of the poor, it was still more desirable.

Public policy did not immediately embrace Sanger's program. The distribution of contraceptive information and devices was the subject of a series of court battles through the 1920s; not until 1929 did birth control proponents win their first important case. But to judge by both opinion polls and contraceptive use, the public, certainly the middle class, was consistently more favorable to it. By 1935, this widespread approval meant that clinics operated in many large cities, and that doctors were completely free to prescribe contraceptives without fear of prosecution or harassment. And by 1950, the position of many states had shifted from initial hostility, and subsequent tolerance, to the active promotion of birth control.

Supporters buttressed their arguments by presenting contraception as the only feasible alternative to abortion. Agreeing that abortion, at least when the mother's life was not in danger, belonged in the category of murder, they insisted that this terrible act could not be prevented unless contraceptive knowledge and techniques were widely available. "The trade cannot be extinguished," argued one president of the American Medical Association. "Methods of birth control offer the only relief from this tragedy." While some doctors in the 1920s and 1930s were prepared to defend the idea of therapeutic abortions, they did not spark a broader campaign to change statutes. Perhaps the battle for birth control had been too recently won to allow anyone to think of expanding the grounds for legal abortions. Perhaps the idea of abortion stood in too sharp a contrast with the definition of a woman's family functions. Sanger herself, after all, still assumed that women would find ultimate satisfactions at home. It would take a very different concept of the nature of womanhood to make abortion a pressing issue for social policy.

The Progressive conceptions of the family quickly, and without much controversy, became the basis for a critique of traditional relief and corrections practices. The brunt of the attack was on caretaker institutions, the reliance on the almshouse to support the needy widow and her brood, on orphan asylums to house abandoned or parentless children, on juvenile reformatories to confine delinquents. As soon as the goals of child-rearing changed from inculcating obedience to shaping a wholesome personality, from instilling discipline to transmitting affection, a search for alternatives to incarceration began.

The first White House Conference on Children, convened by President Theodore Roosevelt in 1909, announced the new principles:

Home life is the highest and finest product of civilization. . . . Institutions represent the line of least resistancee. . . . Childhood is too sacred a posession and too mighty a potentiality to be handled on a ready-made plan. The best of institutions after all must neglect individual differences. They cannot take account of personality. They deal with inmates. And inmates necessarily lapse into the nondescript devitalized value of a number. . . . The inmates are of necessity trimmed and turned into automotons. The result is the institutional type.

Thus the White House Conference advocated, and states rapidly adopted, widow pension programs, what we know today as Aid to Dependent Children.

Public relief was to obviate the need for women who headed households to work, "such aid," the Conference insisted, "being given to maintain suitable homes for the rearing of children." To achieve the goal of substituting family care for asylum care, legislators codified adoption laws and social workers established adoption agencies. At the same time, juvenile courts sprang up. Their judges, freed from the formal rigors of criminal law and empowered to use a sentence of probation as a first resort, were to treat delinquents as children, not as adult criminals. Their vast discretionary powers would allow them to act in the role of parent, to tailor decisions to individual cases, to respond to each child's particular needs.

The sharpened sense of the special character of children also encouraged the passage of truancy laws designed to keep minors out of factories and in schools. The premium once placed on the disciplining effects of work gave way to a rhetorical commitment to individual growth through education. So, too, child guidance clinics grew up, to enhance or to remedy family and school training. The same professionals who helped to popularize the message of personality development stood ready to intervene in the name of emotional health.

Underlying the widow pension program, the founding of juvenile courts, and the passage of truancy laws was a clear commitment on the part of Progressives to promote, and especially to protect, the welfare of women and children through positive state action. One distinguishing mark of the Progressives was their very willingness to use the means of government power to accomplish desirable ends. They were not at all nervous about the possibility that state intervention might create mischievous effects. To the contrary, they confidently assumed that implementation would automatically fulfill the avowed goals of policy. Hence, if truancy laws set out to enhance educational opportunities for the young, or if special codes put limits on when or where or for how long women could work, then clearly women and children would benefit from them. The attack in the 1920s of some feminists on the concept of special protection, and their advocacy of an equal rights amendment, was very much a minority position. To most others, these acts were humanitarian in intent and benevolent in practice.

But the reality was more complicated. The administration of several of the Progressive programs fell considerably short of their founders' goals. The widow pension act was never adequately funded; and rigid distinctions between the ostensibly worthy and unworthy poor kept the numbers receiving aid under its provisions pitifully small. The juvenile courts increased the number of persons under state surveillance without reducing rates of incarceration. The probation lists swelled, while the number of inmates in reformatories remained high. Truancy laws were often evaded in practice, as lower class parents and factory owners acted in concert to keep the young employed. At best, the act may have produced a trade-off: Children remained longer at school while mothers substituted for them at the machines. The effects of protective legislation for women may have been to reduce their incomes, to give employers a pretext for differentiating their wages from that of their male counterparts. In sum, Progressive legislation may have expanded state authority to the detriment of lower class families.

The settlement houses of the Progressive period also organized day care centers to supervise children, particularly those of lower class and immigrant families. But there was no doubt in anyone's mind that these centers were a poor second choice to family care. They were primarily intended to serve mothers who, having been judged unworthy of a pension, had to work, or who, for their own reasons, chose to work. Day care, in fact, remained a program of last resort through the 1920s and 1930s. Even during World War II, when federally-supported centers proliferated in order to facilitate the employment of mothers in war production, day care remained suspect. The Children's Bureau successfully insisted that the centers not be located in the community but near the factories. Otherwise, once the war was over, women might be tempted to use the centers and continue working.

In the end, the focus on the child during these decades was so intense, the definition of its needs so consuming, that child care stood first among the obligations and concerns of the family. The wife-companion was the better mother; affection between husband and wife was a prerequisite for successful child-rearing. Ultimately, both the woman and her children belonged at home.

The Discovery of Personhood

The image of the family in the 1970s has changed radically from the 1920s. That a harmony of interests unites its members, that the institution itself is inherently stable and workable, that the insularity of the family promotes the general welfare are propositions that no longer command automatic assent. Rather, a wide range of observers, from Senator Walter Mondale to anthropologist Margaret Mead, perceive the family to be in the midst of crisis, overwhelmed by pressures and tensions it may not be able to resolve. The nuclear family, says Mead, is a nuclear bomb, and it is about to explode. While one can easily cite earlier spokesmen predicting impending doom, something unique does seem to characterize the contemporary perspective. Predecessors invariably insisted upon the propriety of family norms; for them, the problem was that members were not living up to their obligations. Now it is the very norms that are suspect. The legitimacy of the family, like that of so many other institutions in our society, is being questioned. The issue seems to be not how to but whether to strengthen its traditional role.

To understand the causes and implications of this shift, the links between this new perspective and the realities with which we live, it is appropriate to examine first the position of women. Ideological and social changes in the woman's role have sparked change in other areas. Her unwillingness to play the part set out for her in the 1920s conception of the well-ordered family has made inherited definitions as outmoded as the Model T Ford.

Once World War II was over, the moment arrived for putting the ideal of the woman-companion into practice. Federal funds helped to underwrite a massive development of the suburbs, so that in healthy and pleasant environments women could raise their children and encourage and enjoy the successes of their husbands. It did not take very long, however, for the flaws in the companion ideal to emerge. It had never been clear how a college education, even a major in home economics, fitted a woman to remain home alone all day, or to find a small child a suitable companion for most of her waking hours; nor had it been apparent how a well-educated woman would be satisfied to live vicariously through the accomplishments of her husband, why her college degree would make her content to fulfill herself passively through someone else. Hence, as rapidly as the suburbs spread, so did a sense of cracks in the picture window.

It was Betty Friedan's polemic, *The Feminine Mystique*, which most clearly articulated fallacies in this definition of the woman's role. Hers was a two-pronged attack. First, the affectionate mother who devoted herself exclusively to the care of her children not only lost a sense of self-definition, but invariably did a poor job at child-rearing. Lacking any other outlet for her feelings or ambitions, she tended to smother her children, to deprive them of the opportunity for growth and development. "It is time," announced Friedan, "to stop exhorting mothers to love their children more, and face the . . . fact that most of the problems now being treated in child guidance clinics are solved only when the mothers are helped to develop autonomous interests of their own, and no longer need to fulfill their emotional needs through their children."

Second, and even more damaging, the woman-companion all too frequently turned out to be an inadequate wife. When sex was all there was to make her feel alive, she was as overbearing in the bedroom as she was in the nursery. "Many of the young suburban wives," reported Friedan, "make such heavy demands on love and marriage . . . that there is no excitement, no mystery, sometimes almost literally nothing happens." Freidan's diagnosis was clear: When a woman's response to the question "Who am I?" was inevitably "Tom's wife . . . Mary's mother," she had condemned herself to minimal satisfactions and competence. And her solution was equally simple: Women had to escape the house and enter the workplace, to assume meaningful and challenging jobs.

Even as Friedan was writing, mothers of small children were entering the job market in unprecedented numbers. The 1920s had witnessed one major shift in the sex composition of the work force: During that decade, many women holding jobs prior to marriage continued to work until the birth of their first child. The 1950s and 1960s witnessed another: Women with children were remaining in the work force. In 1950s, 25 percent of all married women worked; by 1972, the figure had climbed to 40 percent, and it was women with children who accounted for this rise. In 1950, only 12 percent of women with children under six years of age were gainfully employed; by 1972 they were 30 percent.

Behind this change was an important economic reality. Expanding service industries had dramatically increased the number of positions available to women. A booming economy also created a number of part-time jobs, which women with children eagerly filled. As more jobs became available, more women decided to limit the number of their children; as the birthrate declined, more women were available and eager to take up employment. Women who had the best record in family planning and limitation, demographers discovered, were those who were most committed to their work or careers. This variable, not religion or husband's income, was the crucial one.

These economic and demographic conditions made the model of the wife-companion even less tenable. And so did the impact of the civil rights movement. As many observers have noted, attempts to elevate women's rights have often followed immediately on efforts to advance the condition of blacks—not surprisingly, reform on behalf of one group spurs the other to action. But the civil rights movement also cast a new light on the idea of "separate but equal," one with special relevance for American women. The crucial effect of the "separate but equal" doctrine as it was understood in the 1950s, was to freeze blacks into one mold, to trap them in low-paying and unskilled positions. In the 1960s, it appeared that the effects of separate but equal facilities for women, whether in the guise of segregated colleges or special courses in home economics, conspired to trap and restrict women to menial tasks. "Our society," wrote two psychologists, "is managing to consign a large segment of its population to the role of homemaker solely on the basis of sex just as inexorably as it has consigned the individual with a black skin to the role of janitor or domestic."

The civil rights movement also had a vital impact on the types of problems that social psychologists set out to solve. After the school desegregation decision, psychologists began to study the differential achievements of whites and blacks in the classroom, hoping thereby to equalize performance. Logically and inevitably, they turned their attention next to differential achievement patterns between boys and girls. To their surprise, they discovered that while girls tended to mature quicker and to learn more readily in pre-school and elementary school situations, they slipped behind late in high school; by the time they reached college, girls were rating boys' achievement higher than their own in almost every respect. A spate of studies in the early 1960s documented what Martina Horner labeled "woman's will to fail," and they put the blame on rigid ideas about femininity and masculinity, as perpetuated in the family, the school, the media, the peer group—ultimately in the culture at large. Hence, these psychologists argued, any woman who entered "the man's world," did so with an overwhelming sense of anxiety, and a predisposition to failure. In effect, by focusing on toys and television images, these studies shifted the analysis of determinants of masculine and feminine behavior from the world of biology to that of sociology. Or, put another way, the inherited model of the woman-companion seemed a self-defeating one.

It was left to William Masters and Virginia Johnson to take the argument its final step, to demolish the biological assumptions upon which the inherited definition of woman's social role had rested. The propriety of a passive role for the wife-companion had been confirmed by the Freudians, particularly in the writings of Helene Deutsch. Raising anatomical definitions to the level of psychological and sociological truth, she linked physiology to sexuality and sexuality to social functioning. As Deutsch argued it, female anatomy made women physically incapable of gratifying "the active and aggressive instinctual impulses," and the normal woman gave up these drives, turning instead to a feminine, that is, a passive role. Only neurotic women became aggressive. The well-adjusted woman, at peace with her biology, became passive, receptive, and masochistic—both sexually and socially.

The primary contribution of Masters and Johnson was to establish a totally different definition of female sexuality. The title of their book, *Human Sexual Response*, conveys the principal finding, that basic similarities marked the anatomy and physiology of male and female sexuality, "that direct parallels in human sexual response . . . exist to a degree never previously appreciated." Experiments in their laboratories in St. Louis revealed to a startlingly ignorant medical profession that women's sexual responses were at least as intense as men's, maybe even more so, and that it was absurd to label men sexually active and women sexually passive.

The psychological and sociological implications of this research rapidly emerged. New York psychiatrist Mary Jane Sherfey, in a widely read and—particularly among woman liberationists—influential tract, was the first to bring them to bear on psychoanalytic theory. *The Nature and Evolution of Female Sexuality*, dedicated to Masters and Johnson, was a world apart from Deutsch's *Psychology of Women*. Combining new findings in biology, which argued that insofar as embryonic development was concerned, males developed from females and not the other way around, with the new data on sexual responsiveness, Sherfey presented a woman who was anatomically whole and sexually active. While careful to remind us that an "Adam and Eve" view did not establish female "superiority," she did shatter the notion that anatomy dictated men's dominance in the marketplace and women's passivity at home. Sherfey also suggested that the relationships between this woman and males in particular and society in general, was marked by conflicts of interest. The act of sexual intercourse, for example, was not necessarily the most satisfying form of sexual stimulation for the female. More important, the female's sexual drive might well have to be tamed, indeed repressed, in order for organized society to flourish. Sherfey, still very much within the psychoanalytic framework, had added another dimension to the discontents inherent in the state of civilization.

The findings of Masters and Johnson also helped to expand the concept of sexual normality. A wide range of stimuli, it seemed, produced satisfying sexual responses. And this premise is crucial to the outlook and counsel found in the latest addition to the advice-to-couples genre, *The Joy of Sex*. The title's play on the *Joy of Cooking*, and the book's organization into main courses, relishes, and condiments, reflects the notion that one can follow instructions in the bedroom to achieve gourmet sex just as easily as one can follow instructions in the kitchen to achieve gourmet cuisine. The recipes, while important, are easy to follow; and, therefore, no barriers need block the attainment of sexual pleasure.

The realities and expectations confronting women in the course of the past decade have added up to a new definition of womanhood. They have not only rendered the concept of the wife-companion obsolete but offered another one in its stead: woman as active, energetic, fully competent, and capable of self-definition as a person in sexual and in social terms. Her essence is no longer to be found in a household role, but in her own self. Having moved over a century and a half from mother to wife, she has now reached the stage of person.

The Quest for Equal Rights

This change, undermining the traditional premises of state action, compelled reexamination and readjustment in social policy. Intervention that had been traditionally sanctioned in the name of "special protection" for women now seemed illegitimate, discriminatory, and injurious. To restrict women's employment was an unnecessary limitation of their freedom of choice; they were person enough to choose their own jobs, without having to cope with laws that defined them as weak or incompetent. In fact, the reorientation from special protection to equal rights occurred relatively quickly in American society, and, allowing one exception, with a minimum of tension. Insofar as the issues have involved the relationships between women and employers, or between wives and husbands, social policy has moved without exceptional difficulty to an equal rights position. The more difficult problems, as we shall soon see, emerge when social policy must confront the implications of this shift for the woman-child relationship. This is the thorny area, raising conflicts which have yet to be resolved.

At first the nation moved with a minimum of debate to adopt a constitutional amendment prohibiting all forms of discrimination on the basis of sex. The Equal Rights Amendment, aimed primarily at inequities in the job market, passed through Congress in 1971; by the start of 1974, it had been ratified by thirty-three states and needed only five more for enactment. After its initial successes, however, the ERA ran into trouble. The opening attacks seemed to be the product of an expensive and well-coordinated effort by some of the most politically conservative groups in society. But then, the defeat of state ERA

Amendments in New York and New Jersey in 1975 pointed to sources of opposition that were far more complex and troubling. Evidently, a large number of women were finding the opposition rhetoric very appealing. A group of educated and financially comfortable women in well-to-do suburban communities helped to vote down ERA.

The amendment had become a battleground for women. On the one side stood the wife-mother, on the other, the working woman. Around the symbolic issue of ERA, the old and the new values clashed. The ERA, in effect, challenged the suburban housewife, questioning her life style. In one grand gesture, it announced that the days of special protection were over; women now had to stand on their own. They would have to gain status by their achievements in the world outside the family; they could no longer rely upon their husband's accomplishments or their children's to validate their personal worth. To these women, the ERA not only legitimated but elevated the status of the working woman. In valuing the office over the home, it seemed to make their life choices obsolete, even stigmatized. So upon being asked why they voted against ERA, these women responded passionately, if inaccurately, that it could force them to go to work to support their husbands; in case of divorce (and they were certain it occurred more often when wives worked), it could force them to pay alimony. This seemingly harmless amendment stood as an affront to the standards by which they had lived.

The ERA, in other words, pitted the highly trained professional woman against the volunteer, the working mother against the housewife. The ERA also pitted the young against the old, the life style of a mother against the life choice of her daughter. In 1975, the victories went to the mother. But given this dynamic, the amendment is bound to pass sooner or later. As the life style symbolized by ERA becomes the choice of a growing majority of women, as prestige is increasingly accorded to women on the basis of their own achievements, the ERA will become law.

The eventual success of the amendment certainly does not mean that discrimination against women in offices, factories, or universities, will disappear. Nevertheless, in time practice may measure up to law, and in the meanwhile the symbolic nature of the act, announcing clearly that women no longer require paternalistic state intervention, is bound to enhance expectations by and for women. To be sure, there are those who would argue that special protection has not died, it has just been reborn under the rubric of "affirmative action." But this charge, while not unreasonable, ignores the essential differences between the two types of measures. Special protection laws were meant to be permanent in operation and rigid in application, assuming the frailty of the woman. The state's ongoing duty was to compensate for her vulnerability. Affirmative action, to the contrary, even at its most grandiose, only sets standards and procedures, and temporary ones at that. Most important, it shifts the definition of the problem from the weakness of the woman to the biases of the man, from her incapacities to his prejudices.

The woman-as-person doctrine has also altered state policy toward husband-wife relationships, particularly in the area of divorce. Even the liberalized codes of the pre-World War II period assumed a wife in need of special protection. Based essentially on a "fault" model, they wished to defend her against the folly or depravity of her husband. Her options, it was assumed, were severely limited since nature and society had put her in charge of the children. Her husband, better able to earn his keep and less restricted by family responsibilities, was easily the more mobile. It made no sense, under these circumstances, to ban divorce—that would only encourage the man to desert, or trap a good-hearted woman in a bad marriage. Rather the divorce procedures themselves had to protect the woman. Alimony payments assured her of support, and a fault model allowed the courts to penalize the errant-husband by increasing the levels of payments. Courts were particularly reluctant to acknowledge the guilt of an erring wife, fearful of endangering the financial well-being of the children. The establishment in the 1920s of family courts, with their reconciliation bureaus, was another effort to protect the woman, this time by trying to persuade the husband of his family obligations.

Once it became inappropriate to base divorce policy on a model of the woman who at once guarded the home and was herself trapped in it, states altered their procedures. Generally they opted for a no fault scheme. Although California passed the first no fault divorce law in 1939, it was not until 1971 that states in number followed suit. These statutes remove the concept of blame from divorce, in effect declaring that both partners are equally able to bear weight of the decision and its consequences. Hence, to dissolve the marriage, the court relies merely on the partners' statement that the marriage is "irretrievably broken."

It is difficult to understand why such a simple formula for dissolving a marriage was not adopted decades ago—difficult that is, unless one appreciates that implicit in the court's acceptance of this formula is the belief that both partners were competent to make it, that wives were not coerced in some fashion or another into giving consent. This same perspective has been carried over into procedures determining financial arrangements after divorce. The two parties are encouraged to reach an agreement among themselves, and the court will not interfere unless it is "unconscionable." Mental cruelty, desertion, and adultery are no longer viewed as causes but as symptoms, and as such irrelevant to alimony decisions. Now what matters is earning power, and so if the wife has the greater capacity and the husband has the children, she will be paying him alimony. Equal rights in entering marriage now has its equivalent in equal rights in dissolving marriage. Again, special protection seemed unnecessary and unwise.

Policy liberalization here will be very difficult to reverse. By facilitating divorce through a simplification of procedures and a reduction in blame and stigma, the new codes make it less and less possible to think in terms of fault. Hence, a backlash response, a tightening of requirements, becomes unlikely. Moreover, once a new policy tests itself in reality, it often does not bring with it the nightmarish consequences that opponents had raised. True, at least one of every three couples get divorced—but most of them remarry. One can then take the occasion to talk not about the death of the family, but about the fluid family, stage marriages for different points in the life cycle—in other words, a new form of family organization. All of this reduces the backlash potential still more.

Indeed, something akin to this message is precisely what the almost two million readers of *Open Marriage* have received. The O'Neills' best seller seemingly presents new criteria for marital success, but in many more ways, it appears to be preparing couples for their impending divorce. The *New Yorker* cartoonist who had beau on bended knee asking belle please to be "his first wife," must have read it. They contrast the closed marriage—with lifelong monogamy ultimately for the sake of the children—with an open marriage, dedicated to "exploring new and different relationships for the sake of individual fulfillment and growth." Not ones to shirk the issue of just how open an open marriage should be, they insist: "We have no intention of course of denying that some people can be sexually monogamous for life . . . in which neither one ever has or even wants extra marital liaisons. But they are rare and becoming rarer." The essence of the open marriage is its impermanence, and hence the O'Neills warn the reader: "Nor will your wife necessarily be the mother of your children. She may be, but don't count on it. . . . This is not negativism, only realism."

As long as the issue focuses on consenting adults, where each understands what the marriage contract means, the O'Neills' tract, and even the possibility that our norms will come to approximate their prescriptions, does not raise complicated policy issues. Equal rights for women and liberalized divorce laws are the only necessary adjustments, and they are being made. When the wife's needs are in conflict with her husband's, one can foresee personal unhappiness, more or less successful accommodations, but no need for state intervention. But as soon as the issue shifts to the place of children in this scheme, matters are not so easily resolved. It is one thing to warn husbands that their wives may not be the mothers of their children—but are we prepared to warn children that their mother of today may not be their mother of tomorrow? The O'Neills understandably prefer to ignore this dilemma. One looks in vain through their pages for a discussion of what open marriage means to children. In occasional asides they applaud the fact that more couples are now deciding not to have children, and they do ask that husband and wife share equally in child-rearing responsibilities. But fundamentally, open marriage is childless marriage, a temporary liaison between two persons to satisfy their own immediate and individual needs.

In fact, numerous arguments have been advanced over the past two decades in favor of a norm of smaller families, even childless marriages. Proponents look not only to the liberation of women from child care responsibilities but to a still broader range of social benefits. And in many ways, as the demographic evidence makes clear, this norm is taking hold.

Limiting the Family

Americans in the 1960s became obsessed with the problem of population control as ecologists began to warn about rapidly diminishing natural resources and the disastrous effects of environmental pollution. Defining resources as finite, they contended that Americans were exhausting them at a rate which not only endangered our environment but took no account of the needs of future generations. At first, these claims were vigorously debated, but by 1970, the ecologists had certainly persuaded, if not a majority of Americans, then many of those in policy-making positions of their validity. One of the most important results of this campaign was to give a new impetus and rationale to programs of population limitation, to achieving zero population growth. Book jackets, magazine covers, even bumper stickers, and lapel buttons all proclaimed the cause.

Once again it was Margaret Mead who effectively summarized the position for a congressional committee.

We have to recognize that we want to keep our family size down because although the American family size is not very large, our stress on the world's environment is high. Every child that is born in this country uses up something like 40 percent more energy and irreplaceable resources than does the child born in India. . . . We have to realize that the small family, well cared for, well educated, well qualified, is our best contribution to the world.

A concern about emotional energy soon matched the concern about industrial energy. The villain here was the "unwanted child," and the burdens it placed on the family and on the society. The category, first invented by Margaret Sanger in the Progressive years, assumed unprecedented importance in the 1960s. As one executive of Planned Parenthood, the successor organization to the Birth Control League, analyzed it: "Mothering and I would add fathering is a task that requires enormous human and emotional resources . . . Done in the spirit of love and fulfillment it is hard but rewarding work. But when the child is unwanted the task may become an onerous obligation, an ordeal emotionally destructive to the mother and disastrous for the child."

Nowhere was the burden more oppressive than among the poor. Senator Joseph Tydings told his colleagues as they prepared to pass the first federal subsidies for family planning that it is "only in the past few years that family size has been perceived as a cause of poverty as well as an effect. A child born into a family with five or more children runs a 350 percent greater risk of being poor than an only child. Raising unwanted children on inadequate incomes drives the poor deeper into poverty, trapping them in a vicious circle of impoverishment and fertility. And so the poor stay poor."

The power of this rhetoric in promoting a norm of small families has had major effects both on private behavior and public policy. The 1960s and early 1970s witnessed a reversal of post-World War II population trends. The average number of children that a woman bore during her lifetime stood at 4.3 in 1900; the number declined to 2.3 in 1940, rose to 3.3 in 1960, and has now dropped back again to 2.4. So too, the average household size of 3.7 persons in 1960 declined by 1973 to 3.5. The number of very large families has decreased steadily. The ideal of the two-child family seems to have spread through the society.

Clearly, the improvements in contraceptive techniques contributed to this change. But the effects of birth control technology can be easily exaggerated. The most precipitous drop in family size occurred in the period 1900-1940, when only semi-reliable procedures were available. Urban families, for example, where the head of the household held a clerical or sales position, had on the average 3.2 children in 1910, and only 2.1 children in 1940 and 1.9 children in 1960. Among unskilled workers the most dramatic shift in family size also took place between 1910 and 1940, from 4.9 to 3.6 children per household. Nevertheless when the norm of a small family combines with available and effective birth control devices, the effect is powerful. The National Fertility Study of 1955 revealed that 57 percent of Catholics and 75 percent of Protestants said they used contraception. By 1965, the number of Catholic families had climbed to 78 percent, and Protestants to 87 percent. There is no longer anything controversial within the family about contraception.

The same can also be said for public policy. Law finally caught up with practice when in 1965 the Supreme Court ruled in the *Griswold* case that the giving of "information, instruction and medical advice to *married persons*," was protected by "the zone of privacy created by several fundamental constitutional decrees." Whatever lingering doubts remained were dispelled by its 1972 decision, *Eisenstadt* v. *Baird*. The Court expanded the Griswold precedent to include unmarried persons. "If the right of privacy means anything, it is the right of the *individual*, married or single, to be free from unwarranted governmental intrusion into matters so fundamentally affecting a person as the decision whether to bear or beget a child." Indeed, by the time of the *Eisenstadt* decision, Congress had approved the Family Planning Act, providing free birth control information to anyone who wanted it, with federal subsidies underwriting the creation of family planning clinics. There was so little opposition to the act, that Senator Thomas Eagleton felt compelled to note that the committee holding hearings on the bill could not find any group to speak out against the concept of planned parenthood!

The intensity of Americans' commitment to effective contraception programs is nowhere more evident than in the incredible rise in voluntary sterilizations over the past decade. In 1965, according to the National Fertility Study, 16 percent of older couples (wives between the ages of thirty and forty-four) practicing contraception, had one of the partners sterilized. By 1970, the number had climbed to 25 percent! This safe but irreversible procedure had actually become *the* contraceptive method of choice for older couples (25 percent compared to 20.6 percent using the pill), and the operations were almost equally divided between husband and wife! As of 1970, some 2.75 million couples of reproductive age had resorted to sterilization, and there is every expectation that the figure will continue to rise. Public opinion polls reveal that nearly 50 percent of the population of child-bearing age would "seriously consider" sterilization to prevent unwanted conceptions.

Data from local institutions confirm these national surveys. One St. Paul hospital which had been performing voluntary sterilizations for women since 1958, reported a rise in tubal ligations from 331 between 1958 and 1967, to 550 between 1968 and 1971. The hospital opened a vasectomy clinic in 1970, performing 40 operations that year. In 1971 the figure increased to 289, and in 1972 to 500. One study of a largely white suburban San Francisco community found that 23 percent of *all* adults between the ages of twenty and fifty-four had undergone voluntary sterilization, and in two-thirds of the cases it was the husband who had been operated upon.

Under this pressure for sterilization, restrictive governmental and medical regulations have evaporated. Connecticut, one of the two last states prohibiting sterilization except for "medical necessity," repealed the ban as of October 1971. The American College of Obstetricians and Gynecologists in 1969 dropped all references to age and number of living children as criteria for voluntary sterilization. The operation could now be had for the asking.

It was inevitable that the expanded view of women's rights and the heightened concern for population control would come into conflict with state prohibitions on abortion. Indeed, the abortion controversy posed in clear and unambiguous terms the ultimate implications of the definition of woman-as-person: women's rights as against the rights of the fetus, the rights of women as opposed to the obligations of motherhood. By comparison, discrimination in the workplace, or the right to obtain contraception, even to be sterilized, were the easy cases. There, the woman-as-person doctrine seemed to elevate one set of rights without endangering those of anyone else. But abortion was an instance of conflict of interest, the test case for how thoroughly the new views would transform policy.

During the late 1960s, a handful of states, including New York, expanded the grounds for which a woman could obtain an abortion. But the crucial moment came in January 1973, when the Supreme Court decided that a woman in her first trimester of pregnancy, in consultation with her physician, had the right to obtain an abortion; state interference in that privilege was unconstitutional. To a remarkable degree, the decision echoed the new rhetoric. In subsuming the woman's right to terminate pregnancy under a right to privacy, the Court cited first the potential medical dangers to the woman. But it quickly left these traditional grounds, noting: "Maternity, or additional offspring, may force upon the woman a distressful life and future. Psychological harm may be imminent. Mental and physical health may be taxed by child-care. There is also the distress for all concerned, associated with the unwanted child." And hence the woman's right to an abortion.

The merits of the decision aside, the opinion itself was neither brilliant nor consistent. It did not persuasively demonstrate why states could not reasonably attempt to resolve so murky a question as when life begins. The Court's reliance upon such criteria as when a fetus can survive outside the mother's womb is bound over the next several decades to open more questions than it closes. Nor is it altogether clear whether the woman can command her physician to perform an abortion. After all, if one of the grounds for abortion is mental health, and she claims this pregnancy is endangering her mental health, what evidence could the physician possibly marshall to refute her? Nevertheless, for all these weaknesses, the decision set off a series of developments with consequences, intended and unintended, for social policy.

The numbers and types of women who underwent abortion, and their fates have effectively put to rest some long-standing objections to the procedure. For one, it became obvious just how safe a procedure abortion was. In New York State, from mid-1970 to mid-1972, 402,000 abortions took place with only 16 deaths. For another, abortion on an outpatient basis, relying upon the vacuum aspiration technique instead of surgery, proved to be a very practical and not dangerous method for women in their first trimester of pregnancy; and it was also the simplest and least expensive to administer. Moreover, the number of women who took advantage of the liberalization of abortion was staggering. In 1973, there were over one and a half million abortions, and estimates put the 1974 figure at one and three-quarter million. And the women, at least on the basis of first studies, seem to have had none of the acute guilt that some psychiatrists had predicted; they were not filling hospital beds with post-abortion depression. The attitudinal changes that were supposed to take a generation to occur happened overnight.

The change in law prompted a change in public opinion—once again, law did shape morality. By April 1973, 66 percent of women under fifty approved of legalized abortion. Initial reports of the abortion clientele revealed that a high percentage were unmarried women (in upper New York State the figure was nearly 60 percent), and they were young (in New York, 60 percent were under twenty-five). In fact, of the 32,351 unmarried women who received abortions between January and December 1971, fully 37 percent were under the age of twenty! Taken together, these findings all point to a massive and safe reliance upon abortion on the part of a group of women who seem to be making sane and sensible decisions.

Yet, the controversies surrounding abortion have by no means disappeared. To the contrary, legalization has sparked a new series of objections. Many gynecologists are now at best ambivalent. Their earlier advocacy of legalization was intended to enable them to practice medicine as they saw fit, to allow them to perform an abortion in those cases where incest or rape had occurred, or where there was evidence of the likelihood of massive birth deformaties. Now, they are apprehensive because that control over abortion has been transferred to the patients. A group of one hundred professors of gynecology recently issued a statement declaring that physicians should realize "that abortion has become a predominantly social as well as medical responsibility. For the first time, except perhaps for cosmetic surgery, doctors will be expected to do an operation simply because the patient asks that it be done." And while they accept this change in order to serve "the new society in which they live," many of their colleagues are less eager. There are numerous stories about hostile physicians, the harrassment of women in large hospitals, indeed of an inability to receive abortions outside of metropolitan centers.

Family planning officials, who spearheaded the fight for legalization, have also become much less vocal in their support. They are not actively lobbying for legal changes that would enable them to perform outpatient abortions in their federally-funded facilities. In part, they are apprehensive about losing funds for contraceptive programs. In part they are fearful that the controversy surrounding abortion will spread to include contraception. In addition, many civil libertarians have discovered for the first time their own ambivalence. So long as the Catholic Church monopolized the anti-abortion position, they gave the arguments little credence. But now they are beginning to worry that legalized abortion may be the first step on the road to legalized infanticide, and eventually, legalized euthanasia. A recent article in the *New England Journal of Medicine*, where doctors reported that 14 percent of the deaths in Yale's special infant care unit were the result of physicians and parents deciding to shut off the machine on defective neonates, increases their misgivings. Thus the abortion issue had become entangled with concerns about medical ethics, contraceptive programs, and the rights of the defective. And while it may seem the better part of wisdom to keep the issues separate, to fight the infanticide battle on its own grounds, it is clear that abortion is sparking a widespread concern about the power that families in general and women in particular can exercise over their offspring.

The Discovery of Children's Rights

It is within this context that the sudden and sharp turn of attention to a concern with children's rights becomes explicable. The doctrine of woman as person implicitly suggests that her needs may not fit with those of her child; and the case of abortion most vividly makes that conflict explicit. Hence, it is not surprising that simultaneously with the liberalization of abortion has come the discovery of children's rights.

One of the most important statements of the new concept of children's rights has appeared in a small book by three psychoanalysts, Joseph Goldstein, who is also a professor of law at Yale, Anna Freud, director of the Hamstead Child Therapy Clinic, and Albert Solnit, professor of pediatrics and psychiatry at Yale. Aptly entitled, *Beyond the Best Interests of the Child*, the tract contends that our traditional allegiance to the doctrine of a child's best interest has in fact been a masquerade, cloaking policy decisions that were ultimately made for the best interest of the parent.

Goldstein, Freud, and Solnit argue the case in only one aspect, child custody proceedings. Heretofore, custody decisions were made in prima facie terms in favor of the biological parent—the right of a mother to her child was almost always paramount, certainly over the foster parent and, usually, over the father. Their plea is for a genuine concern with the child's best interest, that is, custody decisions and policies that favor a child's "psychological" parent. Studiously avoiding the use of the term, "mother," they refer only to parents—and in their definition, the fit parent is the one who is actually fulfilling the child's psychological needs. "Whether any adult becomes the psychological parent of a child is based on the day-to-day interaction, companionship, and shared experiences. The role can be fulfilled either by a biological parent or by an adoptive parent or by any caring adult—but never by an absent, inactive adult, whatever his biological or legal relationship to the child." For them, the crucial consideration is to promote and respect the child's attachment to his psychological parents; in cases of conflict, the decision must support the rights of the psychological parents, in whose care the child feels valued and "wanted." "An absent biological parent will remain, or tend to become, a stranger."

Thus, in that terrible and tragic case when Dutch Jews returned at the end of World War Two to reclaim children left for safekeeping in non-Jewish households, the doctrine would reverse the Dutch parliament's flat decree in favor of biological parents, and substitute instead the decrees in favor of the now "psychological parents." "More interests," the authors conclude, "will tilt the scale toward leaving well enough alone than toward allowing the biological parents to prevail." What seems cruel and heartless from the perspective of the parent is, in fact, in the best interest of the child.

In more general terms, Goldstein, Freud, and Solnit have rendered the current definition of the "wanted" and "unwanted" child obsolete. Until now, the terms have taken their meanings from the sentiments of the biological parent—if she did not want the child, the child was unwanted. But if one views the concept through the child's eyes, it turns out that while he may be unwanted by this parent, he may be wanted by another. So in the first instance, these authors would upgrade the prerogatives of the foster parents, giving them first rights to adopt a child already in their care. They would also insist upon speedy adoption procedures, compelling a biological parent to decide quickly on custody; and the decision once made in favor of adoption would be irreversible. They would not allow agencies to remove the child from the psychological parent except in those cases where the child's interest, and not that of the agency or the biological parent, dictated it. They would also strongly support state adoption subsidies, so that the psychological parents would have full rights to the child without forfeiting financial compensations.

Psychoanalytic doctrines clearly form one basis for the judgments of Goldstein, Freud, and Solnit. Defining the child as one who changes "constantly, from one state of growth to another," who perceives the world in "an egocentric manner," who cannot maintain "positive emotional ties with a number of different individuals," who can "freely love more than one adult only if the individuals in question feel positively to one another," they predictably elevate psychological ties over the biological ones. So too, building on the work of John Bowlby, they stress the special nature of time to children and the detrimental consequences of prolonged separation from the parent; while to a mother, a six-month absence may be brief, to a two-year-old it is interminable, and the effects may be devastating.

But why have these doctrines, basic to psychoanalytic literature for decades, now suddenly been placed in a context of children's rights? The answer rests, first, in the new awareness of the distinction between biological parents' interest and those of the child. Once we can no longer assume that a woman is primarily a mother, that her needs are identical with and indistinguishable from the child's, then child advocacy takes on a new meaning and importance. In essence, these authors are saying, if there is an adult ready and able to care for the child, for goodness sake do not disturb the relationship.

Beyond the Best Interests of the Child also reflects another crucial judgment, that state intervention in family relationships should be minimized. Goldstein, Freud, and Solnit are acutely sensitive to the dangers of hyperbolic rhetoric, terribly aware that the state's promise to do good is not often matched by its ability to do good. "This preference for minimum state intervention and for leaving well enough alone," they write, "is reinforced by our recognition that the law is incapable of effectively managing, except in a very gross sense, so delicate and complex a relationship as that between parent and child." In fact, many of the other battles now being fought in the arena of family policy have aimed to reduce state power, to prevent it from interfering in decisions regarding contraception or abortion. And this distrust is no less acute here. When the child is doing well in one setting, intervention, no matter how grandiose the claims, ought not to be allowed. In effect, Goldstein, Freud, and Solnit have for the first time used psychoanalytic theories to minimize state interference. Until now, these doctrines have provided a rationale for intrusion they have reversed the tradition. At least in this one area of custody, the theories have been marshalled to limit the state.

These same premises inform the programs of one camp of child advocates, those who believe that the welfare of children would be best served by approximating their legal status insofar as possible to that of adults. They have campaigned and litigated successfully to narrow the jurisdiction of the juvenile court, preferring due process to judicial benevolence. They have fought to remove PINS (Persons in Need of Supervision) cases from the juvenile court, unwilling to allow intervention on the basis of a child's status (his ostensible need for supervision), instead of his acts (the actual commission of a criminal offense). They have urged the right of teenagers to live apart from parents, to allow them the choice to run away without subjecting them to court sanction. They have also lobbied effectively to reduce the age of consent for receiving medical treatment; they prefer to have minors, albeit in consultation with doctors, reach a decision about contraception and abortion without prior parental approval.

Moreover, at least some in this camp have attacked the protective legislation that is compulsory schooling. From their perspective, truancy laws have been one major reason why schools do not teach, why they function more as places of custody than places of learning. In each instance, these advocates assume that parental choices may not reflect the best interests of the child, and that state intervention will not ultimately promote the child's welfare.

Their position raises as many problems as it solves. At what age is a runaway to be left to his own devices, or a pregnant teenager to be allowed to choose whether or not to have an abortion? Are the rights of consent for the young to be expanded in all areas, including such irreversible procedures as sterilization? Are we prepared to abolish truancy laws and leave children to the mercy of employers' pressures, as in the instance of children of migrant workers? We may well want to treat children as adults in some areas and not in other areas, but the conceptual framework which would enable us to know where to draw the line is still missing.

An even tougher issue remains. Can public policy enhance the rights of children without simultaneously enlarging the power of the state? Will the expansion of children's rights mean, in effect, that state authority will replace parental authority? Once we allow minors to consent to medical procedures without parental approval, will we not become still more dependent upon state oversight? More generally, once we presume a conflict of interest between child and parent, is it not the state that will have to adjudicate the competing claims? And generalized legislation or court review may operate still less satisfactorily than parental discretion. In essence, can one advocate both a reduction in parental power and a reduction in state power? Children's rights must now confront this dilemma. It can no longer be ignored by assuming either that parent knows best or that state intervention is necessarily beneficent.

The Call for Intervention

There is a second camp advocating children's rights who share many of the assumptions of the first group but have reached diametrically opposed policy conclusions. Also unwilling to equate parental interest with children's interest, they are prepared, in the best Progressive and New Deal tradition, to enhance child welfare directly through state intervention. Their concerns are not so much with rights as with needs. Rather than lobby to equalize the legal status of children with adults, they want to invigorate the doctrine of special protection to insure that the physical and emotional requirements of children are met. They are not so concerned with the age of consent for medical treatment as with the availability of medical treatment. They are not as interested in allowing teenagers a choice of where to live, as in manipulating the environment to improve the quality of their lives.

The 1970 report of the federally financed Joint Commission on the Mental Health of Children summarized the position of these child advocates. They are unwilling to trust to parents to act in the best interest of the child, first, because the job now seems too terribly complex. "Obviously," the Commission notes, "the demands on parents are tremendous." Second, they appreciate that conflicts among family members are real. "Eager as nearly all parents are to do an excellent job of child-rearing, they cannot deny their own human needs—physical, psychological, and social." And third, they assume that the resources to do the job well may not be available. "Fathers and mothers cannot cope singlehandedly with the many handicaps that the social and economic system may impose upon them and their children." Thus, if parents "are to be effective in the tremendously important task of child-rearing, they need the supporting cooperation of other systems outside the home."

Precisely what these outside systems should provide is never made very clear. It is not unfair to say that child advocacy is a program desperately in need of a definition. One report to New York's Governor Nelson Rockefeller in 1971 favoring a state child advocacy system never did move beyond a vague rhetorical insistence upon the need for more action, for "optimal opportunities for growth and development." There does emerge a call for superagencies to deliver services. As Alfred Kahn, one of the leaders of this group has argued: "Since social services are frequently unresponsive to children's needs, special personnel or agencies should be developed to enhance transactions between children and various social institutions." Neighborhood clinics tied to a central planning board would intervene to satisfy these needs and improve the environment. But again, these child advocates are hard pressed to move from a bureaucratic chart to a program's substance.

The closest one gets to specific recommendations is support for "comprehensive day care," staffed by early childhood education experts. The centers, according to proponents, would be integrated, so that rich and poor, black and white children would come together, countering the effects of our class divided and racially segregated society. Day care would also solve problems of malnutrition and inadequate medical care. The centers would serve balanced meals, and bring in physicians to diagnose and treat maladies, and to provide general medical and dental care. Moreover, comprehensive day care would offer instruction in the rudiments of reading, so that all children would enter the first grades equally well prepared. And day care would reduce, maybe even eliminate, the tensions between parents' outside interests and children's needs. It would provide "continuous loving care," thereby allowing mothers to work and pursue their careers without guilt, indeed with the satisfaction of knowing that their children were being cared for at least as well as at home.

Comprehensive day care is also offered as an antidote to a more generalized attack on the role of the nuclear family. Over the past decade, a number of critics have argued that the insularity of the family, its hothouse quality, operates to the detriment of children in particular and the society in general. They reject the Progressive ideology that individual exertions inevitably add up to the public good. Rather, they see private gain at the expense of societal goals. In the insularity of the family, the vision of a community is lost, and the result is private wealth and public paucity. They argue too that the intensive child-rearing practices of the nuclear family are actually dysfunctional. Children raised in self-encapsulated households are not prepared to operate in a bureaucratic, or indeed, a democratic society.

The student uprisings of the late 1960s provoked these kinds of attacks on the nuclear family from both the Right and the Left. The one faction was persuaded that the activists were spoiled children; their political activities had the quality of temper tantrums, for they had never learned how to balance their own desires against the rights of others. The other faction insisted that nuclear families isolated individuals from each other while breeding a myopic social vision. The campus sit-ins, with their commune-like character, were seen to represent a healthy revolt from an excessive privatism, in all senses of the word. In response to these critiques, the advocates of day care promise to liberate children from their families. In the centers, children would interact with peers under the guidance of adults trained to be sensitive to the group. In the end, to its supporters, day care training really is superior to family training.

Child advocates insist that our basic problem is that we have not had a national family policy. If only we would coordinate our resources and intervene in skilled and planned ways, then the needs of children, the desires of women, and the welfare of the family and the polity would be met. "Unlike other democracies," psychologist Edward Zigler told a recent Senate committee holding hearings on *American Families: Trends and Pressures, 1973,* "America has never committed itself to a coherent family policy. We have avoided coming to grips with the problem by taking refuge in the view that the American family is so sacrosanct that the Government should not meddle in its affairs." The solution is obvious: systematic state intervention in support of the family.

But the case is not so easily resolved in their favor; there are good reasons to question this formulation. For one, it is simply not true that government has not intervened in the family. From the construction of the first houses of refuge through the design of the juvenile court and the administration of ADC, from the first anti-abortion statutes to subsidies for family planning clinics, the state has intervened extensively in the family.

More important, the plea for intervention presupposes a consensus on goals, the probability that state action will be accorded legitimacy. But this agreement may not be readily obtained. The very ideologies and realities that seem to make intervention necessary militate against its achievement. A sharp and acute distrust of the exercise of authority now permeates our society. Just as we have restricted the prerogatives of wardens, psychiatric superintendents, school principals, college presidents, and even to some degree corporation executives, we now suspect the beneficence of parental control over children and reject the rule of husbands over wives. In large measure, we perceive society as made up of splintered and segmented groups all vying for power with competing claims that may not allow for mutually agreeable solutions. The ideal of the common weal seems almost beyond realization. Instead, the contest in the public arena has the quality of a zero-sum game—where some win, others must necessarily lose, and the notion of the general welfare may represent only the rationalization of the victors to justify their spoils. In such circumstances, every group had better have at hand its most powerful advocates. But how the contest is to be decided, how the victors will exercise power and how the losers will tolerate it, is far from resolved. Hence, a truly national family policy seems fanciful, a slogan without meaning.

Who Speaks for the Poor?

There is yet another problem with the call for state intervention, one which involves its effects on the poor. In fact, advocates of a national family policy have the economically disadvantaged most in mind. But a review of the way government programs directed at the lower class family have operated, an examination not of promise but of the delivery, makes an interventionist strategy highly suspect.

Once the focus of discussion is on the poor, debates about the desirability of action give way to demands for assistance. Senator Edward Kennedy, for example, in his opening remarks to the Senate committee on American families declared: "It is wrongly assumed that all families function in the structured and narrow definition of the two-parent family, with a working father, a home-making mother, and dependent children." Rather, "the increase of one-parent families has forced us to realize that other family structures are also prevalent in our society." These families "face problems in trying to provide for their children's needs"; and particularly in the case of female-headed households receiving public aid, "the burdens are enormous." Hence for Kennedy, the implications were clear: Government must devise and implement programs to strengthen the family.

But there is an ambiguity in Kennedy's statement that bears all too relevantly on the character of this social policy. Is it the purpose of intervention to provide better financial support, better medical and educational opportunities, so that those in female-headed households can live better? Or is it the very existence of female-headed households which is the problem to be eliminated? Is it the goal of state intervention to enlarge individual choices among the poor, to give them the wherewithal to decide about life styles, or is it to mold them into patterns of behavior which conform to those of the middle and upper classes? In brief, is it the aim of policy to liberate or to transform, to enhance or to coerce?

Government support of day care for the poor graphically reveals just how pertinent these questions are. While the rhetoric promoting federal subsidies was benevolent, the reality was grim. Proponents, taking their cues from the new commitment of middle class women to day care, saw here an ideal way of delivering nutritional, medical, and educational services to the children of the poor, and of enlarging parents' freedom of action. But when translated into a government program, day care became a method first and foremost for reducing the welfare rolls, for giving state officials another weapon in their arsenal with which to coerce the poor.

Until the late 1960s, ADC supported needy mothers of young children at home. But once the option of day care became legitimate, the opportunity to try to reduce the ADC rolls proved irresistable. By 1967, congressional legislation established the Work Incentive Program (WIN)—for the first time, mothers of young children could be compelled to transfer the care of their children to someone else, and undergo job training to qualify for employment. The results of this program were nothing less than disastrous.

First, the majority of centers at which mothers had to leave their children were grossly inadequate. As the director of the United States Child Development Office later testified, a good part of the federal funds went to unlicensed family day care centers which served six or fewer children. "Some of these homes are good, but others are ghastly, and thus we are witnessing Federal funds being spent to place children in circumstances detrimental to their development." Second, the centers were segregated by color and class; a sliding scale of payments made it impossible for anyone except the very poor to use the facilities. The results in New York State, for example, fully warranted the charge that the centers resembled concentration camps for black and Puerto Rican families. And the New York experience was not unusual. A study of 500 centers scattered through the nation reported that fully 75 percent of them were segregated, serving either whites or blacks exclusively.

Moreover, WIN was expensive. "It cost more," one independent evaluation of the program noted, "to provide quality day care to children than most states are willing to pay mothers [under ADC] to take care of their own children." In effect, WIN transferred funds from the poor to the middle classes, with little reduction in costs. Teachers, social workers, and psychologists received eight to ten dollars an hour for taking care of children. The welfare mother received perhaps one to two dollars an hour for doing the same thing.

Finally, the welfare mother who in fact did receive training and entered the job market, could only leave her child in the WIN centers for three to six months. After that, she was on her own, compelled to pay most of the costs of child care. But these mothers were not usually able to earn enough to meet these costs—and hence they had little incentive, indeed little opportunity, for leaving welfare for employment. In the end, the most tangible result of WIN was not to give mothers jobs or children services, but to frighten potential welfare recipients from applying for relief.

Even more disturbing has been the effects of state intervention in family planning. In 1969, the federal government abandoned its traditional hands-off policy to fund a national system of family planning clinics. These clinics were "to make comprehensive voluntary family planning services available readily to all persons in the United States desiring such services." The bill passed readily through Congress, and the provision that the funds would not be used for purposes of abortion pacified spokesmen for the Catholic Church.

The family planners sold this measure on the basis of a very particular explanation as to why the poor had such high birthrates. The large families, they insisted, were unwanted. The poor were victims of an uneven distribution of knowledge about contraception and of implements with which to carry it out. The planners argued,

It is clear that couples in higher socioeconomic groups tended to use more reliable, medical methods of family planning, while poor couples tended to depend on the less reliable, non-medical methods. It is doubtful that these differences were a matter of choice; rather they seemed related to the modal economic structure of American medicine in which the essential precondition for obtaining health services is the financial ability to employ a private physician.

In opting for this approach, the family planners minimized sociological findings, such as those of Lee Rainwater, which contended that poor families received gratification from children that they could not find in other areas of their lives, that they knew well enough about contraception, that techniques were available, but that they chose not to use them! The planners could not accept such a formulation. Obviously, large families and teenage pregnancies trapped the poor in their poverty, so once the pill or the IUD was available, once they were educated to family limitation, they would voluntarily limit births. Government officials, acutely concerned with swelling ADC rolls and illegitimacy, bought this approach, supporting the program to the cost of about $150 million a year.

Once again, the rhetoric of advocates has collided with the realities of administration. The planners had hoped for a generous and voluntary program that would serve a broad spectrum of the lower class population. But the government has steadily moved to narrow the services to the hard-core poor. Moreover, by 1973 the government was eager to transfer the management of family planning from health to welfare agencies. HEW, observes Jeannie Rosoff, one of the directors of the Center for Family Planning Development, is now attempting "to tie the provision of family planning services to state-set welfare eligibility criteria, and to shift the administrative responsibility for the family planning program from its health to its welfare arm, and on down to state and welfare agencies." Increasingly, the coercive aspects of family planning are becoming apparent.

Johan Eliot, professor of population planning at the University of Michigan notes:

Many women on welfare have pointed out that if the caseworker responsible for approving or disapproving and raising or lowering their welfare grants offers them family planning services, a sense of pressure to accept them is almost inevitable. . . . Furthermore, there has been a trend toward evaluation of performance of welfare caseworkers relative to their success in reducing excess fertility and out of wedlock births.

What was to be a voluntary program is turning out to be a way of compelling the poor, under the threat of welfare payment cut-offs, to limit their families.

The coercive character of government intervention is still more starkly visible in the area of sterilization. The Family Planning Act did not actually mention sterilization as one means of limiting births; indeed, family planners argued for the establishment of the birth control clinics as a way of counterbalancing mounting pressures in states for sterilization. But the Act itself has only exacerbated the problem. In 1971, HEW authorized funds for the use of sterilization research for the first time. By 1973, two examples of family planning clinics carrying out sterilization procedures without prior consent had come to public attention. Senate hearings on the use of humans in drug experimentation programs uncovered the case of a white welfare woman in Tennessee who was given a sterilizing drug without being told of its consequences. In another instance, two black teenage girls were sterilized without parental approval. Family planning officials are certain that these are isolated incidents, the fault of overzealous or careless workers. But others suspect that these two cases represent only the tip of the iceberg.

These suspicions are not ill-founded. There is no denying the growing attractiveness to state officials of sterilization programs aimed at the poor. In 1973, five bills were introduced into legislatures to put pressure on welfare clients to be sterilized; and while none passed, they do illustrate the nature of the sentiment. In Illinois and New Hampshire, cash incentives were to be offered to the poor to undergo the operation; in Indiana, Tennessee, and Ohio, welfare payments would have been denied to a woman with more than two illegitimate children unless she agreed to sterilization.

And there are clues that sterilization already may not be so voluntary a procedure for welfare mothers. In 1973, the Joint Program for the Study of Abortion examined the experiences of almost 73,000 women who had legal abortions between June 1970 and June 1971. Of these women, 2,725 had been sterilized—but the likelihood of sterilization at the time of abortion was significantly greater for non-white women and those in non-private wards than for white women and those in private wards. Even when the ages and number of children already born to the two groups were standardized, "there remained a 20 per cent differential between the two groups which cannot be readily explained." It is not unreasonable to suspect the intrusion of non-voluntary sterilization at just this point.

The best evidence for the scope of the problem emerges in the 1974 court test of proposed HEW guidelines to govern sterilization in family planning clinics. HEW contended that the guidelines allowed for the sterilization of minors and incompetents only when a review board gave approval; it insisted that the voluntary consent form for competent adults offered adequate protection against coercion. The opposing brief of the Center for Law and Social Policy, representing the National Welfare Rights Organization, argued that the rights of minors and incompetents were not being protected, that their approval, or the approval of their guardians, was not even required, that the review board represented agencies involved either in welfare or sterilization, and that competent adults remained subject to coercion. The decision of federal Judge Gerhard Gesell found the HEW guidelines "arbitrary and unreasonable." "There is uncontrovertible evidence," declared Gesell, "that minors and other incompetents have been sterilized with federal funds and that an indefinite number of poor people have been improperly coerced into accepting a sterilization operation under the threat that various federally supported welfare benefits would be withdrawn." In one case, a woman at childbirth "was actually refused medical assistance by her attending physician unless she submitted to tubal ligation after the birth."

Gesell disallowed all sterilization in the case of minors and the mentally deficient, finding no possibility for informed consent. He also insisted the regulations be revised to insure that federal funds not be used to compel the poor to undergo sterilization. "Individuals seeking sterilization [must] be orally informed at the very outset that no federal benefits can be withdrawn because of a failure to accept sterilization. This guarantee must also appear prominently at the top of the consent document already required by the regulations." The court did not prohibit all voluntary sterilizations, and the National Welfare Rights Organization did not ask it to do so. They both assume that procedural safeguards can protect the indigent against coercion. Whether their faith will be justified by practice still remains to be seen.

The Worst of Both Worlds?

Thus, over the past decades the dynamic shaping of social policy toward women, children, and the family has had some tragic consequences. When the middle class invites government intervention to improve the quality of life, the results often have been to supply the state with new means for coercing the poor. The calls for government-sponsored day care centers or programs to maximize the availability of contraceptive techniques have been translated into ways of manipulating the poor to reduce welfare rolls. And when the middle classes have attempted to minimize state intervention in order to enhance privacy and individual choice, the result leaves the poor as victims of inadequate resources. To remove PINS cases from the dockets of juvenile courts does nothing to enlarge the opportunities for lower class children. In a society so marked by uneven distribution of wealth and power, a policy of consistent laissez-faire only promises to exaggerate these inequities. In a sense, we have had the worst of both worlds, intervention which has led to coercion, restrictions which have allowed neglect!

The challenge, then, confronting social policy toward women, children, and the family over the next decades is awesome. To escape the effects of the existing dynamic demands not only a genuine commitment to the welfare of all classes but ingenuity and imagination as well. Perhaps the recognition of how this dynamic has operated will begin to enable us to avoid the traps. We stand in desperate need of total honesty both in terms of what we ask of policy and how we go about implementing it. It is simply too dangerous a strategy to advocate day care in order to maximize such other goals as medical and nutritional services. The rationale legitimates too much intervention. It is equally unacceptable to promote contraception and sterilization among the poor in the name of mental health or social mobility when what we really intend is to reduce welfare rolls. And it is no less hazardous to fight the infanticide issue not on its own grounds but on those of abortion.

Given the dismal record of state intervention, it seems preferable wherever possible to expand the rights of privacy, to enhance freedom of choice, to test the limits of allowing competing claims to reach their own resolutions. And when inequities are too gross to be neglected, or when opportunities seem too promising to be ignored, we must be certain that the benefits offered to one class are not translated into the means to coerce the other. In all cases, we must be precise in our rhetoric, and set out to accomplish what we know we can deliver. Slogans, whether in the name of child advocacy or a national family policy, cannot substitute for precise and carefully defined programs. To confuse day care with loving care, or the availability of contraception with the solution to the poverty problem, will not only breed disappointments, but finally, a certain recklessness.

In light of the past, there is little reason to be confident about the future. We may continue shuffling between neglect and coercion. But if we fail to end this tradition, we all will pay the price, and from appearances, it will be high.

IV

Crime, Punishment, and Reformation*

James Q. Wilson

Since the early nineteenth century, the publicly-avowed purpose of the American system of criminal justice has been to "rehabilitate" criminals. At first this reformism had a religious cast: Prisons—"penitentiaries"—were created in America as places where criminals would undergo the moral reeducation that would enable them to rejoin society as productive and law-abiding citizens. Later, the idea of penal reform became secularized: prisons were to help criminals make the psychological adjustments and acquire the social, educational, and vocational skills that would fit them for the world outside. But throughout the system's evolution, it justified itself by the promise that it could reform habitual law-breakers.

James Q. Wilson argues in this essay that the experience of the past 150 years casts doubt on this view of human nature and of society's ability to change it. Social science research has shown that prisons, even the best of them, cannot remake criminals to the extent that criminologists have hoped, and that the deterrent function of the criminal justice system is more important than reformers had imagined. A more balanced notion of man, says Wilson, would imply a system of justice that would maintain prisons to deter and to incapacitate the criminal; rehabilitation would be attempted only for those that show themselves to be amenable.

---

*Parts of this essay appeared originally in James Q. Wilson, *Thinking About Crime* (New York: © Basic Books, 1975). I do not here take into account the substantial body of research and commentary that has appeared since this chapter was written in 1974.

For almost 150 years, the dominant, publicly-avowed purpose of the criminal justice system has been to effect the reformation of the convicted criminal and the redirection of the prospective criminal. This purpose implies that human nature is malleable and thus human behavior can be altered—"corrected"—according to plan. It is a remarkable theory, not wholly American in origin but peculiarly American in application and persistence, and though it has repeatedly been challenged it has, until recently, survived almost intact whatever the partisan dispositions of statesmen who have addressed it.

When Gustave de Beaumont and Alexis deTocqueville published in 1833 their classic report on American prisons, they wrote that the "principal object" of these institutions "is to give him [the prisoner] the habits of society, and first to teach him to obey."[1] Indeed, the very name widely given to these institutions—*penitentiaries*—suggests vividly what was expected of them by their most ardent advocates: that their inmates would, by reflection, become penitent and would thereby undergo a radical transformation of character. Beaumont and Tocqueville were wisely skeptical of these exaggerated claims, noting that moral reformation rarely occurs, in or out of prison, but they were prepared to believe that a more modest improvement was possible:

Perhaps, leaving the prison, he is not an honest man; but he has contracted honest habits. . . . [I]f he is not more virtuous he has become at least more judicious; his morality is not honour, but interest. . . . [H]is mind has contracted habits of order, and he possesses rules for his conduct of life; without having a powerful religious conviction, he has acquired a taste for moral principles which religion affords; finally, if he has not become in truth better, he is at least more obedient to the laws, and that is all which society has the right to demand.[2]

After reviewing such data as they could find, the French visitors concluded, to the pleasure of the many advocates of the American penitentiary experiment, that these institutions had succeeded in reducing the rate at which prisoners are recommitted from one in six (in the old crowded, noisy prisons) to only one in twenty in the new, silent penitentiaries at Auburn and Wethersfield.[3]

Nearly a century later, the National Commission on Law Observance and Enforcement, headed by George W. Wickersham and appointed by President Herbert Hoover, concluded its survey of the rampant lawlessness stimulated by Prohibition and the depression by observing that "the reformation of the criminal" is the best means of protecting society and, therefore, it is "the function of the prison to find the means so to reshape the interests, attitudes, habits, the total character of the individual as to release him both competent and willing to find a way of adjusting himself to the community without further law violation."[4]

The Wickersham Commission was not confident that it knew the causes of crime. Its report on this subject comprised fewer than four pages, the only substantive paragraph of which stated that "we find it impossible comprehensively to discuss the causes of crime or factors in nonobservance of law." But the Commission was quite confident it understood the changes necessary to speed the reformation of the criminal: individualized treatment, extensive use of probation and parole, schools and workshops for prisons, an end to filth and overcrowding, better prisoner classification, and the recruitment of better correctional personnel.

Thirty-six years later, the Commission on Law Enforcement and Administration of Justice, chaired by Nicholas Katzenbach and appointed by President Lyndon Johnson, formed a Task Force on Corrections, which stated that "rehabilitation of offenders to prevent their return to crime is in general the most promising way to achieve" the goal of reducing crime.[5] The focus of the volume was on methods to attain that goal. The full Commission did not state explicitly and categorically what it believed were the purposes of criminal justice, but the thrust of its recommendations and the tenor of its writing leave little doubt that reformation was the objective. It says at one point, for example, that the "most fundamental" of the desired changes in prisons is the "establishment of a collaborative regime in which staff and inmates work together toward rehabilitative goals." The Commission's "model" for corrections would shift the focus away from "banishment" to a "carefully devised combination of control and treatment."[6]

The Katzenbach Commission, unlike its predecessor, advanced a large number of recommendations for preventing crime, but quite like its predecessor, it urged as methods to improve the rehabilitation exactly the same list of reforms proposed by the Wickersham Commission, to which it added the concept of "community-based corrections."

Seven years later, in 1973, Attorney General John Mitchell instructed the administrator of the Law Enforcement Assistance Administration (LEAA) to develop "goals and standards" for criminal justice agencies, a task he undertook by creating the National Advisory Commission on Criminal Justice Standards and Goals, chaired by the governor of Delaware, Russell W. Peterson. The Peterson Commission report, describing prisons as "little more than 'schools of crime'," endorsed essentially the same list of changes proposed in 1967 and 1931, adding an even greater emphasis on deprisonization and community-based corrections."[7] The Peterson Commission was not explicit as to whether deprisonization would aid rehabilitation or if it was simply a more humane and less expensive alternative to a prison system that could not rehabilitate. To a greater extent than its predecessors, this Commission was concerned with the rights of prisoners rather than with the rehabilitative ideal, but the language endorsing probation, parole, work release, study release, and other forms of "supervision" in the community implies that this supervision is intended to help change the offender—else why supervise at all? It is, of course, possible that the Peterson Commission, though created at the instigation of a "conservative" administration, issued a report that was meant to signal the abandonment of the rehabilitative ideal as part of a general abandonment of the system of organized restraint that was always central to criminal justice. This implies a truly radical shift in the perceived nature of man; he is no longer merely malleable, but already perfect.

In this century, statesmen summoned by our highest officials to advise on crime have uniformly spoken optimistically of man; though he may err, he can be reformed, and perhaps even reformed spontaneously, without institutional intervention. But this century also has seen virtually every significant effort at criminal rehabilitation come to nought.

Between 1966 and 1972, Robert Martinson reviewed, initially at the request of the New York State Governor's Committee on Criminal Offenders, 231 experimental studies on the treatment of criminals, including *all* those from here and abroad that were available in print between 1945 and 1967 and that met various tests of methodological adequacy. Martinson's study, which was not published by the New York state authorities, came to a clear conclusion: "With few and isolated exceptions, the rehabilitative efforts that have been reported so far have no appreciable effect on recidivism."[8] Studies done since 1967 do not provide grounds for altering that conclusion significantly.

It does not seem to matter what form of treatment in the correctional system is attempted—whether vocational training or academic education; whether counseling inmates individually, in groups, or not at all; whether therapy is administered by social workers or psychiatrists; whether the institutional context of the treatment is custodial or benign; whether the sentences are short or long; whether the person is placed on probation or released on parole; or whether the treatment takes place in the community or in institutions. Indeed, some forms of treatment—notably a few experiments with psychotherapy—actually produced an *increase* in the rate of recidivism.

The Martinson review is unique in its comprehensiveness, but not in its findings. R.G. Hood came to much the same conclusion in a review published in 1967;[9] Walter C. Bailey, after examining 100 studies of the efficacy of treatment and especially the 50 or so that claimed positive results, concluded in 1966 that the "evidence supporting the efficacy of correctional treatment is slight, inconsistent, and of questionable reliability";[10] Leslie T. Wilkins observed in 1969 that "the major achievement of research in the field of social psychology and treatment has been negative and has resulted in the undermining of nearly all the current mythology regarding the effectiveness of treatment in any form."[11]

One of the most ambitious and conspicuous victims of scientific re-analysis of treatment programs has been the California Treatment Project (sometimes called the Warren study). President Johnson's Crime Commission singled out this experiment for special mention as evidence that rehabilitation was possible, especially if done in a community rather than an institutional setting.[12] Young offenders, classified by their level of "interpersonal maturity," were assigned directly to probation officers in small groups and exposed to intensive and individually-tailored therapy programs. Warren reported, and the Crime Commission repeated, the claim that these youth were much less likely to commit additional crimes than a similar group sent through the regular detention facilities and then placed in conventional probation. Upon later and closer study, however, it became clear that the experimental group not only did not commit fewer offenses, they, in fact, committed *more*. The probation officers assigned to the experimental group were not revoking probation when young people in that group committed new offenses, while the probation officers assigned to the regular youth (the "control group") were revoking probation in the normal way whenever a new offense was committed. In short, the "treatment" program did not alter the behavior of the delinquents; it only altered the behavior of the probation officers.[13]

In retrospect, little of this should have been surprising. It requires, not merely optimistic, but heroic assumptions about the nature of man to lead one to suppose that a person, finally sentenced after (in most cases) many brushes with the law, and having devoted a good part of his youth and young adulthood to misbehavior of every sort, should, by either the solemnity of prison or the skillfulness of a counselor, come to see the error of his ways and to experience a transformation of his character. Today we smile in amusement at the naiveté of those early prison reformers who imagined that religious instruction while in solitary confinement would lead to moral regeneration. How they would now smile at us at our presumption that conversations with a psychiatrist or a "return to the community" could achieve the same end! We have learned how difficult it is by governmental means to improve the educational attainments of children or to restore stability and affection to the family, and in these cases, we are often working with willing subjects in moments of admitted need. Criminal rehabilitation requires producing equivalent changes in unwilling subjects under conditions of duress or indifference.

The origins of the reformative theory of criminal justice and of the theory of human malleability that underlies it are to be found in both religious and scientific impulses. The Boston Prison Discipline Society, founded in 1826, was, through its reports, of great influence in the penitentiary movement; it is described by Beaumont and Tocqueville as a group "which is convinced that religious instruction is the whole system of reform of prisons" and which with its own funds supported ministers in five major prisons.[14] Strong support for the Philadelphia Society for Alleviating the Miseries of Public Prisons, the first modern prison reform society, came from the Quakers.[15] Thomas Eddy, builder and first warden of the Newgate Prison in Greenwich Village in 1796, was himself a Quaker who believed that any man, even a criminal, shared the divine "inner light" and was thus amenable to reform. In close touch with like-minded persons abroad, such as John Howard, he was, in the words of Professor W. David Lewis, "a member of a trans-Atlantic community of the benevolently inclined."[16]

The New York Prison Association was founded in 1843 by, among others, William H. Channing, the noted Unitarian minister, as testimony to what Reverend Channing described as the Christian desire to avoid vindictiveness and to remedy the familial and communal neglect that had produced criminals. Louis Dwight, founder of the Boston Prison Discipline Society, had studied for the ministry and had once been an agent for the American Bible Society. The religious impulse of the Quakers, of Channing, and of Dwight did not result, where prisons were concerned, simply in religious programs. Their concerns in this area were quite secular, convinced, as they were, of the importance of the family in causing crime and of the role of the modern penitentiary as a kind of surrogate family that would produce, through a combination of solitary reflection, moral precept, and useful labor, the human character that fathers and mothers had not.

The progressive ministry of the 1830s and 1840s was opposed to the earlier Calvinist views that asserted the natural depravity of man and thus accepted the inability of society to eliminate that depravity.[17] In the early eighteenth century and before, man was thought to be born corrupt, crime was viewed as a sin, and temporal punishment was required both to deter the criminal and to vindicate divine and human law. Where punishment by pain or public humiliation was inadequate to protect the community, death or banishment would be imposed.[18] *But criminals were not imprisoned.* A prison would be expensive, would offer no greater protection to society than hanging or exclusion, and could not hope to transform the naturally depraved.

In the early nineteenth century, this view was replaced, at least among accepted spokesmen, by the theory that man was born innocent, that he was sometimes corrupted by society, and that to punish crime by pain or death was not only "vindictive," but an abdication of society's responsibility to set right the conditions it had caused. Hence, "enlightened" views *led to the creation of prisons.*

There were, in addition, rationalistic reasons for this development. In Europe, Jeremy Bentham, Cesare Beccaria, Voltaire, and Montesquieu sought to eliminate from the law what they took to be the dead weight of tradition, the capriciousness of monarchical discretion, and the inconsistent and brutal pattern of criminal penalties. In Beccaria, American reformers found a critic of despotic law and an advocate of precision and promptness in applying criminal penalties. But he did not address himself directly to rehabilitation and only by implication to the nature of man, and his remarks on prisons were of little significance, for in Italy and America, at that time, "prison" was merely a holding place for arrested persons awaiting trial. The penitentiary had not been invented, nor did he advocate it.

It was Bentham, especially in his *The Rationale of Punishment*, who provided America with the most systematic examination of the relationship between the criminal law and human nature, together with a detailed consideration of a model penitentiary (the "Panopticon"). Bentham was a radical philosopher, not a churchman, and he was uninterested in the sources or quality of human preferences and values. He had little desire to explain crime as a result of broken homes or communal neglect; his view was that of the economist for whom the social origins of human tastes are less important than their market expression. "Pain and pleasure are the great springs of human action," he wrote, and thus man is led to crime, not because he is driven to it by demons or bad manners, but because it is profitable. If a would-be criminal sees that the "pain" (i.e., cost) of a crime will exceed in value the "pleasure" (i.e., benefit) to be obtained from its commission, he will refrain from it. To prevent crime, therefore, one should devote his energy, not to strengthening the family or improving the community, but to eliminating the physical ability to commit crime ("incapacitation," as by imprisonment), by taking away the desire to offend ("reformation"), and by making persons fearful of offending ("intimidation" or "deterrence").[19]

American prison reformers in the nineteenth century and the members of crime commissions in the twentieth century have by and large ignored the methods of incapacitation and deterrence in favor of reformation as a strategy for reducing crime. The reasons for this are not altogether clear. Perhaps reformers and statesmen have observed rising crime rates and concluded (erroneously) from this that, since they are rising, existing legal penalties have not prevented, and thus cannot prevent, crime. Perhaps it is because reformers have, and seek to arouse in others, a repugnance for existing criminal penalties, and inasmuch as one generation tends to view with moral horror what a previous generation accepted with equanimity, extant penalties are always subject to rising levels of aversion. The steady growth in opposition to the death penalty is a case. Or perhaps it is because the incapacitation and deterrence theories of crime reduction imply that human nature is either immutably evil (some people will always try to steal, and thus they must be forcibly restrained, as by imprisonment) or narrowly calculating (many people will try to steal when it is in their interest to do so). Reformers prefer to believe that man's nature is either benign or malleable.

Whatever the case, it is clear that incapacitation and deterrence were not rejected on empirical grounds. Incapacitation reduces crime by definition: those dead, banished, or imprisoned cannot victimize citizens (except, in the last case, those citizens who are their fellow prisoners). Evidence on whether criminal penalties deter was rarely gathered in any systematic way, except for *post hoc*, scientifically invalid statements alleging that a certain penalty "obviously" does not deter because the crimes for which these penalties might ensue are increasing in rate. The problem with such a view, of course, is that it says nothing about whether such crime rates would increase even faster in the absence of the penalty.

Neither early prison reformers nor contemporary statesmen have been expert in the analysis of the deterrence effects, if any, of criminal penalties. One would suppose, however, that criminologists would long ago have begun to study the matter closely. Though there has been a good deal of thought given to the death penalty, especially in the 1950s, there was not, until the late 1960s, much serious attention paid to the issue of deterrence generally, and even the quality of analysis of the death penalty as a deterrent has been seriously inadequate. Though criminology is one of the oldest social science disciplines in this country, it was not until almost a half century after its founding that many of its members began addressing crime as a problem of public policy. The first National Conference on Criminal Law and Criminology was held in Chicago in 1909; the *Journal of the American Institute of Criminal Law and Criminology* began appearing the following year.[20] Almost from the first, however, criminology became the study, not of the control of crime, but of its causes, and because it was devoted to the latter, it could contribute little to the former.

This seems paradoxical. The popular view is that to solve a problem one must first understand its cause; otherwise, one only deals with "symptoms." If we do not understand the causes of crime, how can crime be reduced? In a limited sense, the statement is true. If cameras are left unguarded in a camera store, we should not be surprised to see thefts of cameras from that store increase. One way, therefore, to reduce this kind of shoplifting is to reduce its (proximate) cause by placing the cameras in locked cabinets and having clerks keep an eye on the customers. Bentham would call this policy a form of incapacitation. But it is not merely the availability of cameras that causes their theft, since most people do not steal them even when unguarded. What then, causes some people to behave criminally?

Criminology has sought to answer this question, partly because of its intellectual interest and partly because criminologists felt an obligation to examine critically popular theories of criminality (for example, that criminal tendencies are inherited, or physiologically determined, or the product of mental aberrations). But criminal behavior is a form of human behavior, and thus to explain the former is tantamount to explaining the latter. Though the full argument is too extensive to be stated here,[21] I would assert that a relentless search for the sources of human behavior, criminal or noncriminal, leads inevitably into man's subjective state—his attitudes, beliefs, preferences—and thus into the social and psychological processes by which that subjective state is formed. Behavior will surely be *influenced* by objective conditions, but it will rarely be *determined* by them. Persons buy fewer large automobiles as the price of gasoline rises—but some people go on buying large cars anyway. Areas of great poverty and social disorganization are also areas of high crime rates—but many people living in those areas never become criminal, and some living in affluent ones become criminal despite their advantages. Most people will not murder even if their chances of being caught are slight—but some will murder and promptly confess to the police.

For policy purposes, it is usually enough to know that the consumption of gasoline varies with the price; the incidence of crime, with the quality of the communal environment; and the rate of murder, with—well, we are not certain. But for purposes of understanding the *causes* of automotive purchases or crime rates, this will not do. We shall want instead to know how individuals form their tastes for cars or their disposition to crime and whether these inclinations are derived from familial instruction or are the consequences of parental neglect and in what way friends form, confirm, or resist attitudes that dictate whether automobiles shall be purchased or stolen. People act (except when they act impulsively or irrationally) because of their preferences and motives, and preferences and motives, in turn, are socially formed—by friends and family, by schooling and culture.

The implications of this approach for theories of man, crime, and criminal control are profound. A modern criminologist, adhering to this perspective, would reject out of hand the Benthamite calculus of pains and pleasures as an "explanation" of crime since it does not explain why one man finds much pleasure in large cars and little pain in being arrested, whereas another prefers small cars and would be mortified by a traffic ticket. Moreover, whatever a man's preferences, the Benthamite approach implies that he alone freely chooses them and the course of action they support. This radical individualism and its attendant conception of free will is anathema to those who believe that human behavior is caused by attitudes that are socially formed.

If man is a creature of society and if criminality occurs in response to attitudes that are socially produced, then the proper approach to crime reduction is to prevent the formation of criminal proclivities or to change them once formed. In quest of crime prevention, criminologists have made a special effort to intervene among youth in ways designed to redirect their gang activities, to make them wards of the state, to provide them with counseling, and to reorganize their communities. If prevention efforts do not prevent, then the task becomes one of rehabilitating the convicted offender by changing his attitudes and by reducing the stigma which society, having produced him, has attached to him.

Criminologists have not supported the rehabilitative approach merely because they are tender-minded or politically liberal, or even because they believe that society has "produced" crime by failing to eliminate poverty and to correct injustice. They have endorsed it in the past because of the theory of human nature that has been implicit in their discipline. As the authors of perhaps the most widely-used text on criminology point out, "attempts to explain criminal behavior have greatly abetted . . . the official use of the treatment reaction."[22] It could hardly be otherwise. If crime is the result of persons behaving on the basis of socially-determined values and attitudes, then the deterrence theory will not work, or work very well; it is the nature of human wants, not the costs of gratifying them, that chiefly influence action. In this view, crime is to an important degree nonrational, or expressive behavior. Indeed, for some the risk of being caught adds to the pleasure of the crime; increasing the risk would only enhance the pleasure. Thus, criminologists spent little time trying to find out, in fact, whether penalties deterred; they argued on theoretical grounds that they did not.[23]

Gradually, however, it has become clear that efforts at rehabilitating offenders were not working. Certain criminologists have been among the leaders in this discovery. The best that can be said for most treatment programs is that they produce no greater rate of recidivism than prison. A dilemma. If rehabilitation ought to be the purpose of criminal justice, but rehabilitation does not succeed, what then? There seemed to be only two possibilities: try harder, with more resources and greater ingenuity, or abandon the criminal justice system altogether.

Both responses can be framed in ways that permit one to preserve a view of human nature as pliant. "Trying harder" has until recently been the more common response. When, for example, the ambitious Cambridge-Somerville Youth Project failed, by intensive counseling and other methods, to reduce juvenile delinquency, the evaluators of this project urged that what was needed was more and better counseling to make up for the "absence of parental affection" and inconsistent discipline, perhaps even to the point of removing the child from the family and placing him in a therapeutic "milieu."[24] There is, of course, very little evidence that any institutional milieu, however therapeutic, can make up for whatever damage has been done by parental neglect and (happily) little support for the idea that the state should take children away from their parents before their habits are formed.

Abandoning the criminal justice system by "deprisonization" and a more extensive use of probation and "community supervision" has become of late a far more actively discussed alternative,[25] but it is not clear on what view of human nature these proposals rest. One possibility is that convicted offenders can be reformed only in the community (on probation or in half-way houses) and not in an institutional setting such as a prison. There is little evidence to support this view. In 1969, the National Council on Crime and Delinquency reviewed all known studies which rigorously compared offenders assigned to half-way houses to those not assigned to them. No differences in recidivism rates were found between offenders who went to half-way houses and those who did not.[26] One objection to this discouraging finding might be that the offenders were first sent to prison, and then to the half-way houses in their communities; perhaps the prior prison experience so hardened them that a return to crime became likely whatever form their reintroduction to the community took. In short, perhaps society cannot improve human nature, but can harm it. The problem with correctional institutions may be that while they cannot make matters better, they can make them worse—by "stigmatizing" the offender, by exposing him to hardened convicts from whom he learns criminal skills and antisocial attitudes, and by degrading his dignity and autonomy.

There is not much evidence to support this theory. Persons put on probation are less likely to commit a new crime than those sent to jail, but the former group's better performance is primarily the result of their special selection—only good risks are supposed to be put on probation and if they succeed, it only confirms the ability of the sentencing authorities to make good guesses. There have been some efforts to compare persons on probation with those sent to jail who are matched in terms of the crime they committed, their prior criminal record, and the like. In a review of these studies in 1968, R.F. Sparks concluded that there was little difference in the success rates of probationers and prisoners—they were about equally likely to commit new crimes.[27]

Proponents of deprisonization have used such findings to argue that probation is desirable because it is as likely as prison to produce rehabilitation. But the more important interpretation of these findings is that *they do not support the theory that, for similar offenders, prison makes them worse.* If prison does not reform, neither does it deform. This is a vital point, because prison serves at least one and perhaps two functions that probation cannot; it incapacitates the offender so that, while imprisoned, he cannot harm society, and the prospect of prison may be a greater deterrent to would-be criminals than the prospect of probation.

Although Bentham outlined in detail the theory of deterrence almost 200 years ago, it was not until the late 1960s that much effort was made to test it. Since then, a number of scholars have compared the crime rates by states with the certainty and severity of punishment in those states. Everyone recognizes that reported crime rates are not very accurate; thus, particular findings employing this method must be viewed with great caution. What is striking, however, is the almost complete uniformity of results, whoever the author. George E. Antunes and A. Lee Hunt reviewed a number of these studies in 1972 and concluded that all supported the conclusion that the more certain imprisonment was for a given offense, the lower the rate at which that offense was committed.[28] Charles R. Tittle and Charles H. Logan published the following year an even more comprehensive review and came to essentially the same conclusion: "Almost all research since 1960 supports the view that negative sanctions are significant variables in the explanation of conformity and deviance."[29] Or to say the same thing more plainly, increasing the prospect of being caught and punished reduces the rate at which many punishable acts are committed. Finally, Isaac Ehrlich, who has done the most sophisticated and comprehensive analysis of crime rates, concludes that not only is an increase in the certainty of the penalty (i.e., a high probability of being imprisoned) associated with lower crime rates, so also are higher levels of severity (i.e., longer, rather than shorter prison terms).[30]

Evidence supporting the deterrence theory suggests a view of human nature quite different from that implied by the reformation theory. Whereas the latter argues that persons commit crimes because of deep-seated attitudes formed by familial and friendship experiences to which they respond without real regard for the prospect of being caught and punished, the former asserts that most would-be criminals take into account, however, crudely, the likely costs and benefits of crime and, as the costs rise or the benefits fall, will commit fewer crimes. Obviously not all criminals are sensitive to costs and benefits. Some husbands will murder their wives even though they are almost certain to be caught; some boys will steal in order to prove they are not afraid of the police; and some madmen will plant bombs that destroy themselves as well as their victims. But if the data on deterrence mean anything, they mean that most persons contemplating most crimes, especially crimes for monetary gain (burglary, robbery, larceny, auto theft) take into account the risks, just as law-abiding persons take into account the changing risks of starting a business, or leaving their homes vacant during their summer vacations, or of learning to ski.

Neither the deterrence theory nor the view of human nature which it implies "explain" crime. A hundred persons may confront equal prospective benefits (say, spending $1,000 stolen from a bank) and equal prospective costs (say, a one in five chance of imprisonment), but ninety-five will not seriously consider bank robbery while five will pull a gun and march up to the cashier without a moment's hesitation. It is intellectually interesting to try to discover why the five steal and the ninety-five do not; no doubt it has much to do with their tolerance of risk, their money need, or their values as shaped by family, friends, and perhaps even the mass media. From the point of view of public policy, however, such explanations are of little value because government has no way of changing in any systematic fashion family backgrounds, deep-seated attitudes, or friendship patterns. And even if government could do these things, the cost would be frightful—not only in money terms, because the programs would have to be directed at the ninety-five who are not likely to be criminal in order to be certain of reaching the five who are, but also in terms of those fundamental human values that would be jeopardized if government possessed the capacity to direct the inner life of the family or to mold the mental state of its citizens.

Some countries, such as the People's Republic of China, are supposed to have greatly reduced crime. If true, we can only speculate on the price of this in social mobilization, the elimination of dissent, and the reduction in personal privacy and autonomy.

Democratic governments have relatively few policy instruments they can use effectively and economically in dealing with crime. They can help make things harder to steal (by locking them up, bolting them down, or rendering them non-negotiable); they can alter the certainty and severity of punishment; they can incapacitate criminals by depriving them of their liberty; and they can help make legitimate alternatives to crime relatively more attractive. What is striking about the history of the public policy toward crime in this country is that our government has tended to employ those strategies that it did not know how to make work (for example, running rehabilitation programs) in preference to those it did know how to carry out (for example, increasing the ability to incapacitate convicted offenders). And when it tried to alter those factors over which it did have control, it either picked the less important (for example, by increasing the severity of sentences), rather than the more important (increasing the certainty of sentences) or it picked an important factor but changed it in an undesirable direction (for example, by reducing the number of persons in prisons during periods of rapidly rising crime rates). And some policies, such as improving legitimate alternatives to crime, it attempted, but not very successfully.

We have made these errors, I believe, because our policy has been informed by a mistaken view of man's nature and of the capacity of government to alter it. In consequence of these errors, we may have increased rather than decreased crime, treated persons convicted of crimes unjustly, and wasted scarce resources.

If we assume, as by and large we have, that crime is "caused," that the causes are to be found in "motives and attitudes," and that these motives and attitudes are socially formed by family and friends; and if we assume, as for the most part we have, that it is the responsibility of the courts and the correctional system to reform the criminal by changing his motives and attitudes and the social relationships that sustain them—then it follows as a matter of course that we will create special juvenile courts to handle youthful offenders in order that they may be rehabilitated before their criminal inclinations are fully formed. The juvenile court movement began early in this century with just this view. A youth who committed a crime gave evidence by that act of a defective or improper upbringing and thereby justified a judge in substituting the guidance of the state for that of the family. Such a youth was not "punished," he was made instead a ward of the state for an indefinite period of time or until he reached his majority. The institutions that were to substitute for the family were called, naturally, "reformatories."[31]

It is now well understood, of course, that the juvenile court system did not realize the hopes of its founders. Reformatories rarely reformed; young persons confined in them saw these institutions for what they were—jails—and not for what they claimed to be (surrogate "families"). The sentences to these reformatories, often being dependent on the prospects for rehabilitation rather than on the nature of the offense, differed among persons who had committed the same offense and thus were seen by them as unjust. Furthermore, the court process leading to this result was deliberately paternalistic and therefore, out of the best of motives, lacking in most of the essential elements of due process. Many scholars criticized the juvenile justice system;[32] the Task Force on Juvenile Delinquency of President Johnson's Crime Commission joined in that criticism;[33] and the Supreme Court in 1967 ruled that the requirements of due process (including the right to a hearing, to counsel, to cross-examine witnesses) apply to juvenile proceedings as they do to adult ones.[34]

But the policy implications of these criticisms are confusing so long as we persist in our view that the "causes" of delinquency can be discovered, that human nature is sufficiently malleable to permit these causes to be corrected, and that the juvenile justice system must be judged solely or primarily by its ability to affect this transformation. Most criticisms of juvenile justice assert that it is our institutional processes that are defective: We have chosen the right goal but the wrong means. Hence, two responses to the failures of juvenile corrections have been made. The first, epitomized by the Crime Commission, has been to call for more and better resources to be invested in the existing approach, modified only by greater procedural fairness. The Task Force on Juvenile Delinquency asserts that the "most promising and so the most important" way of dealing with delinquency is to ameliorate the underlying social causes. But if the family and community has failed, how are we to make them better? The Task Force cannot answer beyond listing a number of banal or unworkable suggestions: "improve housing and recreation facilities"; "provide help in problems in domestic management and child care"; "develop activities that involve the whole family together"; "involve young people in community activities"; "spend more money on the public schools"; and so forth.[35] The report represents a high-water mark of the misplaced optimism of the 1960s about what government was able to accomplish. There was no reason to believe, then or now, that we know how to improve the family or that more money spent on schools or housing would lead to reductions in delinquency.

Those juveniles whose delinquency is not prevented by those means should be dealt with, according to the Commission, in a correctional program that has been improved by limiting the powers of police and courts over juveniles and by providing alternatives to adjudication through the creation of "Youth Service Bureaus."[36] What community services these bureaus would supply or coordinate is not clear, and the capacity of any such services, whether coordinated or not, to reform delinquents or improve character is not discussed. If it had been discussed, it is hard to see how the Commission could have avoided repeating the statement of two distinguished students of delinquency buried in Appendix T to the report of the delinquency task force: "As of now, there are no demonstrable and proven methods for reducing the incidence of serious delinquent acts through preventive or rehabilitative procedures."[37]

The other response to the failure of the juvenile justice system to prevent or reform delinquency is to abandon the effort by closing the institutions and placing delinquents under "community supervision" (which is to say, under very little supervision at all). For example, all the juvenile "training schools" (i.e., prisons) in Massachusetts have recently been closed. The advocates of the program claim that juveniles who are not sent to jail will prove no more likely to repeat their crimes than those that are sent. This may be true, though it is as yet too early to tell. The larger question—larger, that is, for a society more concerned about reducing the number of innocent victims of crime than in increasing the number of rehabilitated perpetrators of those crimes—is whether the absence of any detention facilities will reduce the ability of society to deter future delinquents or incapacitate unreformable ones. Such considerations do not trouble the leaders of the decarceration movement: Since crime is "caused," it cannot be deterred. In this view, would-be delinquents do not choose to commit or avoid criminal acts because their actions, being socially determined, are not the product of choice.

The problem of adult criminality is approached by procedures influenced by essentially the same philosophical premises, though stripped of the inclination to parental guidance. The indeterminate sentence was devised by those who believed that the penalty must fit the criminal, not the crime, with the result that two adults who have committed the identical offense under identical circumstances may serve very different penalties because one is judged to be a "good prospect" for rehabilitation (he is neat, courteous, white, reverent, or obedient), while the other is judged to be a poor prospect (he is long-haired, surly, godless, black, or impertinent). In some states judges are vested with this discretion, leading to the well-known disparities in sentences. Some disparity, of course, is inevitable and desirable as criminals differ in their prior records and in the circumstances of their offenses, but it is inconceivable that any such differences could produce the pattern of sentences we now observe. In Los Angeles, for example, the proportion of arrested felons sentenced to prison ranges from 7 percent by one judge to 57 percent by another.[38]

In other states, sentencing boards or parole authorities set the actual sentences. Whatever the system, the theory that penalties should be tailored to the characteristics of individuals rather than to the nature of crimes confers on the sentencing body a license to discriminate. Sometimes these discriminations are based on the most genuine concern for the welfare of the offender (though how one *knows* his welfare is not clear), but in many other cases the distinctions between long and short terms reflect the personal prejudices or political loyalties of those making the decisions. Such studies as we have of judicial sentences, where the range of permissible discretion is wide, suggest quite strongly that it is the characteristics of the judges rather than the attributes of the offender or the offense that best explain the sentence imposed.[39]

Once an offender enters prison—and of course only a small proportion, unequally selected, do enter—the unjust consequences of the rehabilitative ideal continue. To many, perhaps most offenders, such rehabilitative facilities as the prison may have—libraries, counselors, therapists, work-release programs—are seen as privileges, an attractive alternative to life in a cell. To the guards, whose overriding concern is security, these facilities are also seen as privileges—privileges that can be used to enhance attainment of the custodial objective. Guards and their allies among the inmates have powerful incentives to use control over access to these facilities to further their personal objectives—security in the case of the guards, power and privilege in the case of the convicts.[40] The rehabilitative ideal can scarcely fail to be corrupted in an institution whose animating idea is not and cannot be rehabilitation but only the deprivation of liberty.

The response to this state of affairs has been similar to that observed with respect to juveniles. Some still wish to make prisons rehabilitative; others, to close them entirely. The former do not know how; the latter dismiss as insignificant the deterrent and incapacitative function of such institutions. No one seems to wish to do that which society both knows how to do and will tolerate having done, namely, to increase the number, variety, and quality of institutions that in varying degrees constrain the liberty of convicted offenders.

In no field of government policy has the best been more the enemy of the good. When reformers deplore prisons, they deplore their failure to reform. When their opponents rejoin, it is to oppose "mollycoddling" prisoners. If the reformers win, the schools, counselors, and therapists they manage to hire will fail. Their opponents then feel vindicated, and redouble their efforts to prevent more money being spent on prisons because, to them, more money means simply "more frills." The resultant debate between defenders of reform and advocates of revenge is far wide of the mark, almost entirely insensitive to what either reality allows or justice endorses.

The consequence of this stand-off has been a policy of deprisonization by default. During the 1960s, while crime rates were soaring, there was no significant increase in the amount of prison space and an actual decline in the number of prisoners, state and federal, from about 213,000 in 1960 to 196,000 in 1970.[41] Fewer and fewer persons were sent to prison by state and federal judges. As a result, the prospect of being imprisoned for an offender in New York State fell by a factor of *six* during that decade. To state the matter from the criminal's point of view, the risk of any serious deprivation of liberty as a result of crime was in 1970 only one-sixth of what it was in 1960, and in the latter year it was already quite low, owing to the great difficulty of solving by an arrest most crimes against property. The reason for the decline is not hard to find: if all right-thinking persons believed that prisons were supposed to rehabilitate but, in fact, did not, judges could scarcely be blamed for concluding that prisons had "failed" and, therefore, should not be used—unless, of course, a particular offender outraged some judicial sensibility.

Let us now suppose that in 1960, we had abandoned any hope of discovering the ultimate causes of crime or of finding any way to correct those causes once discovered. Suppose that our view was that man's nature was ultimately unknowable and in the short run (at least an adult lifetime), unchangeable to a significant degree by plan in any large number of cases. Suppose we assumed instead that most persons, criminal and noncriminal alike, behaved rationally most of the time—that is, they compared the costs and benefits of various courses of action and chose that most likely to produce the greatest net benefit. We need not actually believe that people spend much time calculating in this way, or that when they do calculate, they do it very precisely. But we would all agree that most of us keep our hands off hot stoves, try to get the best price when we buy a new car, and avoid illegal parking in cities (such as Los Angeles) where the police enforce the traffic laws vigorously and engage in illegal parking in cities (such as Boston) where they do not. In the aggregate, we tend to be quite rational even though in individual cases we may behave idiosyncratically. If we made these suppositions, we would, of course, acknowledge that people differ both in what they want and in their willingness to take risks. Hence, younger persons, who have little and want much and who are sufficiently present-oriented to discount heavily costs that must be paid in the future, are (as statistics show) much more likely to run higher risks of facing criminal penalties than older persons. There are no doubt also similar differences associated with culture and income, and perhaps even nationality.

With these assumptions, we would then have made plans for the 1960s in view of observable changes in the few key variables that would clearly affect, in a dramatic way, crime rates. One of these was the vast increase, absolute and relative to the rest of the population, of the number of persons in that age group, essentially the late 'teens and early twenties, that is always greatly overrepresented among lawbreakers. During the 1960s, we added over thirteen million persons between the ages of fourteen and twenty-four to the population, an increase of nearly 50 percent. Few scholars saw clearly the consequences of this in 1960; by 1967, it was seen, but little was done about it.

Of course, nothing can be done directly to affect the number of young people in the population, but several things can be done about the pattern of rewards and sanctions these persons will confront as they come of age. This "invading army," as Norman Ryder has described it, clearly was going to tax to the breaking point the labor market and the criminal justice system. Even though the average young person might be no more likely to commit a crime in 1965 than he would have been in 1955, the absolute number of lawbreakers, and especially the number relative to potential victims, rose dramatically. Jobs were found by many millions of the newly-arrived teenagers, but not by all of them, and as a result the teenage unemployment rate increased in the 1960s by one-third over what it had been in the 1950s. While the adult unemployment rate fell, the teenage rate rose, so that whereas the latter figure had been twice the former during the early 1950s, it was *five times* greater by 1968.[42] Meanwhile, the number of persons imprisoned, as already pointed out, fell more or less steadily throughout the decade of the 1960s—indeed, the prison population started down the same year (1963) that the crime rate started up.

Any given teenager or young adult may not have noticed or cared about these trends because he either had a job, did not want one, or was ethically disinclined to crime. Others may have been so pathologically attracted by theft or violence as to be indifferent to any risk, however great, or any job, however lucrative. But at the margin, there were, without doubt, many youth for whom legitimate sources of income (jobs) were not absolutely preferable to or worse than illegitimate sources (crime), and it is hard to believe that all were unaware that the costs of property crime were falling at the very time that the benefits of job-hunting were also declining.[43] No doubt, as criminologists have told us, the factors that predisposed young persons to view with equanimity or even enthusiasm the prospect of stealing were to be found in the family and the peer group, but we would have to assume that these youth were hopelessly misinformed or wildly irrational if they took no account at all of the comparative net benefits of crime and employment in deciding whether, or how frequently, to give way to those "predisposing factors."

A number of empirical studies have confirmed the relationship between the reported rates of various property crimes on the one hand and the rates of unemployment and the probability of being imprisoned on the other. Belton Fleisher found that juvenile arrest rates increase with increases in unemployment.[44] Phillips, Votey, and Maxwell come to the same conclusion.[45] Isaac Ehrlich not only confirmed the effect of unemployment (at least on property crime rates), but also was able to show that the higher the probability of imprisonment for these offenses, the lower the rate at which they were committed.[46] The Ehrlich study, like all studies of crime, suffers from having to rely on reported (and thus inaccurate) crime rates, but it is clearly consistent with the theory that, at least for property crimes, people act as if they were choosing between legitimate and illegitimate opportunities—raising the unemployment rate and lowering the certainty of punishment are associated with an increase in the theft rate; lowering the unemployment rate and increasing the certainty of punishment are associated with a decrease in the theft rate.

These relationships must be viewed against the background of vastly enlarged temptations. The 1960s was not only a decade of profound demographic changes, but also one of dramatic growth in the consumer economy. The affluence of the period did not go unnoticed by young people. They saw no reason why they should defer gratifying those acquisitive instincts that adults were so amply indulging. More things were stolen, in part because there were more things to steal. Leroy C. Gould has shown that during periods of prosperity, and, in particular from the mid-1940s to the mid-1960s, the rates of property crime are very closely correlated with the level of consumer expenditure. For example, simply knowing the number of automobiles enables one to predict the national auto theft rate with 95 percent accuracy; knowing the amount of cash and coins in banks permits one to predict the number of bank robberies and bank burglaries with 85 percent accuracy.[47] This suggests that, short of reducing the supply of money and consumer goods, there are important gains in crime control that would ensue from making things harder to steal—for example, by increasing the use of nonnegotiable alternatives to cash (electronic credit cards and the like).

Over the last ten years, we have done some of the things that a rationalistic rather than characterological theory of crime would suggest. Efforts, albeit belated, were made to cope with teenage unemployment during the late 1960s. Protective devices to discourage theft have come into more general use. A concerted effort to attack heroin trafficking and to provide treatment for large numbers of addicts has made some headway. But we have done rather little about one crucial element: the deterrence and incapacitative features of the criminal justice system. We have tried, a little, to make legitimate jobs easier to find for teenagers and to make desirable things harder to steal, but we have done almost nothing about making the costs of crime, especially the certainty of having to pay those costs, any higher.

We have not done so because, I argue, of our mistaken view of the purpose of prisons and of the nature of man. Our statesmen and scholars, but not the public generally, have created unrealistic expectations about what jails can achieve and thereby have set self-defeating standards by which those institutions should be judged. We have learned, I should think, that there are limits to what government can accomplish in human affairs generally and in criminal affairs particularly. It cannot export democracy, remold human character, or revitalize families; nor can it rehabilitate in large numbers thieves and muggers. Government can transfer money, invent and operate technologies, construct and manage facilities, and administer rules that are clear and simple. With respect to courts and prisons, we have not yet even achieved—because we have not yet tried very hard—those objectives that are *within* our reach because we have so often emphasized those that are beyond it. We do not yet adequately classify and segregate offenders so as to prevent pathologically assaultive persons from terrorizing ordinary convicts. We do not invest in facilities adequate to eliminate overcrowding and to provide sufficient privacy and security to protect both guards from prisoner conspiracies and prisoners from each other.

Beaumont and Tocqueville meant for us to have these modest goals when they suggested that the true object of the American experiment with penitentiaries should not be the radical reformation of human nature, but rather "another kind of reformation, less thorough than the former, but yet useful for society." The object of the "less thorough" change was to produce, not honest men, but men with honest habits, ex-convicts who, if not more virtuous, are at least more judicious, whose morality "is not honour, but interest."[48]

It is precisely this sober view of human nature and thus of the institutions such a nature would animate that informed the thoughts of the Founding Fathers. They rejected those aspects of classical political thought that saw in society the capacity and the obligation to develop and perfect human nature. They may or may not have shared those religious views that thought human nature could be enhanced by providing spiritual nurture for the "inner light" of the human soul, but they clearly denied that government had any business supplying that nurture or claiming a spiritual role. James Madison sought, as Martin Diamond has shown, to base American institutions on a conception of human nature as fallible—indeed, on the very fallibility that made democracy necessary in the first place.[49] In *Federalist* 51, Madison recommended a "policy of supplying, by opposite and rival interests, the defect of better motives," a defect that can "be traced throughout the whole system of human affairs, private as well as public."

Some may feel that prisons are a poor way of "supplying the defect of better motives," and indeed as presently managed they often are. But one must bear in mind that prisons—by which I mean any institution or process, large or small, rigid or casual, distant or communal, designed to deprive persons of liberty—are a peculiarly democratic way of supplying punishment and deterrence. Democracy made possible general human liberty and this liberty, once available, became sufficiently prized so that its loss was a grave matter. Prisons rarely existed before the nineteenth century, in part because liberty rarely existed until then. The serf, the indentured servant, and the perpetual soldier would not have feared prison; indeed, for some it might have been a welcome release. American democracy also implied equality before the law, and thus no system of fines would suffice—the rich could then "afford" crime more readily than the poor. The equal deprivation of liberty for equal offenses, not the rehabilitative ideal, was the sound and proper basis for the American system of justice. Though that justification is rarely offered by the distinguished commissions which have addressed the problem, it is, I believe, the justification widely shared by the American people and for this reason, if no other, deserves our serious attention as we enter the nation's third century.

Notes

1. Gustave de Beaumont and Alexis de Tocqueville, *On the Penitentiary System in the United States and Its Application in France*, trans. Francis Lieber (Philadelphia: Carey, Lea & Blanchard, 1833), p. 24.

2. Ibid., pp. 58-59.

3. Ibid., pp. 68-69.

4. National Commission on Law Observance and Enforcement ("Wickersham Commission"), *Report on Penal Institutions, Probation and Parole* (No. 9), p. 7.

5. Task Force on Corrections, President's Commission on Law Enforcement and Administration of Justice, *Report* (Washington, D.C.: U.S. Government Printing Office, 1967), p. 16.

6. President's Commission on Law Enforcement and Administration of Justice, *The Challenge of Crime in a Free Society* (Washington, D.C.: U.S. Government Printing Office, 1967), p. 173.

7. National Advisory Commission on Criminal Justice Standards and Goals, *A National Strategy to Reduce Crime* (Washington, D.C.: Law Enforcement Assistance Administration, U.S. Department of Justice, 1973), pp. 176-186.

8. Robert Martinson, "What Works?—Questions and Answers About Prison Reform," *The Public Interest* (Spring 1974): 22-54.

9. R.G. Hood, "Research on the Effectiveness of Punishments and Treatments," reprinted in Leon Radzinowicz and Marvin E. Wolfgang, *Crime and Justice*, vol. 3 (New York: Basic Books, 1971), pp. 159-182.

10. Walter C. Bailey, "Correctional Outcome: An Evaluation of 100 Reports," reprinted in Radzinowicz and Wolfgang, *Crime and Justice*, vol. 3, p. 190.

11. Leslie T. Wilkins, *Evaluation of Penal Measures* (New York: Random House, 1969), p. 78.

12. President's Commission, *Challenge of Crime*, pp. vii, 170.

13. Martinson, "What Works?" p. 44. See also James Robinson and Gerald Smith, "The Effectiveness of Correctional Programs," *Crime and Delinquency* (January 1971): 67-80.

14. Beaumont and Tocqueville, *On the Penitentiary System*, p. 152fn.

15. W. David Lewis, *From Newgate to Dannemora: The Rise of the Penitentiary in New York, 1796-1848* (Ithaca, N.Y.: Cornell University Press, 1965), p. 3.

16. Ibid., p. 5.

17. David J. Rothman, *The Discovery of the Asylum* (Boston: Little, Brown and Co., 1971), pp. 53, 69, 73-76.

18. Ibid., p. 51.

19. Jeremy Bentham, *The Rationale of Punishment* (London: Robert Heward, 1830), Bk. I, Ch. 3.

20. Leon Radzinowicz, *In Search of Criminology* (Cambridge: Harvard University Press, 1962), pp. 114-117.

21. I develop this argument in my book, *Thinking About Crime* (New York: Basic Books, 1975), Ch. 3.

22. Edwin H. Sutherland and Donald R. Cressey, *Principles of Criminology*, 7th ed. red. (Philadelphia: J.B. Lippincott, 1966), p. 367.

23. Walter C. Reckless, *The Crime Problem*, 4th ed. (New York: Appleton-Century-Crofts, 1967), p. 508.

24. William McCord and Joan McCord, *Origins of Crime* (New York: Columbia University Press, 1959), pp. 181-184.

25. A popular argument for deprisonization is Jessica Mitford, *Kind and Usual Punishment: The Prison Business* (New York: Alfred A. Knopf, 1973), Ch. 15. A governmental argument for essentially the same policy is made by the Corrections Task Force of the National Advisory Commission on Criminal Justice Standards and Goals.

26. Eugene Doleschal, "Graduated Release," *Information Review on Crime and Delinquency* 1 (1969): 1-10.

27. R.F. Sparks, "Research on the Use and Effectiveness of Probation, Parole and Measures of After-Care," reprinted in Radzinowicz and Wolfgang, *Crime and Justice*, vol. 3, pp. 211-218. See also Dean V. Babst and John W. Mannering, "Probation Versus Imprisonment for Similar Types of Offenders," reprinted in *loc. cit.*, vol. 3, pp. 224-231.

28. George Edwards Antunes and A. Lee Hunt, "The Impact of Certainty and Severity of Punishment on Levels of Crime in American States," paper delivered before the American Political Science Association (1972).

29. Charles R. Tittle and Charles H. Loan, "Sanctions and Deviance: Evidence and Remaining Questions," *Law and Society Review* 7 (Spring 1973): 385.

30. Isaac Ehrlich, "The Deterrent Effect of Criminal Law Enforcement," *Journal of Legal Studies* 1 (1972): 259.

31. National Commission on Law Observance and Enforcement, *Report on the Child Offender in the Federal System of Justice* (No. 6), pp. 25-31.

32. For example, Stanton Wheeler and Leonard S. Cottrell, Jr., *Juvenile Delinquency—Its Prevention and Control* (New York: Russell Sage Foundation, 1965), p. 35; "Juvenile Delinquents: The Police, State Courts, and Individualized Justice," *Harvard Law Review* 79 (1966): 775.

33. Task Force on Juvenile Delinquency of the President's Commission on Law Enforcement and Administration of Justice, *Report on Juvenile Delinquency and Youth Crime* (Washington, D.C.: U.S. Government Printing Office, 1967), Ch. 1.

34. *In re Gault*, 387 U.S. 1 (1967).

35. Task Force on Juvenile Delinquency, *Report*, pp. 47, 49, 52, 53.

36. President's Commission, *Challenge of Crime*, Ch. 3.

37. Wheeler and Cottrell, *Juvenile Delinquency*, reprinted as Appendix T to Task Force on Juvenile Delinquency, *Report*, at p. 410.

38. Peter W. Greenwood et al., *Prosecution of Adult Felony Defendants in Los Angeles County* (Santa Monica, Calif.: RAND Report R-1127-DOJ, 1973), p. 111.

39. John Hogarth, *Sentencing as a Human Process* (Toronto: Univ. of Toronto Press, 1971); Martin A. Levin, *Urban Politics and The Criminal Courts* (Chicago: University of Chicago Press, forthcoming).

40. Sutherland and Cressey, *Principles of Criminology*, pp. 523-537.

41. *Statistic Abstract of the United States, 1972* (Washington, D.C.: U.S. Government Printing Office, 1972), p. 161.

42. This discussion of age and employment changes follows *Thinking About Crime*, Ch. 1.

43. A good discussion of the motives of different kinds of thieves is John E. Conklin, *Robbery and the Criminal Justice System* (Philadelphia: Lippincott, 1972), Ch. 4.

44. Belton Fleisher, *The Economics of Delinquency* (Chicago: Quadrangle Books, 1966).

45. Llad Phillips, Harold Votey, Jr., and Darold Maxwell, "Crime, Youth and the Labor Market: An Econometric Study," *Journal of Political Economy* (1972).

46. Isaac Ehrlich, "Participation in Illegitimate Activities: An Economic Analysis," Ph.D. dissertation, Columbia University Department of Economics, 1970.

47. Leroy C. Gould, "Crime and Its Impact in an Affluent Society," in Jack D. Douglas (ed.), *Crime and Justice in American Society* (Indianapolis: Bobbs-Merrill Co., 1971), pp. 102-103.

48. Beaumont and Tocqueville, *On the Penitentiary System*, p. 58.

49. Martin Diamond, "Ethics and Politics: The American Way," paper delivered to the Marquette University Symposium on Ethics and Politics (March 1974).

V The American Military Tradition

Marcus Cunliffe

It is fair to say that Americans have always been a rather bellicose people with a powerful antimilitarist tradition. It is also fair to say that, as a result of their experiences in the twentieth century, Americans today are considerably less bellicose than they used to be, and also considerably less antimilitarist. Indeed, it was in reaction against an unpopular war that this nation created a large, professional army—the traditional nightmare of the antimilitarists!

What do these changes signify? Have Americans, as some claim, repudiated and in some sense "betrayed" their traditional ideals? Professor Marcus Cunliffe, in exploring the history of American attitudes toward the military, suggests that we can learn much from comparing the evolution of American attitudes with that of such other democracies as Britain and Switzerland. He further suggests that these venerable attitudes, as they encountered an ever more complex reality in foreign affairs, were destined to be transformed. The implications of this transformation for the American democracy's conception of itself are bound to be momentous—but the antimilitarist heritage may yet be of a great value in helping a great power use its military strength acceptably.

A crucial problem in the modern world is how to reconcile historic tradition with present-day needs. Twentieth century mankind, and *Homo americanus* perhaps above all, is unsure whether the past is a solace or a burden. Tradition is supposed to provide a foundation—lessons, precedents, principles. But suppose change brings about not only a quantitative but a qualitative shift. How can precedents help us deal with the unprecedented? Or suppose the tradition itself

111

proves to have been illogical, ambiguous, evasive? In such circumstances may not a national heritage turn out to be irrelevant and even harmful? Some political scientists feel that America's governmental headaches derive from the attempt to apply an eighteenth century mechanism to a twentieth century situation. May not the same be said of America's military attitudes—which can for the moment be defined as ways of thinking about when and how to fight, or not to fight?

America did begin to evolve a military tradition even before there was an independent United States. This tradition, enlarging its terms yet still resting upon early ideas, appears to have remained prevalent in American minds—possibly as late as the 1940s. Since then, it is commonly said, the American military situation has been entirely transformed—by world-power status and by nuclear technology. So let us begin by outlining the elements of the tradition and of the new realm. We can then consider the implications. For instance: Was the old tradition really as consistent, rich, and influential as it can be made to sound? Has it much, or any, relevance for the second half of the twentieth century? If not, have Americans been facing up manfully, but painfully, to an unavoidable severance from the past? Are they unique in their military predicament? Or, if there still is value in the heritage, where does it reside and how best can it be encouraged? In short, which is the more significant, the tradition or the transformation?

The American Military Tradition

Most historians would say the tradition came to embody the following features.

Hostility to Regular or Standing Armies

If the United States was to have an army at all, numbers must be kept to the bare minimum. Such hostility, as Alexander Hamilton remarked in *Federalist* 26, was part of the British heritage. Seventeenth century England has learned to mistrust the army as an instrument of tyranny, whether controlled by the crown or by Parliament. Remembering these crises, Hamilton claimed, the American people absorbed "an hereditary impression of danger to liberty, from standing armies in times of peace." The clashes leading up to the Revolutionary War, symbolized by the Boston "massacre," when British troops opened fire on a local mob, heightened American antipathy. So did the hiring of "Hessian mercenaries" by the mother-country. Several of the new state constitutions declared that a peacetime standing army should be forbidden in America, except with the express consent of the legislature. During the next hundred years, Americans of almost every stripe—Congressmen, pacifists, businessmen, authors—reiterated their dislike for regular soldiers (and, to a lesser extent, sailors: see Herman Melville's novel *White-Jacket* or *The World in a Man-of-War*, 1850). The enlisted men were "hirelings," the officers snobs, "kid-glove gentry": in a word, un-American.

The Purse and the Sword

If a (small) standing army was a necessary evil, it must in any case be controlled in policy and finance by civilians. Here, too, British lessons helped to form the American tradition. Parliament had learned to subject the power of the sword to that of the purse. Appropriations for the British army had to be approved annually by the legislature; no money, no army. Under the Constitution, it was stipulated that Congress must scrutinize the military budget at least once in every two years. The principle of civilian control was soon entrenched in the American creed, as a dogma that no one dare openly challenge.

The Moral Superiority of the United States

In the *Rights of Man* (1791), Tom Paine expressed what was to become another cherished American conviction. Republics, he said, do not foment wars, because the government and the people have the same interests at heart.

All the monarchical Governments are military. War is their trade; plunder and revenue their objects. . . . What is the history of all monarchical Governments, but a disgustful picture of human wretchedness, and the accidental respite of a few years' repose? Wearied with war, and tired with human butchery, they sat down to rest, and called it peace. This certainly is not the condition that Heaven intended for Man. . . .

War was seen as the endemic condition of Europe—a feuding, cynical, dynastic, imperialistic snakepit. In such a view, 1914 was one of the inevitable climaxes of the European system, 1939 another—each bringing the Old World to the brink of collective suicide, and dragging in other, innocent peoples. According to its tradition, however, the United States would never start a war, and would never wage war for conquest, but only to maintain its honor or independence. For these reasons America, after getting out of the French alliance of 1778-1800, must avoid further entanglements. The Old World would have to play its sordid war-game without America for partner. And, of course, the United States did steer clear of alliances until World War II. In 1917-18, America was merely "associated" with Britain and France.

Providential Geography

The War for Independence and the War of 1812 seemed to prove strategically that Americans were a chosen people, set by God upon a favored continent whose ocean boundaries made foreign invasion a hopeless task. If Britain, the strongest military and naval power in the world, could not manage to crush the numerically inferior United States, then nobody could. Isolation as a geographical fact supported isolationism as an ideological tenet. Several things followed in consequence.

Bulwarks of Defense

Thus, a large standing army was deemed unnecessary as well as undesirable. A modest priority should be given to naval strength, because the coasts were the first line of defense, because the merchant marine needed protection, and because—yet another adoption of a British sentiment—sailors were thought less menacing than soldiers. For this reason the Constitution did not subject the navy to the biennial legislative check. "A naval force," as Thomas Jefferson assured James Monroe in 1786, "can never endanger our liberties, nor occasion bloodshed; a land force would do both." Coastal batteries should be the second line of defense. That was how places like Fort Sumter came to be constructed. If an enemy nevertheless succeeded in landing, the chief military response would be from militia and volunteer units. In American rhetoric, the country's true defenders were the citizenry: Massachusetts Minutemen at Lexington and Concord, Andrew Jackson's Kentucky riflemen at New Orleans, the volunteer regiments who formed the majority of Zachary Taylor and Winfield Scott's corps in the Mexican War—patriots who would answer the call eagerly and invincibly.

All of the attitudes sketched so far are epitomized in President Jackson's first annual message to Congress (1829):

Considering standing armies as dangerous to free governments in times of peace, I shall not seek to enlarge our present establishment [an army of about 6,000], nor disregard that salutary lesson of political experience which teaches that the military should be held subordinate to the civil power. The gradual increase of our Navy, whose flag has displayed in distant climes our skill in navigation, and our fame in arms; the preservation of our forts, arsenals, and dockyards, and the introduction of progressive improvements in the discipline and science of both branches of our military service are . . . plainly prescribed by prudence. . . . But the bulwark of our defense is the national militia, which in the present state of our intelligence and population must render us invincible. . . . Partial injuries and occasional mortifications we may be subjected to, but a million of armed freemen, possessed of the means of war, can never be conquered by a foreign foe.

Swift Victory

America would not be the aggressor, but once committed, the nation would act with irresistible speed and vigor. European armies, according to the popular belief, were clumsy and hidebound; effete aristocrats in charge of a plodding peasantry. American soldiers, by contrast, were democratic and briskly unorthodox. Being basically civilian, they regarded war not as a profession but as a cross between an escapade and a temporary emergency. In Europe (so the American tradition went), the authorities monopolized and manipulated violence. In the United States, where Article II of the Constitution recognized "the right of the people to keep and bear Arms," the ordinary citizen was already a marksman. As the story was interpreted in balladry and orations, the American amateur invariably beat the foreign professional. An American frigate or privateer would outmatch a British ship. Wars were therefore bound to end swiftly with American victory.

Of the conflicts America engaged in up to 1918, not all in fact fitted the specification. But they could be believed to have done so. The War of 1812, for instance, was remembered for ship-versus-ship encounters and for Jackson's dazzling triumph at New Orleans. The four-year struggle of the Civil War claimed more American lives, North and South, than any other war in the nation's history. But then, the best fighting spirit in the world was pitted against itself: How could such a confrontation fail to be bloody? On other battlefields the outcome was gratifyingly right. The "splendid little war" against Spain in 1898 lasted only six weeks in its main phase. Pershing's citizen army in the Meuse-Argonne offensive of 1918 took Montfaucon on the second day, when Marshal Petain had predicted a whole season's weary effort.

Plowshares into Swords, and
Back Again

Apart from being short and decisive, wars were expected to make no great difference to the nation. At the end, the victory parade would resemble the war's opening rally—played in reverse like a film run backward. Mobilization and demobilization would be symmetrically rapid. Having rushed off to war, the boys must be rushed back to peace—and compensated by land grants and bounties, and later by pensions. The *Shorter Oxford Dictionary* defines a *veteran* as "one who has had long experience in military service; an old soldier." On the telescoped American time scale, three months in uniform might suffice to qualify a youngster for veteranship. Except for the Confederate South, warfare in truth left behind very few reminders. Since 1815, no foreign war has touched America: no invaders, no bombs. Even for the South, invasion and occupation are far remoter memories than for France, Germany, or Japan. Apart from the

Civil War, American casualties were relatively light. In World War I, the British and French dead outnumbered the American by twenty to one. For the United States, the tradition was that wars closed as they began, contraceptively: no alliances, no strings, no offspring.

Voluntarism

The traditional American soldier, to repeat, was not a regular. He was a patriot, responding to a sudden crisis as a passer-by might attach himself to a bucket team to put out a fire. Indeed the volunteer fire companies were very close in outlook and sometimes in personnel to military companies. In theory, the militia, America's "bulwark," were held to compulsory peacetime training. Article II's "right of the people to keep and bear Arms" is actually prefaced by: "A well regulated Militia, being necessary to the security of a free State. . . ." But that part of the "militia clause" was forgotten. The private right was stressed—the right to a gun—not the public duty. As early as the War of 1812 the predominant American battle force was composed not of the embodied militia but of volunteers. This was the case in the Mexican War and for much of the Civil War. Conscription was regarded as a European expedient. The absence of peacetime conscription was one of the things that made the United States attractive for young Europeans contemplating emigration. For America it was a last resort, such as in the special wartime circumstances of 1861-65 and 1917-18. Where conscription did prove necessary, official language borrowed the old militia concept of a "universal" form of emergency aid—on the lines of George Washington's statement that "every Citizen who enjoys the protection of a free Government, owes not only a proportion of his property, but even of his personal services to the defense of it. . . ."

The Regular Nucleus

After the Revolution, it was nevertheless gradually accepted that the United States must retain a small regular army and navy—raised by voluntary recruitment as with the British army. The role of the regular army, expounded by several Secretaries of War beginning with John C. Calhoun, was to provide a skeleton or armature for the mass of volunteers. The trained cadre would instruct the untrained mass in drill and other rudiments. It was also recognized that some aspects of warfare were becoming more complex, especially gunnery and engineering. Hence the establishment in 1802 of the U.S. Military Academy at West Point, laying particular emphasis on the technical branches. (The Naval Academy at Annapolis came later, in 1845). In Jackson's 1829 message, it will be recalled, he did—in praising the "million of armed freemen"—mention "discipline and science" as *professional* attributes. But the peacetime regular services of the nineteenth century, and military spending, were much smaller than in Europe. As late as 1937, a mere 1.5 percent of the American national income went on military appropriations, as against 5.7 for Great Britain, 9.1 for France, 23.5 for Germany, 26.4 for Russia, and 28.2 for Japan.[1] Even so, the generalized antimilitarism of the American tradition made the army's position equivocal. Some people, including such enthusiastic volunteers as Congressman Davy Crockett, insisted that West Point cost too much and produced an elite that was incompetent and supercilious. The Academy was criticized for being too professionally military, and—since many graduates became civil engineers, teachers, and administrators—for not being military enough. Attacks on West Point's rigidity and mediocrity redoubled during the Civil War. But by then, the Academy, and the notion of professional expertise, were within limits fairly well entrenched. During the next half-century Americans were, sometimes a little grudgingly, accustomed to the fact that the nation's top-ranking officers would nearly all have gone through West Point or Annapolis. They were ready to admit the professional into the tradition—if he demonstrated that he was no martinet or theoretician.

Masculinity and Heroism

There are some other, more diffuse attitudes—not all of them strictly military, and not necessarily related to one another, yet needed to complete the picture. Thus, the nation achieved its independence by fighting; and as peace advocates complained, the martial spirit continued to figure quite prominently in America's imaginative life. A high proportion of the nation's heroes were men who carried a weapon and knew how to use it, whether against foreign enemies or Indian tribes, or in brawls and duels. The sequence of wars, large and small, was by no means negligible. The South, in particular, prided itself on its warrior qualities. There was more armed peacetime violence (and more homicide) in the United States than in most parts of Europe—for example, in vigilante movements and in clashes between strikers and strikebreakers. A surprising number of presidential candidates were able to trade upon their military experiences. For a country supposed to dislike regimentation, there was also a surprising quantity of military schools; VMI (Virginia Military Institute, 1839) is probably the best known, but there were a good many others, north, as well as south. There was even covert and intermittent admiration for the regular officer, as a gentleman who had, in placing "service before self," also opted out of the national preoccupation with money-making.

It is impossible to draw all these elements together into a neat diagram. This is a key factor in the so-called tradition to be explored later: It pulls in different directions. The contradictory aspect can, however, be accommodated to a degree by suggesting that the American military tradition breaks into three categories: antimilitarist, antiprofessional, and professional.

Antimilitarism ranged from outright pacifism of the kind preached by the young (later Senator) Charles Sumner of Massachusetts to the more common-sensical outlook of, say, Abraham Lincoln of Illinois. Lincoln's adversary, Jefferson Davis, president of the Confederate States, was a West Pointer who had led a volunteer regiment in the Mexican War. Lincoln's only military experience was a short, and grotesquely hilarious, involvement in the Black Hawk "war."

Antiprofessionalism, shading off from antimilitarism, embraced both re-formers like Henry George, who thought regular forces a waste of money, and spokesmen for citizen soldiery like Senator Ben ("Beast") Butler—these the kind of men who, castigating West Point, later lobbied successfully for the establish-ment of the National Guard.

Professionalism, sometimes encouraged by the Army and Navy Departments and a few sympathetic members of Congress, but usually carried on within the service enclaves, was exemplified by such men as Admiral Alfred T. Mahan and Major General Emory Upton. Mahan became famous as the exponent of sea-power. Upton's *Military Policy of the United States* (published in 1904, but written in about 1880) maintained that the nation's antimilitary and antiprofes-sional sub-traditions had brought it near disaster; what was needed was a coherent permanent structure—regulars at the top, active militia or National Guard underneath, sustained by a larger base of trained, but inactive citizen soldiers.

I have suggested in other writings that these three categories approximated to three historic American personality types: Quaker, Rifleman, Chevalier.[2]

The *Quaker* (Quaker by temperament, if not religious affiliation) stands for "simplicity, shrewdness, ingenuity, diligence, decency, piety.... All the features associated with war—parades, weapons, display, hierarchies of rank, collective anger—are alien to him."

The second type, the *Rifleman*

likewise an individualist,... represents ... the volunteer spirit.... Though sometimes an officer, the Rifleman is more usually in the ranks—Johnny Reb, Bill Yank.... He ... yields no automatic obedience to those in command, and believes firmly in his right to vote his commanders in and out of office as if they were a pack of political candidates—which of course they also sometimes are. Being intolerant of long enlistments, the Rifleman, on occasion, marches away from the battle, not because he is a coward but because his time is up and he feels he is a civilian again. Resourceful in combat, he is also sometimes resourceful in the base military arts of scrounging, looting and desertion.

The third type, the *Chevalier*, is

a mounted figure, an officer, a gentleman, proud of his family, proud of his calling.... The Chevalier model has more elements of make-believe than the other two. It is naturally represented for the most part inside the regular army, but cannot find an altogether comfortable niche in an organization so small, so dispersed, so often called upon to deprecate or deny those very features which distinguish the Chevalier: dignity, breeding, display.

The three types were found in all parts of the nineteenth century United States. They can be seen as broader divisions, respectively, of "reason, appetite, and sensibility." The Quaker looks to the future, the Rifleman to the present, the Chevalier to the past. The difference between North and South, in this typology, is that the Quakerism mode became less and less admired below the Mason-Dixon line, and the Chevalier mode more admired. The Rifleman was common to both sections.

So much for the historic military tradition in the United States. To judge from the library shelves, it still has a sizable following, at least so far as campaign history is concerned. The public clearly likes to read about combat.

Transformation Scene

There is, however, another rapidly-growing class of material on the shelves, most of it produced since 1945, which rests upon very different assumptions. Its contributors, though they disagree on many points, share a conviction that the underlying military realities have altered profoundly for the United States. In their general picture, the United States swung during the 1940s from a tradition of small, inexpensive regular forces, supplied by voluntary recruitment, to a huge and extremely expensive establishment (army, navy, marines, air force, missile bases), backed by ancillary institutions (the CIA, "think tanks," research programs contracted out to universities) and dependent upon peacetime conscription.

In the old conception, civil dominance was conspicuous. Peacetime regulars were obscure figures, stationed out on the frontier or, later, tucked away in the Philippines or the Canal Zone. Military affairs were decided by a handful of men in Washington—the president, department heads, chairmen of congressional committees. In the new scene, the prominence, if not the dominance, of the armed services became no less conspicuous. President Eisenhower, himself a military man, was worried enough by the growth of "the military-industrial complex" that he warned the nation of its implications in his farewell address of January 1961:

Until the latest of our world conflicts, the United States had no armaments industry. American makers of plowshares could, with time and as required, make swords as well. But now we can no longer risk emergency improvisation of national defense; we have been compelled to create a permanent armaments industry of vast proportions. Added to this, three and half million men and women are directly engaged in the defense establishment. We annually spend on military security more than the net income of all United States corporations.

"This conjunction of an immense military establishment and a large arms industry," Eisenhower added, "is new in the American experience." In his memoir, *Mandate for Change* (1963), he said of the mid-1950s: "Our military structure and equipment were changing so rapidly that even the comforting old slogan 'Tried and true' was gone. In its place had sprung up a disquieting new one: 'If it works, it's obsolete'."

During former days the United States has shunned alliances. Now it was not only a member but a prime instigator of military pacts—NATO, SEATO—and underwrote the budgets of groups like CENTO where it was not a full member. Instead of long periods of peace interrupted by short wars, America entered the puzzling twilight of the cold war. Civilians now bowed to the military technologists in accepting their esoteric rationales for ballistic and other weaponry. Huge appropriations were approved by Congress, usually with little question; the experts were presumed to know best, and the layman felt inhibited by his ignorance and by the assent-commanding propositions of "free-world" preparedness. Americans found themselves committed to undeclared wars, notably in Korea and Vietnam, fought against intangible ideologies with no definite conclusion in sight. "Escalation" was one of the words in a vocabulary that exemplified the new era. The apparent transformation from earlier times can be recapitulated as follows:

Traditional America	Cold-War America
suspicion of standing armies	acceptance of huge military establishment
civil dominance	military prominence; interfusion with civilian heads
no entangling alliances	global alliances and commitments
short wars, rapid demobilization	protracted conflicts, permanent semi-mobilization
parsimonious economy	lavish expenditure
amateurism	professionalism
volunteering	compulsory service

Reactions

There is no need to go into further detail on America's post-1945 circumstances. Our interest lies in the juxtaposition of newer and older attitudes, and the ways in which their relationship has been interpreted. Among many reactions, these may be singled out as representative:

The old tradition, good in its day, has been rendered largely obsolete. The nation and the world have changed: thinking must change with them. Dwight D. Eisenhower observed in his autobiography:

The Army in which I was commissioned a second lieutenant in 1915 underwent phenomenal changes in the thirty years from then until the German surrender in 1945. Auto-firing guns, motor transport, fighter and bomber airplanes, tanks, and many, many types of rockets all came into common use. But those changes, startling as they were, faded into insignificance when compared to those of the postwar period, particularly during my first three years in the Presidency.

At the end of World War II, the United States was obliged to re-frame its assumptions and reorganize its military establishment. The National Security Act of 1947, which set up the CIA, replaced the Secretary of War with a Secretary of Defense and made the U.S. Air Force a separate service, was a logical response to the pressure of events. It was not only the military experts who argued thus. During World War II, the columnist Walter Lippmann began to insist that traditional attitudes to defense and foreign policy offered most inadequate guides to current reality. A similar view was taken by the historian C. Vann Woodward in "The Age of Reinterpretation"—his 1959 presidential address to the American Historical Association. Woodward suggested that the United States had once enjoyed "free security" as result of geographical remoteness and the accident of being able to rely upon British naval strength. Sheltered and cushioned in this way, America had done things differently from other countries. For instance, Woodward speculated, the United States was

the only major country since Cromwellian England that could afford the doubtful luxury of a full-scale civil war of four years without incurring the evils of foreign intervention and occupation. Had such evils been as much a foregone conclusion as they have been among other nations, it is doubtful that Americans would have proved as willing as they were to fall upon each other's throats.

The old tradition failed to correspond to the realities even of its own day. It was often self-righteous and hypo-critically moralistic. It nourished the illusion that, alone among large nations, the United States was virtuous. In their treatment of regulars, for example, Americans (in peacetime at any rate) behaved as a Southern slaveholder might toward a slave dealer, or a European town to its public hangman: They could not do without him, but preferred to pretend he was not there. The tradition encouraged claptrap. Thus, the "brinkmanship" and the talk of "agonizing reappraisals" indulged in by Secretary of State John Foster Dulles were a carry-over of old moralisms, already outmoded when Woodrow Wilson showed himself their prisoner in the Paris peace negotiations of 1919. Americans were innocents for too long. The "end of innocence" was the beginning of wisdom. Hard, realistic analysis must replace the old fondness for woolly rhetoric.

The old tradition, instead of defining a military policy, amounted to an attempt to do without one. It was a loose congeries of bits of unexamined folklore. Emory Upton, recounting the discouragements he had met, even among fellow officers, in trying to write his book, said that merely to mention the words "military policy" was usually enough to "provoke the reply that 'We have no military policy';... everything is left to luck or to chance." As early as 1880, the prescient Upton believed the United States had come perilously close to disaster but had failed to interpret the lesson. "It has," he said, "been truly remarked by one of our philosophers that 'We follow success and not skill'."

The newer outlook has built selectively upon the least attractive portions of the old tradition, and enlarged them to a terrifying extent. These portions include admiration for gunplay and violence; belligerence of the "my-country-right-or-wrong" sort; overconfidence in one's own martial prowess; and underestimation of the enemy, especially where the enemy is of different racial stock. The more modest and pacific sides of the old tradition have been neglected. The Rifleman, one might say, has been exalted at the expense of the Quaker and the Chevalier—and had his firepower infinitely increased through modern technology. Reflections of this type have led historians to explore the deep roots of contemporary violence; and to contend that several of America's previous wars were unpopular and unnecessary.

The old military tradition is part and parcel of the nation's basic heritage, together with the Declaration of Independence, the Constitution, and certain other fundamental texts. It appealed to the same essential set of democratic, republican, libertarian, humanistic values. To jettison it would be to betray the nation's birthright. Moralistic attitudes, whatever their deficiencies, are far preferable to amoral attitudes. "Right makes might" may not be invariably true; but that is a more wholesome proposition than the amoral converse, "might makes right." According to C. Wright Mills in *The Power Elite* (1955), the nation had acquiesced in a dangerous abandonment of the old creed. In Mills' view the service chiefs of Eisenhower's America associated on intimate terms with the top administrative echelons in Washington, and with heads of business corporations—often joining the latter as vice presidents on retirement from the armed forces. Mills conceived of this civil-military managerial group as an interlocking directorate—indeed as a "military-industrial complex" in President Eisenhower's term. He maintained that they lay outside the democratic political process. They were appointees, not persons who had been elected to office, and therefore were answerable to no one but themselves. Congress had little authority over them, the American public none at all. Their form of realism, said Mills, was "crackpot realism."

Mercifully, in this view, the old tradition might still retain some vitality (though Mills himself was too pessimistic to think so). President Truman was old fashioned enough to abide by at least some parts of the heritage—notably when he relieved General MacArthur of the Far Eastern command in 1951 for challenging the civil government. Eisenhower, too, it could be argued, was aware of the heritage, if not always effectively so.[3] In his autobiography, for instance, he reiterated the conviction that "the United States on its own initiative would never start a major war." To be sure, this led him to conclude that the nation must, in consequence, "maintain forces of greater strength . . . than would be necessary if our purposes had been aggressive." But at least he meant well; and so long as the old tradition remained alive, the "crackpot realists" might be held in check.

The Transformation Transformed?

These alternative arguments do not exhaust the range of reactions to America's military evolution. But they are varied and characteristic enough for our purposes. They all reflect a hope or a fear that we have seen an "end of innocence" in the United States—a healthy or a disquieting break with tradition. Some historians would locate this as early as the Civil War, seeing that as the first of the world's "modern" wars, in which mass armies contended for "total" victory instead of for limited ends employing limited means. Some would locate the break in the late nineteenth century—when the Senate and the nation divided over the momentous question of whether to annex the Philippines. No less than twenty-seven senators voted against the Spanish treaty; they came within a single vote of defeating it. Charles Francis Adams, of the famous presidential family, gave a lecture on "Imperialism and the Tracks of Our Forefathers" in which he said the proposed imperialist policy would "on every one of the fundamental principles discussed—whether ethnic, economic, or political . . . abandon the traditional and distinctively American grounds." Most historians, perhaps, think with Eisenhower that the atom bomb and the onset of the cold war marked the crucial transformation.

As a student of America, I find plausible elements in most of the arguments this essay has outlined. But, perhaps because I am a foreigner and in particular a British foreigner, I am not altogether persuaded by any of them. To my mind, in brief, the tradition has never been uniquely "American," for good or for ill: There have been flaws in the conventional wisdom of all periods of American military thought, but these are not always the ones that critics have stressed; there is no complete, irrevocable break in the nation's evolution.

The post-1945 change is undeniably important. Some factors are obviously irreversible. The United States cannot return to the conditions known by the Founding Fathers: a scattered, mainly rural population with rudimentary armament. Life is vastly more complicated: so must be its military aspects. But we should reconsider the actual past record before deciding that it holds few or no relevant messages (other than nostalgic memories or cautionary tales) for the America of the 1970s. Some parts of the tradition might be dead, for example, while others might be as germane as ever.

Perhaps we can agree, for a start, that the tradition was never internally consistent. Antimilitarism, antiprofessionalism, and professionalism form a discordant trio. Nor did portions of the tradition respect their own logics. This can be illustrated with reference to two possible lines of development, the "Swiss policy" and the "China policy." Both assumed that the United States was and ought to be different from monarchical Europe in military as in other respects. So there was an interest in other nations with comparable situations.

Switzerland, like the United States, was a republic of pacific but sturdy disposition. If the United States was to be a modest trading nation, content to stand on the defensive, then the Swiss military system appeared highly apropos. This was how the analogy struck George Washington; and it was to be revived at intervals by American theorists during the next two centuries.[4] The Swiss, it was said, deterred potential invaders by maintaining a citizen army—an efficient militia with active and inactive components, based on short-term conscription. It did not cost much, it was equitable, and it operated locally, at canton level, with control exercised ultimately by the federal government. The American militia of colonial days had been quite active: Why not expand the pattern? Yet, this seemingly admirable solution was not adopted. In the United States, the militia was almost everywhere moribund by the 1830s. The state militias of subsequent decades tended to exist only on paper, or they were fleshed out by volunteer companies which were allotted militia designations but actually ran their own affairs as almost sovereign entities. New York's Seventh Regiment, still in being today, is a prosperous example of one such independent formation. So the Swiss parallel was neglected. It was simply not possible to convince Americans of military age that they should give two or three weeks of annual training as a patriotic obligation. The notion of a citizen army remained, in patriotic rhetoric; but in fact it came to signify an instant wartime army of untrained volunteers.

In the early national period, Jefferson was among the Americans who saw a parallel with China. Both nations were territorially large, civilized, peaceable, and determined to preserve themselves from European contamination. Jefferson's vision of defending America by means of a flotilla of coastal gunboats, and various early schemes of non-intercourse and embargo, were sometimes labeled a "China policy." The dream of separation from Europe underlies the Monroe Doctrine of 1823. But of course the United States, unlike China, was not territorially static; in this respect, it was more like nineteenth century Russia. As the Monroe Doctrine also revealed, Americans asserted special claims to authority over their whole hemisphere. The acquisition of Canada was a war-aim in 1775 and 1812, and annexation of Canada was conjured up now and then (by Walt Whitman, for instance) for several more decades. The Mexican War of 1846-48 was in this context a war for territory; and so in part was the Spanish-American War of 1898.

Again, the United States differed from China in maintaining an active overseas trade, as well as in welcoming immigration. The Americans wanted to be modest, but also to grow and prosper. There were citizens in some numbers who opposed the wars of 1812, 1846, and 1898. Senator George F. Hoar of Massachusetts, an anti-imperialist at the end of the century, gloried in the nation's old tradition of moral grandeur: "I believe that a republic is greater than an empire." The weakness of his position, and that of Charles Francis Adams, was that one side of the tradition was in implication expansionist. What of Manifest Destiny? Could moral greatness be achieved without physical, material greatness? It must be added that the Chinese analogy seemed less and less applicable as the Western powers broke in upon the isolation of the Celestial Kingdom: "numbering 400,000,000 people," Upton grimly noted, "she has been twice conquered by a few despised Tartars, and only a few years ago 20,000 English and French dictated peace at the walls of the capital."

These are only two examples of the failure of the early tradition to furnish lessons that the next generations could take seriously. Indeed, it is hard to find evidence of any sustained public interest in military affairs. One can reinforce the point by looking at a good anthology by Walter Millis, *American Military Thought* (1966). The passages he reproduces consider how to make the nation's armed forces more effective. They debate the comparative merits of regular units as against militia or volunteers, theories and technologies of defense, and the respective (sometimes rival) claims of military, naval and (later) air power. Important issues, yes—indeed "vital" issues, to use one of those words that somehow signals to an audience that the subject is going to make them yawn. Military issues have not as a rule *felt* vital to the average American, or for that matter to the American intellectual. Public involvement has been fitful, and generally cynical or unenthusiastic. In the ordinary run of events, Americans traditionally have not found military affairs as relevant, as centrally symbolic to them, as the nation's political, religious, or educational institutions. Millis's anthology belongs to the *American Heritage* series, whose aim, according to the editors, is "to provide the essential primary sources of the American experience, especially of American thought." It is in truth a thoughtful book. I suspect, however, that college courses on the history of American ideas ignore the Millis text (leaving it to the ROTC stream)—though they may well prescribe other titles in the same series, such as Staughton Lynd's *Nonviolence in America*.

If he were an intellectual, the American of former days would tend to comment very little on military matters, except with distaste. One instance would be Ralph Waldo Emerson's note in his journal: "A company of soldiers is an offensive spectacle." He was almost certainly unaware of the pun in the word "offensive." Another illustration would be James Russell Lowell's reaction to the Mexican War, put into the mouth of his New England farmer-spokesman, Hosea Biglow:

> Ez for war, I call it murder—
>   There you have it, plain and flat;
> I don't want to go no furder
>   Than my Testyment for that.

In moments of emergency, especially the Civil War, the Emersons and Lowells might change their tune. But such conversions were apt to be temporary.

The tradition, then, can be argued not to have engaged the American imagination or intellect in any profound way, but to have been left to a handful of rather obscure scholar-strategists, and to have been carried on in public discourse mainly through platitudes. The apparent irresponsibility and stupidity of this brand of conduct is a theme in several post-1945 commentaries. If a number of them have gone in for ancestor scolding instead of ancestor worship, then they are arguably correct. Thus, there would seem to be a good deal of weight in the post-Uptonian charge. This accuses Americans of having evaded their responsibilities. They should, we are told, have thought, planned, and acted far earlier, instead of living in intellectual torpor. Their new sense of responsibility came much too late in the day—eighty years after a calamitous Civil War, half a century after the nation was groping toward big-power status by constructing a modern navy and acquiring bases overseas. In the rueful and penitential atmosphere of the 1970s, we may likewise incline to blame the past for not having taken the correct *moral* decisions. Bygone America, in this light, drifted into wars and aggrandisement because it refused to admit that choices had to be made. Trying to be both isolated and expansionist, peaceable and martial, virtuous and tough, the United States almost gained the whole world, but in doing so almost lost its own soul.

Ancestor scolding can be fun. But it is apt to counter cliché with cliché. If the old tradition perceived America as uniquely good, the newer spirit is apt to perceive America as having been uniquely immature, self-indulgent, confused, etc. But were Americans unique in their thinking and behavior? For me, the parallels with Britain are closer than with Switzerland or China or Russia. Significant parts of the American military heritage—especially the grudging attitude to standing. armies and the emphasis on civil control—were directly absorbed from Britain. Other parts, while not borrowed, reflected similar responses to similar situations. Geography protected Britain as well as the United States from invasion. Both nations prospered in the nineteenth century from industry and trade. Both fought a number of short, remote, and usually successful wars and campaigns. Both avoided permanent alliances: "splendid isolation" was the British phrase. Both, in the act of expanding territorially, prided themselves on not being militaristic or amoral. George Bernard Shaw's ironical comment, "You will never find an Englishman in the wrong," could easily be adapted to describe the American tone of moral superiority. And both countries prided themselves on *ad hoc* pragmatism—otherwise known, in Britain, as "muddling through." Secretary of State Elihu Root recognized the kinship when he observed, at the dedication of the Army War College in 1908: "We are warlike enough, but not military. In this we are singularly like the English, and unlike other nations. We have political ideas, but no mould of military ideas."

Of course their situations were not identical, and after the end of the nineteenth century the dissimilarities became more striking. But the previous parallel has at least two useful functions. One is to challenge the cliché about American uniqueness—which, having once been a boast for the United States, now threatens to be treated as some sort of terrible curse afflicting America and only America. It is much healthier, and historically more correct, to regard the United States as neither angel nor monster, but a nation among other nations. The second function of the British comparison is to remind us that nations, like people, rarely commit themselves to conscious policies unless they have to. The Swiss, the Germans, the French and some other nations developed coherent military policies—wise or unwise, defensive or aggressive—because they had to. Vulnerable land frontiers, population pressures, emulative jealousies forced them into active roles; and the continuing tensions of Europe kept them on the alert. The Americans, on the other hand, in common with the British but with even greater leeway, enjoyed the boon of not having to be rigorous about military affairs. In a real sense, the American military tradition was a non-tradition, an absence rather than a presence. Having other, more urgent and more congenial things to think about, the United States gave a low priority to almost every aspect of warfare—including how to avoid it.

Uptonian rebukes are therefore often beside the point. Present-day American analysts follow a determinist line in assuming that power realities shape military and foreign policy. They invoke the primary idea of national self-interest, and suggest that other considerations such as morality are secondary—mere luxuries, flourishes, rationalizations. But according to their own logic, American military behavior in the past was also determined by circumstance. The American circumstance was a remarkably fortunate one; so, *of Uptonian necessity*, military thinking was correspondingly elementary. Perhaps the Anglo-Americans ought to have refrained from congratulating themselves so complacently upon their wisdom and virtue, when much of the credit should have gone to sheer geographical good luck.

It is also true that the United States could have fought its wars with more economy, and with fewer deaths from disease. But such improvements could only have been purchased at a price. This price—a greater attention to military issues—was one that Americans were not willing to pay. Why should they think the unthinkable when they did not have to? In the abstract, a stronger awareness of public duty might have been desirable. The United States may now be paying a heavy price for a whole heritage of private selfishness. But that was an entire heritage, of which the military aspect was only a portion. Within the military realm, though, why should Americans—in the terms of their society—have accepted militia duty on the Swiss model? Switzerland (which incidentally had not been able to put up much of a resistance to Napoleon) was surrounded by powerful neighbors. The United States, as was truly said by July 4th orators, was surrounded by big oceans and weak neighbors.

We might wish to amend Tom Paine's thesis that republics do not start wars, perhaps with reference to Alexis de Tocqueville's chapter on warfare in *Democracy in America*, to read that they merely fight different *kinds* of wars; and that once in a fight, they carry it through implacably. We could certainly answer the Uptonian preparedness thesis, which would contend that American unpreparedness was wrong because it took a heavy toll in lives and money. At least, we could in relation to the Civil War, which to Emory Upton supplied the most convincing proof of American folly. His theory supposes that a militarily prepared Union would have defeated the Confederacy in much less than four years. But then, the extent of preparedness would also have been greater in the South—a region which in any case is commonly said to have been more receptive than the North to military activity. So the Union's task would not have been lightened; and with better marksmanship and gunnery on both sides, the casualty lists might have been even longer.

Nor, by the test of events, are post-Uptonian doctrines very encouraging. Between 1950 and 1970 the United States built up the best-trained, best-equipped armed forces in its history. Military and para-military expertise was copiously available—and listened to, not pigeonholed. The technological advances, viewed technologically, were most impressive. Realism had supplanted sentimentalism. But the results of this formidable concentration of weapon-power, brainpower, and manpower, in Korea and Vietnam, were disquieting. Cost-benefit analysis began to appear as naive as the sloganizing of the old days. Professional morale, especially in the army, slumped lower than ever before. Quite senior officers produced books with titles like *Militarism, U.S.A.* There was widespread revulsion from the new dispensation, and a drive to rethink the unthinkable in opposite directions from those recommended by Herman Kahn. After a generation of experiment with universal and selective conscription, the United States is now back with the old principle of voluntary recruitment throughout the services.

Then what conclusions are we left with?

First, I think, awareness that there has never been any single "watershed" or dividing line in American history. The reversion to a volunteer army; General Eisenhower's warning against the "military-industrial complex," and his desire to disengage from Korea and promote world peace; ex-Captain Truman's dismissal of General MacArthur—these are instances of the carryover of old attitudes into the new period. So has been the intense debate of the 1960s and early 1970s over American military postures. The new antimilitarists can and do reprint the antimilitary writings of earlier times: Thoreau, for example, on *Civil Disobedience* in the 1840s; William James, Mark Twain, and the sociologist William Graham Sumner, on antiimperialism in the 1890s. Conversely, supposed characteristics of the new military realm can be traced back long before the 1940s. If one can detect the seeds of Vietnam as far back as 1812, which some American historians might argue, what becomes of the supposed break between old and new? The United States has never been a static society. Outwardly, the America of 1840 was already markedly changed from that of 1790; and 1840 would hardly have felt at home in 1890. This is not to argue that change has been smoothly continuous. It is simply to maintain that there was no long, comfortable run when Americans felt that some set of traditional principles existed to guide them straightforwardly.

What was intellectually novel after 1945 was the necessity to focus intensively and for a possibly unlimited period upon military problems. The results were not in my view altogether unprecedented, or lamentable. Some time-honored assumptions proved under scrutiny to be of dubious value. For example, the old suspicions of "standing armies" ceased years ago to mean much. A modest amount of training and experience swiftly obliterates the difference between professionals and amateurs. Exposure to danger ceased some while ago to be a crucial distinguishing feature. Even in World War II, only one soldier in ten was involved in combat. In missile technology and other sophisticated fields, it does not signify whether a man holds a colonelcy or a doctorate (he may have both). So the rule of civilian control might also be of little relevance. Defense Secretary Robert S. McNamara was as civilian as one could wish; but under his aegis the Pentagon grew prodigiously. Certain congressmen out-hawked the armed services. At the end of the 1960s, it began to seem as though the issue of control was not between the civilians and the services, but between the White House and Capitol Hill.

In old American antimilitary critiques, the army was sometimes compared to the unreformed medieval church. Both, it was said, absorbed men and money unproductively. Indeed, in every decade since the United States achieved independence, peace advocates have reckoned up what could have been done if such resources had been put to productive use. It is a somewhat ingenuous argument, for even as a mere economic calculation, it ignores the cash that pours into civilian sectors as a result. And it refuses to accept that less tangible but more fundamental benefits might be placed on the credit side of the ledger. No one can prove that the astronomical expenditure on nuclear armament after 1941 had much actual deterrent effect. But that cannot be disproved either. Despite the most alarming predictions, from hawks and doves alike, the superpowers have not warred with one another. Our descendants may come to think that mutual terror, as an alternative to mutual annihilation, was worth the money.

Even so, there would be grave cause for alarm if the military experts had continued to be able to justify their policies. We might then have been confronted with an irreversibly profound alteration in American attitudes. The systems analysts might have convinced themselves and most other Americans that they had cleared up the old muddles and ambiguities in military thought: rigor instead of torpor, *Kriegsraison* (military self-interest) instead of confusion between morality and power. In retrospect, I believe the almost traumatic shocks to American military and strategic planners suffered recently in Southeast Asia will seem blessings in disguise. Congress, the executive branch, the services, the nation have been shaken to the core. In the process the expert has been dethroned. Esoteric doctrine and technology have lost their magic. We are back again with old, part-commonsensical, part-ethical propositions. They do not furnish a military blueprint: they never did. But in diminishing the prestige of the pundits and hierarchs, they reintroduce America to a homelier, more honestly perplexed atmosphere—one which the Founding Fathers would still recognize, and still speak to.

Notes

1. Quincy Wright, *A Study of War*, 2 vols. (Chicago: University of Chicago Press, 1942), I. pp. 666-72, quoted in C. Vann Woodward, "The Age of Reinterpretation," *American Historical Review* 66 (October 1960): 4n.

2. Marcus Cunliffe, *Soldiers and Civilians: The Martial Spirit in America, 1775-1865* (Boston: Little, Brown, 1968; repr. New York: Free Press, 1973), especially pp. 412-23.

3. See T. Harry Williams, "The Macs and the Ikes: America's Two Military Traditions," *American Mercury* 75 (October 1952): 32-39.

4. For a fairly recent statement of the presumed parallel see Fritz Martin Stern, *The Citizen Army* (New York: St. Martin's Press, 1967).

VI

The Schooling of a People

Mortimer J. Adler

Democracy is always about equality, as well as other things. The exact degree to which it is or should be "about equality" is always a matter for controversy. But even more important than the question of degree is the question of direction: What kind of equality do we have in mind? What is equality itself "about"?

In the area of education, this latter question takes the form: should we "level up" or "level down"? Should we insist that the democratic citizen become an educated man or rather that our educational system adapt itself to democratic man as he exists at any moment? Professor Adler shows that this debate is endemic in the history of American education, and is still at the root of most educational controversies today. And one's point of view will, in the end, depend on one's estimate of the nature of human nature, and of the potentialities for the perfection of this nature in a democracy.

If we were to survey the history of educational thought and practice from its beginning to the middle or end of the nineteenth century, we would not find the answers to the major problems of education in our day and in our society. The best answers we could find—answers to the perennial questions about education, answers on which substantial agreement had been reached across the centuries—would not lead us to the solution of those problems which are peculiarly our own. On the contrary, they would intensify our sense of the difficulty of the problems we face. The better grasp we had of the wisdom about education gained during the preceding twenty-five centuries, the more appalled we should be by the magnitude of the problems that have arisen in the last hundred years.

The double impact of democracy and industrialization has created problems both new and difficult.

Before the last hundred years, the two most serious crises in Western education occurred with the transition from Graco-Roman antiquity to medieval Christendom, and with the widespread changes effected by the Protestant Reformation and the Renaissance. What is common to both can be briefly summarized in terms of issues concerning the relation of church and state, the place of religion in human life and in the formation of society, and the emphasis in education on temporal or eternal goals. These two crises in Western education have left us with a legacy of certain problems, even though, with the progressive secularization of our society and culture, we have moved further and further in the direction taken at the Reformation and with the Renaissance. Nevertheless, these two crises did not disrupt the basic continuity of Western education from the Greeks to the nineteenth century.

Only with a sense of that continuity can we fully appreciate the sharpness of the break that has occurred since 1850. During the whole preceding period, education had certain common aims and methods, not unrelated to the fact that it was always restricted to the few. No society up to that time was concerned with the schooling—much less the education—of all its people. Thomas Jefferson's proposal to the legislature of Virginia in 1817 (not adopted at the time it was made) that *all* the children should be given three years of common schooling at the public expense marks the emergence, in our country at least, of the central problem that our kind of society faces and that it has yet to solve in any satisfactory manner.

In a letter to Peter Carr in 1814, Jefferson outlined the basis of a Bill for Establishing a System of Public Education, which he submitted to the legislature in 1817. He wrote:

The mass of our citizens may be divided into two classes—the laboring and the learned. . . . At the discharging of the pupils from the elementary schools [after three years of schooling] the two classes separate—those destined for labor will engage in the business of agriculture or enter into apprenticeship to such handicraft art as may be their choice; their companions, destined to the pursuits of science, will proceed to the College. . . .

The suggestion that *all* children, even those destined for labor rather than for the arts and sciences as pursuits of leisure, should be given at least three years of schooling is the beginning of the democratic revolution in this country. But the explosive force of that revolutionary idea could not spread until the economic and political barriers to universal public schooling had been removed. Two basic changes—in the constitution of government and in the production of wealth— had to take place before society was fully confronted with the problem of how to produce an *educated people*, not just a *small class of educated men*. The two changes, dynamically interactive at every point, were the extension of the franchise toward the democratic ideal of universal suffrage and the substitution of machines for muscles in the production of wealth.

An industrial democracy, such as we have in America today, is a brand new kind of society. It represents the most radical transformation of the conditions of human life that has happened so far. Hence it should not be surprising that the problems of education in an industrial democracy are startlingly new problems and much more difficult than any that our ancestors faced.

The novelty and difficulty of our problems cannot be accounted for solely in terms of the quantitative expansion of education from the schooling of a relatively small portion of the population to that of the people as a whole. It is also necessary to consider a profound qualitative change in our culture. This change, in preparation since the seventeenth century, has reached its peak only in the last fifty years. We live in an age of science fully matured, an age of specialized research, dominated by the centrality of the scientific method and by the promises or threats of technology. Our educational problems are what they are—both in novelty and difficulty—because of the interplay of these two sets of factors: the quantitative extension of schooling to the whole population and the qualitative alterations in the content of schooling demanded by science and technology.

To understand the difficulty of our problems, it may be useful to consider briefly why the educational wisdom of our ancestors, developed in undemocratic societies, in nonindustrial economies, and in eras not dominated by science and technology, does not solve our problems for us. On the contrary, it appears to accentuate the difficulties we face in trying to solve them.

It is not necessary to pretend that there was perfect unanimity among educators and philosophers of education in the twenty-five centuries prior to our day in order to summarize the basic insights and convictions that they shared. The institutions and practices of education have changed, of course, with successive epochs in Western history. In addition, the great contributors to educational theory have differed and disputed on many points. One need only mention the names of Plato, Aristotle, Cicero, Quintilian, Augustine, Bonadventure, Aquinas, Montaigne, Erasmus, Francis Bacon, Comenius, Locke, Rousseau, Kant, J.S. Mill, and Cardinal Newman to have some notion of the controversial questions. Nevertheless, with few exceptions, the differences of opinion tend to be more concerned with particular policies and practices than with general principles; and the prevalence of common practices throughout the whole period during which schooling and education was restricted to the few, together with the sharing of basic theoretical insights, indicates a substantial agreement about general principles.

That measure of agreement can be summarized in the following six statements. As we consider each of these statements, let us ask ourselves three questions. *First*, can we still affirm the truth of what is being said when our concern is with the schooling and education of the people as a whole rather than a small portion of the population? *Second*, if we do affirm the truth of what is being said as still applicable to the conditions of life in an industrial democracy and in a culture dominated by science and technology, do we know how to apply that truth to the schooling and education of the people as a whole? *Third*, if we must reject what is being said as no longer applicable, at least not without substantial modifications or qualifications, then how shall we formulate the principles that must replace the ones we have rejected?

1. The aim of education is to cultivate the individual's capacities for mental growth and moral development; to help him acquire the intellectual and moral virtues requisite for a good human life, spent publicly in political action or service and privately in a noble or honorable use of free time for the creative pursuits of leisure, among which continued learning throughout life is pre-eminent.

2. Guided by the aim of education just stated, basic schooling must be liberal in character; that is, a preparation for liberty or a life of freedom—the political freedom enjoyed by citizens (or the ruling class in society) and the economic freedom of time free for the pursuits of leisure, time free from labor in the production of wealth, and time free for political activity and intellectual or artistic pursuits. Such basic schooling, in method and content, should be the same for all, involving little or no specialization. It does not include the specialized training of workers in the skills required for earning a living. The kind of specialized schooling that may be required beyond basic schooling is the schooling needed to impart the knowledge and skills required for vocations which are essentially liberal in character—the learned professions and the professions of learning.

3. Basic schooling, even when followed by professional schooling, does not complete the education of a man. The satisfactory completion of school requirements merely certifies that the individual is equipped to carry on learning by himself in any sphere of knowledge or skill. Education cannot be completed in school because of the limitations intrinsic to youth or immaturity and the inherent limitations on any course of study that is appropriate for youth. One of the essential forms of leisure activity is the continuation of learning after school, for which schooling at its best is only a preparation. The pursuit of understanding and wisdom involves the effort of a lifetime. It cannot be accomplished in youth, nor can the obligation to go on learning be fully discharged while any capacity for learning remains.

4. Society's interest in the schooling and education of human beings is twofold. On the one hand, it seeks to enhance its own welfare by deriving from

well-educated persons the contribution they can make in the service of society. On the other hand, it seeks to put the resources of society at the service of the individual by contributing through schooling and education to his own pursuit of happiness or a good human life. So far as it is agreed that society and the state exist for the perfection of human life, and that the individual human being, while under an obligation to act for the social welfare, has ends beyond that, society's concern with schooling and education cannot be limited to their utility for its own welfare. On the contrary, that interest must be pursued in a manner that does not conflict with or detract from society's obligation to facilitate and enhance the education of the individual for the sake of his own development as a human being.

5. The profession of teaching is both a learned profession and a profession of learning, and so it involves knowledge and skill beyond basic schooling. Since the liberal arts are the arts of learning and teaching, the preparation of teachers involves, in addition to basic liberal schooling, special training in the liberal arts. The teacher must know what to teach as well as how to teach. Hence the best teachers are those who not only perfect their teaching through practice of its arts, but who also deepen their grasp of the subjects they are teaching by further study of those subjects.

6. Not all who teach or study may be able to contribute to the advancement of learning, but the vitality of education in any society depends on the efforts of those who augment learning as well as on the efforts of those who disseminate or acquire it. Such efforts normally prosper through the cooperation of scholars. The advancement of learning, therefore, depends on the condition requisite for such cooperation—a community of scholars which exists only to whatever extent scholars can and do communicate with one another across all the specialized fields of learning.

In the context of the questions that must be asked about them, the foregoing six propositions raise more problems than can be discussed within the confines of this essay. I will, therefore, concentrate on the problems raised by the first four and, even so, I will try further to narrow them down to what I regard as the most important and far-reaching critical choices that confront us in the field of public education. But before I attempt to define the alternatives that challenge us, I would like to review briefly the American commitment to public education; and, following that, to indicate the altered circumstances which have in turn altered the nature of that commitment.

Beginning with the earliest days of the American republic, and even before that in the years of its formation, the commentators on the genius of its institutions called attention to the education of its citizens as a prime requisite not only for the preservation of their liberties, but also for the effectiveness of their engagement in public affairs. The institution of public schools, Noah Webster wrote in 1785, "is the necessary consequence of the genius of our governments; at the same time, it forms the firmest security of our liberties. It is scarcely possible to reduce an enlightened people to civil or ecclesiastical tyranny." Two years later, in 1787, Dr. Benjamin Rush told an audience in Philadelphia on the eve of the Constitutional Convention, that "to conform the principles, morals, and manners of our citizens to our republican forms of government, it is absolutely necessary that knowledge of every kind should be disseminated through every part of the United States."

In his Inaugural Address as president of Cumberland College in Tennessee in 1825, Philip Lindsley began by saying that

a free government like ours cannot be maintained except by an enlightened and virtuous people. It is not enough that there be a few individuals of sufficient information to manage public affairs. To the people, our rulers are immediately responsible for the faithful discharge of their official duties. But if the people be incapable of judging correctly of their conduct and measures, what security can they have for their liberties a single hour?

Elementary schooling, for the poor as well as for the rich, is not enough for this purpose, Lindsley argued. Colleges must be provided, not only to make better citizens but also to enable those citizens to lead better lives. Against the view that "superior learning is necessary only for a few particular professions," Lindsley maintained that "every individual who wishes to rise above the level of a mere laborer at taskwork ought to endeavor to obtain a liberal education."

In a somewhat similar vein, William Seward, in a speech delivered at Auburn, New York, in 1835, observed that elementary instruction in reading and writing was not enough. "Without some higher cultivation of the mind," we become "the sport of demagogues, and the slaves of popular passion, caprice, and excitement. . . . To discharge the duty of electors, we should understand some of the principles of political economy, of the philosophy of the human mind, and, above all, of moral and religious science." For the preservation of our free institutions and for their conduct to the maximum advantage of all, he urged that "the minds of all the people should be thus instructed."

In contrast to those who advocated enlarging the scope of public education for the political benefits it can confer, John H. Vincent, in a speech about the Chatauqua Movement in Boston in 1886, insisted that "education, once the peculiar privilege of the few, must in our best earthly estate become the valued possession of the many. It is a natural and inalienable right of human souls. The gift of imagination, of memory, of reason, of invention, of constructive and executive power, carries with it both prerogative and obligation. . . . No man has a right to neglect his personal education, whether he be prince or playboy, broker or hod carrier." If a just society is one that secures human rights, it is obliged to do all that it can to provide human beings with such schooling as will facilitate the exercise of their right to an education and, through it, their personal development.

These themes are echoed again and again, changing slightly as we pass to later generations. In *The Promise of American Life* published in 1909, Herbert Croly declared that "democracy must stand or fall on a platform of possible human perfectibility. If human nature cannot be improved by institutions, democracy is at best a more than usually safe form of organization." But for democracy to prosper as well as to endure, Croly looked to the benefits of education. "It is by education that the American is trained for such democracy as he possesses; and it is by better education that he proposes to better his democracy. . . . It helps to give the individual himself those qualities without which no institutions, however excellent, are of any use." Thirty years later, James B. Conant, in his Charter Day Address at the University of California in 1940, pointed out that the three fundamentals of the Jeffersonian tradition were "freedom of mind, social mobility through education, [and] universal schooling." These, he said, have represented "the aspirations and desires of a free people embarked on a new experiment, the perpetuation of a casteless nation." Though his theme on this occasion was education for a classless society, Conant concluded his address by insisting that "extreme differentiation of school programs seems essential," in support of which he referred to Jefferson's differentiation between the schooling of those destined for labor and the schooling of those destined for leisure and further learning.

Two other themes make their appearance in the historic record of the American concern with public education. One is the educational significance of vocational training in the public schools. Jane Addams and John Dewey, who defended such instruction when it was first introduced into the curriculum, did *not* do so on the ground that vocational training served the purpose of preparing the young to obtain jobs and earn their living. They would not have espoused it for that reason. On the contrary, they argued for its educational value as contributing to an understanding of "the social meaning of work," in Jane Addams' words; or, as John Dewey put it,

scientific insight into natural materials and processes, points of departure whence children shall be led out into a realization of the historic development of man. . . . When occupations in the school are conceived in this broad and generous way, I can only stand lost in wonder at the objections so often heard that such occupations are out of place in the school because they are materialistic, utilitarian, or even menial in their tendency.

The other theme is the role that public education plays in promoting the equality of conditions that constitutes a democratic and supposedly classless society. Horace Mann was one of the most eloquent spokesmen for education as the great equalizer. In a report to the legislature of Massachusetts in 1842, he asserted that "individuals who, without the aid of knowledge, would have been condemned to perpetual inferiority of condition and subjected to all the evils of want and poverty, rise to competence and independence by the uplifting power of education." Six years later in another report to the legislature, Horace Mann summed up his conviction on this point by saying

education, then, beyond all other devices of human origin, is the great equalizer of the conditions of men, the balance wheel of the social machinery. . . . It gives each man the independence and the means by which he can resist the selfishness of other men. It does better then to disarm the poor of their hostility towards the rich; it prevents being poor.

As we pass from the last century into the present one, the hope that Horace Mann held out came to be looked upon as illusory. Writing in 1892, President Eliot of Harvard reported

serious and general disappointment at the results of popular education up to this point. . . . Skeptical observers complain that people in general, taken in masses with proper exclusion of exceptional individuals, are hardly more reasonable in the conduct of life than they were before free schools, popular colleges, and the cheap printing press existed. They point out that when the vulgar learn to read they want to read trivial or degrading literature. . . . Is it not the common school and the arts of cheap illustration, they say, which have made obscene books, photographs and pictures, low novels, and all the literature which incites to vice and crime, profitable, and therefore abundant and dangerous to society?

After citing a long list of similar complaints, all of which might be made in the present decade as well as in the 1890s, President Eliot pointed out that the laboring classes "complain that in spite of universal elementary education, society does not tend toward a greater equality of condition; that the distinctions between rich and poor are not diminished but intensified, and that elementary education does not necessarily procure for the wage earner any exemption from incessant and exhausting toil." In addition, they allege that education "has not made the modern rich man less selfish and luxurious than his predecessor in earlier centuries who could barely sign his name . . . [and] also that the education of the employer and the employed has not made the conditions of employment more humane and comfortable. . . ."

The question, which President Eliot did not answer, was whether the fault lay with defects in the educational system itself, defects which might be remedied to produce the opposite results, or whether universal public schooling, even with all its defects removed, could never be the equalizer of conditions that Horace Mann claimed it would be. Both answers have been given in this century. Professor George Sylvester Counts of Teachers College, Columbia, and an educational reformer in the line of John Dewey, claimed in 1922 that the selective character of American secondary education made it, in effect, anti-democratic—a major factor in the perpetuation of class differences. Much more recently, the Coleman report on equality of education opportunity, published in 1966, and the book by Christopher Jencks and his associates, *Inequality, A Reassessment of the Effect of Family and Schooling in America* (1972), tend in the opposite direction, pointing out that no improvement in the system of public education by itself can produce either an equality of educational opportunity or an equality of social and economic conditions.

The statements quoted and the views reported in the foregoing brief survey of the American commitment to universal public schooling are submitted as a sketchy sampling of opinion from the beginning of the republic to the present day. They should not be read as accurately reflecting the facts about the school system, much less as giving us reliable appraisals of its effectiveness or accomplishments. They may generate the impression that, almost from the beginning, this country was dedicated to the schooling of all its children at the public expense, both for the perpetuation of our free institutions and for their own fulfillment as human beings, but not until the present century—in fact, not until very recently—have the number of children in our schools and colleges and the duration of their attendance at these institutions come near to approximating a system of universal public education that looks as if it might be serving the aims which our ancestors had in mind.

Even if, prior to this century, all or most or a majority of the children had the benefit of primary or elementary schooling, that could not be expected to achieve more than a rudimentary literacy and numeracy. It was certainly not adequate to the task of producing an educated people—a citizenry or electorate capable of exercising a free and critical judgment on public issues and on the performance of public officials, and a society of cultivated human beings, each of whom had been helped by schooling to realize his capacity for learning in a measure proportionate to the degree of his native endowment. Not until this century does the extension of schooling, both in the number of children it accommodates and in the number of years it provides instruction for them, reach a quantitative scope which warrants us in saying that we are now engaged in the schooling of a whole people. Unfortunately, no one who has any acquaintance with how the system works would feel warranted in saying that the qualitative level attained by the products of our educational institutions, taken in aggregate, remotely resembles what we have in mind when we contemplate the ideal of an educated people.

This striking discrepancy between the quantitative and the qualitative measures of educational achievement underlies the alternatives which, I submit, constitute the single most important—the central or focal—critical choice that confronts America in the field of public education. How we decide it will determine how we approach all the other options that are open to us. It is important to remember that the choices we face have never been faced by any society prior to this century, and are being faced in this century only by societies with political and economic arrangements like our own. Remembering this, we should not be surprised by our failure so far to create a system of public education that is qualitatively as well as quantitatively adequate to the task of producing an educated people. But though the novelty and the difficulty of the problems involved may extenuate our failure to solve them, they do not excuse failure on our part to open our eyes and see clearly the magnitude of the problems themselves.

Let us remind ourselves once more of the changes that have brought us to our present plight, and also of the realities of contemporary society and culture—the circumstances which have generated problems so novel and difficult that the traditional principles and practices of Western educational theory, *even if they were completely valid*, would not solve them.

In 1850, 5 percent of our productive power was supplied by machines, the rest by human and animal muscle. In 1950, 84 percent was supplied by machines, the rest by muscle; and a quarter of a century later, the percentage differences are even more striking. In 1850, more than half the adult population of this country was disfranchised; less than half exercised the suffrage that is indispensable to political liberty and participation in self-government. By 1950, the franchise had been extended to include the whole adult population, and a quarter of a century later steps had been taken to ensure that all those who possessed suffrage could freely exercise it.

The revolution in education has followed in the wake of industrialization and democratization. In 1850, a very small percentage of the children who went to school went beyond the elementary school, and not all went to school. In 1900, less than 10 percent of the children of eligible high school age were in high school. By 1950, over 85 percent of the children of high school age were in high school, and twenty-five years later that figure has increased substantially.

With universal suffrage, all normal children are destined to become citizens— members of the ruling class. In line with the democratic conception of citizenship, the basic schooling of future citizens, both elementary and secondary, is necessary and is, therefore, made compulsory. Under conditions of industrial production, it is economically possible and, perhaps, even economically desirable for compulsory basic schooling to be lengthened to twelve years, and for another two or four years of schooling at the public expense to be added on a voluntary basis.

Along with the abolition of slavery and the attenuation of economic servitude in all its myriad forms, the industrial economy has either abolished or blurred the separation between a leisure and a laboring class. All human beings are citizens with suffrage and, with exceptions that are rapidly becoming anomalous, all are also both workers and persons with sufficient free time at their disposal to be engaged in the pursuits of leisure (over and above the time that is devoted to recreations and amusements). The division between labor and leisure is no longer a division of society into distinct classes; it is now a division of the time of citizens into distinct activities—the activities of labor, on the one hand, and the activities of leisure as well as play (which is quite distinct from leisure) on the other.

With the shortening of the work week, the increase in the time available for leisure pursuits has made the continuation of learning in adult life possible for all workers; and since basic schooling by itself, even at its best, could not possibly suffice either for their proper functioning as citizens or for their personal fulfillment as human beings, continued learning in adult life would seem to be necessary for all, if our educational aim is to produce an educated people. Furthermore, with the lengthening of the period of compulsory basic schooling for all, there is less and less need for adults to go back to school to make up for insufficient schooling in childhood; adult education can become the kind of education which continues and sustains learning after sufficient schooling has been completed.

But many problems confront these possibilities. The great increase in the number of students in school and in the number of adults who can and should be helped to go on with learning places an enormous burden on society with respect to the housing and expenses of education and the preparation and support of school teachers and of leaders in adult education. Also, the number of learned professions, or of vocations requiring specialized schooling beyond basic schooling, has increased with the intensified division of labor in an industrial society, with the demands of its technology, and with the social ambitions of occupational groups. The advancement of learning in a culture dominated by science and technology calls for more and more intense specialization in both study and research; and this has not only affected the organization of our higher institutions of learning, but has also tended to influence the content of the curriculum in the years of basic schooling.

To state the central critical choice that a society such as ours faces, it is necessary to make certain underlying assumptions explicit. They all rest on the proposition declared self-evident in the Declaration of Independence; namely, that all men are by nature equal (if human equality is to be self-evident, "by nature" must be substituted for "created"). The equality affirmed is the equality of all persons belonging to the same species, having the same specific human nature and the species-specific properties and powers appertaining thereto. Such equality of all human beings as persons is quite compatible with all the inequalities which differentiate them as individuals—inequalities in the degree to which they possess the same specific endowments and inequalities in the degree of their attainments through the development and exercise of their native gifts. In fact, the only respect in which all human beings are by nature equal is the respect in which they are all persons, all human, all members of the same species. In all other respects, they tend to be unequal as individuals.

Against this, consider the ancient doctrine that some men are by nature free and some are by nature slaves—some destined from birth to the free life of a citizen engaged in self-government and in the pursuit of human happiness, and some destined by their meagre native endowments to be subjected to rule by others and to serve by their labor the pursuit of happiness by others. While it may be true that this doctrine is no longer espoused by anyone in the harsh form which would justify the ownership and use of human beings as chattel, it is far from clear that a softened form of the doctrine has no exponents in modern times or in contemporary society. Until the twentieth century, there were many who held the view that only some human beings were fortunately endowed with native capacities that made them genuinely educable. It would be folly to try to educate the rest; suffice it, in their case, to train them for the tasks they would have to perform, tasks that did not include the duties of enfranchised citizenship or the pursuits of leisure. Even in the present century, there have been some distinguished educators who have held similar views.

Less than forty years ago, for example, President Darden of the University of Virginia recommended that compulsory education beyond grammar school should be abandoned. He urged a return to Jefferson's dictum that we are obliged to teach every child only to read and write. After that, Darden said, "it is our obligation, as Jefferson visualized it, to provide a really fine education beyond reading and writing for the students who show talent and interest." Albert Jay Nock went further in urging a return to the aristocratic notions of the past. "The philosophical doctrine of equality," he wrote,

gives no more ground for the assumption that all men are educable than it does for the assumption that all men are six feet tall. We see at once that it is not the philosophical doctrine of equality, but an utterly untenable popular perversion of it, that we find at the basis of our educational system.

Nock accepts the philosophical doctrine of equality only to the extent that it calls for the abolition of chattel slavery. He does not think that the doctrine calls for universal suffrage or for equality of educational opportunity. While he endorses a minimum of compulsory schooling for all, he thinks that it should be directed toward training "to the best advantage a vast number of ineducable persons." To require the public school to provide, over and above their function as training schools, forms of education that are appropriate only for the gifted few is to impose upon them an obligation that they cannot possibly discharge.

In stating what I regard as the central critical choice confronting us today in the field of education, I am proceeding on an assumption diametrically opposed to that implicit in Nock's theory of education. I call it an assumption only because, within the confines of this essay, I cannot fully present the reasons that would show it to be true, and so not something that must be postulated without argument. From the self-evident truth that all human beings are by nature equal (or from the truth of what Nock calls "the philosophical doctrine of equality"),

I think it can be shown not only that chattel slavery cannot be justified, but also that all human beings are by nature fit to lead free lives—the lives of self-governing citizens, with suffrage, and with lives enriched by engagement in the pursuits of leisure, preeminent among which is learning in all its many forms. If that can be shown, it must follow that all human beings are educable, though in different degrees proportionate to differences in their native endowments. Without spelling out in detail the reasoning involved, suffice it to say that we live in a society which has assumed that these things are true—that all human beings have the right to be politically free, to be citizens with suffrage, to have enough free time and other economic goods to be able to engage in the pursuits of leisure; and assuming these things to be true, our society has committed itself to two consequent propositions—that all human beings are educable and that all should be given, through public institutions, equal opportunity to become educated.

On these assumptions, the central critical choice we face can be stated as a decision between the following alternatives: On the one hand, (A) differentiated basic schooling, such as now exists in this country; on the other hand, (B) undifferentiated basic schooling which would require a radical reform of the present system. Each of these alternatives needs a word of further explanation in order to make the issue clear.

Differentiated Basic Schooling. By basic schooling is meant the whole sequence of years in which schooling is compulsory—either ten or twelve years from the first grade through the tenth or twelfth. Beyond that, if the young do not elect to leave school, they can voluntarily go on to further schooling, either to senior high school or to two- or four-year colleges. For reasons that will become clear, let me proceed as if basic schooling extended over a period of twelve years and was divided into two levels—primary (the first six grades) and secondary (junior and senior high school)—each taking six years. Now, such basic schooling is *differentiated* when its aim and curriculum are the *same only at the primary level*, and when, beyond that, at the secondary level, students are shunted into different courses of study which are motivated by quite different educational aims, such as vocational training on the one hand, and what is called "college preparatory training" on the other. The situation is not greatly altered if the differentiation occurs after eight years of elementary school and the children pass on to quite different kinds of high school.

Undifferentiated Basic Schooling. On this alternative, it is requisite that the period of basic schooling cover at least twelve years, six years of primary or elementary and six years of secondary schooling. Such schooling is *undifferentiated* when its aim and curriculum are *the same for the whole period of compulsory attendance at school*—at the secondary as well as the primary level. The curriculum may include the study of vocations or occupations, but not, as

John Dewey pointed out, for the sake of training the young for jobs, which is the training of slaves, but rather as one aspect of their introduction to the world in which they will live. Furthermore, while the curriculum is such that it would prepare the young for further schooling, in college or university, that is not its essential aim, because all who have been thus schooled will not necessarily go on to higher institutions of learning. Rather the aim of undifferentiated basic schooling is to make the young competent as learners, and to prepare as well as inspire them to engage in further learning whether that takes place in higher institutions of learning or in the course of noninstitutionalized study through a variety of facilities or means.

Exponents of both alternatives subscribe to the proposition that all should be given equal educational opportunity, but they interpret this proposition differently. Exponents of differentiated basic schooling think that such equality of opportunity is provided if all the children attend school for the same period of years, even though during some portion of that time the schooling they receive is different in content and motivated by different aims. Exponents of undifferentiated basic schooling think that equality of educational opportunity is provided only if the quality as well as the quantity of basic schooling is the same for all; and they mean by this that the curriculum and method of basic schooling as a whole should be directed toward the same goal for all—their preparation for a life of learning and for responsible participation in public affairs.

There is one other fundamental difference in the views of those who defend differentiated basic schooling as it exists today and those who advocate the reform of present institutions and practices to make basic schooling undifferentiated. The former hold to the ideal of the educated man conceived in terms which makes it unrealistic to suppose that all human beings can aspire to some measure of fulfillment of that ideal. The latter so conceive the ideal that it is within the reach of all, with the qualification, of course, that its attainment will vary, from person to person, in a manner proportionate to their initial differences in endowment and their subsequent use of their abilities. It is this difference which leads the exponents of differentiated basic schooling to reject undifferentiated basic schooling as unrealistic: A realistic appraisal of the human potentiality for education, they maintain, supports the conclusion that one portion of the population, the larger portion perhaps, should be treated differently at the secondary level, because they are not truly educable in the same way and toward the same end as the other and smaller portion. If we call them the realists, and their opponents the idealists, we must also acknowledge that both are, in their different ways, democratic rather than aristocratic in their views of public education, for both adhere to the tenet of equal educational opportunity and both regard that as an inescapable corollary of the truth that all men are by nature equal and endowed with the same inherently human powers and rights.

If it is within the purview of this essay to go beyond a statement of the alternatives and to argue that the decision should be made in one direction rather than the other, I would like to spend a moment more saying why I favor undifferentiated basic schooling. The rudimentary literacy and numeracy, which is a large part of what can be achieved in the primary grades, is certainly not adequate as preparation either for discharging the duties of responsible citizenship or for engagement in the pursuits of leisure. Six more years of schooling at the secondary level should be devoted to those ends—for all, not just for some, since all will be admitted to citizenship with suffrage and all will have ample free time for further learning and other pursuits of leisure. The realistic democrat is inconsistent in thinking, on the one hand, that all normal children have enough innate intelligence to justify their right to suffrage and free time, and enough intelligence to exercise these rights for their own and for the public good, while also thinking, on the other hand, that all do not have enough intelligence to receive the same educational treatment at the secondary level. At this level, they say, some—probably a majority—must be separated from the minority among their fellows who are educable in a different way and with a different purpose in view.

Having gone this far, it is also incumbent upon me as an idealistic democrat to answer the objection that the realists raise against the alternative that I favor. The objection has two prongs. One is the point that the wide range of individual differences in educational aptitude calls for differentiation in educational treatment when we pass beyond the primary level of instruction. Great inequalities in intelligence and other native endowments must be acknowledged; but to acknowledge them does not require us to adopt different aims in the schooling of the less gifted and in the schooling of the more gifted. A pint receptacle and a quart or gallon receptacle cannot hold the same quantity of liquid; but, while differing in the size of their capacity, they can all be filled to the brim; and if, furthermore, the very nature of their capacity craves the same kind of filling, then they are treated equally only when each is filled to the brim and each is filled with the same kind of substance, not the smaller receptacles with dirty water or skimmed milk and the larger receptacles with whole milk or rich cream.

The other prong of the objection is that, while we have for many centuries known how to help the large receptacles imbibe whole milk or cream, we have *not yet* been able to discover ways of helping the smaller receptacles get their proportionate share of the same substance. The operative words here are "not yet," and the answer to the objection is that we have not yet given sufficient time, energy, and creative ingenuity to inventing the means for doing what has never been done before. If whole milk or rich cream is too thick and viscous a substance easily to enter the narrow apertures at the top of the smaller receptacles, then we must invent the funnels needed for the infusion. Until a sustained and massive effort is made to discover the devices and methods that must be employed to give all the children the same kind of treatment in school, motivated by the same aim and arising from a conviction that they are all educable in the same way, though not to the same degree, it is presumptuously dogmatic to assert that it cannot be done. All that can be said, in truth, is that it has not yet been done.

In the light of evidence recently amassed, it may be further objected that an attempt to carry out the mandate of equal educational opportunity by undifferentiated schooling is doomed to defeat by differences in the children's economic, social, and ethnic backgrounds and especially differences in the homes from which they come—differences which affect their educability and which cannot be overcome by the invention of new educational devices and methods as, perhaps, their differences in innate endowment can be. Does this require us to abandon the effort to carry out the educational mandate of a democratic society, or does it require a democratic society to undertake economic and social as well as educational reforms to facilitate carrying out that mandate?

I have dismissed without discussion an issue that is antecedent to the choice between differentiated and undifferentiated compulsory schooling. The question whether compulsory schooling should be abolished or maintained has been much agitated of late, but I do not think it presents us with a genuine option. In a recent essay on the subject, "The Great Anti-School Campaign," Robert M. Hutchins reviewed the various attacks on compulsory education and the proposed substitutes for it, and he argued persuasively to the conclusion that what is needed is not a substitute for the system of compulsory schooling but rather radical improvements in the organization, aims, and methods of the schools that constitute the system.

However, I would like to deal briefly in these concluding pages with another set of alternatives which, in my judgment, do present us with a genuine option and a critical choice that I think we shall have to make in the years immediately ahead. The choice is between (A) retaining the present organization of our system of educational institutions and (B) substituting for it a quite different scheme of organization. Let me make this choice clear by describing the alternatives.

The Present Organization. It consists of twelve years of schooling beginning at age six and normally ending at age eighteen, and usually divided, as we have seen, either into eight years of elementary school and four years of high school or into six years of primary school, three of junior high school, and three of senior high school. The period during which school attendance is compulsory may, under certain circumstances and in certain states, be less than twelve years; but, in any case, schooling at the public expense is open to all during this period. Beyond secondary or high school, the system includes two-year municipal or junior colleges, four-year colleges, and universities; and many of these institutions, especially the municipal or junior colleges, provide further schooling at the public expense, and beyond that attendance at state colleges and universities involves the payment of only nominal fees. On the principle of "open admissions," which has become wide-spread in recent years, nothing more than a certificate of graduation from high school is required for admission to our so-called "institutions of higher learning." Schooling at the public expense has thus been extended from twelve years to sixteen, and even more if graduate instruction at the university is involved; it is, moreover, open to all, though it is not compulsory but voluntary at whatever age the law allows the young to leave school without being truants.

The Proposed Reorganization. In place of the existing sequence of three or four levels of continuous schooling at the public expense, it is proposed that the system be divided into two main parts, quite different in their aims and character and not continuous in sequence.

The first part would be twelve years of basic schooling, beginning at age four rather than age six in order to terminate at age sixteen instead of age eighteen. This would be compulsory for all. It might, for convenience, be subdivided into a primary and secondary level, but this would have little educational significance if this whole period involved *undifferentiated schooling* for all. Since the aim of such basic schooling would be to inculcate the arts of learning and to introduce the young to the world of learning—to make them competent learners, in short, rather than to try to make them genuinely learned (which is impossible for the young)—it would be appropriate to award the Bachelor of Arts degree at the completion of such basic schooling. Doing so would return that degree to its original educational significance as certifying competence in the liberal arts, which are the arts or skills of learning in all fields of subject matter. Basic schooling, thus conceived, might be terminal schooling for some and preparatory schooling for others—terminal schooling for those who would engage in self-education in adult life without further formal attendance at higher institutions of learning for the purpose of getting advanced degrees; preparatory schooling for others who would attend higher institutions and seek advanced degrees. In one sense, basic schooling would be preparatory schooling for all, in that it would prepare all for continued learning in later years whether that occurred in educational institutions or by other means and facilities.

The second part of the system proposed would consist of what I shall call *advanced* schooling in contrast to *basic* schooling; it would be voluntary rather than compulsory schooling. Though attendance at higher institutions of learning would be at the public expense or involve only nominal fees, it would not be open to all who had completed their basic schooling, but only to those who qualified by criteria of aptitude, competence, and inclination. Advanced schooling would include both further general education and also specialized training in all the learned professions and in all vocations requiring technical proficiency, as well as specialized training for the profession of learning itself—all the forms of scholarship and research involved in the advancement of learning. Certain aspects of what is now collegiate education would be integrated with the final two years of basic schooling, and certain aspects of it would be reserved for the first two years of advanced schooling; but, in either case, the curricular elements would be retained only insofar as they constitute general not specialized education. Differentiated and specialized education, of whatever sort, would begin only after undifferentiated and general education had been completed.

The proposed reorganization of the educational system involves one further innovation which, in my judgment, is an essential ingredient of the plan. It consists in the introduction of a scholastic hiatus, either for two years or four, between the completion of basic schooling and the beginning of advanced schooling in institutions of higher learning. With graduation from high school at age sixteen, and with non-attendance at school made compulsory with few if any exceptions, advanced schooling would begin for those tested and qualified at age eighteen or twenty. For those going on to institutions of higher learning, the period of the enforced hiatus would be spent in remunerated work either in the private or public sector of the economy.

The hiatus is designed to serve a threefold purpose: (1) to interrupt the continuity of schooling and save the young from the scholastic ennui that results from too many successive years of sitting in classrooms and doing their lessons; (2) to counteract the delayed maturity induced by too many years of continuous schooling and thus to remedy some of the disorders of adolescence; and (3) to populate our institutions of higher learning with students who have gained a certain degree of maturity through the experiences afforded them by non-scholastic employments, as well as with students who return to educational institutions for further schooling because they have a genuine desire for further formal study and an aptitude for it, instead of students who occupy space in our higher institutions as the result of social pressures or because to continue on with more schooling is following the path of least resistance.

In the course of describing these alternatives, I have made no attempt to conceal my partisanship in favor of the proposed reorganization. The reasons why I favor it should also be sufficiently apparent not to need further comment. However, I might add two observations. One is that to initiate schooling at age four rather than age six would take advantage of the child's lively capacity for instruction in these years. This is confirmed by everything we have recently discovered from researches in early learning. Two years that might otherwise be wasted would be put to good use; and, in addition, starting at age four rather than age six would bring basic schooling to an end at age sixteen rather than age eighteen. If it were at all possible, it might even be better, for the cure of adolescence and the achievement of earlier maturity, to terminate basic schooling at age fourteen or fifteen.

My second comment concerns the ideal of the educated man under the circumstances of contemporary life—in our kind of society and our kind of culture. As an idealistic democrat, I have tried to reconceive that ideal in a way which makes it attainable in some degree by all human beings, not just the exceptional few for whom the ideal, as traditionally formulated, was exclusively realizable. If our kind of society and culture is dedicated to the education of a whole people, not just the development of a small class of educated persons, then the notion of *the educated person* must hold out a goal toward which every human being can strive and which, given facilitating circumstances, he can achieve in some measure. This makes sense if we define *being educated* not in terms of the traditional intellectual virtues or in terms of certain high attainments with respect to the arts and sciences, but rather in terms of having competence as a learner and using that competence to continue learning throughout a lifetime and to engage in other of the creative pursuits of leisure. Every human being, from those with the humblest endowments up to the most gifted among us, can become an educated person in this sense.

Since the purpose of schooling is not to produce educated men and women but rather to facilitate their becoming educated in the course of a lifetime, it serves that purpose well only if basic schooling for all tries to make the young *learners* rather than *learned*, and tries to make them avid for learning rather than turn them away from it; only if advanced schooling for some initiates them in the process of becoming learned, both in general and in specialized fields; and only if other facilities for becoming learned, whether in educational institutions or by other means, are provided by society for all, for those who have had advanced schooling as well as for those who have had only basic schooling. A choice in favor of undifferentiated basic schooling and in favor of the proposed reorganization of our educational institutions would, I submit, help us to school a whole people in a manner that would facilitate their becoming an educated people as a whole.

The Idea of
Mental Health

Robert Coles

For the past century and more, the United States has maintained institutions and programs for the treatment of the mentally ill. Implicit in these was the notion that there was such a thing as a normal or healthy range of human behavior, and also such a thing as behavior that was outside the bounds of the normal. Implicit also was the belief that defining those limits, and curing the people whose behavior put them outside them, was the proper function of an objective science: psychiatry.

Though psychiatry does have many of the attributes of an objective science, argues Robert Coles, it also incorporates a healthy portion of the moralistic and rationalistic myths around which nineteenth century society was organized. In recent decades, psychiatrists and social critics have increasingly argued that mental health is not so starkly separable from mental illness—and in some instances they have even argued that it is only society and society's prejudice which makes the distinction between "sane" and "insane." To some extent, this development in psychiatric doctrine reflects a growing cultural uncertainty that pervades all Western societies; we no longer are as sure as we once were about what is and is not right, or healthy, or desirable in human behavior. But, in addition, this development also reflects a growing sophistication in psychiatry, which has come to recognize the limits of its knowledge and its ability to treat the mentally ill.

In the United States, more than any other country, psychiatry has become familiar to ordinary men and women, even to children. Each of our states has a system of hospitals, clinics, and sometimes schools designed to help those considered or declared to be "mentally ill" or "psychiatrically disturbed" by themselves, their relatives and friends, or upon occasion, no one familiar, only a strange doctor or judge. The federal government spends millions on "mental health research." There is a National Association of Mental Health, an influential lobby made up of thousands of dedicated citizens who keep careful watch on governors and state legislators, and if need be, on Congress and the president. Will they all pay the right amount of attention, including the financial kind, to "mental health issues," as they are often called? Once those who argued on behalf of the mentally ill were thought by many to be in the vanguard of social reform—advocates of "progress" against people who, out of prejudice and fear, wanted only abject confinement or moralistic censure for men and women who felt unaccountably "nervous," or fearful, or plagued by nightmares and obsessions. Now it is safe to say that, for the most part, the mentally ill and those who argue their cause obtain at the very least respectful attention in every region of the country, from both political parties, and from those who consider themselves "liberal" or "conservative."

Yet, if the "mentally ill" and the care they receive are no longer a subject of acute controversy, they nevertheless present us, at every level of government, with definite matters of public policy—arguably all the more serious, because they are not sufficiently examined, debated and made more explicit. Exactly *what* if anything, is "mental health"? Who is "mentally ill"—as opposed to the rest of us, who make do, if not prosper psychologically? When ought a person be confined to a mental hospital—against his or her will? For that matter, ought there *be* mental hospitals as we have known them in the past? Put more sharply, more controversially, is the whole subject of "mental health" a phantom—a means by which different people, possessed of different notions about life and its purposes, turn on one another categorically, morally, and even, it can be said, politically: I am "healthy" (good, saved, favored by God or fate) and you are an outcast of sorts? And finally, but not insignificantly, what are we to do with federal and state funds? To what kind of psychiatric research or care ought we devote those funds, in view of the suspicion and truculence, the ideological passion, it seems, which can characterize the various "approaches," as advocated by their spokesmen?

Since the dawn of recorded history, at the very least, men and women have had various notions of what is normal or pathological in the behavior of others. The ancient Greeks tended to regard certain eccentric individuals as objects of the gods' displeasure. Those who acted especially strangely were believed to be possessed by demons. Priests prayed hard, sang incantations, and hoped that a friendly ear of some god would be reached. On the other hand, over eight centuries before Christ, a few Greek observers of their fellow man looked inward rather than to the heavens; wondered what specifically (that is, in everyday life) prompted the behavior of those who behaved in a bizarre or peculiar way, and came up with surprisingly contemporary recommendations—rest, quiet, sensible involvement with activities which engage the person's interest, and above all, an attitude of compassionate interest in the person's life, as opposed to a sense of awe and bewilderment, if not outright fear, and one of its expressions, hateful rejection.

In the sixth century B.C., Alcmaeon went further. He dissected the brain, showed that it is connected to our ears and eyes, and insisted that it is where we do our reasoning. He even dared connect the mind to the soul; they both are located in the same place, he speculated, and perhaps are one and the same thing. Soon thereafter the philosopher Empedocles was able to point out the significance of love and hate; in their various manifestations, which he took pains to document, they determine our behavior. His ideas influenced Plato, whose notion of Eros as a psychological force of great subtlety and influence may seem familiar today, but for long centuries was ignored by those who had any say in how people we might call "mentally ill" were treated. Hippocrates, no stranger even now to doctors, regarded mental disturbance more or less as we do. He rejected the notion of supernatural intervention, and instead tried to show how fluctuations in mood were connected to events in the person's life. He pointed out that fevers induce delerious states; that pregnancy in some women prompts psychotic behavior after the child is born. And very important, he took a strong and important stand on the rights of the mentally disturbed; they were, he held, entitled to their full legal rights as citizens of Athens. Further, if they could be shown to be seriously troubled (such as afflicted with paranoia, which he had described in rich clinical detail), the courts should show them special regard.

Well before the Christian era, guardians were being appointed by the Greeks for their fellow citizens, and serious efforts were being made by physicians and pathologists to understand what we would refer to as the neurological, psychiatric and, yes, sociological elements in mental illness. In fact, human behavior was regarded by a succession of Greek physicians as not a subject for theological or even philosophical speculation, but as a natural phenomenon to be observed, fathomed, and eventually, when gone awry, brought under control. By the second century A.D. the Roman physicians Galen and Soranus had developed an impressively rational and sensitive viewpoint about the causes and treatment of psychiatric disturbances. It was especially important, they held, to regard each person as somewhat unique, rather than to submit symptoms to a categorical explanation: if x develops, then y is the "problem."

Soon enough Rome would collapse entirely, the Greek city-states be but a memory in the minds of a relative handful of people, and the "Dark Ages" settle on Europe. Enlightenment would persist among the Arabs of North Africa and, in Asia, among the Chinese who accepted as inevitable—and not a matter for self-righteousness or persecution—a wide range of behavioral differences among human beings. But among the "barbarians," and later, in the Middle Ages, among the professed Christians of Western Europe, the notion of mental illness eclipsed markedly. Instead, the devil was blamed—or witches or "spirits." The English had founded Bethlehem (hence bedlam) in 1247; in places like that, or in Paris' Bicêtre, those judged mad were chained, beaten, starved, and in countless ways insulted. They had sinned; they had sinned grievously. They had caused the Lord to frown on them. They were in league with Satan. The Devil had entered them. They were witches. They were evil—signs of impending catastrophe. Perhaps Armageddon would, finally, come; if so, the enemy was at hand. The mentally ill were regarded as spies or harbingers of doom. In a world plagued by violence, instability, serious outbreaks of illness, as a result of which thousands inexplicably died, the hand of God and the hand of His rival or protagonist, Satan, was everywhere anticipated or visualized.

Scapegoats have not been the privilege of any particular century, nation or people; but those considered mad have at certain points in the West's history been particularly vulnerable objects of anxiety and contempt. And perhaps the highly personal nature of Christianity (God becomes man, then is persecuted and betrayed) lends itself to such social scapegoating. As one goes through accounts of the treatment of the mentally troubled in the late Middle Ages, or the Renaissance, one wonders who was more agitated and frightened, the confused people who were hospitalized—sometimes tarred, beaten, even killed—or those who hunted them down and regarded them as sources of contamination, infection, extreme danger. Men of learning and wisdom struggled against that kind of attitude, but with limited success. And when the puritans crossed the Atlantic, they brought with them a willingness to "cleanse themselves," in Jonathan Edwards' words, of all that is "foul, wicked, sinful"—certainly including the aberrant words or deeds of friends, neighbors, relatives.

In eighteenth century America, every effort was made to exert social and psychological control over the individuals who belonged to various communities. Men and women who behaved eccentrically or spoke strange (or dissenting) words were punished, then released. Prisons, never mind asylums, were by and large unknown. The point was to express disapproval—through the stockade, the pillory, and if necessary, the guillotine or gallows. The indigent were fed and reprimanded by strangers, as well as by those they knew or lived near. Those who violated laws were denounced and made to feel physical pain as well as disapproval; then they were sent back to their former lives, hopefully chastised enough. The peculiar or bizarre ones were treated likewise: a spell of embarrassing public contemplation, then a sober return home. In moments of panic, of course, witches (in the form of various persons) were pursued, found, and banished—not "for life," but through a termination of life.

In the nineteenth century, as the historian David J. Rothman has shown so persuasively (*The Discovery of the Asylum*), a new approach emerged to the various exiles, the poor and indigent, the lawless, and the "deranged," as so many troubled people were called at that time. Institutions of various kinds were built to feed and clothe such people, to detain them for various lengths of time, and—very important—to reform them. Today, as we look at the old and battered mental hospitals in many states, or at pictures of their predecessors, we are likely to stress the punitive side of that mode of "treatment," that social and cultural movement really. Men and women were herded together, we correctly insist, simply because they were penniless; or in various ways were unwilling to comply with the prevailing political and economic order; or because, like Blake, they had their own vision of what things are or (in a New Jerusalem) would or ought be.

In fact, those in the nineteenth century who fought hard on behalf of the downtrodden and ostracized, who were most sensitive to the plight of wayward and hurt men and women, were reformist visionaries, determined to build institutions which would, once and for all, bring Heaven close to Earth. They may not have had Blake's dreams, but they were not unlike some of our most militant critics of psychiatric institutions, among others. Dorothea Dix, Benjamin Rush, and others struggled against prevailing orthodoxies, often at considerable personal risk. They foresaw an era when poverty was no more; when the social order was just, hence not plagued by criminals; and not least, when agitated or depressed people, the *mentally* lawless, would also be brought under control—vanish, no more an unsettling presence among a people marching (as opposed to slouching) toward Jerusalem.

The large sums expended on alms houses, correctional houses, enormous prisons, increasingly large asylums (later called mental hospitals) were not regarded as wasted by those who asked for them and eventually secured their construction. The Puritans had dreamed of a "city on the hill," only to face, generation after generation, harsh struggle. By the middle of the nineteenth century, America could foresee its greatness; a whole continent was being opened up, and the harsh, Calvinist, messianic streak of the previous century was giving way to a new kind of meliorism—steady, noticeable improvement in the East, while the West, that "glorious frontier," remained always there: a source of comfort, a sanctuary for misfits, a promise of what simply had to be, given time, patience, and of course, a nation's commitment. Those enormous buildings, so grim and unsightly to us, were meant to change people, to help them return to an increasingly demanding society: more hands to enable more "growth." No longer were witches feared. No longer were strange and brooding people mocked and assaulted. They needed protection; they were wayward if not ill outright, and they could be brought to their senses, given rational and sympathetic support in a special environment.

To some extent the movement toward asylums reflected the spirit of the Enlightenment. Francis Bacon, in the seventeenth century, had urged philosophers to study "mental functions" as closely as other aspects of the "natural order." As one goes through Hobbes and Locke, one sees how subtle, psychologically, those philosophers were—and how substantial the lag between their knowledge and the "public policy," in words we use, of Britain or its American colonies. Locke, in particular, had developed by the end of the seventeenth century an extraordinarily sophisticated analysis of the mind's structure and function. He understood the nature of what we call "free association." He understood that we tend both to engage in reverie and to organize our thinking, depending upon the circumstances—*and* that the behavior we demonstrate at any given moment can be explained: this idea prompted that deed, and so on. But as his views became known, England's mentally disturbed continued to remain in chains, or near starvation; and in the Massachusetts Bay Colony similar people were at best scolded publicly, made a display of, and warned about God's impatience with those whose sin of pride takes the form of egoism and the self-centeredness that was thought to prompt aberrant behavior.

True, in 1766 a state asylum had been opened in Williamsburg, Virginia; and in England William Tuke, with the help of his son Henry, and the Society of Friends, had opened York Retreat—a sincere and dedicated effort to work with the mentally disturbed in a humane and rational way. But it was not until the middle of the nineteenth century that asylums became an integral part of American life—places to which a wide range of troubled people would be regularly sent. And if humanitarian motives were an important part of the reason for the confinement of such a significant number of men and women, the requirements of an energetic, hopeful republic were also at work: why ought people languish at home, become a source of concern or worry to others, when they could, no doubt, be changed, turned into respectable, unremarkable citizens who bothered no one and, incidentally, pulled their fair share of burden in a nation which God himself (so it was fervently declared in many sermons) had chosen to smile on?

Only in recent years has the confinement of "mental patients" been seriously challenged. At the end of the Second World War, when psychiatry suddenly earned the attention, if not (universally) the high regard of America's intellectual community, including its various journalistic media, a number of muckraking reporters, as well as some discursive and scholarly essayists, stressed institutional reform rather than the eradication of asylum life. The critics questioned the availability and character of nursing or medical care, the quality or quantity of food; in sum, they lamented the dreary, faceless lives so many men and women had to endure. The hope was for more expenditures by the federal and state governments, so that psychiatric hospitals would be places where patients received kind, thoughtful, and above all, personal attention. The ideal was a comfortably furnished building with each patient able to see a doctor daily, if need be.

By the late 1940s, psychoanalysis had begun to catch the imagination of more than a scattering of writers, artists, doctors. The profession of psychiatry, for some time quite hostile to Freud's ideas, became increasingly accommodating, then enthusiastically accepting. A new image of mental illness became prevalent. Formerly psychiatrists had been preoccupied with the intricacies of diagnosis and with various kinds of manipulative procedures. They had developed an elaborate system of classification; and if they could not easily cure their patients, they at least could fit them into one or another category: schizophrenic, manic-depressive, and on and on. They applied various "techniques": baths, diets, hypnosis, nitrous oxide or chloroform, and later, electricity. Persuasion was explicit; exhortation was vigorous and no cause for shame. With the advent of psychoanalytic thinking as at least a model for psychiatric practice, even in many areas of the country where there were no psychoanalysts, a much greater emphasis was given to talk—the patient's, as opposed to the doctor's. Before psychiatrists had been given to preachy enthusiasm, hopefully delivered with tact and encouragement, but not rarely with the vengeance that frustration generates. Now psychiatrists were taught to be wary, more silent than talkative, exceedingly guarded about what to promise (or ask from) their patients.

Freud's view of man, as any number of his followers and critics have pointed out, was pessimistic, an irony in view of the welcome he received in this country: the man who at last had brought hope to psychiatry, through the therapeutic possibilities claimed for psychoanalysis by not only misguided analysands, but all too confident analysts. He saw all of us as troubled, though in different ways; what separates us is not the presence of neurotic tendencies, but the manner in which we deal with them. The Puritans had talked of the saved and the damned. The nineteenth century optimists had viewed mental patients as flawed of character; somehow they, too, must become successful citizens of a burgeoning republic. In the past few decades we have been taught that there is only so much we can do about the way we think and feel—and at great cost of money and time; moreover, in the end we will still be, with respect to the psychiatrically ill, fellow sufferers, though perhaps more aware, more tolerant of ourselves, less given to inexplicable outbursts or periods of disintegration. Ours is a relativistic viewpoint, a psychological counterpoint to what Darwin and Einstein had come up with: No neat distinctions, no *this* as against *that*, but the insistence that all distinctions are, at best, comparative—only a matter of degree.

Freud's skeptical and sometimes morose picture of man's nature has been taken seriously indeed. We are all a touch mad, said Freud. We are all more, quite a bit more than a touch mad, say R.D. Laing and his followers. We go through a transference neurosis, said Freud, in the midst of analysis; thereby we get as "better" as it is permitted any of us to become. We go mad, says Laing, because we are trying to indicate to others, and ourselves, what we perceive, how we feel; thereby (if psychiatrists only realized it!) we come to terms with ourselves, are enabled to live as honest and open lives as is possible in this world. Not that Freud would necessarily approve of what Laing and others have said and urged. Freud was a cautious observer, and in many ways a conservative; he fitted his radical notions of mental function into a view of history not unlike that of Hobbes: man as by nature possessive, demanding, self-centered, and hard to tame—hence the need for a long spell of childhood and adolescence. Once, in his New Introductory Lectures, Freud permitted himself a messianic moment: maybe if more and more people became analyzed, the world would become a kinder, more hospitable place to live. But he directly challenged no political "powers and principalities," and he never tried to "apply" his ideas to the institutional structure of psychiatric treatment, apart from the recommendation that a relative handful of carefully selected patients visit analysts daily, lie down on a couch, say what comes into their minds.

Freud was not really interested in the economic, political, and social forces which impinged upon his patients. There were, he knew, the poor, the vulnerable, the hard-worked but underpaid. He was determined, however, to explore the *psychological* unconscious, as it develops in childhood; and had to take for granted, mostly, the process by which a society enters a household, makes felt in the unconscious of millions of citizens a whole range of values and assumptions, ambiguities and imperatives: the development of a superego which responds not only to a family's oughts or naughts, but those of a given political and economic order. Today a number of analysts—again, Laing predominant among them—lay emphasis on the *world's* madness, the lunacy of various nations, as expressed in their policies, to the point that the mad individual becomes peculiarly sane; others adjust to what is described as being so evil and murderous, whereas he or she who gets called "psychotic" or "schizophrenic" (and oftentimes gets carted off to a state hospital) is one of the few who dare indicate, through various symptoms, an appreciation of what really obtains, once various hypocritical veneers are penetrated.

In his more anarchic moods, and they are not infrequent, Laing would scoff at the very words "public policy." All he and the relatively small number of people he works with (or, for that matter, reaches and convinces through his writing) can do is withdraw from the madness of those who determine or implement "public policy" in favor of a particular kind of household here, an arrangement there, a commune or collective—the name means less than the approach to that mass of "others" who are regarded as, at best, hopelessly lost. Such a perspective turns around—in Nietzsche's word, transvalues—the meaning of any number of psychiatric words or methods. The sane are the mad; the mad are, at the very least, trying to come to their wits. Those who run mental hospitals, not to mention governments, are hopelessly compromised, if not outright criminals. Those who defy, protest, revolt, are struggling toward some version (for themselves, for others) of "real" health, as opposed to the kind most people think of themselves as possessing, or wish they might obtain—and doing so, reveal themselves to be deluded, nothing less.

Our various notions of what constitutes "mental health" or "mental illness" do deserve the increasing scrutiny they have recently received. Laing and others, so-called "radical therapists," are not the first to look askance at the way we regard those who are socially or psychologically deviant. Thomas Szasz's work is well known; he has emphasized the "uses" we find for psychiatrists; they help us in the West to segregate idiosyncratic or "different" people—keep them under watch, label them, stigmatize them, if necessary confine them. For Szasz, psychiatric procedures—diagnosis, "treatment," hospitalization—are social acts; a particular person is different, enough so to discomfort us. Therefore we act, by resort to a mode of psychological analysis which soon enough becomes a social and political step. Once such individuals were branded accomplices of the devil or witches; now they are called "sick," and if need be, "committed." Though Szasz has incurred the wrath of many psychiatrists, his views are not all that revolutionary, psychologically speaking. Nor are Laing's, or those of the neo-Freudians—Fromm, Horney, and Harry Stack Sullivan, for instance. Common to all those psychological theorists is a way of looking at man's "nature and destiny," to draw upon Reinhold Niebuhr, who would both accept and reject that way.

Whereas the Puritans—and in his own manner, a contemporary theologian like Niebuhr—embraced the Augustinian tradition, acknowledged unashamedly their own sinfulness, but took pains to distinguish among men, and, too, their societies, Freud and *all* his followers try to avoid explicitly normative judgments. They are not moralists but scientists or, if self-admittedly gone astray, social critics. Not that all sorts of implicit value judgments don't insinuate themselves into psychiatric and psychoanalytic terminology. There are, by implication, "good" defenses and "bad" ones, often called "healthy" or "mature," as against "primitive." There are "appropriate" responses, and "grossly inappropriate" ones. Or, for Laing, there are those who are candid, who seek after the "authentic," and those who dissemble, tricking others and fooling themselves. Still, the moral tone is indirect; millions of ordinary (and especially) middle class citizens of England or the United States might read Laing and feel grossly insulted by what he insists their lives are about; but he is, finally, a doctor who has made certain observations, followed by generalizations—as opposed to a man who calls upon the Word of God, a faith, a creed, a moral philosophy.

If one asks what it is Freud considered "normal," never mind desirable or important, the answer would be the one he tersely gave: "To (be able to) love and work." He was shrewd enough not to go into details or specifics. An actively transvestite, vigorously energetic migrant farm worker fits the bill—and if he-she happens to feel, upon occasion, moody, resentful or anxious, so it goes with everyone. Moving on to analysts like Fromm and Horney, and to the magnificently complicated yet pointed ideas of Harry Stack Sullivan, the emphasis is on social "pathology," on the ways a given society causes people to have "neurotic personalities" (Horney) or to be Fromm's "constricted person," "authoritarian" and "alienated." Sullivan, in rich clinical detail, describes such people; they have progressively lost their sense of personal authority and become pawns in a social and psychological "network" he evokes convincingly.

Sullivan, Fromm, and Horney would no doubt emphasize how constricted that farm worker is, and connect his-her sexual "pathology," the state of his-her "mental health" to the burdens and oppressiveness of a particular social and economic situation. Still, someone has to pick tomatoes, or drive the machine that does so; and none of the neo-Freudians have spelled out for such people—the millions of working people of the West—what they might do to live the more ideal life that analysts like Fromm suggest as alternatives to what so many of us experience. Fromm is especially disdainful of the working class, the bourgeoisie. As one goes through his books, one wonders what the man who works on an assembly line or in an office is to do, never mind migrant farm workers, who at least elicit, as members of the "oppressed," his sympathy. The really "healthy" ones, psychiatrically, for the neo-Freudians, are the upper middle class, socially conscious, psychoanalyzed, politically liberal-to-socialist men and women who work, say, in universities, or write, or are doctors, architects, social scientists. They are not "authoritarian." They have become "creative," "spontaneous," "flexible." For the rest, life is dull, dreary, common-place; and those who live it are, let's face it, the same—if not "sick." If the transvestite migrant farm worker somehow became an interesting abstract expressionist painter, his sexual life would not especially go against him in the minds of many socially conscious, politically liberal psychoanalysts. He would be a productive person, perhaps eccentric, but all to the good—a nonconformist in an all too restrictive society. If he were somehow to become quite conventionally heterosexual, and remain an efficient, unprotesting fieldhand, or again, by a magical turn of fate, become a vigorous, effective stockbroker or municipal bureaucrat or production manager for the Ford Motor Company, his chances for approval from many neo-Freudians, or from Laing, might well be low indeed.

For Freud, man is driven by sexual and aggressive "drives," only able to come to terms with them within certain limits. Briefly here, he struggles as best he can to tame yet give reign to his desires, all under the watchful, often stern and unforgiving eye of his conscience (superego), not to mention his sense (ego) of what is possible, anyway, under the circumstances of a particular life. If all that is familiar, it has to be stated and examined for its implicit assumptions—that there is just so much that any social or political order can do to make life "easier" or "better" for individuals. Something, yes; Freud connected Victorian hypocrisy and prudery to the misery of his patients. But he also knew that under the same climate of opinion, others (including himself), didn't do all that badly.

So, he never took after the Hapsburgs; never embraced a political or economic "solution" for international (or domestic) turmoil. In contrast, the neo-Freudians have stressed the role of all that turmoil (and inequality and exploitation) in the growth and development of individuals. For Fromm and Horney, man is not utterly perfectible, but he can come fairly close to all sorts of virtues. He can become neurosis-free, "generative," his own person; he can develop a series of psychological qualities which may not earn entrance to

Heaven but which sound, to secular ears, enormously impressive. Laing, too, holds out hope for man: through madness, through relentless and truly honest self-scrutiny (much of what is ordinarily called that, he suggests, is fraudulent, deceiving, misleading) one comes out clean, aware, a stronger person because he is no longer prey to the clever manipulations of others, be they relatives and friends or bosses and politicians.

The political extrapolation of Laing's ideas has been only sketchily spelled out by him and his followers—though one can more easily picture a Laingian analysand on a barricade than in an office of the White House or the Kremlin; as for factory workers in America or Russia, their presence is no more common in Laing's clinical "cases" than in Fromm's or Horney's, though all three devote much *abstract* discussion to the plight of just about everyone, except perhaps industrialists and generals, in the Western, capitalist democracies. And again, for all the grimness of Laing's view of Western man and his society, there is great promise, too: radical social change and radical introspection will give us a much better time here on earth. In so hoping, he makes more explicit and insistent the claim of Fromm and Horney: a combination of psychoanalysis and social activism will, if pursued with vigor, enable the most honorable and decent (and, let's face it, admirable) life possible.

Freud had no reason to believe that his ideas would become influential among those who make decisions about the treatment of hundreds of thousands of hospitalized men and women, or those who go to outpatient clinics, or for that matter, ordinary citizens who claim to have no serious psychological "problems" but do indeed have ideas of what they want out of life. As for many so-called neo-Freudians, and certainly Laing or his followers, they have a good deal of animosity toward the social and economic structure of nations like the United States, England, France and even feel with a certain pride like outcasts or exiles, rather than policymakers or candidates for the position of hospital administrator. Nevertheless, it is arguable that, in fact, some mixture of psychoanalytic theory, orthodox and modified and radicalized, is as good an ideological handle as any for expressing the implicit assumptions of those who make public policy, including the kind that determines the fate of psychiatric patients in or out of hospitals.

We are proud that we no longer run at the whim of kings or popes to convert alien people. We are proud that we are acknowledged certain rights and "needs." We require privacy. We require bread, a roof over us, a job. We require respect for our "individuality." Governments (not unlike therapists) ought to "help" people, respond to them. True, some leaders say that the government ought to be more demanding—summon the lazy, the indifferent, the discouraged, to idealistic self-sacrifice. But even that approach gets interpreted as "healthy," as "good" for the young, as conducive to the "maturity" and "creativity" which many desperately seek to possess. What American leader in his right mind would tell his audience that he is, really, rather indifferent to their various economic, psychological, and sociological needs, because man's time on earth ought be spent in contemplation of God, or death, or that he himself is a man without faith, however obvious and ornamental his religious practices? Conservatives, liberals, radicals—they offer different programs, but they all think of man as the center of things, and of his various requirements or inclinations as a measuring rod: how well does party X or leader Y of political system Z meet the individual's subjective sense of well-being? The point is not to guarantee "life, liberty and the pursuit of happiness"—and needless to say St. Augustine or Calvin would have many doubts about an emphasis on those "inalienable rights"—but to bend one's "life" and "liberty" toward the *achievement* of "happiness."

Not that even the boldest and most messianic psychoanalytic theorist has spent thousands of words on the definition of what "happiness" is. Freud shunned the word; he started out studying those manifestly unhappy, and ended up saying that maybe, given luck and enough psychoanalyzed people, the world would be spared destruction. For the neo-Freudians, or Laing, happiness, however implied or spelled out as a "goal," is only one of several objectives; others are honesty, authenticity, a feeling of being "accepted" by oneself and certain others. Or perhaps happiness, rarely mentioned, is the ineffable sum of all other realized "goals," states of mind or "orientations." Nevertheless, some men and women obviously live better lives than others; they eat better, they have better jobs, they smile rather than cry, delight in the morning's arrival rather than turn their backs on it. And insofar as it can, a government ought help the latter get a taste of what the former possess, or so a broad range of policymakers would say: directly through political action (liberals or radicals) or indirectly, by helping to restrain the excesses of one or another segment of society (conservatives).

Barry Goldwater and the SDS both favor "the good life" for all Americans— not as an incidental in some larger quest, but as something which one quite naturally wants with all one's mind and heart: a ranch in Arizona, or a house in a suburb, along with a car or two, and if necessary, a good doctor who pays one close regard. Mr. Goldwater hopes, *expects* that those who want all that hard enough will realize their ambition, and those who don't will be frustrated— hence, hopefully "motivated" one day, at last, to join the ranks of the more "successful." The SDS members say that there is every reason for everyone to have what now only some have—without the exertion Mr. Goldwater demands or the strenuous frustrations he is quite willing to accept as inevitable.

In contrast, Puritans were religiously obsessed; they wanted freedom alright— not freedom from want or fear, but the freedom to reform themselves, to show themselves worthy of God. In England their nearly frantic preoccupation with the smallest details of living—all in the name of God—had earned suspicion and anger from an established church whose leaders knew the virtue of a relaxed, practical involvement with the "powers and principalities." America offered the kind of freedom needed if men and women were to be turned away from sinfulness—we would, perhaps, say away from their very humanity. Those afflicted with what we consider to be "mental illness" were, like everyone else, objects of chastisement and reform.

America, in a sense, was founded by men and women who were willing to accept exile and the distinct likelihood of death in order that their vision of man, and their vision of a society, be achieved. But by a decade or two into the nineteenth century that kind of "puritanism" had been secularized—turned to good account by various burghers, intent on improving their situation, their position. On Sundays, one could always persuade oneself that success is divinely sanctioned. As for those who couldn't seem to get on, because they thought differently or had strange ideas, or fell into impossible moods, there was no point in persecuting them *ad gloriam Dei*; rather, they ought be beckoned, maybe coaxed a little, into a fast-growing world—the City of Man, rather than the City of God, but still, a "city" full of hope and promise.

To this day we persist in addressing those "others" who strike us as peculiar or bizarre with the same secular nineteenth century message, though we have been, year by year, losing some of our zeal—as if we ourselves have a few doubts about the world we want everyone in sight to join. Almost certainly this trend will continue. Moreover, by the end of the twentieth century there will be relatively few asylums left in this country. In state after state, psychiatrists (and police officers and judges) have been losing more and more of their authority over mental patients. I know what I could once do with a signature, was encouraged to do in a university-connected hospital in Boston, and what I now simply cannot do. One doesn't commit a person these days without long and hard thought—followed by a determined and usually necessary effort to enlist the man's or the woman's cooperation. In the 1950s, mental hospitals were bulging, were being built and built, were places where psychiatrists not only confined people but took them for "observation and evaluation." In the 1970s, mental hospitals, increasingly, are closing down, giving way to community-based homes or strong efforts to keep the individual at work and in his or her own home. Yes, the rationale is "therapeutic": the patient doesn't "regress" so much, is apt to "function" better, even if there is no "cure," in the sense that long-standing inclinations or hesitations really go away. But some day a social historian, writing up the twentieth century's experience with "mental illness," as David J. Rothman did for the nineteenth century, will observe that Americans progressively lost the very convictions that prompted "the discovery of the asylum."

It is hard to exhort or persuade the disturbed when the country itself seems, at the very least, unsure of itself. Most people in the United States, no doubt, have never heard of R.D. Laing, and if told his ideas, would reject them. Americans are, by and large, not prepared to declare themselves madmen, violent paranoiacs, dangerous lunatics about to destroy the world. Nor are they ready to applaud as potential sages those who go berserk or seem caught in hallucinatory, delusional states. But there is no great wave of self-assurance sweeping this nation, and it is especially hard, these days, even for psychiatrists to draw a firm line between the sensibly troubled and those beside themselves for utterly irrational reasons. Psychiatric journals carry article after article about the changes in symptoms: once diagnosis was relatively easy, because psychiatrists (like Freud) saw people who behaved quite differently from everyone else. Now patients come to offices complaining of vague unrest, malaise, nonspecific anxieties, a loss of nerve rather than a "case of the nerves," a suspicion that all does not and will not go well rather than a specific fear or worry. Now, too, an experienced and thoughtful analyst like Allen Wheelis, uninterested in a quick fortune or a faddish moment of celebrity, suggests (in *How People Change*) that old-fashioned willpower is, after all, what a psychiatrist must ultimately depend upon: the patient's desire, in the clutch, to *do* something, as opposed to sitting or lying down day after day—the recipient of another's words.

Yet, Wheelis also knows how hard it is for anyone, "sick" or "well," to know precisely what to do with his or her "willpower." Many so-called problems are regarded as "existential," rather than "psychopathological," meaning they confront each of us and have to do with life's inevitable twists and turns, as well as its severe limitations. The psychiatrist's authority is not diminished by virtue of some lag his profession has encountered; rather, he himself, along with his patients, feels closer and closer to at least one aspect of the psychiatric patient's existence: the doubter, the one who feels at loose ends or all too blindly driven. Medical students read hungrily books like *The Stranger*. Young psychiatrists, like Ivan Karamazov, question everything and wonder what, if anything, they ought believe. (See Wheelis' *The Moralist* and Leslie Farber's *The Ways of the Will*.) Karl Menninger (*What Ever Happened to Sin*) suggests that doctors, as well as patients, know neither what to believe in, or what to call wrong. Under such circumstances how are keepers to hold on to their keys with any confidence, or make decisive policy decisions, and how is anyone to be sure that he is sane—and not a fool, whistling in the dark?

All of which is *not* to say that Laing's vision has become a profession's, a whole nation's. He ideologically upholds madness as a way, potentially, to salvation—at the very minimum a cry for it—whereas, for most of us (as sensitive, socially aware analysts like Wheelis and Farber keep pointing out), it is a matter of not by any means being so sure of ourselves any longer, hence a significant degree of bewilderment, and at times, outright panic. Witches are no longer possible. Scapegoats come and go. Wars don't work to unite us any more; they even make matters worse. We experience simultaneously inflation and a recession. Words like "ecology" or "energy crisis" come upon us, out of nowhere, it seems, and with them news that the death of the entire planet may be as much a prospect as our own death. That being the case, we may decide that it is best to go easy on the man who mutters to himself, talks about the end of the world, looks with despair or apprehensiveness at strangers or friends alike. Instead, we turn on ourselves rather than make bold plans for others. We watch patients stay in analysis longer and longer; or join a "group," leave for a commune, take drugs or alcohol, develop a good, socially permitted "hate"; or go wild while seeing the "Exorcist," after standing in line for hours and hours—yet another "response" for critics of many kinds to analyze and analyze: Americans, what ails them?

So it has come about that the "liberty" many of us take for granted derives, historically, from a progressive loss of religious faith. The Puritans came here as if on an Exodus; they wanted everyone to build yet another Canaan. Those who resisted, showed "fits" or strange ruminations, deserved no "liberty," no "understanding." One resists evil, hopes to tame it. Not that it won't reappear, requiring a new struggle; but that struggle is, in fact, life. In the nineteenth century the nation became our God. Through expansion we would achieve a heaven on earth: manifest destiny. The result: restraint on individuals so that the national purpose would be realized. Lincoln once referred to "this almost chosen people"; a nation smiled upon by God had a right, an obligation, to tame its excesses—meaning those who were idle or disruptive because of their "thoughts" or "mental disposition."

In this century, God does not exist for many influential people. As for the nation, it has been criticized with increasing severity. Patriotism is hardly a welcome posture for many of our educated people who set and implement public policy. In place of God we have various secular pieties; in place of the Nation, we have proudly idiosyncratic communes, or social and political movements which in various ways end up being exclusive, sometimes by design, sometimes because an initially broad or tolerant ideological position becomes increasingly narrow or polemical. Under such circumstances "liberty" becomes everyone's demand—and authority, from policemen and teachers and mayors, from Washington, never mind God, highly suspect. At this point Thomas Szasz, or the editors of a conservative publication, like the *National Review*, find themselves, not necessarily with pleasure, on common ground with the "radical psychotherapists": both demand "freedom" for, among others, those people who have hitherto been called "mental patients"—freedom from the power of the state, mediated through judges and policemen, and not least, from psychiatrists and their various "commitment" procedures. By implication that "freedom" extends beyond the law's territory; "life-styles" ought be thoroughly various—and let those who don't go along die off, as surely they will!

We have become perplexed wanderers, proudly so. It was for others in the past to seek God, or try to avail as a great nation. Two hundred years ago Pilgrims looked upon American soil as a mere stopping place; ahead were Dante's Heaven or Hell—maybe, alas, Limbo or Purgatory. America could offer no more (and no less) than a chance for achievement: salvation. Those who strayed with nightmares or terrible bouts of despair, those who behaved in odd or bizarre ways, needed rescue. The search for God's Gracious Presence, the journey toward Him, ought not be interrupted by the Devil's workings. One hundred years ago, Kierkegaard's description of what people were like, how they lived, in cosmopolitan Copenhagen, was beginning to fit America's eastern seaboard, and even the outlying provinces: the self as a pursuit or indulgence (the aesthetic stage) or the self (and by extension, the nation) as a solemn responsibility (the ethical stage). Those who strayed psychologically in Copenhagen or New York a century ago also had to be rescued—lest a whole community, a whole purpose or "general Will" (on and on the abstractions go) be damaged. And besides, Reason, like God, has its power, its requirements, which each of us ought respect. (Needless to say, Kierkegaard was both amused and appalled by what he saw—hence his stage III, so seldom reached by modern man, he knew: the "leap of faith.")

I do not know what will obtain one hundred years from now; it is a measure of our times that one doesn't easily take for granted the very existence of this country, or indeed the world. I rather suspect that so long as we remain a political democracy (and that, too, cannot be assumed as a permanent "condition"), there will always be those who, because of what enters their minds, because of what they are prompted to do, will strike others as "different," even others grown quite accustomed to a thoroughly diverse (socially, culturally) society. We know that the walls that have kept such "different" people apart are being brought down. We know that in the future there will be for them open spaces, small places, halfway houses, a host of "groups," and maybe on a few blessed occasions, an unselfconscious period of contemplation, the "retreat" some ministers and priests embark upon. Only if the people of this nation come upon a new and summoning sense of their "nature and destiny"—one that possesses the ideological power that other "visions" have had—is it likely that any of us, "different" or all too "the same" (or "normal," or "regular") will be regarded in a new light psychologically by policymakers. Right now I see no such "vision" working its way around any corner.

Meanwhile, for thousands of men and women in positions of responsibility—policymakers in the "mental health professions"—there are the vexing decisions I alluded to at the start of this essay. Conflicts rage over the rights of the "mentally ill," over the correct manner of "treatment" for them, indeed over the very use of a term like "mental health." It is, at the very least, ironic, and maybe an occasion for a good deal of further analysis and discussion, when hundreds of millions of dollars are spent in the maintenance of a vast system of "psychiatric service"—while, simultaneously, and from a wide range of political and philosophical perspectives, the very definition of either "mental illness" or "mental health" (even the possibility of ever arriving at a suitable definition) is strongly contested. At issue are different, and often conflicting, notions of man's nature, not to mention his "purpose" here on earth. Perhaps, for many, concepts like "mental health" or its opposite, "illness," have served to blur some of those differences—or have become congenial ways for us to set them aside. Until recently, many of us could not agree on moral principles, on religious and philosophical issues, but we could make certain common assumptions about the "good" and the "bad," the "desirable" and the "unfortunate" through our acceptance of a certain secular ideology, of which psychiatry is certainly a prominent part. Now, it would appear, that relatively short-lived "consensus" is breaking down. Arguments are becoming heated—psychiatrists and much of what they (and allied professionals) have stood for are subject to new and intense criticism from many directions. Is it any wonder that a good number of those who make policy may feel confused—and ultimately, forced to fall back on their own particular values? Nor is such a development a bad thing, either, especially if a degree of self-scrutiny is first entered upon. Freud himself, no stranger to authoritative statements, once remarked: "Do not ask me to predict the future of psychiatry or psychoanalysis. The future always defies the present."

I suspect that we have now entered that "future." A certain period of relative ideological stability has given way to rising strife—even as social and political schisms in our society suddenly appear, one after another, out of nowhere it seems. It is no accident that a number of women, homosexuals, and political activists strike so hard at psychiatry and its various definitions of, or assumptions about, the "normal" or the "abnormal." At stake, again, are fiercely held ideas about, in Niebuhr's continually arresting phrase, "the Nature and destiny of man." Nor, in my experience, are those ideas merely tacit or vaguely felt. I have heard, day after day, working people cling all the harder to certain ideals and values, in the face of an assault which those people, rightly or wrongly, sense being made upon what they hold most dear. "They'll let them all out, the kooks and the nuts and the crooks, the murderers and rapists, the people who want to destroy society," I once heard a factory worker say. Needless to say, one can hear his outcry put even more strongly—the desperate sense, the sure conviction of many that something incomprehensible at the least, and quite often, something believed to be dangerous and corrupting, is at work in this nation; the sense, too, that many in the academic world, and increasingly, in the world of public policy, do not appreciate the depth of their feelings, the sense they have of being deserted, mocked, ignored, reproved. Often I do not at all agree with what I hear, but I believe it is unwise for me or others like me, and certainly it is not wise for policymakers of various kinds, to ignore how such people feel, and to fail to understand that it is not only intellectuals or political activists who have strong feelings about how one ought to conduct oneself in public and private, about how people ought live a life.

VIII

Planning the Cities of Man

Nathan Glazer

"Urban planning" is today more or less universally accepted as a necessary and desirable feature of democratic societies everywhere, and people called "city planners" are no longer the exotic characters they were once thought to be. No sooner had this new profession become established, however, than its members ceased to agree on what kind of city ought to be designed for what manner of American. Historically, American planners were committed to the ideal of what Ebenezer Howard called the "garden city"—a perfect union of rural and urban amenities. But more recently some planners have come to a new appreciation of the values of the densely-populated central city, as a focus of creativity in a liberal society. At the same time, observes Nathan Glazer, the very idea of planning itself has come under increasing attack, in many instances from planners themselves. For if density, diversity, and spontaneous change are the key virtues of the central city, planners cannot very well plan without freezing the city into patterns which it does not "choose" for itself.

In the end, suggests Glazer, the planners' image of "garden city" man has given way to a new vision of a diverse "urban" man—a being who chooses freely according to his own lights, and who in the process shapes society, and is shaped by it, in ways neither he nor any planner fully understands or intends.

A recent issue of the *Journal of the American Institute of Planners* (May 1974) bears on its cover a monster, with what appears to be a number of heads, endless arms, branching tails, and other undefined excrescences. It is the monster of planning, or rather of planning theory. The chief slogans and themes that characterize the confusion of modern planning can be read off along the branching and writhing arms and tails. One stocky branch begins with "User need," and moves on to "Disjointed incrementalism," "Advocacy, common, and action planning," with little tags reading "To the victor the spoils," "Don't blue print America—just make money." Another branch reads "National Planning, Resource Planning Board, Jurisdictional Planning, Feds., States, Counties, Council of Economic Advisors, Bureau of the Budget." Still another reads "Functional planning—Econ * Soc * Poli Educ * Psyco—all together now," and goes on to "Future oriented." Perhaps the most "robust" branch includes "Open-ended, future option (previously long-range), non-foreclosing (robust)" planning. There is also, of course, room for "transactive planning," "learning environments planning," "planners anonymous" on one branch; for "structured competitive planning" on another; and "meta-multi-multi-planning (formerly comprehensive)" flies off, detached from the monster completely.

The artist, Julio San Jose, seems very up-to-date, but he has missed "post industrial planning," introduced in a lead article by Kas Kalba in the very same issue of *JAIP*, and has not yet incorporated the themes of a second article on "Some New Directions for Planning Theories," by Martin Krieger, which suggests that phenomenology, language philosophy, and developments in linguistics also have a good deal to offer the planner.

Clearly American planning theory today is nothing if not (to use another popular term) "pluralistic." New styles of thought come—and stay, cohabiting uneasily with the styles of yesteryear, and of tomorrow. A recent innovation, "advocacy planning" is now so well institutionalized that the term is hardly necessary. It was the fervent and seemingly utopian hope of critics of urban renewal and other massive schemes in the 1960s that those affected by them would not only have the opportunity to go to court against them (which they have always had), to have their litigation fees paid (which the rise of public legal services made possible), but also should have the opportunity to employ their *own* planners, so that their opposition to prevailing proposals should be not only efforts to halt them, but efforts to revise and transform them.

It all happened, though not quite as expected. "Advocacy planning" emerged in the many planning disputes of the 1960s, particularly where there was poverty program money to support neighborhood groups. But it became solidly established by the subsequent need for "environmental impact" statements for any project that involves federal funds. It is by now a settled matter of law and politics that environmental impact statements should deal not only with the natural environment but with the man-made environment, not only with the open spaces and wilderness but with the city. They include everything about a project but its aesthetics—its impact on streets, service facilities, surrounding institutions, land costs, apartment rentals, and the like. Tense battles are fought over the question of who should undertake the "environmental impact" study: Since the study is undertaken by outside consultants, public money is thus now available in principle for what may be a counter-study.

It is fair to say that, at the moment, city planning in America displays a breakdown of dominant ideas, such that the planner no longer is quite clear what his skills and competences should be, in whose service they should be placed, to what end, judged by what standards. In this respect, the city planner is not unique. A number of other professions have also shown a startling breakdown in recent years of established modes of preparation and practice; social work is perhaps the most prominent.

What makes the present breakdown so striking is that it comes at a time when resistance to city planning as an idea is at its lowest point in American history. Planning was once considered a "socialist" idea. Yet, when was the last time any such criticism entered into public discourse? Planning in general—planning in more and more functional areas, covering larger and larger geographical areas, and with greater and greater powers—has been steadily on the increase since the development of public housing and urban renewal in the early 1950s. A city, to get federal funds for public housing or urban renewal, had to have a "workable program." The workable program had to include a master plan, as well as much more. As more and more benefits were added to those that cities could get from the federal government in the 1950s and 1960s, each was made contingent on meeting the requirements of the "workable program." The endless variety of housing subsidies, the different types of urban renewal, sewer and water grants, open space grants, beautification grants, and the like—all these required a city plan drawn up by a professional city planning department or by professional city planning consultants, and approved by other city planners for its professionality. Of course, it was the federal government that paid for the planning.

In the 1960s, as low income housing and black and poor populations concentrated in the cities, there was more and more concern for area-wide planning. "Councils of Governments" (COG) came into being, and the federal government could require—and it did—that every proposal emanating from the area covered by a COG be accompanied by a professional evaluation by the COG's planners as to how it related to other projects in the region. A similar development has taken place in the field of health care planning, where new facilities may be stopped, or at any rate, be denied access to federal funds, by metropolitan health councils. We may expect similar developments in planning for higher education facilities. While those whom we may call critics of planning have much more intellectual and academic respectability than seemed possible thirty years ago, planning itself is more solidly established than ever before.

Our concern here is primarily with "land use" planning, what was once meant by "city planning" before it began to include "social planning," and to intersect with educational, health, environmental and other forms of planning. Planners— as perhaps all professionals or all scholarly disciplines—of course have an inherent tendency to imperialism, to expand wider and wider the scope of their powers (or at least the functions and areas for which they plan), for all things are indeed interrelated: the various functions of government; the central city with the suburbs; the metropolitan area with its region; the region with its river basins, and so on. But at the core of the work of the city planner, the planner as related to the problems of cities, is land use planning—what function would best go here, and what there.

That such planning should take place is almost universally accepted. Land use planning is now freed almost completely from the charge of socialism, and is broadly accepted by every major interest group in the country. As William H. Whyte, Jr., points out in *The Last Landscape*, a very wise book on planning, major businessmen and establishment figures always are prominent when a new city or regional plan is unveiled, even though the uninformed think of them as opponents of planning. Indeed, it was such figures who used to give the money for planning; with the broad stream of planning aid funds available from the federal government, they generally now give only their presence, interest, and prestige. So generally accepted are the principles that planning should be broader, wider, deeper, more powerful, that it was only the *Wall Street Journal* (June 17, 1974), among major organs of public opinion, as far as I can tell, that did not react in horror when the House of Representatives, by a narrow vote, turned down a bill for nationally-mandated state land use planning. In effect, as the *Journal* pointed out, the expanded planning activities and powers of states, and previous federal legislation, as well as the flow of a variety of funds from the federal government, already make possible land use planning on a statewide level on the part of any state that is so inclined, and many do it. The purpose of the bill—hardly thought out—seemed to be to require some last holdouts (North Dakota?) to come into the fold.

But if the idea of planning is triumphant, the kinds of people we are planning for, and the kinds of lives we assume these people will want to lead, has become blurred. The broad sweep of Mumford's *The Culture of Cities* takes us through a number of types of planning (or at least building on the land), each of which can be given a name and an objective and has implicit in it an idea of man. The medieval town: Its purpose is protection, but it also provides within its walls for the humanistic handling of the small scale, for the enhancement of town life, for religious spectacle. The baroque city: It celebrates pomp and parade with its long straight streets, its endless facades and vistas. The industrial town: The dominance of the factory, and the bending of everything toward the efficiency of the factory, is evident. In each, one feels, whether or not a planner was at work (and modern history reveals a planner, a mind, or at least a sensibility was almost always at work, whether to lay out crooked and narrow streets or straight and broad ones, or to locate a factory, or to locate its workers' housing), a dominant conception was.

But the modern American city? We have few "specialized" cities, except for state capitals and university centers, for which a clearly defined function, an objective, can be set. There are few one-industry towns in the United States any more, and developments in our economy tend to reduce the dominance of a single industry in any city. A common land use pattern does emerge in American cities, with only minor variations: Gridiron patterns, the commonness of central business districts, of decaying areas around them, an industrial center or centers, older housing areas of various sizes and degrees of maintenance, extending suburban areas (the older ones showing on a reduced scale the patterns of the city), freeways, etc.

Even spatial arrangements of social groups in American cities, despite their enormous ethnic diversity, are remarkably similar (with regional variations). A common pattern of urban development reflects a common political system, common values, common ways of handling problems, a national economic system, a national social system. A common pattern of urban development reflects thus a great deal more than an "image" of urban life and an appropriate design for it. It reflects varied interests, varied political arrangements, a fixed heritage of invested capital and of political and legal arrangements that are difficult to change, and a good deal else which is in no way an "idea" or an "image." But it *also* reflects—to some extent, to some degree—ideas and images of American man. It is these on which we shall concentrate here, not in an effort to fully explicate the details of the urban environment—for as already said, more than images are significant there—but to indicate how these images have changed, who has held them, and to suggest, if only cautiously, what contribution they have made to the built urban environment.

It is widely held that one of the prominent images of man that has shaped the American city is the one that asserts the city is *bad* for man. This has come in many variants, as Morton and Lucia White pointed out some years ago.[1] There was Jefferson's fears of what large cities and their underclasses would do to American democracy; Emerson's favoring of Concord as against Boston (and certainly New York); Thoreau's favoring of the woods as against even Concord; Melville, Hawthorne, and Poe described the large city as dusky and fearful, a proper setting for misery, sin, and crime; Henry Adams liked Washington for a while, but in the end found every city he had lived in or visited a prey to what he termed the "Jew spirit" of the age; and even that elegant urbanite Henry James had little good to say for American cities. And so it goes, with variants, through William Dean Howells, Frank Norris and Theodore Dreiser, William James, and Jane Addams, even Robert E. Park and John Dewey. I will not go into the details of an analysis that persuades one that these men and women who lived in and worked in cities, who studied cities and led reforms in cities, were not quite at ease with the American city. They preferred the country or the town, and all looked back, in one way or another, on its virtues.

In a well known essay, C. Wright Mills exposed the small town biases of early American sociologists,[2] and, undoubtedly, the same was true for early political scientists. But I doubt whether we could make this case against American sociologists and political scientists since, let us say, the 1950s: they have been friends of the city.

There has been much discussion and analysis of the presumed agricultural and anti-city bias of American legislators; and even after one-man, one-vote, the beneficiaries were, as we know, the growing suburbs, rather than declining central cities. Indeed, one may say that when the big cities increased in population, they were hobbled by rural and small town biases in thought and in political structures, while in their decline they are hobbled by suburban biases.

One could say all that, and more. It is true that we set both our state capitals and our state universities in small towns, that the American dreaming of success dreams of a larger house, on a large piece of land, further from the city, and the dream of truly urban success seems now limited to the movies of the 1940s. And yet, I sense an exaggeration in the view of the American bias against the city. Without making the case, the fact is that between the 1880s and the 1920s, the cities of the United States were extravagantly embellished with great civic monuments, parks, railway stations, libraries, museums which the far wealthier cities of our own day can barely maintain; that leading businessmen (if not leading statesmen) combined with distinguished architects, planners, and landscape architects to produce a glorious heritage for very new and very raw cities. We have been engaged in the mindless destruction of that heritage for the past twenty-five years, but that scarcely reflects a turn against the city; it rather reflects in many cases a turn *toward* the city, the pouring of great sums of money, public and private, into the rebuilding of cities, or parts of them.

Whether cities are favored or not in the disbursement of federal funds is one of those incredibly complex questions to which easy answers are continually given, but a convincing case has not been made out. After all, until very recently the cities wanted the freeways as much as the suburbs and the countryside; now that they want them rather less, the political process is bending to provide considerable funds for more traditional urban forms of public transportation. I wish the turn had occurred fifteen years ago, but that was not then the feeling of most mayors and city councils and the people who vote for them.

As against attitudes toward the city in general, it is the more discrete and specific images I will analyze in their effect on the American city. We must, of course, speak of "images" rather than "image"; various images held by different social and professional groups at the same time, and changing images, succeeding each other in time. To the outside world, all the professionals involved are often summed up in the general term (used pejoratively, despite our new acceptance of "planning") as *planners*. And indeed, there is a profession of planning, with professional planners, planning organizations and publications and theorists and schools, and this is the center from which new ideas are launched, or more likely taken from other places, adapted to the needs of planning and planners, and then diffused to policymakers. There is also a profession of planning officials— many of whom are professional planners, but also many of whom are civil servants or lawyers. But there are subgroups, too, within this profession, of housing and renewal and redevelopment officials, who are often likely *not* to be planners. Then there are landscape architects and urban designers, the publicists of planning, of urban affairs and urban design (these latter not professionally planners, for the most part). There are finally those remarkable figures who have affected what planners think and say (it is harder for them to affect what planners *do*), the theorists of planning whom we may include, to one degree or another, in the category of the *anti*planners—Charles Lindblom and David Braybrooke, Aaron Wildavsky, Martin Meyerson and Edward Banfield, Herbert Gans and Jane Jacobs and W.H. Whyte. Antiplanners though they may be, they create the flux of ideas that affects planners and planning, because as a matter of fact their works are part of the curriculum of planning schools, and help eventually to form the thinking of planners. All these differences mean little to those who observe the built environment and who assume that, if they see something large, and something that clearly was designed by someone, planners are responsible.

One dilemma of planning, as of other professional fields, is that while the theorists in each field can demand the abolition of its institutions—schools, hospitals, churches, and planning agencies have all been denounced as the chief centers of miseducation, misguided health care, inauthentic religion, and poor planning—while the theorists may argue planning must fail, their followers, insofar as they are professionals and have a task and functions, *must* plan. Morale in a number of professions such as city planning is rather low, because so many of the leading developers of ideas in these fields have been so critical, not only of the common level of practice but, rather more unsettlingly, of the whole *possibility* of good practice. The unfortunate planner can solace himself with the thought that, by entering a planning agency and proposing plans, he at least becomes part of the system of pluralism and process of conflict and compromise by which the world moves. Indeed, what would the advocate planner advocate, what would the pluralist planner propose, what would the open-ended planner criticize as "too closed"—did we not have the official planner presenting, at least at the end of some process, his inevitably public, single, and closed proposal?

The ideas of the planners, this harried and confused group, denounced for creating our urban mess, yet insisting in their defense it was someone else who did it because others did not really follow or understand their plans, must be taken seriously, because while the planner indeed does not rule, he does influence, and in particular he influences rulers and decisionmakers and influential others—elected officials, investors, civil servants, publicists.

The process of *how* the planner influences them is still obscure and uncertain: most of the literature on planning describes how he does *not* wield influence, how in the end interests and politicians determine what is to be done. But this is much too narrow a view. It is the planner, in the end, who provides a good deal of the ideas that the legislators put into lawyers' language, as in the case of the national land use act to which I have referred. Even more significantly, it is the planners who then write the guidelines on the basis of which our grant and formula legislation is administered. The fact that nationally-mandated state planning did not pass in 1974, it will be said, demonstrates also the inevitable power of those who want private property developed untrammeled by land use legislation; but, as against this view, we would point out (and any developer can report), land development is already very much trammeled by mountains of legislation and serried ranks of administrators and boards. National land use legislation would only have added one more obstacle to be overcome here and there. It would hardly have mattered in many states. Its defeat does not mean land use development is unhampered, just as its passage would not have meant that all the benefits its supporters insisted would follow from it would really follow. The planners, I would argue, do provide the ideas for the legislation, do write the guidelines; those influenced by them do impose these guidelines. Their influence is real. The fact that the benefits that are expected to follow from this influence do not, in fact, always follow, does not demonstrate that they have no influence. Nor does it demonstrate that the interests can ride roughshod over them. No one who represents the interests would ever give this picture of his dealings with the federal, state, county, and local agencies who have the power to stop or hamper him, nor are these stories of the difficulty of development all crocodile tears.

But since the promised land does not seem to follow the implementation of the mountains of legislation and the ever more stringent guidelines, one must ask why. Private interests are one reason; another is that we do not have a means of utilizing a complex democratic machinery to implement ideals; a third is that ideals differ—not only between groups, but within the same individual (or group) as he contemplates the national scene, the regional scene, his city, and his neighborhood. It is interesting, for example, that among the supporters of national land use planning legislation was the AFL-CIO. Presumably, this means the national legislative office, which would naturally be influenced by planning experts in determining what legislation to support in their area, and which would naturally take the national view. Yet, local labor groups quite regularly support larger and more rapid development—whether of houses, civic centers, freeways, urban renewal projects, or whatever—as against planners with a comprehensive planning approach who tend to slow down the adoption of such projects, and who indeed, if they follow the newest developments in planning theory, must evoke through public hearing, organization, polls and other techniques such a storm of apparent opposition that large projects and modern planning approaches seem to become mutually exclusive. It was, after all, Robert Moses who was the bugaboo of planners (even before they developed theories of advocacy planning and local participation), and he was the one who kept the construction unions happy.

The *idea* of planning is, I would argue, triumphant, but that is because everyone hopes that planning will fulfill the more concrete ideas and images that planning evokes *for them:* protection of the single-family home for the homeowner, of residential environments for those who live in them, the protection of mixed environments for those who like them, better housing for those in slums, the availability of convenient land and facilities for industrial development for manufacturers, protection of the natural environment for the environmentalist, availability of large-scale aid for the planned communities of the big developer, and so on. But is there any integrating idea or image that pulls all these varying interests together? Is there a unifying idea that the planner can set forward to accommodate the wide reach of interests that are ready to band together under the general slogan of planning? Here planners—used in the broad way I have taken the term, to include professional planners, planning officials, planning teachers, theorists of planning, and influential intellectuals—seem in the past seventy-five years to have come up with two central ideas which have been put forward with the hope that they would serve as integrating ideals for urban development.

The first—and in itself one of the most powerful ideas of the twentieth century—was the Garden City, which we know today under the name of its direct if somewhat different descendant, the New Town. The idea was launched by Ebenezer Howard, a man of remarkable pragmatic ability, even though a reformer and visionary, in his little book, *Tomorrow: A Peaceful Path to Real Reform,* in 1898 (republished in 1902 as *Garden Cities of Tomorrow*). Howard not only launched the idea, but he was instrumental in founding two Garden Cities fulfilling his model, one before World War I, one after, both of which survive and prosper. More significantly, the Garden City idea became one of the important bases of English urban land use planning policy during World War II; and because of the enormous influence of England on planning everywhere, the idea has survived to influence planning education and planning practice in countries as various as Sweden, the Netherlands, Canada, Israel, Japan, and most recently the United States, which since 1968 has had legislation supporting "New Communities," our own modest and very distant descendant. Lewis Mumford has written, without exaggeration: *"Garden Cities of Tomorrow* has done more than any other single book to guide the modern town planning movement and to alter its objectives." Somewhat more extravagantly, he continued: "At the beginning of the twentieth century two great new inventions took form before our eyes: the aeroplane and the Garden City, both harbingers of a new age: the first gave man wings and the second promised him a better dwelling place when he came to earth."[3]

In practice, the urban growth of very few nations has been taken up by New Towns; in theory, it remains the favored way to accommodate the growth of cities and to solve problems as various as inner city congestion of dwellings and traffic, the despoiling of the countryside for urban uses, the separation of work and residence, and the "anomie" of modern town life. Even the problems of American race and income segregation—far from Howard's mind in the writing of *Garden Cities of Tomorrow*—is now seen as another urban problem that may be substantially mitigated by a New Towns policy.

It would only be a form of ironical historical justice if the Garden City came back to affect American urban land use policy. For the Garden City idea itself was deeply affected by American utopianism, American reform, American socialism, and American town-planning practice. Howard, born in 1850 in London, the son of a small shopkeeper, went to the United States as a very young man, homesteaded in Nebraska, failed, worked in an office in Chicago, then in England. He was an inventor—though his major invention was an idea—and in connection with his inventions revisited the United States twice. F. J. Osborn writes:

In his spare time the young Howard moved in earnest circles of Nonconformist churchmen and less orthodox religious enthusiasts, circles overlapping with others of mild reformists who in those days were largely concerned with the land question. Henry George's Single Tax, Land Nationalization, and many other proposals relating land ownership and land values to the problems of poverty and urban squalor, were the mental food of such groups. . . .
     If any one book can be said to have "triggered off" the charge accumulating in Howard's mind, it was Bellamy's *Looking Backward*, the American edition of which aroused his enthusiasm in 1888 and which he was instrumental in having published in England. . . . Its two basic assumptions—that technological advance could emancipate men from degrading toil, and that men are inherently co-operative and equalitarian—were the essence of Howard's own optimistic outlook, in which there was no proletarian resentment and class bitterness. . . .[4]

Presumably the heritage of the Garden City-New Town can be traced even further back, to the utopian communities of the United States, and the proposed utopian communities of the early French Socialists. But this would be to taint what has turned out to be an eminently practical idea—an almost necessary one, so necessary that one doubts whether it should be called an invention—with the charge of impractical utopianism. Further, let us not exaggerate the role of Socialist predecessors and contemporaries. Yes, Henry George and Peter Kropotkim were important, "but no little stimulus came to him," writes Mumford, "from his visit to America, where he had before him the constant spectacle of new communities being laid out every year on new land. . . ."[5] These new communities were being laid out by businessmen; and Howard had nothing against businessmen: he expected the Garden City to return a good rate of interest. Our own interest must be in what has become of the Garden City idea, where it stands today, what it tells us about the image of man, rather than with its distant forbears.
     Osborn, a follower of Howard, is somewhat unfair to him when he says Bellamy's two basic assumptions became Howard's. Howard, as I read him and his proposals for Garden Cities, was more skeptical that men were inherently cooperative. They needed self-interest to be cooperative, and the most ingenious part of the Garden City idea was not so much that it was to be limited to fixed size and have a fixed greenbelt around it, but that the profits from rising land

prices and rents would go to the community. He counted as much on self-interest to make men cooperative as does any modern corporation.

I have said the Garden City idea was inevitable. What made it inevitable, to my mind, was first, that urbanization was a natural and powerful force in modern societies, for reasons which are well known: the shift basically from the primary sector of the economy—agriculture and extraction—to the secondary (industrial) and tertiary (service) sectors. But this need only have led to further extension of urban areas, or to shantytowns—as it does in developing countries. A second factor was necessary: the growing wealth of society and the growing demands of people for an expensive environment and an elaborate infrastructure. While this could be (and for the most part is) accommodated by simply stretching out streets, sewer lines, utility lines, and the like, it is increasingly accommodated by new development on distant and cheaper land, and on an ever larger scale in order to get economies of scale. Of course, there are other reasons for New Towns—defense in Israel, to accommodate workers in extraction industries in Canada, the desire to limit the growth of large cities in England and Japan; but even in the absence of these specific motives—and none of them plays any major role in American New Town interest—urban development in the form of large, somewhat self-contained urban units would be inevitable.

Thus the expansion of urbanization and the demand for a fully-equipped and up-to-date and expensive urban environment, which can best be met on new land and by large-scale development, seem to be the chief factors that led to new development in the form of New Towns. After all, Levittown did not need Howard to come into being: one may say Howard's idea was in tune with the future, in ways that he could not foresee. Similarly, Mumford advocated New Towns for reasons that were quite irrelevant to the reasons New Towns later came into being. He was concerned with providing "an urban environment just as favorable to fertility, just as encouraging to marriage and parenthood, as rural areas still are. . . ." What worried him in 1945 were "the prospects of a dwindling population if the past tendencies toward urban concentration continue."[6]

But no ideas—whether those of Marx or Howard—achieve whatever realization they do because of the reasons for which they are originally set forth. Nor is any idea which requires practical realization in the world ever realized in just the way its originators set forth. Nothing so displays an improper grasp of the character of action in the world than to say, after a great idea has been implemented: "But that is not what we meant! The idea is still fine, the realization was just awful." Whether it is the institution of socialism in a variety of countries, the nationalization of British industries, the creation of New Towns, the building of housing projects, or the carrying out of a scheme of urban renewal, the *way* the idea is realized in a world of existing people, institutions, interests, and intractabilities must form part of its meaning. So while Osborn and Mumford, true believers, would insist that Garden Cities have still rarely been tried, and if they were tried as the founder intended, all would be well (Osborn: "Everything [the Garden City] has been used persistently in a sense entirely different from, indeed opposed to, the author's definition"), still we must look to its progeny to judge this most important single component of the city planning outlook.

There is an idea of man and of life that is projected by Garden Cities-New Towns: It is the idea of balance. It is a balance between town and country, to begin with; between residence and work (one of the chief criticisms New Town purists make of many actual New Towns is that they do not have sufficient workplaces, or, if they do, that too many of the working inhabitants commute to the central city); between different social classes. It is also a place for a balanced life, one that stands halfway between the cultural deprivations of the countryside and the cultural superfluity of the city. And, as Mumford empha- sizes, it is envisaged as a family-centered life. There are—even in New Towns with tower apartments—few places for single young people, or young couples without children. Thus, it becomes a child-centered community.

But once we state the conception of man that guides the Garden City, we have already just about stated the criticisms that have been made of it. There is no place for the essentially "urban" side of man. Perhaps we may put it more broadly: There is no place for the central city; and the conception of what happens to the central city in a fully developed New Towns approach has never been made fully clear.

We have no better guide to the fate of the central city under a newly developed system of New Towns than Howard himself, in the remarkably prophetic last chapter of *Garden Cities of Tomorrow*, "The Future of London." Howard asks us to assume that the Garden City movement is successful—new towns are springing up everywhere, taxes are lower (because the municipalities' own sites are increasing in value), and the environment healthier and cleaner— and to imagine the effects on London. He points out that as more and more people move into the New Towns, rents in London must fall. As rents fall, taxes must rise. This process is self-maintaining, for as people in London compare their situation with its rising taxes to that in the pleasant New Towns, more will move out. Under these circumstances, more and more housing will become available in London, at lower rents; thus, the housing of the remaining London poor will improve. "Slum property will sink to zero, and the whole working population will move into houses of a class quite above those which they can now afford to occupy. Families which are now compelled to huddle together in one room will be able to rent five or six. . . ." Finally, "the wretched slums will be pulled down, and their sites occupied by parks, recreation grounds, and allotment gardens."[7]

So it was already clear, seventy-five years ago, what must be the fate of the central city with the steady expansion of urbanization to newer areas, on cheaper land, with more modern facilities, and lower tax burdens. Note that these effects would follow—and have followed—even in the absence of expansion through New Town schemes. Simple suburban sprawl will do the job. It was indeed prophetic of Howard to see as one effect the improvement of the housing of the poor—this has been happening on an enormous scale in many American cities. It was prophetic of him to see the import of an increased burden of taxation on a city population become poorer, living in cities with heavier financial obligations. We should not fault him for what he did not foresee: the social decay that inevitably must accompany the decline of the city, and the political problems in the way of making use of this decline for a rebuilding of the central city. First, the power of those concerned with the central city—the landowners, the mortgage holders, the great commercial stores, the newspapers, the central city mayors and political machines, the whole alliance that makes urban renewal such a powerful political force—is used to arrest the process of decay, at least in some areas, before land values drop low enough for this healthy process of renewal as described by Howard to take place; and second, despite urban renewal, the process of decay, accompanied by social dangers—crime, drug addiction, poor schools, ineffective city services—goes so far that even when land drops greatly in value, no one is tempted to rebuild.

So, while New Town advocates were clear as to what they expected the fate of the central city to be, and while some crude economic reasoning supported them, their political reasoning and their social reasoning were awry.

In New Town thinking, the proper fate of the central city was to be transformed into a somewhat larger Garden City or network of Garden Cities. But what was overlooked were the positive social processes which would continue in the declining central city. The central city, even with its zones of decay, attracted headquarters for businesses, governments, nonprofit organizations; it attracted as a place of residences those who found a "balanced" life-style unattractive—the bohemians, the young people escaping from their families and not yet establishing families of their own, the deviants, the very well-off, the very badly off. All these, I would argue, were *attracted* to the city: for some, perhaps, there were no alternatives, for the well-kept Garden Cities had no room for them. Thus, while some rents dropped in the central cities, others rose, and London, far from being abandoned and rebuilt, is so attractive to so many uses today that its rents are enormously high, and it is being rebuilt (or was, until the recent recession) by private interests expecting substantial profits. It is not being turned into parkland.

The New Towns image of man, in short, did not accommodate certain important aspects of human needs: it was a powerful image, relevant to most people and perhaps to almost all people at some point in their lives; but it left out, at any given time, a very substantial part of the population.

Perhaps the Garden City image was at its height (even without any New Towns legislation) in this nation in the 1950s, when families were becoming larger after the low birthrates of the 1930s and first half of the 1940s, when 80 percent or more of new housing units were detached single-family houses, when suburbs sprouted with relatively little support from government. I have never felt that this suburban growth was *principally* to be explained by federal subsidy, as so many enthusiasts of urban renewal and of public housing for the poor insisted. FHA was no subsidy; highway building was for the most part demanded rather than imposed on an unwilling nation of public-transit users; and, as we know now, subsidy to central city rebuilding was inevitably far, far heavier per unit of building than whatever federal aids encouraged suburban growth.

But apparently no central image dominates for long in a changing society, though our tendency is always to extrapolate into the future what is dominant at the moment. Four striking developments checked the New Towns vision of the 1950s. First, the birthrate began to drop again in the middle 1950s, and it has been dropping most precipitously in the last few years—from 25.0 per thousand in 1955, to 18.2 in 1970, and to 15.6 in 1972. Second, the well-established overwhelming dominance of the single-family detached home—a dominance I took for granted when writing about housing in the 1960s—was reduced considerably: from 79 percent of all private housing starts in 1960, single-family homes dropped to 55.5 percent in 1972, and many of these are now town houses.[a] Third, the mobile home suddenly became very rapidly a major part of new housing; from 18.3 percent of all new single-family homes (if we include mobile houses among them) to 30.5 percent in 1972. And finally, the energy crisis of 1973 brought home to all that the heavier energy-using pattern of single-family detached homes on distant sites would never be restored to the dominance it had held in the 1950s and 1960s.

I have earlier pointed out how hard it is to disentangle image from necessity: what men want from what they are forced to accept. Earlier, it was argued by many urbanists that men did not want suburbs, they were forced to take them. Now the New Towns theorists argue that men do not want apartment houses, town houses, mobile homes, and public transportation, they are being forced to take them. I do not know how we can decisively settle these questions, but I do believe that necessity is not all, as desire is not all. Some balance is always struck, and the unexpected developments I have just described are to be accounted for not only on the basis of what people are forced to take, but also on the basis of what they want. Thus, I will take declining birthrates, more town houses and apartments and mobile homes, and more investment in public transportation as at least in part an index of the influence of changing images.

The Garden City, then, despite its overwhelming dominance in the planning profession, has not ruled supreme: there was an urbanist counterattack, as I will label it, one which emphasized, as against a spread-out, low-density, family-cen-

---

[a]But in December, 1975, as this footnote is being written, single-family houses once again dominate the new housing industry, now shrunken.

tered type of development as the norm, a dense development of the central city. The counterattack took two forms.

The first were the proposals of Le Corbusier for a Radiant City, a city of sixty-story skyscrapers, on cleared central city land, set at considerable distances from each other so that every room could be reached by sun, raised on piles so that the entire surface of the land (most of which in any case would not be built on, owing to the height of the towers) could be devoted to park, playground, and pedestrian walks. These were to be automobile cities—and automobiles would reach their destination at ninety miles an hour because they would ride on roads raised above the parkland, and would not have to stop for pedestrians. The vision was first proposed in the 1920s for Paris, but a better account of it, for our purposes, concerned as we are with the United States, is the remarkable book, *When the Cathedrals were White*, written by Le Corbusier after a trip to the United States in 1935.[8]

Urbanists have developed a tolerant and amused air at the imaginings and proposals of architects, who make visions without thinking of practical objections. One should wipe that expression off one's face when one considers Le Corbusier. He did after all design one city, Chandrigarh, though in the country most inappropriate to his vision—the enormous distances of Chandrigarh are suited for cars, but most of the population must use bicycle or foot. Further, his ideas were carefully thought out. He was an inveterate opponent of the Garden City idea, and cavalierly dismissed all American suburbs—undoubtedly to the outrage of all Garden City purists— as "Garden Cities":

We [Europe] always live under the burden of current ideas. While New York was rising into the air, London and the towns of Germany were satisfied with the illusory idea of garden cities: a rural humanity, living idyllically in cottages, served daily by a purgatory of transportation systems. Every day they sank more deeply into the paradox. And New York also, and likewise Chicago, since that was the fashion, at the very moment when a vague feeling drove them to set up, straight and inflexible in the sky, the first landmarks of the new times.[9]

The Garden City enthusiast will cry out, "but Garden Cities are supposed to eliminate the need for long transportation trips by combining work and residence." Le Corbusier, in his imperious dismissal of such a hope, is clear-sightedly concentrating on what a Garden City, in the ambit of a large metropolitan center and in a society with a free choice of employment, must *become*, rather than what its planners insist it *should be*.

Undoubtedly, it was an aesthetic vision that seized Le Corbusier, but it was worked out (somewhat) in practical detail. One *could* build densely and leave a great deal of open space. One could thereby save transportation, utility, sewer, and street-building costs incurred when the city stretched out infinitely into the countryside. One could also save countryside in this way. And, undoubtedly, the new skyscrapers expressed the technology of our age, and every great work of building by man, whether pyramid or cathedral, had expressed the technological potential of the times. This was Le Corbusier's vision of the past applied to the future and it was truly breathtaking: The pyramids were once made of sharply cut granite, sharp edges, gleaming in the sun! "When the cathedrals were white, the stone was raw from the blows of the axe or chisel, the features clean, the faces hard, everything was new...."[10] A vision: and yet, with some historical reality:

About three years after the year 1000 the churches were renovated throughout the universe, especially in Italy and Gaul, though most of them were still beautiful enough not to require repairs.... One would have said that the whole world, in a common accord, had shaken off the rags of its past in order to put on a white robe of churches.[11]

Many of his practical details make considerable sense. Thus, Le Corbusier argued that the street pattern of New York had simply too many streets for automobile traffic, which had to be stopped too often. His proposal that the city be reorganized in superblocks, and, of course, the further proposal that automobile and pedestrian traffic be separated, has been the proposal of every "practical" city planner, whether Garden City or Central City enthusiast. Le Corbusier insisted that we should not be weighed down in the dross, as he saw it, of the past. That was the problem of Paris, with its dirty monuments, its crowded streets, its offices in buildings designed for other uses, its regulations against building high. In New York he thought he saw a city half-emerging from this prison of the past—only half, for as he said on his arrival to the reporters, and was quoted in the *Herald Tribune:*

FINDS AMERICAN SKYSCRAPERS MUCH TOO SMALL

Skyscrapers not big enough says Le Corbusier at first sight. Thinks they should be huge and a lot farther apart.[12]

I feel I am almost playing a monstrous trick on Le Corbusier when I report that we do now have many skyscrapers in parks, even in Manhattan—I am thinking of the many housing projects, for the poor, the middle class, and the affluent, under public housing or urban renewal, that have created free-standing tall buildings, that have placed them in greenery, that have closed the streets and created superblocks. Admittedly, the full program of Le Corbusier has not been carried out. They are not on piles and there is not a full separation of pedestrian and automobile traffic. And yet, they have gone part of the way toward realizing his image—though one must report that these do not provide the most desired housing of New York or of other cities in which they have gone up. It is true there are enormous waiting lists for public housing in New York City; but housing projects built to such models in other cities have vacancies; one at least has, to great publicity, been destroyed less than twenty years after it was built;

and the middle classes prefer, if they can find them, older apartments in well-maintained buildings or town houses, all of which of course crowd the land.

Once again, as in the case of the Garden City, the advocate of La Ville Radieuse will react in horror, and say, "This is not what we meant!" Of course not. But the fact is that, in a real world in which Le Corbusier does not rule as absolute dictator, this is what you will get. The advocate may also say: "But you did not build these monstrosities because of Le Corbusier—you built them for economic reasons." One will have to answer that that is, in part, true, but we also built them for the same reasons that led Le Corbusier to design his radiant city: to free the ground for greenery, to open up every apartment to the sun, to create play spaces free of the danger of auto accidents, and indeed to maintain, while doing all this, high density on the expensive land of the inner city. No, the advocate of La Ville Radieuse cannot get away so easily if we test his proposals by what we actually have. And indeed, we could add, since much of the objectives for which we built these skyscrapers in a park could have been attained through other means, the fact is that the *idea* itself, the *image* created by Le Corbusier and other architect-planners enamored of the possibilities of modern technology, and calling on men to free themselves from the worn-out styles of the past, did in some substantial measure influence what was actually done.

One might say the idea of skyscrapers in a park or something like it is an inevitable consequence of modern technology, the high costs of land, the desire to maintain high densities, the desire to maintain access to nature. Kenzo Tange's plan for the city of Tokyo proposed an enormous megastructure to be built in a continuous line through present-day Tokyo and Tokyo Bay and which would contain all the necessary infrastructure for building, and thus, on which and in which sections of buildings could be inserted, with internal transportation through elevators and moving sidewalks or similar technology. The megastructure could be extended as long as one wanted in either direction, with nature nearby on either side—it is only a further development of the idea of La Ville Radieuse.

What was the image of man projected? Certainly it was man as urbanite, who wanted to be close to everything, and to find everything he needed rapidly at hand. It was man as conductor of business, talker in cafes, as sun worshipper, and, at least in Le Corbusier's variant, man as purposeful athlete using the grounds immediately adjacent to where he lived and worked.

What was absent was man as almost all men are for part of their lives, man as raising a family and living in a family. Everywhere in the modern world, where people have choices, those raising families resist the megastructures. The well-to-do middle class can make do in it, because it has other resources—a second home, cars, the opportunity for extended vacations. But even among the well-to-do middle class, only minorities choose this type of living in preference to the suburban home against which Le Corbusier railed. The fact is that while economic necessity and architectural ideology led to the building of large numbers of high-rise dwelling units surrounded by parkland, where choice is possible, where the citizenry is organized and makes its voice heard—in the United States, in England—high-rise living for families is in disfavor. Indeed, Congress has, at least on paper, banned it in public housing except in exceptional circumstances.

The office skyscraper in a park is rather more popular. Much urban renewal does call for large office buildings with a good deal of landscaping and room for car parking around them. A major development in Stockholm has transformed much of the city center according to this model. New corporation headquarters are often built in a park—but if one has enough land to build in parkland, corporations seem to decide that building low has more advantages than building high.

But all skyscraper-in-a-park building, whether for residences or workplaces, has come under attack from the second wing of the urbanists, the school that stretches from Jane Jacobs to Jacquelin Robertson. The argument against the Garden City of the second wing was the same as that of the first: The city needs density, and if it does not have density it is not a city. But it also argued against opening up the ground within the city, against clearing it of old buildings so that it would consist only of the most contemporary structures, enormous, gleaming in steel and glass, functioning efficiently. And the arguments against this replacement for the central city were hugely convincing: the city street must not be abandoned: it was a human form and a human need, as much a need as the sun and grass which La Ville Radieuse made available. The mixture of city uses—commercial, industrial, residential, entertainment, cultural, educational— was another essential human need, and it could not be accommodated in tall new buildings. Also a city needed a variety of small enterprises: artists, inventors, bookbinders, sandal makers, umbrella manufacturers, and the like, all of whom needed cheap quarters—such quarters, could not be found in fancy new buildings. If, as Le Corbusier proposed for his Habitation, one had a shopping street in the sky, it could not possibly support the variety that the busy city street, with its many passersby, could. Indeed, even the most conventional grouping of stores, providing less variety than a suburban shopping center, could not, it turns out, find enough patronage if it were stuck on the tenth or twentieth floor of an apartment tower, and was limited to the residents for trade.

In other words, the second school of urbanists pointed out to the first that there was a contradiction between the desire for *density* and *variety* on the one hand, and the *physical forms* that were proposed to attain it on the other. One needed city streets, and one needed old buildings, and one could not wipe the slate clean of them and hope to come up with the city of excitement that Le Corbusier wanted and loved—after all, it was New York he saw as the answer to Paris, not Los Angeles. (Los Angeles is not mentioned in his book.)

There was an additional twist that was perhaps the most persuasive single argument in Jane Jacob's *Death and Life of Great American Cities*: diversity with density made for safety. Filling up every bit of space with active uses made for safety. Parks were dangerous. The closing up of the street—the blank wall instead of the line of stores—was dangerous. This was a particularly American touch, and one which would not bother city planners in most other developed countries, but it perhaps suggests what has been at fault with every image of man projected by the planning professions—they cannot fully take into account all the social problems that an ethnically and racially and religiously heterogeneous urban population throws up. They design for family man—but many Americans (increasing numbers) don't live in families, leave them early, have longer and longer periods before marriage, or between marriages, or in marriages but without children. Or they design for the new urban, mobile man, who seeks diversity and excitement—but most people after all do eventually get married and have children and want peaceful and fairly homogenous and not-too-exciting environments in which to raise them.

For ten or fifteen years now, or more, American planners have been saying that we should therefore design for *diversity*. Not all the poor want to live in high-rise public housing, or in public housing of any kind; not all the middle class want suburban free-standing, single-family homes with lawns to take care of; not all the aged want leisure villages, not all the young unmarried want inner city apartments; and the like.

In a recent address to the American Society of Planning Officials, Harvey Perloff, Dean of the School of Architecture and Urban Planning at the University of California in Los Angeles, who has argued along these lines, and who as his contribution to diversity coined the expression and the concept of the "New Town In-Town," urges that we must plan for more varied life-styles, emphasizing the word *plan*, with greater powers to planners than they have ever had before. He realistically points out:

My proposition [for more large-scale planning to accommodate more varied life-styles] unfortunately presents a catch—"Catch-22": how does one convince people largely disenchanted with the results (or lack of results) of urban planning and development that still larger scale planning and development—even if of a very different kind—is needed in the future?[13]

But one can raise a larger objection: *How* does one plan for diversity, for change, for varied life-styles which cannot be predicted? To plan for varied life-styles, for diversity, is to say there is *no* dominant or stable image of man to plan for. Not only do many images compete; we do not know how long any image will remain dominant, or will maintain whatever position it has. I have indicated that, in the 1960s and early 1970s, a number of things happened that were simply not expected by any planner, or any image, in the early 1960s: The birthrate dropped, the single-family detached home lost its dominance, mobile homes and town houses achieved great popularity, the energy crisis undermined support for distant suburban building, highway building, and the building of glass skyscrapers. In the middle 1970s, it would be foolhardy to predict even as far as the early 1980s. We know how many people there will be, because the persons involved have already been born: that is about all we know. We are not sure at what rate they will marry or have children, where they will want to live, or what technical developments may introduce influences on these choices now which do not exist today.

Plan for diversity, thus, is now the cry: Open-ended planning, don't cut off future options. But there is a contradiction here. If they mean anything, "future-oriented," "open-ended," and all similar forms of planning really mean *less* planning—they mean we will *not* say this piece of land must be a park, and that must be low-cost housing, etc., or we will say it less often, or when we say it, we will be willing to change our minds and our ordinances more often. In other words, planning for what we cannot predict really means less planning.

It may not, however, mean less planning *activity*—that is, making plans, having hearings on plans, researching alternative plans, building models to help planning, etc. We do a great deal of this already, more than any other country, and there is no reason why we cannot maintain or increase the level of planning activity—strengthen the neighborhood level, the metropolitan level, the river basin level, along with the city, county, and state level. But when we do that, let us recognize we are choosing *less planning* in reality, even if we are choosing *more planning activity*. Indeed, the multiplication of levels in itself is a way for one to checkmate another, and for less planning that sticks—that really limits activity or that requires activity—to take place. That, I think, is a choice that is not uncongenial to many people today. Having had enough experience of planning, the poor may prefer their decaying slum tenements to what may replace them, the West Siders of Manhattan may prefer a decaying West Side Highway to what may replace it, the opponents of the Crosstown Expressway in Manhattan may prefer the existing lofts for small-scale industry to the broad expressway that will uproot them. More planning activity, as a kind of choice for less planning reality, has a large and growing constituency.

What is the image of man appropriate for this new development in planning, with its advocacy groups, its varied levels, its access to litigation, its endless appeals? Certainly neither New Town nor urbanist. Stalemated man, perhaps?

But stalemate need not mean disaster. Behind all discussion of various ideas in planning, there stand the economic realities. New Towns are not only built because Howard proposed them, Radiant Cities because Le Corbusier argued eloquently for them, and mixed and diverse city areas are not maintained because of Jane Jacobs's convincing demonstration of their virtues. They also serve diverse economic interests—the interests of builders, homeowners, employers, mortgage-lenders, slum-dwellers, etc. Whose interests are served at any given moment by any given project is a complex issue that the students of political influence, even after the most detailed case studies, have not yet resolved to their own satisfaction, let alone the satisfaction of others not of their tribe. But these economic influences do mold the development of the city—clearly. That is why we build high in the center and low on the outskirts, why industry seeks flatlands near transportation, why offices seek places accessible to young women, why the rich live near in or far out (some trading space for accessibility and some making the reverse trade), why the poor live in the oldest dwellings, and so on. As we observe how economic influences mold the development of the city form, I at least find it difficult to argue vehemently that a process of planning would have been better. (My *own* plan would of course be better, but that is not likely to evolve from a process of planning in a democracy.)

Certainly we must—and have—set political limits on development. Too much, too little? It varies. Perhaps too much in one place, too little in another. Is Houston worse than other cities of its type because it has no zoning legislation? It is a hard question to settle. Clearly not *markedly* worse off, because people, including scholars, still argue about the matter. Is Washington better off because it has such strict controls—people argue about that, too. (And we will not allow the position, "the controls are good, the way they are implemented—to negate the possibility of any decent modern architecture—is bad." The goal implies the way—in reality. In fantasy, we are all free of such complications.)

When no single image of man rules, or can rule, perhaps only Economic Man can be trusted—people doing what their interests dictate. Economic Man moderated, of course, by other Economic Men, working through a democratic political system to control them.

Notes

1. Morton and Lucia White, *The Intellectual Versus the City* (Cambridge, Mass.: Harvard University Press, 1962).

2. C. Wright Mills, "The Professional Ideology of Social Pathologists," *American Journal of Sociology* 49, 2 (September 1943), reprinted in C. Wright Mills, *Power, Politics and People* (New York: Oxford University Press, 1963), see pp. 540-544..

3. Lewis Mumford, "Introduction" to Ebenezer Howard, *Garden Cities of Tomorrow* (Cambridge, Mass.: M.I.T. Press, 1965), p. 29. Reprinted with permission.

4. Ibid., p. 20.

5. Ibid., pp. 29-30.

6. Ibid., p. 38.

7. Howard, *Garden Cities of Tomorrow*, pp. 155-156.

8. Le Corbusier, *When the Cathedrals Were White* (New York: Harcourt Brace Jovanovich, 1947. McGraw-Hill Paperback, 1964).

9. Ibid., pp. 36-37.

10. Ibid., p. 130.

11. Chronicle of Raul Glaber, Benedictine monk of Burgundy, quoted in Le Corbusier, *When the Cathedrals Were White*, p. 28.

12. Ibid., p. 51.

13. Harvey Perloff, Dean of the School of Architecture and Urban Planning, UCLA, 1973 Dennis O'Harrow Memorial Lecture to the American Association of Planning Officials, "Life Styles and Environment," in *Planning*, June 1973, p. 22.

# IX Economics and "Economic Man"

Thomas Sowell

It is often said that one of the crucial flaws of capitalism, as both an economic and social system, is that it is based on an overly narrow, even perverse, vision of human nature. Certainly many critics have recently been expressing their dissatisfaction with capitalism in terms of its supposed debasement of humanity to the level of "economic man." But does capitalism really believe in "economic man" as either an ideal or a reality? Or is the conflation of capitalism with the notion of "economic man" the result of a widespread intellectual confusion?

Thomas Sowell explores this issue and finds that, while modern economic theory gives the impression of relying on the abstract concept of "economic man," this impression is misleading, and has in any case nothing to do with capitalism. We are all "economic men and women," to some extent—but that is true whether or not one lives under capitalism, and it turns out to be a matter of indifference to economic theory whether we are or not. The protest against "economic man" can best be understood as a revulsion against certain aspects of modern civilization that have no necessary connection with capitalism, in fact or theory. It has much to do, on the other hand, with the weight one gives to the "materialistic" aspirations of ordinary men and women.

Politics has been called "the art of the possible," though electoral politics certainly may more aptly be called "the art of the plausible." Economics, however, really is restricted to what is possible—to the study of choice among competing alternatives—and with the knowledge that even the possible may not be achieved. For these and other reasons, economics have never been popular.

191

Conservatives, liberals, and radicals have all denounced it at one time or another—while using selected parts of it for their own purposes.

In recent years economics as a science has suffered from the more general criticisms of existing economic institutions, the societies of which they are part, and the value systems which they represent. Thus, those who question the desirability of economic growth, who are appalled by poverty and dislike inequality, who fear the effects of environmental pollution and natural resource exhaustion, turn their attacks on economics as the embodiment of tendencies and values which they find intolerable. Economics is attacked, not only for its particular theories or applications, but more fundamentally for its image of man and of social existence—an image which is supposed to be the cause of a deplorable reality.

Critics see in economics a picture of "man as nothing but the sum of his desires"[1]—a driven creature, rather than a conscious creator of his own destiny. Classical economics especially is seen as an early attempt to depict as "basic traits of human nature" what were only "time- and culture-bound value attitudes"—notably "the acquisitive orientation."[2] The technical developments of modern economics are viewed as an attempt "to convert all moral-political problems into technical ones, to be 'solved' by appropriate expertise."[3] Defenders of the existing social order join its critics in deploring the role of economics in general and laissez-faire economics in particular. The degradation of a stable culture into a tasteless pursuit of novelties is blamed on "the free market."[4] Those who defend middle-class values see the "libertine tendencies" of laissez-faire economics as ignoring the possibility that human nature may be "utterly corrupted" by the permissive economy.[5]

Individualism

The long historical struggle against despotism has left a tradition of defending individual freedom—perhaps our most precious tradition, but one which can also degenerate into a defense of individual irresponsibility toward others and a blindness to interdependence in both the benefits and costs of various actions and policies. For a long time, the vastness of America left enough elbow room around many individuals to permit the principle of individualism almost unlimited scope. But urbanization and industrialization have meant that we must now drink and breathe each other's pollution and have our peace shattered by each other's noise. Moreover, material prosperity has taken the edge off economic need for most Americans and has permitted us to consider our psychological or spiritual needs, which cannot be satisfied within a framework of pure individual self-seeking. The question now arises of a *modus vivendi* between the still urgent need for individual freedom and the unavoidable interdependence and interrelationship among the members of a society.

As an all-embracing principle, individualism is operationally inadequate and spiritually unsatisfying, even aside from its conflict with other values. Individualism as a principle tells us *where* the locus of decision-making should be, but it provides no guide as to what those decisions should be. A one hundred percent individualist might spend his whole life in leisurely wandering through the woods, or working day and night in his science laboratory, or contemplating religious revelation, or pursuing novelty and excitement wherever they are to be found. Individualism is a principle or a theory as to *who* should make crucial decisions rather than a philosophy that says *what* the actual content of those decisions should be. Increasingly, Americans—and particularly young Americans—are seeking philosophic guidance as to the content of their decisions and of their lives.

What can economics contribute to this philosophic pursuit? The answer is simple: *nothing*. Economics is a study of the nature and consequences of certain decision-making processes. It can evaluate the efficiency of various means of achieving particular goals, but it can say nothing about whether those are the goals that are really worth pursuing. Economists, as human beings, have had all sorts of personal philosophies as to what they and/or their fellowmen should be doing, but those philosophies are not economics, even if they sometimes turn up in economics books. Typically, economists' philosophies are nothing more than the philosophies of their time and place: In capitalist economies, economists espouse capitalism; in Socialist countries, economists espouse socialism; in Victorian times, they shared Victorian values; and in contemporary times, economists are likely to reflect contemporary values.

A serious problem arises when a rejection of existing values leads to a rejection of a certain system of logic and body of experience—such as economics—merely because its practitioners show signs of accepting the prevailing values that are under attack. With the questioning of materialistic goals has come a questioning of economics as the intellectual discipline most associated with materialistic pursuits. Such a rejection, though mistaken, is not entirely without foundation. Unfortunately, there are important groups of opinion-shapers and decisionmakers who do believe that financial interests are people's "real" interests and that other motives such as patriotism, ethnic loyalties, or moral scruples, are both causally residual and intellectually "irrational." Adherents of this view range from neo-Marxian theorists to hard-headed politicians who believe that delivering a good economic package to their constituents outweighs all other questions of their statesmanship or even honesty. This view has no connection with economics and, in fact, goes much further back in history than economics—at least as far back as the belief in the Roman Empire that "bread and circuses" were all that the masses needed. The decline of the Roman Empire, the setbacks suffered by Marxism, and the passing of machine politics suggests that people do want something more. Economics cannot help them find it; it can only help them weigh the costs of alternative options.

Nowhere is the desire for philosophic values and moral codes more strongly pressed than among a younger generation reaching maturity in a time of disillusionment and crisis. Because economics is morally barren, they often cast it aside as useless or denounce it for such "false" values as "growth at all costs." But even though economics cannot shape their central moral and social concern, it can nevertheless clarify their understanding of actual policy alternatives and bring out the implications of existing and prospective institutions. For example, the concern for nonfinancial qualities of life and for generations yet unborn is a philosophic value to which economics has nothing to add or subtract. But in translating this principle into concrete policy, economics has much clarification to offer.

Thus, economic principles can help explain why much alarm over the possible exhaustion of natural resources has little or no basis, though alarm over water and air pollution are only too well founded. Although American petroleum reserves may only be sufficient to last about fifteen years, this is not so much a geological fact as an economic artifact. It does *not* mean that in five years there will be only a ten years' reserve left. Rather, given the huge costs of exploring for petroleum, there is an economic limit on how much reserves it pays to discover at any given time, and that limit is about fifteen years' supply. In other words, there were only about fifteen years' reserves of known petroleum deposits thirty years ago, and there will probably be only fifteen years of known petroleum reserves a hundred years from now. But this does not mean that petroleum reserves are close to drying up.

Because there is a large gap between general philosophic values and specific social policy, economics has an important contribution to make in formulating policy. However, that contribution is in clarifying cause and effect, not in making value judgments. Problems arise when the very process of economic analysis produces concepts whose connotations have implications for moral and social values—or appear to have such implications. The primary example of this is the concept of "economic man."

"Economic Man"

While economists deal in "facts and figures," the great economists have always recognized that fundamentally they deal also in fictions—systematic fictions, used to organize and direct their analysis. As Walter Lippman observed, in a different context, "the alternative to the use of fictions is direct exposure to the ebb and flow of sensation."[6] But that "is not a real alternative," for "the real environment is too big, too complex, and too fleeting for direct acquaintance." Man is simply "not equipped to deal with so much subtlety, so much variety, so many permutations and combinations."[7] Some schematic view of events, some skeletal picture of society, and some simplified image of man are essential.

But then the particular kind of image of man becomes crucial. Our image of human beings is not just a passive reflection. The image itself helps shape the reality, as we cope with each other and with the complexities of life through simplified preconceptions—which are as necessary as they are misleading. These simplified images range from popular stereotypes to scientific "models." For medical science, man is an organism; for religion, he is a soul; and for economics, he is "economic man."

"Economic man" is always consistent, rational, and far-sighted in choosing courses of action which maximize his economic gain. He is a very convenient fiction for economists, who build elaborate systems of analysis around him, but critics question whether economists are always fully aware that he is a fiction—and that he is certainly not an ideal type of human being. "Economic man" derives from one aspect of modern capitalist civilization and even in this culture there are other traditions which ask, "What does it profit a man to gain the whole world and lose his soul?"

There are also secular traditions which find selfishness unattractive and financial preoccupations constricting. Critics have asked how economics can claim to be scientific when it operates on assumptions which are only partially correct, and then only for a portion of human life, for a portion of the globe, and for a recent portion of history. The narrow focus of economics has caused many critics to question how sensitive economists are to such things as the suffering of the poor, and how open economists are to ideas of different kinds of economies and societies, moved by different kinds of values.

Both economics and economists have a better record than these questions imply, though not a spotless record. Most economists, most of the time, are fully aware that "economic man" is a convenient fiction, not a reality, certainly not an ideal. However, the fact that so much controversy has always surrounded economics is evidence of at least a failure to communicate. Still, what is important is not to condemn or exonerate economists or economics, but to understand what economics is and is not trying to do, and how that fits into the larger question of the well-being of society as a whole. For, ultimately, economics is a means to an end—a method of analyzing and solving problems involving oil, ecology, education, housing, etc. In the course of analyzing these concrete problems, it may project an image of man, or of society, which affects our whole vision of who we are and what we are seeking. These images represent the connotations of economics, and often give rise to misunderstandings. But what economics actually is, and how people misconceive it, are two different matters.

The Role of Economics

The criticism of economists' methods and approaches goes back at least two centuries. In the eighteenth century, the conservative statesman Edmund Burke sadly observed that "the age of chivalry is gone" when he saw the rise of economists, among other undesirable types. In the nineteenth century, Walter Bagehot declared that no real Englishman "in his secret soul" was ever saddened by the death of an economist. At the turn of the century, Thorstein Veblen satirized both economists and their creation, "economic man," in a series of articles in leading economic journals. In recent years, the greatest satirists of economists has been John Kenneth Galbraith, whose election as president of the American Economic Association suggests that economists themselves have doubts about some of the things they are doing.

One of the problems in trying to discuss what economics is or does is that economists do many different things, and there is no authoritative word on which of these things is "really" economics. The best that can be done is to consider in order some major features of the profession.

One thing economics does—and does very well—is analyze cause and effect relationships. If you want to know the effect of a balance of payments deficit on an economy with given monetary conditions, economics can tell you. If you want to know the effect of price control on a competitive market, economics can tell you. The success of economics is even more impressive as the problems become more complex—*provided* that the complexity is of a kind that can be specified like an engineering problem. But if there are missing pieces of information—including information about volatile human emotions—then economics becomes very chancy, even with relatively simple problems. No one can really predict the stock market, for example, and those who manage to come out ahead on its ups and downs typically rely on qualities other than strict economic analysis. However, for suitably defined cause-and-effect problems, economics can be as "scientific" as meteorology or medical science.

Economists, however, not only predict what will happen under specified conditions, they attempt to say what *ought* to happen—and this is where most of the criticism and controversy begins. Sometimes these normative judgments are couched in terms of "efficiency," but this is little more than an elegant evasion. Efficiency can be measured only in terms of some predetermined goal. An automobile engine is 100 percent efficient in the sense that all the energy it does not use for moving the car forward is expended in friction, radiated heat, and random shaking of the vehicle. It is only when we define our goal as the forward motion of the car that we can say that the engine is more or less efficient *for that purpose*. Still, there is nothing to prevent an economist from simply accepting whatever goal is specified for him (by a governmental agency, a private corporation, a political group, for example) and working as a technician to achieve that goal with the least cost. The problem comes when he begins to refer to the achievement of these predetermined goals as greater "efficiency," "productivity," etc., in a general and unrestricted sense, as if it were an objectively determined benefit to society. What is good for General Motors—or the Sierra Club—is not necessarily good for the country.

A key complaint about economists is that they *implicitly* project their personal values under the guise of giving objective, scientific analysis. Whether this is conscious apologetics or merely an inability to escape inbred values is not crucial, as far as most critics are concerned. Walter Weisskopf says that economists' "implicit assumptions about human nature" do not represent "empirical and logical truth" but rather "an image of how man should be in order to function in the economy."[8] Instead of judging the existing economic system by how well it serves people, economics tries to determine "the kind of human nature required by the economy," thereby providing a "justification and legitimation of existing economic institutions. . . ."[9] Such charges against economists are at least a hundred years old, and it would be very surprising if in all that time there were not some economists who were guilty of this thoughtless reversal of ends and means.

The question is whether this has been or still is true of economists in general or of the leading economists—and whether it is inherent in economics as a field. To what extent is economics tied up with "the ethics of acquisition" in general or to capitalism in particular? How are economic problems to be dealt with when they involve non-economic values? Before discussing such questions as these, it is necessary to consider how economics itself has developed over the past 200 years.

Classical Economics: Myth and Reality

The first great work of classical economics was Adam Smith's *The Wealth of Nations* in 1776. This monumental work combined cause-and-effect analysis with moralistic observations, policy prescriptions, and shrewd guesses about human nature. It was also a polemical book, attacking the prevailing "mercantilist" policies which aimed at an export surplus (still called a "favorable" balance of trade today) in order to acquire gold. Smith argued that the wealth of nations does not consist of gold but of production, and that methods which attempt to maximize the gold inflow may reduce a nation's output—that is, its true wealth. More fundamentally, Smith argued that the elaborate network of economic controls which the mercantilists had developed were largely self-defeating, and, in fact, reduced the wealth which they were designed to increase. Smith did *not* select economic wealth as the be-all and end-all of human life. He simply dealt with the goal chosen by others and claimed that this goal was not being served by the policies they proposed. In his personal life, Smith was by no means preoccupied with money. When his estate was examined after his death, it was found that he had engaged in numerous secret acts of charity over the years, out of relatively modest resources. Among the classical economists in general, generosity and unselfishness were the rule rather than the exception.[10]

Long before he wrote *The Wealth of Nations*, Smith had written a celebrated treatise on ethics, entitled *The Theory of Moral Sentiments*, whose central theme was that our ability to imagine ourselves in someone else's place is the basis of all morality and law and is essential to the survival of society. But while Smith saw this as the basis for establishing enduring institutions of law and customs for controlling day-to-day behavior, he was not prepared to rely on each individual's own voluntary adherence to the golden rule. As a cause-and-effect explanation of how people actually behave, *self-interest* was Smith's central variable. But this did not imply either moral approval of selfishness or any assumption that decent self-restraint would accompany it. No work in economics—not even *Das Kapital*—paints a more sour and sordid picture of businessmen and greed than does *The Wealth of Nations*.[11] Smith's argument for laissez-faire was not that businessmen were good fellows, but that competition provided a better safeguard than governmental intervention, which he saw as typically pro-business, anti-consumer, and generally creating corruption and inefficiency.

While Adam Smith's personal philosophy and judgments are liberally sprinkled through his economic analysis, the real question is not how they were interspersed in a literary sense, but whether they are separable in a logical sense. Perhaps the best—or quickest—answer is that Smith's economic concepts and analytical structure provide the basis for a wide variety of later economic analyses, ranging from those by arch-conservatives to the economic theories of Karl Marx. There was a central core of cause-and-effect analysis, which was independent of the philosophical ideas with which it was garnished. Moreover, the philosophy which is attributed to Smith in retrospect is quite different from the philosophy he actually espoused. As the patron saint of laissez-faire, Smith has been cited by conservatives and denounced by liberals and radicals, largely on the basis of their contemporary preoccupations, rather than on the basis of historical fact. Those who see in Smith a justification of greed or a partiality to businessmen are not expressing a political or philosophical disagreement; they are merely exhibiting their ignorance.

There were, of course, some classical economists who were apologists for the status quo. The foremost of these was T.R. Malthus, whose *Essay on the Principle of Population* in 1798 was written explicitly in response to contemporary radical doctrines. Yet, out of Malthus's work ultimately evolved the law of diminishing returns, which is independent of how anyone feels about British society in Malthus' time or about capitalism, socialism, or any other system or philosophy. The next great landmark of classical economics was David Ricardo's *Principles of Political Economy* in 1821. Ricardo was a nineteenth century liberal, both in politics and in economics, but his theories were used to justify doctrines ranging from conservative opposition to unions and social reform to the economic theories of Fabian socialism, and much of his analytical apparatus was incorporated into the structure of *Das Kapital*. In short, there has been no determinate relationship between a particular analytical approach and a particular socio-political philosophy.[12] Sometimes, in the heat of polemics, the author of a proposition may try to show how the economic analysis leads straight to a specific political position. Seldom does history provide much support for this linkage, and logic usually provides even less.

To say that there has been a "scientific" core of cause-and-effect analysis in economics which is independent of political or philosophical influences is not to say that economists themselves have been objective or unbiased, nor does it even imply that the "scientific" analysis is correct. Even the physical sciences can make no such claim. Chemistry and astronomy were begun by men with a desire to prove certain preconceptions (the transmutability of lead into gold; the stars' control of human destiny) which few chemists or astronomers would still take seriously today. There is no a priori reason to believe that science has been right more often than myth. The great enduring beliefs which we call myths often contain some profound (if partial) truths about the human condition, and scientists have been demonstrably wrong innumerable times. What makes science different from myth is that science contains structured processes for proving itself wrong, while myths place themselves above such processes. In this sense, economics has been scientific, and the fact that economists have been proven wrong on particular occasions supports rather than undermines its scientific claims.

Modern Economics

Although scientific analysts are as susceptible to error as anyone else at any particular time, the great power of scientific methods is that their conclusions tend to converge over time, as they are experimentally verified. By contrast, different myths can only continue to war, sometimes figuratively and sometimes literally. The development of a body of tested and accepted principles in economics is obscured by (1) the tendency of economists who agree on 90 percent of their analyses to spend most of their time debating the other 10 percent, and by (2) the vulnerability of even the most solidly established principles—in economics or in chemistry, physics, etc.—to *apparent* refutation by exceptional cases. Even the law of gravity can be challenged by the observable behavior of clouds or airplanes; even in ordinary cases of falling objects, their actual falls do not coincide with the theoretical gravitational formulas in textbooks. None of this means that it is safe to step off the tops of skyscrapers.

In economics, it has been repeatedly—sometimes tragically—shown that governmental imposition of a price below the market price causes a shortage, and that imposition of a price above the market level causes a surplus. It is not absolutely inevitable that this happen, and clever people can easily construct theoretical circumstances or point to a few real instances where this seems not to hold. Overwhelming evidence is not refuted by special circumstances (clouds do not refute the law of gravity), but in economics some people regard the general principle itself as a special circumstance. In a narrow and peculiar sense, they have a point. The theoretical model which rigorously leads to the conclusion that price ceilings cause shortages and that price supports cause surpluses has abstract assumptions never met in the real world. So, too, does the law of gravity, whose formula assumes that objects fall through a perfect vacuum, even though no perfect vacuum has ever been created or observed. Only abstract formulations lead to absolute inevitability. But real life proceeds with something less than inevitability, and what makes abstract theories useful at all is that they are *approximately* correct even under circumstances less extreme than those assumed for theoretical simplicity and logical rigor.

For example, in abstract economic theory, it is assumed that every worker, employer, consumer, and seller, acts with perfect knowledge of costs and benefits. This extreme assumption is made for the simple purpose of avoiding the unmanageable complexity of estimating the widely differing degrees of ignorance and prejudice which are possible among the thousands of people who are engaged in economic transactions at any particular time. Yet, for the analysis of economic problems, the results which are logically inevitable with perfect knowledge become virtually inevitable with considerably less than perfect knowledge. If a major industry begins shutting down plants in Pennsylvania and opening new plants in Illinois, abstract theory would say that every worker in the occupations affected would know that jobs had changed location, and workers in Pennsylvania would instantly move to Illinois. In reality, a massive increase of jobs in Illinois would probably cause local labor shortages in the affected occupations, which would attract some workers from an adjoining state such as Ohio (between Illinois and Pennsylvania). As their departure in turn created new labor shortages in their communities, additional workers would be attracted from further away to take their place, ultimately reaching Pennsylvania where the laid-off workers would be available to make a move to Ohio where jobs are opening up. Probably relatively few workers would move directly from the shutdown plants in Pennsylvania to the newly opened plants in Illinois—but the net result would be very much as if they had.

Economics is simply a means to an end. What matters about the assumptions of economic theory is not their plausibility or symmetry, or even whether they accurately describe the complete sequence of events in the real world. What matters is whether the same *principle* described in the theory leads to the *same end results* in the real world. If it does, we can use it; if it doesn't, we can't.

What economics does besides making cause-and-effect analyses of discrete problems is to present a general framework within which many different problems can be analyzed. This framework or overall picture is called "the economy." An economy might seem at first to be simply a system of production and distribution. However, the Garden of Eden was a system of production and distribution; so was Sir Thomas More's picture of Utopia—but an Eden or a Utopia is *not* an economy. In an economy, the total resources available are insufficient to satisfy people's desires. Each economic system—whether capitalism, socialism, feudalism—must use various institutional devices to *prevent* each individual from getting all he wants. Every economy must *deny* access to consumer goods and productive resources to many who seek them, and each economy must have some method of choosing who shall in fact use or control them. Each economic system tends to emphasize the benefits it brings, but what makes it an economic system in the first place is its systematic pattern of denial. This denial is inherent in the circumstances, and the man-made institutions only determine the particular form of that denial.

This all seems as simple and obvious that its implications are easily overlooked. For example, social commentators often point to particular "unmet needs" as evidence of the "failures" of the economic system. But, since economic systems are all basically systems of rationing—via money, government policy, nepotism—*any* successfully functioning economic system must have such "unmet needs" *everywhere*, rather than completely satiating the desires for some things while leaving other things even more drastically short. Rational arguments may be made as to which needs have been favored and which have been curtailed, but "unmet needs" are inherent in any economy.

One of the political problems with *any* man-made system of denial is that people come to believe that the denial originates in the particular system, or in the particular policies of officials, when it is in fact inherent in the circumstances. An obvious case is wartime rationing. The available goods divided by the population determines the limit of average individual consumption. A rational rationing system can therefore issue coupons entitling each consumer to that amount. But this average amount might be less than people are used to consuming, and could, therefore, be regarded by the public as "unreasonable." Political pressures for larger amounts (more "reasonable," "fair," or "equitable" amounts) can force the government to issue more ration coupons, but this creates no more goods and simply forces a breakdown of the rationing system. An excess number of coupons means more potential buyers than sellers, long lines, favoritism (including bribery), quality deterioration, and a reduction or elimination of auxiliary services—and all this on top of the inherent reduction of consumption.

Had the same goods been rationed by price rises, similar problems could have arisen if the public has similar misconceptions of the situation. Successful rationing by price increases requires that the price rise high enough to force consumers voluntarily to cut back consumption as a result of the expensiveness of the good in question. But if the public regards the price increase as "unreasonable," it can cause the government to impose legal limits on how high the price can go. Often such price controls have strong moralistic overtones, as in the "profiteering" of those who are "taking advantage" of national urgencies, and there are sometimes intimations of plots which have supposedly caused the whole problem. The search for villains is always more exciting than an analysis of causation. Moreover, there is seldom a complete absence of villains. But since villians are with us always, they may have little explanatory value for particular problems.

Economics, at its best, can help us understand the essential nature of the process of denial underlying the social institutions peculiar to a particular culture and a particular period of history. The classic definition of economics is that it is the study of the allocation of scarce resources which have alternative uses. "Resources" here is not simply a genteel word for money. On the contrary, for the economy as a whole it is not money that is scarce (the government can print as much as it wants) but *real* resources—brawn, time, talent, minerals, etc. It is these scarce resources which determine the limits of output and the human costs of approaching those limits. If resources were not scarce, there would be no problem—that is, no "unmet needs" anywhere. If resources had no alternative uses, then each resource could be used to produce as much of its unique product as it could. But in a complex world where the same resource (coal) can be used to make steel, generate electricity, or manufacture dyes, we are faced with the basic problem of economics—the optimum allocation of scarce resources which have alternative uses.

The Nature of Rationing and the Nature of Man

Scarcity and alternative uses have weighty implications. Scarcity means that there are *no* "solutions" to economic problems. There are possible *resolutions* of varying degrees of acceptability. But under any rational resolution, the inevitable "unmet needs" still offer a fertile field for everything from intellectual panaceas to political "leadership." Indeed, these panaceas and "leadership" may be sufficiently irrational to actually solve some particular problem "at all costs" in terms of resources far more urgently needed to keep other problems under control. With sufficient single-minded determination any city can even solve its downtown traffic and parking problems. But to make every street a freely flowing artery and have ample parking available to all in the downtown area would involve such massive spending as to leave little or nothing for the education of children, the hospitalization of the indigent, or the provision of clean drinking water. It is, of course, unlikely that any particular solution will be pushed to this ultimate limit. What is far more likely is that intellectuals and politicians will continue to offer programs to "solve" social problems as if they were academic exercises with answers in the back of the book. In short, no optimal allocation of scarce resources is realistically possible; even if momentarily achieved, the inevitable "unmet needs" would bring a reallocation in hopes of a "solution" to "social problems." For intellectuals and politicians, the mere *search* for "solutions" can be a full-time job—indeed a prosperous career—whether what they actually propose or do makes matters better or worse.

Alternative uses have far-reaching implications as well. Once we fully accept the fact that every use of resources is at the expense of some other use, we can no longer say that (1) we have moved beyond "scarcity" to "abundance"; that (2) we should not "put a price" on some desirable good, such as education or opera; that (3) we must meet our "real needs" and not indulge in "waste"; or that (4) there are "non-economic" values to take into account.

Scarcity and the principles involved in coping with it remain the same as long as what we want exceeds what we have or can get. Increasing prosperity has great social impact, but it does not change the basic principles of economics. Moreover, the notion that we have entered a "new era" is itself quite old. In 1815, Sismondi wondered what we could possibly do with more production, now that we had already met the essential needs of man.[13]

The objection to "putting a price" on something socially valuable or esthetically special ignores the fact that prices are not something which we simply choose to "put" on things. The ultimate "price" of any good in the economy consists of the resources used to produce it, and their price, in turn, consists of the *other* goods they could have produced instead. These are facts of technology, not philosophical principles, or even features of any particular economic system or economic policy. Everything necessarily has a price in this sense, whether or not social institutions cause money to be collected from individual consumers. The pricing system under capitalism is not simply a mechanism for transferring wealth among persons; it is one way of carrying out the rationing function inherent in all forms of economic systems. To refuse to "put a price" on something does not take it out of the economic realm. It simply allows it to be used in that realm past the point where consumers themselves would have stopped if presented with the real alternative facing the economy as a whole.

Thus far we have avoided what is perhaps the most difficult problem in economics—both in theory and in practice. Alternative uses of a resource means that "output" consists of different things, even from a given input. *How then can we decide what is "more" or "better" output?* In turn, how can we decide what is a more efficient use of resources, a wiser economic policy, or a better economic system?

There is no general answer, without further qualifications or additional assumptions. Obviously if policy A leads to *more of everything* than policy B, we can say which is more efficient—but this is almost never the case. More often, one course of action leads to more aerospace activity, less housing, more education, less medical care, etc. Among the possible ways of resolving the question of overall efficiency would be (1) a democratic vote, (2) an establishment of value priorities by some individual or set of individuals, or (3) individual choices according to individual schemes of values.

A democratic decision on values implies that each person chooses values, not for himself, but for everyone, with the result an "average" set of values for all. Values imposed from the top down are another possibility, and while this would probably be unacceptable in this explicit form to most Americans, it is the implicit principle involved when moralists, politicians, and others denounce economic "waste" which does not meet our "real needs." Obviously, the activities described as "waste" exist only because those engaged in them prefer them to activities described by others as "real needs." Individual choices by individual priorities mean, philosophically, the abandonment of any effort to make the economy pursue "real" or transcendant values. Intellectually, it allows economists to construct analyses in which each person is as "well off" as possible (given the inherent constraints of technology and resources), according to his own individual scheme of values, and to use that as a benchmark for optimal resource allocation. There is no logically compelling reason to use this approach. But once accepted, it does allow an objective basis for judging the efficiency of particular economic actions, policies, and—in principle—systems. Economic problems can then be reduced to the mathematical principles involved in maximizing subject to specified constraints.

The economists' preoccupation with "maximizing" has been widely misunderstood, especially as regards the image of man it presents. It has seemed to be a philosophical justification of selfishness and greed. In fact, it has been an intellectual expedient for coping with the ultimately insoluble problem of comparing values among differing individuals. More importantly, the economic principles of maximization do not imply selfishness or greed, or the existing economic system, or even the use of money. The most unselfish philanthropist, if he wants to do what is best for his fellowman and not merely divest himself of wealth, must follow the same general principles of maximization as the most greedy speculator, though what the philanthropist is trying to maximize is the return to society from his programs and grants. The most benevolent ruler must pick and choose where to invest the time, material, and talent at his disposal along lines very similar to an investor choosing among alternative places to put his money. The most socially conscious hospital administrator is making essentially economic decisions when he decides how many of his staff to assign to the emergency room and how many to assign to the wards and the clinics. All are maximizing subject to constraints.

The image of man suggested by the economists' maximization theories has been far too rational, calculating, and amoral for many critics. A businessman who "maximizes profit" conjures up a Scrooge or a robber baron, when economic maximization *subject to constraints* means: within bounds set by the competition of fellow-businessmen, the requirements of the law, and a sense of common decency. All that "maximization" means in this sense is that—other things being equal—the businessman prefers making more money rather than less. When people speak in the popular sense of "maximizing profit," they usually imply *without regard* to ordinary legal or moral standards. This is not what economic analysis implies.

The eternal calculating suggested by the "economic man" stereotype is overdrawn and unnecessary for economic analysis. Indeed, economic principles themselves suggest a limit to how much deliberate calculation to engage in. Since deliberate calculation has a cost in terms of time and emotional pressures, there is some optimal amount of calculation, covering major decisions, but leaving less weighty actions to be determined by rules of thumb, habit, tradition, or snap judgments. It is not rational to be too rational.

The notion that there are "non-economic values" to be taken into account in economic decision-making reveals a fundamental confusion about the nature of economics. Of course, there are "non-economic values." Indeed *there are only non-economic values.* Economics is simply a method of weighing one value against another. It is not a value in and of itself.

Many critics of the extreme individualism sanctioned by economic conceptions of optimality say that the economists' scheme overlooks the role of pervasive supra-individual forces—advertising, fads, traditions, and herd instinct—which dominate many economic decisions. Liberals deplore the effect of advertising and conservatives deplore the vulgarization of tastes. Thorstein Veblen argued that if decision-making were in fact as individualistic as depicted by economists, "the institutional fabric would not last over night,"[14] for there would be no mosaic of shared values which we call a culture. This leads ultimately to questions of free will or, more modestly, to questions about the decision-making process.

Decision-Making and Personification

Edmund Burke once observed that, "We are afraid to put men to live and trade each on his own private stock of reason; because we suspect that the stock in each man is small, and that the individuals would do better to avail themselves of the general bank and capital of nations and of ages."[15] This is in fact what most people have always done. Many of the crucial decisions of their lives—whom to marry, where to live, what career to follow—may reflect special knowledge or tastes peculiar to the individual, but usually the less momentous decisions (how to dress, what form of speech to use) are heavily influenced by the society or social class in which they live. In short, culture is one way of economizing on decision-making. We simply are not prepared to invest the same time or emotion in choosing footwear as we put into choosing a mate, a home, or a career, so we allow "society" to play a more dominant role in the less critical choices than in those choices which affect the individual more deeply as an individual. The individual has not relinquished his free will in these cases, which may constitute the mass of his decisions. Free will does not imply individual caprice in a vacuum. One of the exercises of free will is to determine where and to what extent a particular decision requires inputs of individual time and values, and where it is just as well to rely on existing cultural patterns and beliefs—not because the latter are infallible, but because they cost so much less in mental fatigue and emotional drain.

Although it can be said that "society" makes many decisions in some general, allegorical sense, it is a fatal mistake to reason as if society really does make decisions where it clearly does not. The actual locus of decision-making power is crucial for understanding why the decisions are what they are and lead to the consequences they do. Pollution of air and water occur not because "society" is "irrational," but because the individuals and organizations who actually make the decisions to pollute do not pay the costs entailed by those decisions. "Society" does not decide to pollute or not to pollute; particular subsets of individuals make those decisions—and under both capitalism and socialism, the economic institutions do not convey the resulting costs to those who create them, but diffuse them over the general population. A special governmental decision can be made to so modify existing institutions as to charge the costs directly to those who create them—via fines, taxes, or differential subsidies— thereby forcing those decisions to change. Alternatively, the government could in fact make pollution a decision of "society" by having a referendum on pollution policy or ad hoc "public representation" on particular issues as they arise. The latter would be a profound change from what happens already under either capitalism or socialism, and while there is no a priori reason to avoid profound changes, it is nevertheless very advisable to know that it *is* a profound change—that is not just a question of "society" deciding between A and B. Rather, it is a plan to move the whole locus of decision-making from individuals or organizations to society at large. The wisdom of such a change depends upon the nature of the issues to be decided.

For some elements of a decision, individuals have a knowledge which can never be had by a remote expert. Knowledge of the relative values of things to those actually using them is knowledge keenly felt at the individual level, but virtually impossible to acquire directly or assess at the distant expert level. Knowledge of details is almost equally difficult for the distant expert to acquire, aggregate and evaluate. For example, heads of lettuce differ greatly from one another according to their individual age and storage conditions, and these change from day to day, if not from hour to hour. To the expert, there are 100,000 heads of lettuce in a certain province, but only the millions of individual consumers themselves can evaluate how many are in excellent condition and how many are so bad that they are hardly edible. (This is one reason why it is so difficult to centrally plan the production and distribution of lettuce, while it is relatively easy to centrally plan the production and distribution of steel and other standard-quality, nonperishable products.) On the other hand, where the crucial decision-making elements are obscure and complex, requiring specialized knowledge, then the balance swings more toward the expert as the locus of wise decision-making, though even here the individual non-expert may be able to judge the results, except where these are hidden from him (slow poisons) or where his acquisition of knowledge *ex post* would not be effective (fast poisons).

One of the problems of decision-making at the society-wide level is that such political processes—whether democratic or dictatorial—tend to be "yes or no" decisions rather than fractionalized, incremental, variable, and individualized decisions, such as are common in economic processes. A consumer can buy his soap at Safeway, his vegetables at A & P, and his meat at Grand Union—and can shift to an entirely different pattern next week if he chooses. But a voter has to get his foreign policy, domestic spending, legal reform, and offshore oil regulations all from one national administration and continue to do so for four years. He may have preferred one candidate on some issues and the opposing candidate on some other issues, but on election day he has to simply choose one whole "package" over another. In the legislatures as well, members must ultimately vote yes or no, just as jurors must ultimately vote innocent or guilty. The rigidities of political and legal processes are among their disadvantages relative to economic processes. In particular instances—or perhaps even in general—it may nevertheless be desirable to transfer some decision-making from the individual economic sphere to the collective political sphere. What is important is to understand the implications of the transfer.

There is no obvious or general rule as to the level at which decision-making power ought to exist. What seems much clearer is that the locus of decisions ought not to be drastically changed merely because of a figure of speech, such as "society." There is no one named "society." There are individuals, families, organizations of various sizes, and governmental units at various levels. "Society," for example, does *not* engage in any process that can accurately be described as "income distribution." There is such a thing as a distribution of newspapers, but there is in general no such thing as a distribution of income—under either capitalism or socialism. What actually happens under either system is that millions of subunits decide how much to pay particular individuals for particular services rendered (and smaller amounts—relief, unemployment benefits, etc.—are distributed from a central pool independently of services rendered). To shift those decisions to a central body at a society-wide level would be a revolutionary change in *either* system. Whether such a revolutionary change is desirable or not is a complex question that can be analyzed in its own right. The point here is that it is far too big a question to be settled semantically by allegories about how "society" distributes its income and a simple discussion of how society should perhaps distribute it differently. It is also too important a question to be decided by simply *defining* "planning" as society-level planning,[16] ignoring the overwhelming bulk of planning which actually takes place at the level of individuals, families, and autonomous organizations.

The locus of decision-making power is also crucially misstated in discussions in which multitudes of individuals are summarized, characterized, or personified by some one individual or organization which happens to hold the center of the stage. For example, when desirable and sparsely settled land now inhabited by affluent families is being bought up and converted to apartments or small-home use by less affluent families, the cry that goes up is directed at spoliation by "developers." In economic terms, it is simply the classic and pervasive situation of alternative uses of given resources which are insufficiently abundant to satisfy all potential users. That in this case the lower-income users are able to outbid the wealthier users suggests a more urgent need, even if for use in individually smaller quantities and perhaps less esthetically pleasing forms. In any event, it is not a case of the beautiful land versus the ugly developers. It is a question of competing groups of human beings—one small and affluent, the other larger, less well-off financially, but able in the aggregate to bid some of the resources away. The resolution of the conflict may be open to debate, but the misstatement of the issue should not be.

Summary and Conclusions

"Economic man" is a fiction. So is "society." So is "income distribution." The question is which fiction leads toward, and which leads away from, generally correct predictions about economic behavior. More generally, how does each fiction affect our image of man and of the social world around us? Perhaps the best that can be said in this regard for "economic man" is that he is largely confined to economics textbooks, where he does relatively little harm. By contrast, such concepts as "society" and "income distribution" are allowed to roam at large and create mischief with little or no check.

The image of man has to be more than that of a money-maker, its scope broader than self-interest, and its preoccupations extending beyond cold calculation. Culture helps man to transcend all of these things. Economics is a valuable part of that culture, in making people's options clearer. In doing so, it increases rather than reduces the scope of human existence. It is facile but wholly misleading to speak of "the destruction of moral and spiritual values wrought by the primacy of economic considerations."[17] It is precisely economic advancement that has brought higher human considerations within range of large masses no longer pressed and driven for physical survival. Probably more people have heard the music of Beethoven in the past generation than in the preceding century. Certainly more have had the leisure to travel, to read, to think, or just to enjoy their family and friends. Insofar as economics has contributed to this prosperity it has not turned men into economic man, but has instead freed them to realize their higher human potentialities.

Notes

1. Marc Plattner, "The Attack on Economics," *Claremont Journal of Public Affairs*, Spring 1973, p. 19.

2. Walter A. Weisskopf, "The Image of Man in Economics," *Social Research*, Autumn 1973, pp. 551-552.

3. Plattner, "Attack on Economics," p. 15.

4. Daniel Bell, "The Cultural Contradictions of Capitalism," *The Public Interest*, Fall 1970, p. 16.

5. Irving Kristol, "Capitalism, Socialism, and Nihilism," *The Public Interest*, Spring 1973, p. 13.

6. Walter Lippmann, *Public Opinion* (Glencoe: The Free Press, 1965), p. 10.

7. Ibid., p. 11.

8. Walter Weisskopf, "Image of Man," p. 547.

9. Ibid., p. 548.

10. See Thomas Sowell, *Classical Economics Reconsidered* (Princeton, N.J.: Princeton University Press, 1974), pp. 26-28.

11. "People of the same trade seldom meet together, even for merriment and diversion, but the conversation ends in a conspiracy against the public, or in some contrivance to raise prices." Adam Smith, *The Wealth of Nations* (New York: Modern Library, 1937), p. 128; "Merchants and manufacturers. . . . have generally an interest to deceive and even to oppress the public, and. . . . upon many occasions, both deceived and oppressed it." Ibid., p. 250; ". . . the mean rapacity, the monopolizing spirit of merchants and manufacturers. . . . cannot perhaps be corrected . . . " Ibid., p. 460; ". . . like an overgrown standing army, they have become formidable to the government, and upon many occasions intimidate the legislature." Ibid., p. 438; ". . . the interested sophistry of merchants and manufacturers confounded the common sense of mankind." Ibid., p. 461.

12. See Thomas Sowell, *Say's Law: An Historical Analysis* (Princeton, N.J.: Princeton University Press, 1972), Chapter 9, *passim.*

13. J.C.L. Simonde de Sismondi, *Political Economy* (New York: Augustus M. Kelley, 1966), pp. 132-133.

14. Thorstein Veblen, *The Place of Science in Modern Civilization* (New York: Russell & Russell, 1961), p. 251.

15. Edmund Burke, *Reflections on the Revolution in France* (London: J.M. Dent & Sons, Ltd., 1967), p. 84.

16. See Charles A. Reich and Burke Marshall, "Needed: A Government That Governs," *New York Times*, December 28, 1973, p. 11.

17. Plattner, "Attack on Economics," p. 20.

The Ethos of American Law

Philip Selznick

Is man made for the laws or are the laws made for man? To this eternal question, posed most dramatically in Western civilization by St. Paul, the American democracy has always responded by insisting that no abstract answer was necessary or desirable—that both perspectives on the relation between law and human society are legitimate, and that there is no need for any a priori statement of subordination and superordination. Americans have always made their laws; Americans have usually venerated their laws; Americans have constantly been changing their laws.

Professor Philip Selznick analyzes the degree to which different conceptions of human nature lies beneath this ambivalent American attitude toward the legal order. Even while insisting on the necessity of legal constraints if man is not to become worse than he is, Americans have simultaneously asserted that the law is a proper vehicle for the realization of democratic aspirations. It is this latter "optimistic" view of the possibilities of the legal order which has, over the past century, gradually become predominant, and helps explain the "legal activism" that is such a distinctive aspect of American society today.

The American legal order holds in tension two views of man and society: moral skepticism and moral confidence. Skepticism underpins what is most apparent in the law: an array of devices to hold men in check. Confidence is more subtle, yet no less pervasive. It is evident wherever law hinges on trust, cooperation, goodwill, and self-interest.

The themes of skepticism and confidence evoke contrasting notions of law

211

and justice. One view, founded in moral skepticism, takes the law to be a system of restraining rules. Law exists because without it there would be chaos on the one hand, repression on the other. Its main work is to keep the peace and control the abuse of power. For many, this focus on restraint and on practical urgencies carries a welcome note of realism. Law is known by its cutting edge. And there is no confounding of law and justice.

The alternative is to think of law as a vehicle of human aspiration. On this view legal experience points to a *kind* of order and a *kind* of social control. Where there is fidelity to law, order is not to be purchased at any price. It imposes costs upon those in power and generates expectations among citizens. The outcome is a vision of law as a realm of value, a potential embodiment of ideals, an avenue of civic participation.

Every legal system is a unique blend of skepticism and confidence, restraint and aspiration. In the American experience, activism and democracy have generated a near-irresistible pressure to make confidence the keynote of the legal order. Skepticism has been a residual resource, embodied in a heritage more taken for granted than self-consciously affirmed, more likely to be neglected than nurtured. It is this special configuration, not the abstract opposition of skepticism and confidence, that defines the peculiar problems of law and society in the United States.

The Constitution, which contributed so much to the nation's character and identity, was suffused by an ethos of restraint. It established the supremacy of law, created powerful agencies of government, and demanded accountability. There was conveyed a message of balance and order, continuity of tradition, limited powers, contained aspirations. But the Constitution did not produce an austere, disciplined, Roman polity, despite some Federalist predilections. The Federalist spirit could not embrace the whole of the law any more than it could long be successful in the political arena. In a setting of restless energy and open frontiers, the work of judging, lawyering, and lawmaking took on a more formless, more exuberant, more democratic cast.

As children of the Enlightenment, the Founding Fathers had ample faith that human reason, embodied in institutions, could govern disorderly passions. One senses a confidence in institutions even as there is dispriase of man. Thomas Jefferson wrote,

free government is founded in jealousy, and not in confidence, it is jealousy, not confidence, which prescribes limited constitutions, to bind down those whom we are obliged to trust with power; . . . in questions of power, then, let no more be heard of confidence in man, but bind him down from mischief by the chains of the Constitution.[1]

Here the suspicion of human nature has a special focus; it is not a general indictment. The argument is not that *any* man, given the chance, would misuse power; rather, the premise is that there is sufficient *risk* of such misuse to forbid *reliance upon* the idealism and good will of men in authority. Nor does Jefferson's pessimism necessarily deny that power and authority can be ennobling, summoning ordinary men to political and moral heights.

Although confidence is a keynote, it is not undiscriminating. Confidence in institutions is one thing, confidence in officials is another, confidence in the common man something else again. Not even the common man, though often celebrated, has a sure hold on confidence. Although the democratic ethos must embrace civic participation and majority rule, there is a fundamental understanding that popular decision may be marred and distorted by ignorance and apathy, collective excitement, or irrelevant symbolism. The common man may be unfit for self-government if his participation is divorced from the stabilizing continuities of settled interest, deeply felt values, and practical judgment.

It is not abstract man but the situated being—the person in context—who is the subject of skepticism or confidence. This principle has both liberal and conservative implications. For the liberal, it signifies that the social context can be regenerative: a reconstruction of the environment will bring forth and sustain the better side of human nature. For the conservative, man-in-context vindicates the concreteness of human experience, the futility of abstractions, and the moral worth of a socially embedded life. Conservatives have confidence in people *as they are* so long as they act within constraining contexts. Liberals express confidence in what people *can be* if only the circumstances will be set right.

These contrasts and ambiguities are softened, though not eliminated in that distinctive product of the American mind—democratic pragmatism. The pragmatic temper distrusts abstractions and abhors dualisms. It finds reality in active, questing, problem-solving experience. The person is the touchstone of worth and all institutions are to be judged by what they cost, in human terms, and by what they can do to help people get on with the business of living. Pragmatism knows little of alienation, for it is a philosophy of commitment and a philosophy of the present. The given world is accepted, even loved, for it is the indispensable arena of action and fulfillment. Yet, that acceptance is neither supine nor self-effacing. Pragmatism presumes a posture of criticism and a strategy of reconstruction.

In this peculiarly American perspective, ideals are of little worth if they are not rooted in practical assessments of what men and institutions are like—their vulnerabilities, no less than their potentialities. Genuine values emerge from experience; they are discovered, not imposed. A pragmatist is sensitive to the latent, unrealized values that inhere in social arrangements. Friendship, responsibility, leadership, love, and justice are not elements of an external ethic brought to the world by Promethean fire. They are achievements founded in mundane needs, practical opportunities and felt satisfactions.

Pragmatism is democratic because it takes as its starting point the ordinary human being and ordinary experience. Every person, high or low, every institution, however exalted, partakes of that ordinariness. The veil of pretense is pierced to reveal the commonsense aspects of all decision-making and, indeed, of all excellence. Thus, pragmatism is not friendly to an heroic view of history.

In the world of jurisprudence, three themes reflect the influence of democratic pragmatism:

1. *The continuity of legal and nonlegal phenomena.* Despite a clear need to preserve the integrity of legal institutions, law cannot be treated as a realm apart. Every vital aspect of doctrine and decision is rooted in a more pervasive, more inchoate social process. Legal rhetoric has its own dynamic, but it is inescapably enmeshed in considerations of policy; legal cognition demands an appreciation of social fact; legal rules shade into the environing normative order; legal decisions are complex vectors of fidelity to principle, adaptation to circumstance, and the play of vested interests. A pragmatic outlook blurs conceptual and institutional boundaries and does so with an easy conscience; it happily puts law in its place, derogating the claim to a special worth and dignity. In this way, the stage is set for criticism of law in the light of social needs and aspirations.

2. *The celebration of process.* At least among law teachers and jurists, the American idiom is more comfortable with "legal process" than with "law" or "legal order." This reflects a preference for the palpable and the concrete, and a recognition that law is an enterprise, a way of providing certain services and striving for certain outcomes. Legal process suggests that the ends of law are emergent and open-ended; that legal resources are available for elaboration as new needs and opportunities arise; that the values associated with law decisively depend on whether institutional arrangements are kept in good order. The approach to process is clinical and diagnostic; it presumes that a legal order is corruptible and that its pathologies stem from inherent dilemmas of lawmaking and administration.

3. *Justice as quest.* The grand formulae of commutative and distributive justice, of natural law and natural right, have at best an insecure place in American legal thought.[a] Justice is not an abstract ideal to be captured once and for all in a few fundamental postulates. Rather, it is something at once more definite and more fluid, a remedy for specific grievances, informed by only a dim conception of an ultimate ideal; justice is something striven for, a product of awakened conscience, historical opportunity, and available resources. In this tradition, it is more important to find a firm footing and take a next step than to invoke a philosophy. Justice is *experienced* fairness, and that experience is always tied to the legitimacy of expectations within particular situations.

These perspectives are revealed in all that is distinctive about the American legal experience and American legal thought. Democratic pragmatism is most clearly manifest in the practical, purposive, institution-building spirit of much of private law; in the commitment to a living constitution and the expansion of citizenship; in legal realism and sociological jurisprudence; in the perennial call for a responsive legal order.

---

[a]This is not to deny that, in one form or another, concepts of fundamental justice and natural right have played a part in American jurisprudence. But there has been a recoil from formulations that identify rights in absolute or ahistorical terms.

The Common Law Tradition

All of these themes place the common law tradition at the center of American legal experience.[b] It is there that the perspective of democratic pragmatism comes to the fore; it is there we find a process that defines the moral premises of law and gives life to the Constitution itself. It may be said, indeed, that it is the spirit of the common law, more than the philosophy of Locke, that has inspired the course of constitutional development.

Common law is law fashioned by judges in the course of deciding particular controversies; it is the emergent product of case-by-case rule-making. Therefore, a common law system presumes and encourages judicial inventiveness. More generally, a common law cast of mind is evident whenever an open framework of decision is preferred, leaving the details of policy to be filled in as issues arise and experience accumulates.

From the standpoint of political theory, the significance of the common law tradition lies in the nature of its authority. The authority of the common law does not derive from political will. That explains why, in the interpretation of law, the judges have the strongest claim to the last word. Legislators and executives are agencies of political will; they have only limited credibility as spokesmen for objective principles or as guardians of a legal heritage. The common law is respected because it is presumed to articulate a set of historically established principles of obligation, at the same time transforming those principles into a working system of rule-making and decision. The community says: Be a judge, make sense of our laws and apply them fairly. To make sense of law is to make sense of society, and that truth has deeply informed the common law.

The inherently obscure foundation of judicial authority has generated a quest for special doctrines of justification, such as the idea that judges speak for a "higher" law. But the fundamental fact is that legal authority in the common law tradition derives from the cumulative, diverse, and textured experience of doing justice in a particular society. It is the task of the judges to interpret that experience and give it effect. The principles that emerge are products of social learning; they are not the offspring of philosophical reason.

Substantively, the common law has had two main strands. One is constitutional, reflected in the struggle of the English judges to limit the authority of the Crown. For the American colonists, it has been argued, this was the main significance of the English common law. "They conceived of the common law as being a limited set of essentially constitutional principles—principles of public or constitutional law."[2] On the other hand, common law refers to the regulation of private affairs, as in the law of contract, tort, and property. In either case,

[b]For this reason, like most commentators, I have chosen to focus on the common law rather than on legislation or administration. As my purpose is to draw out underlying values and perspectives, it seems best to keep in mind what is central in the legal tradition.

however, the preoccupation of the common law is with society, that is, with the standpoint and the interests of those who are engaged in the ordinary business of life.

This background suggests two corollary themes. First, the common law counterposes state and society. As they settle disputes and vindicate claims, the judges uphold a private sphere of life. The protection of individual and group rights, including modes of conduct hallowed by tradition, comes to define a legal order that is independent of political authority. The judges invoke social experience and social necessity to postulate rights against the state. This experience feeds into and supports the common law commitment to constitutional government.

Second, authority in the common law tradition is not given, but remains to be worked out. If experience is the book of law, then what is authoritative is to be understood in the light of changing circumstances. It follows that common-law authority is neither an awesome presence nor a clipped command. It is something fluid, variable, and problematic, in which competing doctrines and alternative justifications bid for respect.

In the American setting, the openness of the common law was strongly reinforced by the special role of the courts in (1) adapting English law to American conditions, (2) finding legal coherence within a federal system, and (3) providing for the needs of an expanding nation and a rapidly developing economy. These circumstances lent vigor and legitimacy to judicial creativity. At the same time, "differences among the states in their approach to identical legal problems frustrated belief in inexorable solutions."[3] The quest for such solutions was active enough and, for a time, dominated legal thought and decision, but in a contest for the spirit of American law, it could not prevail.

The theme of openness may, however, grossly distort our picture of the legal process. In fact, the common law, like any law, must look to its legitimacy. The courts find their legitimacy in an institutional morality which includes, above all, a distinctive mode of reasoning. Legal reason is, in Coke's phrase, "artificial reason," because it must start from premises that are authoritative and not merely sound. A scientific assessment, or a moral judgment, is free to use whatever ideas are helpful in arriving at assertions warranted in fact and logic. But a legal conclusion must demonstrate continuity with what is received and established.

Thus, artificial reason is the language of legal legitimacy. Its excesses are notorious, and Americans have been impatient with tortuous legal logic, fictional classifications, and slavish deference to outmoded thought. At an early stage,

... American devotion to the common law was based not on a respect for its crabbed technicalities nor on its many reactionary features, but on its emphasis upon fundamental law and the liberty of the subject. Americans abhorred Coke's disquisitions on feudal tenures; they venerated the Coke who sought to fix limits on the royal prerogative, who declared that the common law will void an act of Parliament that is against common right. . . .[4]

The American quest is for principles that are at once rational and traditional. They should be capable of reasoned elaboration; yet, they should also be founded in propositions that define the historic commitments of the political community. The outcome, it is hoped, will be legality without legalism.

In legal reasoning, at its best, we find a union of legitimacy and cognition. The law insists upon received premises, but (1) those premises are open to reconstruction as their logic is explored and (2) in formulating legal rules, it is the responsibility of the courts to take account of social reality. Put another way, the common-law tradition *commands inquiry*. Knowing the operative law requires scrutinizing the connection between legal abstractions and the practical workings of industry, government, or family life. This is the more true as "fundamental principles" are articulated. The transition from general principle to specific rule requires a confrontation of idea and reality. That confrontation is not meant to be an intuitive leap or a raw acting-out of judicial preference. Instead, the judges are to undertake faithful inquiry into what must be done if legal principles are to be realized in action.

It follows that, despite much skeptical comment, common-law judges are in the business of *discovering* the law even as they exercise discretion and display creativity. Holmes wrote that

in substance the growth of the [common] law is legislative. And this in a deeper sense than that what the courts declare to have always been the law is in fact new. It is legislative in its grounds. The very considerations which judges most rarely mention, and always with an apology, are the secret root from which the law draws all the juices of life. I mean, of course, considerations of what is expedient for the community concerned.[5]

As so often in such remarks, the question is avoided: What is distinctive about *judicial* legislation?

In the common-law ethos, the courts make law but they do not make it out of whole cloth. They legislate, but they do so in their own way. That way is perhaps best captured in Lon Fuller's concept of "implicit" law.[6] Implicit law is law warranted by what is required to give effect to legal aims or standards. It is the product of inquiry into the formation of contracts, the exercise of authority, the maintenance of order, the distribution of risks, indeed, inquiry into virtually every facet of social life. That investigation takes legal policy as its starting point and then considers the interplay of policy and fact. The outcome is a rule that, in purport at least, is a way of making the policy effective.

In the crisis of Watergate, the quest for implicit law was painfully revealed. If "separation of powers" (itself implicit in the structure of the Constitution) is to be given effect, is not executive privilege a corollary, as the Supreme Court has recently suggested? If so, what is its *necessary* ambit? Executive privilege is a concept of implicit law because it derives, not from an act of legislative will, but from a conclusion as to what is institutionally necessary if a constitutional policy is to be upheld.

To be sure, not everything is so cleanly an exercise in policy science. The policy itself may be heavily obscured and its *legitimacy* may depend on a reading of history. The grounds of impeachment are troublesome in this way. Yet, it is ultimately the duty of the courts to inquire into the objective constitutional function of impeachment and to draw from that inquiry the implicit law of impeachable offense.

These are only highly charged examples of routine judicial interpretation. Holmes' "secret root"—what is "expedient for the community"—makes the discovery or finding of law a dynamic and empirical process, but it need not reduce judicial law-making to an exercise of political will. What Holmes and other critics of legal formalism meant to say was that legal reasoning is not a purely logical exercise; it is not logic alone, but the broader operation of inquiry that must inform the legal process. The judge should be able to distinguish his own preferences from what he concludes as he assesses social fact in the light of legal purpose.

Thus understood, the common-law tradition makes the law forever debatable.[7] And that debate turns on what the law *is*, not what it should be.[c] Anyone can argue for a proposition of implicit law because the process of interpretation is open to all. Although the courts may be given the last word, there can be no more certainty in their rule-making than in the most settled forms of moral argument, and there can be no final assurance that the assessment of what is factually required to give effect to legal policy has taken account of all the evidence. Law, like science, is subject to a basic norm of self-correction.

With the development and refinement of common-law method, there is a waning of "artificial reason" insofar as it refers to an opaque and insular mode of thought. The common law has made judges into oracles, but it has been increasingly unfriendly to the idiom of oracular utterance. The demand is that reasons should be given to justify decisions, and these reasons should reveal the interplay of legitimacy and cognition. Yet, with the advance of cognition, including the clarification of policy premises in received law, the legitimating function of a "mysterious science" is inevitably weakened. As the judges win purchase on rational discourse, they lose the protection of an arcane tradition.

In this respect modern law and modern religion share a common fate: In the struggle for adherence and consent, symbolism is a dwindling resource. The result is an ever-greater reliance on autonomous judgment and on self-restraint. If God is dead, so is Justice. Unlike religion, however, law is deeply rooted in the needs and exigencies of a working society. It is inherently less dependent on symbolic resources. Therefore, the common law can more readily overcome recurrent crises of legitimacy by proving its worth as a practical vehicle for resolving conflicts, fulfilling aspirations, and facilitating action.

---

[c]There is, of course, a close connection between what the law is and what it should be. I am concerned here only to emphasize that the debate over implicit law cannot be reduced to dialogue over legislative preference.

The decision for a legal order that is subject to reconstruction in the light of social knowledge reflects a pervasive confidence in the capacity of society to endure ambiguity. Common law is problematic law, and it asks of citizens the maturity to accept an "open texture," an incompleteness, that leaves much for the future to decide. The common-law tradition offers a prospect that, with patience and experience, the materials of the past can be refashioned to help find a just solution to *any* legal problem. In principle, the law is there to be discovered. But that expectation carries a price tag—the acceptance of law that is, to a large extent, implicit, indefinite, and inchoate.

At the same time, if the common law is to be effective, *there must be a functioning social order.* This is not an abstract truism, but a sobering premise. If the law is to be articulated by judges, if their work is a process of social learning, then time is an indispensable resource—time for tentative groping, for piecemeal solutions, for caution born of ignorance. The common-law tradition is not well suited to the management of crisis. Furthermore, common law decision-making presumes a going concern whose needs and circumstances can be studied. If the social world is itself "absurd," if there are not touchstones of shared tradition and common fate, then legal principles are hard to come by.

Confidence in society is also qualified by a continuing commitment to legal technique. The critique of formalism cannot be taken as a rejection of expertise. Law as inquiry is a professional enterprise. There may be good reasons for broadening dialogue and widening participation. But there is no abatement of the need for thorough understanding of legal resources, skill in combining legitimacy and cognition, sophistication in identifying values and interests. Legal expertise mitigates openness and restrains overreaching. And it maintains a social group that has a special commitment to the underlying values of a legal order.

Nevertheless, openness and confidence are hallmarks of the common-law tradition, at least in its American version. That tradition, therefore, should be a major resource for American democracy—to extend its scope, to deepen its commitments, and to discipline its aspirations. In what follows I shall consider some of the ways that potentiality is made manifest. I shall also consider some risks and limitations.

The Release of Energies[8]

In the common-law perspective, "social fact" is not a neutral object of inquiry, something to be taken account of by rulers who seek to impose their will upon the community. Rather, social fact—insofar as it predicates and sustains organized group life—makes its own claim upon the legal process. When Roscoe Pound said that the task of law is to give effect to social interests,[9] he was articulating this promise of the common law. For that mode of governance has given a central place to the *facilitative* work of law. Every legal order makes private action easier, if only by providing a context of stability. But in the

United States, the effort to vindicate interests, confirm expectations, and encourage cooperation has been in the foreground of legal experience. The legal expert comes into his own when he finds a way to move things along and get a job done. He can do this best by releasing energies; he has few resources for harnessing them.

This posture is, in part, a reflection of the peculiar history of Anglo-American common law. By the eighteenth century, it was more or less settled that large areas of social life—especially commercial and property relations—would be governed by judge-made law. In this "private" area legislation was secondary and was largely limited to confirming or amending common-law rules. In effect, the judges (and with them the lawyers and their clients) were delegated responsibility for managing private arrangements. The judges drew guidance from the claims of the litigants, with but little reference to political authority. They worked out policies, and legislated without guilt, because they did not suppose they were in the business of making political decisions. Their law was derived from a private ordering, which is to say, from the implicit requirements of trade and industry.

Thus, the development of the common law was closely tied to the evolving needs of business. The law became unabashedly *bourgeois* as it responded to demands for more flexible ways of amassing capital and deploying it. The corporation was divorced from its traditional role as an agent of the sovereign and became wholly subordinate to private purposes and market mechanisms; new instruments of obligation, new ways of holding and transferring property, were devised and accepted; the law of master and servant was revamped to enhance both the mobility of labor and the authority of employers. In all this the common law was *selectively* responsive, but it created an ethos that could, in time, serve other constituencies and larger interests.

The classic example of facilitative law is the law of contracts. Contract law releases energies by enforcing the terms of a valid agreement; it thereby encourages private arrangements and makes them more secure. The law of contract is suffused by a spirit of voluntarism. The parties decide for themselves whether and on what terms a relation between them should be established. The law of contracts does not define their obligations; it only certifies and enforces what they themselves have accepted. To decide what they have accepted, or whether a contract has been formed at all, may require considerable interpretation and many special rules, but the basic policy of the law is to facilitate agreements and not to impose them.

The idea of contract presumes a certain confidence in the viability of private arrangements. An agreement based on reciprocity will, it is supposed, be largely self-enforcing. And the premise is that a mature person is the best judge of his own interests. The history of the law of contracts shows a steady growth in confidence, reflected in the drift of the law away from narrow, formalist interpretations of contractual duty.

For a long period, the law of contract was especially concerned to *limit* obligations. The parties would gain an island of assurance within an uncertain world; and the courts themselves could find welcome comfort in rules that limited their own responsibilities. The principle of limited commitment still dominates the law of contract, but the courts have been able to expand obligations in the light of changing practices and expectations. In the nineteenth century, American courts broke through the wall of "privity"—the idea that only parties to a contract may claim its benefits or be required to meet its obligations—by recognizing the rights of "third party beneficiaries." More recent developments include recognition of a duty to *negotiate* in good faith and not merely to *perform* in good faith, thus modifying the common-law rule that obligations accrue only after a contract is formed; and the acceptance of flexible pricing arrangements contrary to the traditional rule that a valid contract cannot exist in the absence of definite terms.[10]

It may seem paradoxical to say that new rules, backed by sanctions, presume a growth of confidence. Obviously, there would be no need for a sanction without some doubt about conformity. But the larger truth is that the new rules confirm routine expectations; they are based on an assumption that, on the whole, the norm reflects ordinary business practice. There is confidence that most people can and want to abide by the rule, and confidence in the competence of the courts to frame a workable standard.

The idea of contract is not wholly suited to modern experience; it does not help the law to grasp the realities of an administered society.[11] Voluntarism is eroded when standardized "contracts of adhesion" leave little or no room for negotiation and when "private governments" largely determine the conditions of participation in economic life. The contract model presumes a world of independent, roughly equal actors who enter relationships of limited duration and limited commitment. A world of large-scale organizations, with their clients and constituencies, is forced into that mold only at the cost of significant distortion.

Nevertheless, contract remains a pervasive and powerful instrument of facilitative law. Its premises have sometimes required reconstruction to account for stubborn realities, as when a new type of "collective" contract was evolved to make sense of labor relations. But the appeal of contract as a general idea has not waned significantly. In part this is so because contract, being firmly embedded in common-law experience, casts a benign light of legitimacy over rules and relationships elaborated in its name and applied to new contexts. Furthermore, the law of contracts since the nineteenth century has embodied values of freedom, equality, self-government, and legal competence. Contract preserves the integrity of the parties and upholds the principle of authority founded in consent.

Thus, in the early days of collective bargaining, when the legal status of labor-management agreements was still in doubt, contract took on a political meaning. A trade union reached a political milestone when it was recognized as a party to a written agreement. And however imprecise as a sociological category, or even as a legal idea, the *imagery* of contract could convey a vision of equal parties, reciprocal engagements, and conditional consent.

The American experience with labor law is best understood as an exercise in constitution-making. The collective agreement is a special kind of contract—a constitutive contract. It is constitutive in that new and continuing institutions are created, such as the bargaining unit and grievance machinery; and responsibilities are generated that go beyond what can be spelled out in an inclusive set of detailed provisions. In effect, an arrangement is made for the governance of an enterprise, and the rules apply, not only to the contracting parties but to an indeterminate number of present and future employees. Moreover, the needs of a going concern require that rules be elaborated over time, in response to changing circumstances. Hence abstract principles of uncertain meaning must be tolerated (employees will be dismissed only for "just cause"), leaving specific policies for future elaboration. The collective agreement is a constitutional framework for labor-management cooperation. It creates a structure of authority, a procedure for rule-making, a statement of principles, and a reservoir of implicit law.

Although the collective agreement is the clearest example, the constitutive aspects of other contracts should not be ignored. Many commercial agreements are meant to establish continuing relationships and are correspondingly open-ended in their terms. The thrust of recent contract law is to accept as valid a broad framework of agreement, so long as it can be shown that there was an intention to create a relationship. Agreements among government agencies, though not enforceable in the courts, often establish policy commitments and arrange for long-term cooperation.

Constitutive contracts are institution-building devices. They bring the support of law to "the art of associating together."[12] As this occurs, the idea of contract is subtly transformed. What began as a vehicle of individual action becomes a resource for collective life. What began (in its modern form) as a market mechanism, a legal device for limiting commitments and calculating costs, becomes a social form instinct with obligation. The political philosopher may take some comfort from a perennial rediscovery of the social contract.

Facilitative law is the law of starting-mechanisms and frameworks; it shrinks from the imposition of prescriptive rules; it avoids detailed surveillance. This suggests a special continuity between the common law and constitutionalism. Constitutionalism usually refers to a system of law that transcends and limits political will. As such, of course, it is a major aspect of the common law tradition. But constitutionalism can also be thought of as a style of decision. It is a way of upholding principles while recognizing the demands of a changing social reality. Constitutionalism provides a perspective of continuity and a resource for the future, but it also insists that each generation be its own master. In this it shares with the common law a fundamental commitment to relevance and renewal. Together they establish a preference for law that is more emergent than imposed.

The Postulate of Competence

As a corollary of its preference for emergent law, the common-law tradition gives great weight to self-help and self-assertion. Party initiative and party responsibility are leitmotifs of the adversary system, itself a bulwark of the common law. Judicial lawmaking, characteristically, begins with the assertion of a claim or the making of an accusation. The process is set in motion by partisan advocates, and that advocacy contributes decisively to the framing of issues and the interpretation of law. In an adversary model, "the litigants themselves largely determine the scope of inquiry and the data upon which the judicial judgment is based."[13]

Thus, legal development depends on the mobilization of resources by those who have a stake in a particular controversy. It follows that, if justice is to be done, the system must assume that appropriate resources will be forthcoming; it must also assume that everyone knows his own interests and is capable of asserting them. These presumptions are often quite false and to that extent undermine confidence in the law as a dispenser of justice. I shall return to this issue presently. At this point I wish to consider how the adversary principle, within the common law tradition, contributes to the ethos of democracy.

Most important, perhaps, is a posture of criticism. Advocacy does not take law as given. Rather, the authority of a rule, as applied in the circumstances, is testable and problematic. The skilled advocate (in the context of judicial lawmaking) is known by his exercise of legal imagination. He uses to the full the resources of the law to demand precision in the application of precedents, to justify the elaboration of new rules, and to argue for application of one rule or principle rather than another. Thus advocacy presumes and encourages searching criticism of received authority. Indeed, it is committed to the view that legal materials of all kinds have *variable* authority. If all legal rules, precedents, statutes, doctrines, concepts, and principles are authoritative, some are more authoritative than others.

The law is too often conceived in global terms, as a unitary phenomenon, and especially so when claims to obedience are made. In fact, legal authority is heterogeneous and uneven. The weight of authority depends on many factors, including the explicitness and clarity of rules and opinions, consistency of enforcement, attenuation of consent. The relatively weak authority of a statute is manifested, for example, in restrictive interpretations by the courts. And a judicial decision may be eroded over time, sapped of vitality, even as it retains some measure of authority. The variability of authority provides leverage for legal criticism.

The intimate connection between advocacy and criticism is more a product of institutional dynamics than of legal ideology. The invitation to argue about the applicable law generates a forensic style marked by eager readiness to reconstruct authority. The outcome is a reinforcement of the constitutional premise that each citizen stands on an equal footing with the state. The government has no special claim to legal prescience; it must participate in the dialogue and justify its cause.

A critical spirit *domesticates* authority. Justification, not sanctity, is the keynote. The American legal experience does not sustain a conservative image of the received word. In this it is consonant with a political heritage that takes truth to be "the daughter of time, not of authority."[14] In the legal and political culture of this nation, there are no self-certifying agencies and no truly self-evident principles, despite the rhetoric of the Declaration and the accrued grandeur of some Constitutional clauses. Even the claim that a Supreme Court decision is the "law of the land" has a hollow ring when it is used to summon uncritical consent.

Legal criticism also contributes to the *diffusion* of authority. The courts may have the last word, but it does not follow that they have exclusive authority to interpret the law. Others share in that process and they may, in the absence of legal finality, make their own assessments of what the law is and how they may act. Members of Congress enact statutes that *may* be declared unconstitutional, and they do so as of right, relying on their own notions of what the Constitution requires. A city attorney properly issues his own "authoritative interpretations" of applicable law. In exercising discretion, public officials are constantly called upon to assess the legality of their own conduct. For the most part, their conclusions are unchallenged and constitute the operative law.

More fundamentally, legal authority is diffused because, in the common-law tradition, there is no monolithic source of law and no monopoly of legal truth. The courts decide, but they do so within a context that invites participation. When a legal argument is accepted, a claim to authority is vindicated. Even a rejected argument may persuade in part and prevail in due course. In this sense the legal ministry has a Protestant cast—every individual is, in principle, competent to read and interpret the authoritative text.

It is a striking feature of our legal system that *lawful* opportunities exist, for citizens as well as officials, to decide for themselves when they can disobey an apparently obligatory rule.[15] One illustration of "discretion to disobey" is the criminal jury's non-reviewable decision to acquit, a decision which may be made in plain violation of judicial instructions regarding the applicable law. Another is selective enforcement by police and prosecutors, despite a contrary obligation in the statute. In these and similar instances, the rule-departure is justified on the ground that conformity would interfere with effective performance of an official responsibility. A similar logic applies where the citizen refuses to obey a law he believes invalid and, on subsequent vindication, is not punished for disobedience.

Like the official, the citizen has duties which may require him to make an autonomous inquiry into his legal responsibilities.

This approach points to a distinction often overlooked: There is a radical difference between fidelity to law and submission to authority. Fidelity to law is a commitment to *valid* rules and procedures, including basic principles of legality and fairness. Therefore, criticism and competence are inherent attributes of "legal man," at least as we know him. To appreciate this issue one has only to contrast a military setting with the ordinary expectations of civilian life. The military establishment places very great emphasis on unhesitating obedience to authoritative commands. Although there is obvious variation according to echelon and unit, and some awareness of the subordinate's obligation to scrutinize the legality of a military command, there is only weak recognition of criticism and competence. Therefore military organization, though replete with rules, is hardly a model of institutionalized legality.

Since no system of law can be effective without a prima facie claim to obedience, fidelity to law entails respect for authority and self-restraint in the face of flawed judgment and arbitrary decision. Civil disobedience is not a gun in a holster, to be whipped out at every provocation. There must be tolerance for the right of a legitimate decider to prevail for the time being, despite some acting out of prejudice or whim. Nevertheless, the presumption of obedience is rebuttable and deference to authority is always conditional.

Elsewhere I have argued that "the obligation to obey the law is one of the more subtle and variable of human commitments."[16] It *is* a commitment, but it is not unconditional. This follows from the nature of consent in a polity that takes law seriously and encourages legal criticism, even if it is not formally democratic. Hannah Arendt has written that "consent, not in the very old sense of mere acquiescence ... but in the sense of active support and continuing participation in all matters of public interest, is the spirit of American law."[17] This may be characterized as consent in depth, that is, consent to particular norms and decisions. The *presumption* of obedience arises from a tacit consent that is the corollary of participation in the community—an implied promise of self-restraint made, in part, in consideration of the self-restraint of others. Consent in depth reflects the *quality* of participation which may, in a sophisticated age, provide many opportunities for remission of the obligation to conform to a specific rule or policy.

It is confrontation, not disobedience as such, that threatens the legal order. That is why, in a context of fidelity to law, civil disobedients are called upon (often vainly) to narrow issues, to display self-sacrifice, and to appeal to the conscience of the community. By the same token, those who enforce the law are called upon (often vainly) to approach critical situations with flexibility and self-control. At a more remote level, it can be said that much legal ingenuity is expended on the task of avoiding confrontations among partially autonomous legal actors, especially courts, legislatures, and executive agencies. Confrontation places the funded authority of a legal institution at risk, and this occurs mainly when the authority of the last word (too often confused with authority in general) is challenged. The problem is to husband authority by minimizing occasions for confrontation, and this is done by asserting ultimate authority as infrequently as possible. If civil disobedients can be trigger-happy, so too can men who are uptight about authority. That is surely one of the more compelling lessons of the 1960s.

As the law opens opportunities for autonomous judgment, and more readily recognizes what was there all along, we come face to face with a basic issue: What burden of decision and of self-restraint can we place upon ourselves? What orientation toward authority is most appropriate to American aspiration? What kind of a people do we think we are?

The postulate of *legal* competence presumes an underlying *social* competence, that is, the capacity for effective and self-preserving participation. Social competence depends in turn on both psychic and institutional resources. Psychologically, legal man requires the capacity to assert his own judgment, criticize authority, and exercise self-control. In Freudian imagery, this means that a mature, autonomous ego replaces a weakly developed "sycophantic" ego. The autonomous ego can endure frustration, tolerate ambiguity, assess reality, and adjust behavior to particular circumstances. It can escape the costs and forego the gratifications of submissive compliance; it can accept the burdens of freedom.

As we assess the significance of psychic maturity for the legal order, we should bear in mind the difference between what we can aspire to and what we can rely upon. It is wisdom to appreciate human frailty and to recognize that legal institutions cannot rely upon optimum mental health, any more than they can rely upon protestations of good will or good intentions. For this reason, the legal order must include safeguards against the abuse of power, including the power of democratic majorities. It does not follow, however, that the law can know nothing of aspiration or that we need to take seriously a pedagogical gambit which led Holmes to place "our old friend the bad man"[18] at center stage. A developed legal order is a structure of opportunities no less than a system of constraint. How those opportunities are used has much to do with the quality of justice, that is, with the capacity of the system to provide a high standard of service rather than only a minimal standard. To realize its aspirations, the system depends on the commitment and competence of "good" men.

The Impoverished Public

Thus far, I have discussed our legal tradition in accents of appreciation. But the common law is not exempt from the hard truth that "every virtue hath an humbling vice." The release of energies and the affirmation of competence are solid values and have created, up to a point, a people's law. At the same time, the very attributes that have made the common law an integral part of social life limit its effectiveness as a vehicle of the public interest. This is so because integration has been won at the price of commitment to fragmented interests and foreshortened perspectives.

These limitations arise from (1) the workings of the adversary system, (2) the law's deference to private ordering, and (3) the focus on procedural rather than substantive justice. Each of these methods and thoughtways tends to weaken the legal process as an arena within which the general welfare is pursued.

The adversary principle is in part a device for limiting the scope of judge-made law. The courts deal with cases and controversies; they do not act on their own initiative. Whether and when an issue is raised depends on what some interested parties want to do, and on what they *can* do, including how they perceive the state of the law. Moreover, recognized changes in the common law are made by appellate courts, which means, of course, that the case must be pursued beyond an initial judgment. Thus, legal development is tied to party initiative and party perseverance, as well as to the parameters of the case at hand. It thereby takes on an ad hoc, fortuitous character; it is something less than a comprehensive exercise of public will.

In such a setting, a heavy burden of responsibility is placed on partisan advocates. As in the perspective of laissez-faire, the assumption is that public welfare will be best served if private interests are the prime movers of decision and policy. In fact, however, advocacy is highly selective. In the classic model of an adversary proceeding, the parties are presumed to have private resources, a reasonable assumption when the law is geared to an exclusive club of propertied interests. The affluent and the powerful come to court evenly matched. They can gather facts, hire adequate counsel, endure lengthy litigation and do all the spadework, leaving the court to choose between well-prepared proofs and arguments. By bringing new cases and appealing adverse judgments, they can make sure that the law takes account of new interests and circumstances.

Powerlessness, on the other hand, bespeaks an impoverished law. Given the premises of the adversary system, legal development is necessarily uneven. In recent years this fact has been most widely noted in the area of so-called "poverty law," for example, the law of landlord and tenant (including public housing), consumer rights, and welfare administration. Similarly, criminal sentencing has had a meager history of appellate review. More generally, wherever there are limited resources for advocacy, the law tends to lack sophisticated elaboration. There is less leverage for change and there are fewer opportunities for discriminating judgment. It is not surprising, therefore, that the American law of employment has mainly served the interests of organized labor and offers less protection to the unorganized.

The significance of the adversary principle for public policy goes beyond a pervasive bias for the haves and indifference to the have-nots. For the adversary model is by no means restricted to private law. In significant areas of public action, the adversary proceeding is taken as a paradigm of responsible administration. Recent administrative law has afforded enlarged opportunities for interested parties to participate in formulating rules that will govern their activities. This is altogether consonant with the spirit and style of common-law rule-making. Rules are made in contemplation of need and authority is exposed to sustained scrutiny. In bringing due process to administrative life, the architects of reform have drawn upon the funded experience of the legal order to fashion procedures of criticism and participation.

The outcome is often a failure of leadership. Philippe Nonet has traced an administrative pattern that probably has relevance far beyond the context he examined.[19] In a study of California's Industrial Accident Commission, which handles workmen's compensation claims, he found that what began as a welfare agency, with a mandate for social action, ended up as a passive adjudicator of partisan interests. An adversary relation between business and organized labor came to dominate the scene, and the IAC evolved into a judicial body operating within a framework of received rules. The emergence of a court was signaled by a withdrawal from policy initiatives and by a self-imposed loss of administrative competence. Whereas earlier, the agency had formulated legislative proposals in furtherance of its mandate, now it adopted a posture of neutrality and allowed organized labor to carry the ball. Whereas earlier, there was some commitment to reviewing *patterns* of industrial practice affecting safety on the job, now the focus was on individual claims and discrete cases.

If regulation of business is the chief failure of American law, Nonet's cautionary tale may offer a clue to the underlying institutional dynamic. Outright venality, including the easy flow of public officials to executive suites, is surely a major factor in the timidity and subservience of regulatory agencies. But that pattern is facilitated when the adversary model, with its corollary judicialization of public policy, offers a respectable alternative to initiative and leadership.

Preference for the adversary model reflects a legal ethos uncomfortable with imposed authority, forever in quest of an harmonious union of law and society. That union, however, is always specific, always selective, always vulnerable to the play of power. The optimistic premises of the common law tradition are rudely undermined when effective participation in the legal process is a scarce commodity and unevenly distributed.

Public purpose is not readily vindicated in a legal order that celebrates the release of energy through facilitative law. Facilitative law encourages a deference to private arrangements. The true springs of order and achievement are thought to be found in cooperative organization for private purposes, not in the schemes and directives of government officials. The preferred role of government is more responsive than affirmative, better adapted to providing incentives than mobilizing resources. If there must be regulation, it should be as restrained as possible, indirect wherever feasible, and, above all, tender of the groups that actually carry on the work of society. In this perspective, the erosion of public purpose is a lesser evil than law that lays a rough, intrusive hand on the delicate fabric of private ordering.

It would be naive to suggest that the facilitative spirit of the common law is a direct determinant of palsied public will. Obviously, effective deployment of private power is, what really counts. But if public officials are to resist pressure and exercise leadership, they need confidence and reinforcement. These they do not get from a legal tradition that takes private interests to be palpable and real, while the public interest is elusive and remote.

The pragmatic underpinnings of American law have ill prepared it for public responsibilities. Pragmatism is process-centered and it rightly perceives that the moral character of a person or an institution resides in means used more than in goals sought. But character is not all. It is an irony of modern thought that the most articulate philosophy of instrumentalism should turn out to focus on integrity than on achievement, more on character-defining choice than on substantive outcomes. John Dewey's doctrine of the continuum of means and ends is a message of self-scrutiny and self-restraint, within a framework of open alternatives and reconstructed goals. The main commitment is to method and the faith is that a sound method will discover social needs and release the energies to serve them. Whatever the great merits of this position, it is not a prescription for leadership.

Law and Politics

A preoccupation with method is hardly a fault in a legal system. Procedure speaks to the very origin of law in the emergence of rules for certifying obligations as peculiarly binding. Procedure is at the heart of a legal tradition whose hallmark is a mode of reasoning that at once binds and frees the judicial process. It is procedure that includes most of what is meant by fairness in the settlement of disputes; it is procedure that most clearly points to a close affinity of developed law and the democratic ethos. Therefore it must seem churlish to offer only two cheers for procedural justice.

The trouble is that the quest for justice is ultimately substantive, not procedural. Justice is sought for concrete human ends and, in the long run, will not be bought off by procedural regularity. Confidence in legal institutions depends on their *efficacy*, which means, in part, their capacity to vindicate legitimate expectations. If it ever was true, it is certainly not true today that the law can consider itself separate and aloof, untouched by a crisis of confidence that afflicts the larger sphere of government. That crisis stems from a sensed impotence, a feeling that public institutions are unable to define critical choices, let alone meet them.

If the legal process is to contribute all it can to substantive justice and social efficacy, it must both enrich the democratic experience and enhance the affirmation of public purpose. These objectives involve each other and together they can draw on latent resources of the common-law tradition. There has always been a strain in that tradition toward making the law "common," not only in creating a unified jurisdiction, but also in the sense that community need and community aspiration are to be discovered and made good. And the postulate of competence, as we have seen, makes criticism and participation salient themes of the legal ethos.

In the contemporary situation, "separation of powers" is no longer the key to political wisdom.[20] The community needs all the help it can get, in channels of action and modes of judgment, no less than in the mobilization of material resources. Cooperation and complementarity, not distance and division, are today's institutional needs. Without yielding the principle of check-and-balance, of power taming power, the system must be open to new ways of infusing public policy with direction and commitment.

Herein lies the truth, the historic relevance, of the call for "participatory democracy." That appeal has sometimes produced more a parody of democracy than a fulfillment of it. Nevertheless, there is validity in the criticism of severely channeled majoritarian rule. What is pointed to is a special form of the tyranny of the majority—not the tyranny of direct oppression, but the tyranny of complacence, vested interest, and inertia. The majority entrenched in its representative institutions may effectively contain new claims and interests. And the formation of new majorities is often frustrated by outmoded forms of political representation.

There is nothing new in the idea of supplementing electoral politics with other forms of group representation, including litigation. The well-organized and the affluent never supposed that they participated in politics only by choosing among competing elites. They decisively influenced who the competitions would be, and they took it for granted that they had a voice in the formulation of policy. Participatory democracy is a demand that these benefits be spread through society, and that every major institution provide at least some avenues of civic participation.

In recent years, the most striking contribution of the legal process to the enrichment of democracy has been the rise of social advocacy. Prefigured in the work of Brandeis half a century ago, pursued with specialized vigor by the NAACP lawyers, sustained by a wide variety of public-interest advocates, and brought to institutional fruition by the Legal Assistance Program of the OEO, the use of litigation to affect public policy on behalf of the socially disprivileged has become a lively aspect of the American legal order.

Social advocacy draws heavily upon the common-law tradition. It projects a view of law as problematic and of advocacy as the imaginative and critical use of legal resources. Social advocacy works within the framework of the legal process, for it entails the representation of group interests through an appeal to norms that have some color of authority. It uses forums that can be held responsible to those norms. Hence, the characteristic locale of social advocacy is the court or the administrative agency, rather than the legislature. The appeal is to legal entitlement, not to political will. And yet, paradoxically, politics is made an engine of justice.

The Legal Services Program, and specifically its law-reform aspects, has had remarkable success in winning political support, despite a militancy that has been hair-raising to many conservatives. That support, which has included the leadership of the bar, testifies to the resonance of the program in the American legal tradition. The justification of widest appeal lies in the adversary principle itself: The poor and the legally disprivileged should have effective representation. Donald Rumsfeld, the Nixon-appointed OEO director, put it this way:

What is described as law reform is really nothing more than providing full legal services to the client. If a particular case points up inequities in the application and structure of the law, by attempts to correct those inequities in the course of litigation, legal services programs are following the *traditional role* of a lawyer in representing a client. Taking appeals, advancing legal theories and exploring possible remedies represent an obligation on the part of legal services attorneys to their low-income clients. Indeed, those activities are an inseparable part of the services which all attorneys provide their clients.[21]

With less compelling logic, the program has also been justified as a means of channeling discontent. In his 1971 Message to Congress, President Nixon endorsed the program as providing "a most effective mechanism for settling differences and securing justice within the system and not on the streets."

Although social advocacy is a legal strategy, it is deeply implicated in the political process. Litigation is carried on with the express intent of furthering group interests and changing legal rules, including administrative policies. Insofar as *particular* group interests are at stake, there is strong continuity with the traditional view that adjudication should only be triggered by determinate parties suffering determinate harms. The transition from individual interest to group interest is easy to make and has many precedents. In the new context, however, the social advocate may find himself in the business of mobilizing group effort and raising group consciousness. He is vulnerable to the charge of political lawyering, and he may have to lay the ghost of barratry.

More challenging is the demand for liberalized rules of standing so that, in effect, any citizen may appeal to the courts, on behalf of the community, to right a general wrong. Insofar as this principle is accepted (and the law is in flux), it opens the door to direct advocacy in the public interest. When a legal starting point is available—an argument founded in a preexisting principle, rule, or statute—advocacy becomes an unequivocal supplement to political action through legislative channels.

It is hardly surprising that social advocacy has, in some quarters, excited rosy hopes and stimulated political and legal overreaching. There is little reason to believe that such a strategy can make a *major* difference in achieving social justice. The great issues of opportunity and welfare depend on the commitment of large resources and on the development of programs for action. The courts are greatly limited in what they can do. In the field of welfare law, for example, social advocacy has been fairly successful in winning better procedural justice for recipients, and in striking down obnoxious efforts to invade privacy and regulate morality. These considerations touch closely on the expertise of the courts; and the remedies they frame have a relatively modest effect on welfare budgets. Demands for enlarged distributive justice, that is, wider entitlements and higher benefits, have been less successful. Insofar as social advocacy becomes a permanent feature of the legal process, it will have to accept a defined role and limited aspirations.

Whatever the outcome of these new developments, they may be taken as signaling a creative interplay of law and politics. The division of these spheres has been, historically, an anchor of legal legitimacy and a promise of legal integrity. These are not small benefits. But the wall of separation between legal and political decisions has never been unbreached, even in the heyday of transcendent law and judicial prestige. Contemporary society can even less afford that universal nostrum of institutional history: Purity through isolation, salvation through detachment.

If the intersection of law and politics is a threatening prospect, we may take some comfort from a distinction between "low politics" and "high politics." Low politics is power politics; it is the play of will, faction, interest, and domination. High politics is the realm of dialogue where the ends of group existence are defined. High politics is not divorced from self-interest but it sees politics as debased or ennobled, depending on how far self-interest is blended with a broader public interest and ideals of justice and citizenship are upheld. In high politics what is at stake is the character and integrity of the political community.

The recent debate over presidential impeachment has vividly contrasted low politics and high politics; it has also told us something about the place of law. Low politics is the doctrine that "an impeachable offense is whatever a majority of the House of Representatives considers it to be." No deference to principle is required, only an expression of majoritarian will. High politics takes another tack: An impeachable offense is a systematic abuse of official authority or a pattern of conduct that otherwise undermines the integrity of government. The offense is both legal and political. It is political because it is committed by political actors against the political process; it is legal in that it states a principle the Congress should apply to any president and not merely to a hapless incumbent.

Some have argued that an impeachable offense to be truly legal must be assimilated to the criminal law. The accused must have committed an indictable act. This point of view (insofar as it is more than a defense counsel's gambit) can be understood as upholding a radical separation of law and politics. In denying legal merit to "high" crimes peculiarly relevant to the exercise of authority, it may, in part, reflect a tradition of resistance to political crimes. But that position, in the case of impeachment, has not prevailed.

The law of impeachment is only a highly visible illustration of a more pervasive interplay of law and high politics. High politics reaches beyond procedure to discover the core values and fundamental commitments of the political community. The legal order participates in that process by building public purpose into the texture of law. It is the business of law to articulate principles that are neutral vis-à-vis particular outcomes, thereby preserving the integrity of adjudication. But in a larger sense, legal principles are not neutral. They are the moral foundations of a committed polity. If this is so, there can be no escape from an ultimate union of political, legal, and social doctrine.

Democracy and the Rule of Law

There can be law—even good law—without democracy. Many institutions are effectively guided by principles of legality, yet do not rest on the explicit consent of the governed. Both ideals are enriched, however, when the *affinity* of law and democracy is appreciated. That affinity is perhaps best revealed by contrasting two notions of the rule of law.

In one version the rule of law is "a government of laws rather than men"; it is a system that strives for legal autonomy, especially the separation of law and politics; husbands legal authority; demands unqualified obedience to the law's commands; and has as its distinctive competence the control of official discretion and the achievement of procedural fairness. This "rule of law model"[22] has a minimal connection with democracy, although it may include, of course, a principle of legislative supremacy.

An alternative view invests legality with a larger meaning. In this perspective the rule of law is a master ideal—the progressive reduction of arbitrariness in positive law and its administration. Positive law always includes some element of brute command, some abridgment of wisdom and sensibility, some failure to take account of all the interests at stake in rule-making and decision. At an extreme it may be "congealed injustice."[23]

The reduction of arbitrariness begins with a demand for legitimacy and for elementary constraints on political authority. From there it progresses to formal equality and the traditional model of the rule of law. We might well wish to rest content at that point. But the concept of arbitrariness embraces more than a want of procedural justice. Decisions and rules are experienced as arbitrary when the legal consumer senses a divorce of means and ends. He is asked to honor a system within which his own interests are but dimly perceived. From his standpoint, the autonomy and integrity of the legal process, if it has a low yield of substantive justice, may be purchased at too high a price.

Arbitrariness cannot be minimized unless there is a union of procedure and substance. To that end the legal process must be open to influence at many points so that all legitimate interests will be heard. As that occurs, legal competence shades into civic competence, and the democratic ethos lends its support to the rule of law.

The two conceptions of the rule of law are not antithetical. Each finds arbitrary authority repugnant. The second builds upon the first and takes its achievements for granted—procedural regularity, formal equality, judicial independence. Yet it is impatient with a restrictive, self-limiting vision of the place of law in society. The larger conception of the rule of law, as it strains toward a union of law and democracy, vindicates the pragmatic, purposive, outreaching impulse in American institutions. At the same time, it reaffirms a basic confidence in human nature, a sense that no a priori limits can be placed on the potential capacity of ordinary people to be full participants in the making of a legal order.

If American law gives to confidence an historic priority, it does not follow that skepticism is erased, or even muted. A pragmatic outlook can readily appreciate how precarious and fragile democratic law must be. There need be no embrace of a romantic fallacy that what is morally desirable and historically feasible is thereby especially fit to survive. On the contrary, just because the legal ideal (like any other) is fragile and needs special support, a certain skepticism is warranted. This means that, at any given time, civic competence is to be tested, not assumed, and adequate safeguards of institutional integrity are to be devised and maintained.

Modern society has created irrepressible demands for more widespread and more effective participation. In part because of those pressures, the need for a revitalized moral order becomes ever more acute. The challenge to the legal imagination is this: To accommodate those social necessities, to help rebuild the moral order, while retaining the framework and the spirit of American law. If this challenge is met, we may well discover that a synthesis of legal and democratic ideals has been the fundamental contribution of American jurisprudence.

Notes

1. See E.D. Warfield, *The Kentucky Resolutions of 1798* (New York: G.P. Putnam's Sons, 1887), pp. 157-158.

2. George A. Billias, *law and Authority in Colonial America* (Barre, Mass.: Barre Publishers, 1965), p. xiii.

3. Yosal Rogat, "Legal Realism," *The Encyclopedia of Philosophy*, vol. 4, pp. 420-421.

4. Leonard W. Levy, *Origins of the Fifth Amendment* (New York: Oxford, 1968), p. 338.

5. Oliver Wendell Holmes, Jr., *The Common Law* (Boston: Little, Brown, 1881), p. 35.

6. Lon L. Fuller, *Anatomy of the Law* (New York: Praeger, 1968), p. 43ff.

7. "Nor does the common law system admit the possibility of a court, however elevated, reaching a final, authoritative statement of what the law is in a general abstract sense. It is as if the system placed particular value upon dissension, obscurity, and the tentative character of judicial utterances." A.W.B. Simpson, "The Common Law and Legal Theory," in A.W.B. Simpson (ed.), *Oxford Essays in Jurisprudence*, Second Series, (Clarendon Press: Oxford, 1973), p. 90.

8. This theme has been stressed, with more attention to legislation, by James Willard Hurst. See especially *Law and the Conditions of Freedom in the Nineteenth Century United States* (Madison: Univ. of Wisconsin Press, 1956).

9. Roscoe Pound, *Jurisprudence* (St. Paul: West Publ. Co., 1959), vol. 3, Chap. 14.

10. See Lon L. Fuller and Melvin A. Eisenberg, *Basic Contract Law* 3d ed. (St. Paul: West Publ. Co., 1972), pp. 428-459; also Friedrich Kessler and Grant Gilmore, *Contracts: Cases and Materials*, 2d ed. (Boston: Little, Brown, 1970), p. 145.

11. See Philip Selznick, *Law, Society, and Industrial Justice* (New York: Russell Sage, 1969), Chap. 2.

12. "If men are to remain civilized, or to become so," wrote Tocqueville, "the art of associating together must grow and improve in the same ratio in which the equality of conditions is increased." *Democracy in America*, vol. II, Bk, 2, Chap. 5.

13. *Sale v. Railroad Commission*, 15 Cal. 2d 612 (1940).

14. Bacon's words are quoted in Norman Jacobson, "Knowledge, Tradition, and Authority: A Note on the American Experience," in Carl J. Friedrich (ed.), *Authority* (Cambridge: Harvard University Press, 1958), pp. 113-125.

15. See Mortimer R. Kadish and Sanford H. Kadish, *Discretion to Disobey: A Study of Lawful Departures from Legal Rules* (Stanford: Stanford University Press, 1973).

16. Philip Selznick, "Berkeley," *Commentary Magazine*, March 1963, p. 83.

17. Hannah Arendt, "Civil Disobedience," in Eugene V. Rostow (ed.), *Is Law Dead?* (New York: Simon and Shuster, 1971), p. 231.

18. Oliver Wendell Holmes, Jr., "The Path of the Law," in Julius J. Marke (ed.), *The Holmes Reader* (New York: Oceana, 1955), p. 63.

19. Philippe Nonet, *Administrative Justice: Advocacy and Change in a Government Agency* (New York: Russell Sage, 1969).

20. "We have gone far beyond Montesquieu. We have learned that danger of tyranny or injustice lurks in unchecked power, not in blended power." Kenneth Culp Davis, *Administrative Law Text* (St. Paul: West Publ. Co., 1959), p. 30.

21. Statement before Subcommittee on Employment, Manpower, and Poverty, U.S. Senate, Nov. 14, 1969.

22. See Kadish and Kadish, *Discretion to Disobey*, pp. 40ff.

23. Howard Zinn, *Disobedience and Democracy: Nine Fallacies on Law and Order* (New York: Vintage Books, 1968), p. 4.

XI The Great Polarity: Heredity v. Environment

Donald Fleming

From the beginning it has been clear that man is capable of changing both himself and his environment—and, of course, of changing himself by changing his environment. But it has also always been obvious that this ability is a limited one. Where and what those limits are has been one of the age-old questions about man, and the answer has profound implications for social policy.

In the past hundred years, the debate over the limits of man's power to define himself has passed out of the hands of theologians (the "predestination" versus "free-will" debate) and into the realm of biology and psychology, where it is cast as a discussion of the relative importance of heredity and environment (or "nature" and "nurture"). Yet though it is now a "scientific" question and presumably capable of being settled, no definitive answer has yet emerged. Indeed, the debate continues as furiously as it ever did before. In this essay Donald Fleming recounts the intellectual history of this fascinating debate within modern science, and suggests why it is so difficult to achieve any kind of unequivocal answers.

Men think in polarities. One of the most potent of these in the Western world, from antiquity into modern times, has been the balancing of fate against free will in determining the outcome of a person's life. The perceived boundary between them has frequently shifted, but the sense of man's condition as a resultant of the two forces has persisted. On the face of it, this way of looking at the world might have been fatally undermined by the decline of conventional religion in the last hundred years. In fact, however, Darwin and Spencer as the arch-subverters of the religious world view merely supplied the terms for a new version of the old polarity, now defined as the tension between heredity and environment.

Though some vague notions about heredity did come in before Darwin and Spencer, they were extremely vague indeed throughout the nineteenth century. By the same token, people had long been aware of something roughly corresponding to our notion of "environment," but even Darwin had to make do without the word itself and substituted clumsy expressions like "the external conditions of life." Spencer, on the other hand, seems to have been the principal agent in launching the word "environment" upon its prosperous career. Yet it was not so much the idea of heredity, or the idea of environment, but the polar relationship between them that Darwin and Spencer planted in the minds of men.

The same polarity was expressed by Darwin's cousin Francis Galton in terms of the opposition between Nature and Nurture. All such discussions were given a new turn by the quickening pace of research and speculation on heredity in the closing years of the nineteenth century, culminating in the "re-discovery" of Mendelism and the dawn of genetics.

From the beginning, the political and social import of this family of polarities revolved about the possibility and desirability of adjusting the lever-arm to make the environment either balance or outweigh heredity in shaping the actual human being. The emotional animus behind the harsher Spencerian forms of "Social Darwinism" was the conviction that the environment could be all to effectively manipulated, chiefly by sanitary and medical advances and the proliferation of public charity, to compensate for many hereditary weaknesses and the less fit thereby enabled to survive and procreate. Spencer's doctrine that such manipulations of the environment would constitute an intolerable interference with natural selection constituted the chief intellectual obstacle to social activism in the period from 1859 to 1914. But social activists could and did appropriate Spencer's environmentalism intact by merely reversing the emotional charge upon it from minus to plus and rejoicing in the efficacy of the environmental reforms that Spencer deplored.

Thus Lester Ward (1841 to 1913), as the main American defender of the compatibility of Darwinism and social activism, argued that natural selection, by perfecting the mind of man, had enabled the human race to take its future evolution into its own hands—to escape from the tyrannical adjudication of natural selection into the freedom of making and remaking itself. The most significant *human* environment was the realm of cooperative endeavors to achieve deliberately chosen goals, including the exploitation and transformation of the physical environment and the blunting of its immediate impact upon constitutionally weak or handicapped individuals. This modified version of environmentalism quickly established itself as the characteristic strategy of many socialists and liberals.

Yet there was nothing inevitable about the embrace of environmentalism by reform-minded activists. In his would-be science of eugenics, which was the very type of science-as-reform, Francis Galton fixed upon the other pole of the argument and tried to focus the impulse toward social planning on the calculated improvement of the breeding stock. Almost inevitably, eugenics was tainted by what would later be called elitism and racism and always carried with it the implication that many existing human stocks ought to be eliminated. In this sense, eugenics was the hereditarian equivalent of Spencerian individualism, informed by an identical intolerance for allegedly inferior types. Thus eugenics rapidly became as hateful to twentieth century liberals as Spencerism itself.

The other principal factor in undermining hereditarianism as an acceptable posture for Western liberals and radicals was the parallel decline in the fortunes of Lamarckism. As long as it was scientifically respectable to invoke the inheritance of acquired characteristics, many socialists in America and abroad welcomed the possibility of impressing desirable changes upon human heredity by social reforms that would thereby acquire greater permanence. This was the easy compromise between extreme environmentalism and extreme hereditarianism that constituted "Social Lamarckism." Only when the ill-repute of eugenics was compounded by the discrediting of Lamarckism in the 1920s did hereditarian modes of thought become almost entirely excluded from the range of intellectual options that Western liberals and radicals were prepared to entertain in framing their social philosophies. The situation was different in the Soviet Union, where the Western verdict on Lamarckism was resisted.

Ward's environmentalism and Galton's hereditarian eugenics shared the premise that the biological destiny of man was no longer ineluctable, that conscious endeavors could bring evolution under human control. They differed profoundly on which pole of the opposition between heredity and environment to tackle for this purpose, but both supposed that man had transcended his biological origins to become a fundamentally different organism from any other. Yet, as they well knew, one of the conditions of making plausible social and political discourse after Darwin was to accept the persistence of instinctive behavior as an evolutionary legacy from the lower animals to man.

The modern study of instincts dated from Darwin and Spencer and constituted the main impetus given by them to psychology. In less academic terms, the original skittishness about acknowledging man's animal kin became increasingly concentrated on the overlap between the instincts of the dominant animal and those of all others. Man no longer looked like the apes, but did he still behave like them?

The initial response to the broaching of this theme by Darwin and Spencer was the burgeoning of an anecdotal and anthropomorphizing literature about animals, unjustly associated with the name of George Romanes in England and more fittingly with that of Alfred Brehm in Germany—a literature oscillating between science and sentimentality with the net effect of promoting many beloved domestic species, sage cats and trusty dogs, to the status of honorary human beings. The shock of admitting the link with other animals was blunted by assimilating many of the latter to mankind, though seldom the ones that were postulated in evolutionary theory as man's closest relations.

In the not-very-long run, this provoked a more austere science of "animal" or "comparative" psychology, pioneered in the English-speaking world by C. Lloyd Morgan and E.L. Thorndike and committed to minimal interpretations of animal behavior in keeping with Lloyd Morgan's famous "canon of parsimony" (actually a form of Occam's razor):

In no case may we interpret an action as the outcome of the exercise of a higher physical faculty, if it can be interpreted as the outcome of the exercise of one which stands lower in the psychological scale.

Less resoundingly at the time, the American C.O. Whitman, the first director of Woods Hole, and the German Oskar Heinroth dwelt upon the taxonomic value of instinctive behavior and minutely observed the behavior of pigeons and ducks respectively.

Ideologically, the new science of comparative psychology produced two highly divergent traditions. One of these was epitomized by Jacques Loeb's concept of "tropisms"—obligatory and invariable physiological responses by a given organism to specific stimuli. Loeb's theory of tropisms was justifiably regarded as a kind of reflexology. J.B. Watson originally intended to write his dissertation under Loeb. When first enunciated in 1913, Watson's "behaviorism" was a methodological rather than substantive pronouncement: Henceforth he and other animal psychologists ought to confine themselves severely to the overt behavior of the organism in question without attempting to conjecture about any accompanying mental processes. Watson's thought, as it subsequently developed, was an unstable amalgam of this methodological simplification and an appropriation of Pavlov's concept of conditioned reflexes to the rearing of human infants. In the resulting confusion, some critics conceived of behaviorism itself as a reflexology—a brutal form of environmentalism consecrated to wrenching predictable responses from biological robots.

If this was either a caricature or a misapprehension of the more fastidious versions of behaviorism, the critics were undoubtedly correct in sensing that they were confronted with a basic temperament that relished the irresistible molding of the organism to the natural or social environment. The bluntest defense of this attitude was destined to be B.F. Skinner's *Beyond Freedom and Dignity* (1971), in which the greatest of the behaviorists proclaimed the desirability of controlling people to the utmost through the manipulation of their environments. If, as he freely acknowledged, environmentalist reformers had often failed to accomplish anything in the past, it was because they had contented themselves with an abstract allegiance to the primacy of the environment or had not known how to take hold of it for their purposes. Now, thanks to himself and other psychologists in the behaviorist tradition, there were highly specific techniques of social control for extinguishing undesirable impulses or, better still, reenforcing desirable conduct. The converse of Skinner's environmentalism, and an almost invariable accompaniment of behaviorist philosophies, was his tendency to minimize the intractability of an individual's gene-complex and the obstacle that this presented to achieving unlimited external control over the human organism. Skinner emphasized that the gene-complex was itself the product of environmental selection over the ages. This was true enough, but did not speak to the practical problem of overriding the genetic bounds within which a given organism was currently operating.

The scientifically respectable alternative to all reflexologies was a tradition stemming directly from Lloyd Morgan and his kindred spirit in America, E.L. Thorndike. Expanding upon a hint thrown out by Spencer, they postulated an inherited repertory of standard behaviors by which the organism responded at random to new stimuli till an appropriate response was hit upon by "trial and error"—Lloyd Morgan's phrase. The man who expressly turned this concept against Loeb was the fittingly named Herbert Spencer Jennings, who showed in his *Behavior of the Lower Organisms* (i.e., bacteria, Protozoa, and lower Metazoa) that many even of these simple organisms, on being confronted with an unfamiliar stimulus, engaged in random permutations of their usual spontaneous activities till they chanced upon some course of action that relieved the discomfort induced by a new situation.

The basic issue at stake between Loeb and Jennings was how abruptly and how directly the relevant factor in the organism's environment acted upon its physiological heredity. The implication in Loeb was that the organism passively "awaited" the tropizing stimulus and instantly yielded the one possible response. For Jennings, in contrast, the organism was continually rehearsing a variety of inherited behaviors, actively exploring its environment, till some stimulus organized and focused a particular response. In Loeb's scheme, if the stimulus in question never occurred, the appropriate physiological reaction would never be mobilized. The inherited capacity to make the response could only be awakened from dormancy if something in the environment released it. In Jenning's scheme, the underlying physiology would always be erupting into instinctive behavior even if no stimulus should ever appear toward which the behavior could profitably be directed. He was expounding the physiology of spontaneity.

In retrospect—very much in retrospect—the key figure in perpetuating the tradition of Lloyd Morgan, Thorndike, and Jennings was Whitman's student Wallace Craig. In ultimately classic studies, of which the most important appeared in 1918, Craig investigated the instinctive behavior of pigeons (Whitman's own favorite experimental animal) and demonstrated that, on being deprived of the company of females of his own species, the male would successively lower his sights and direct his instinctive courtship dance, in turn, toward females of other pigeon species (normally ignored), stuffed pigeons, rolled-up pieces of cloth, and (after solitary confinement for a long time) the empty corner of his cage. The threshold that had to be surmounted by an activating stimulus for the dance was continually lowered till the instinctive movement occurred in a psychological vacuum or near-vacuum, when there was virtually no surrogate-stimulus at all.

In Craig's interpretation of his own findings, every instinctive motor pattern created an appetite for its own discharge, an irresistible internal craving presumably correlated with mounting physiological pressures in the organism. Thus an instinct, if starved of its normal stimulus, *must* erupt into a restless questing for something to discharge it. This phenomenon he described as "appetitive behavior" cheated of the consummation to which the instinct would normally lead on. The fact that the appropriate "consummatory behavior" had been blocked was powerless to extinguish the appetitive behavior. In the absence of the appropriate stimulus, the appetite did not disappear or even lie dormant but triggered an irrepressible and autonomous questing that might be turned to very different purposes from those that had been subserved by the original instinct. This possibility, of the "ritualization" of instinctive behavior that passed over from being directly functional into something that craved release for its own sake and became a form of self-expression, was vividly broached by Julian Huxley in his memorable paper of 1914 on the courtship dance of the great crested grebe.

The period from 1910 to 1930 was in fact remarkably rich in major contributions to animal psychology. Oskar Heinroth published in 1910 an account of the phenomenon later christened "imprinting," and his four great volumes on the birds of Central Europe appeared between 1913 and 1929. Huxley published on the grebe in 1914, Craig announced his discovery of appetitive behavior in 1918, and Whitman's voluminous pigeon studies (the nearest American equivalent of Heinroth on birds) were published posthumously in 1919. In 1920 the British ornithologist H. Eliot Howard published the book that firmly established the concept of the territoriality of birds among English-speaking naturalists (actually enunciated as early as 1868 by a German). In 1922 the Norwegian Thorleif Schjelderup-Ebbe announced his discovery of the pecking order in domestic fowls, the source of all subsequent research on dominance relations among animals. Two American investigators were active in following up these leads—W.C. Allee in generalizing the dominance concept, and C.R. Carpenter in extending the territoriality and dominance concepts specifically to primates.

The man who bound all these themes together into a new science of "ethology" was the Austrian Konrad Lorenz, active from the early 1930s onward. Obliged by a teacher to read widely in the already voluminous literature of animal behavior, he was favorably impressed by Jennings and overwhelmingly impressed by Heinroth, with whom he constructed a master-disciple relationship though never his student in any formal sense. He also read the virtually unknown Wallace Craig with great enthusiasm and engaged in extended correspondence with him in the mid-1930s. In spite of what he later regarded as some early lapses of his own into reflexology, Lorenz became increasingly insistent upon the "spontaneity" of organisms in Jenning's and Craig's sense—the physiological welling-up of motor impulses that do not require an external stimulus to activate them, at least preliminarily.

In some ways the most remarkable aspect of Lorenz's work was the total absence of the nervousness about anthropomorphizing animals that had long been almost religiously inculcated in students of animal behavior in reaction to Romanes and Brehm. In this respect, Lorenz had the sympathy of Heinroth, who had originally been attracted to the subject by reading Brehm as a boy and, though infinitely more rigorous in his observations, was equally disinclined to be parsimonious in attributing higher impulses to animals. Lorenz, for his part, quoted with glee the comment of an associate that, after all, geese were "only human." Moreover, some of his most important research, beguilingly chronicled in *King Solomon's Ring*, consisted of taking geese and other birds into the family circle and actually getting himself "imprinted" on some of them at birth as a member of their own species. Lorenz clearly regarded himself as suffering, like Darwin, from many people's persistent refusal to see themselves as animals. The humane import of his work, as he saw it, was to wring this concession from them.

It followed for Lorenz that ethology always had direct social and political bearings for the human race—not that man was identical with any other animal but that he shared fundamental instincts with the rest and could never be realistically understood in isolation from his animal kind. Behavior, as well as anatomy, had come down in the family. Accordingly, Lorenz did not hesitate to say that there could be "no correct political system, no sound ordering of society," without grasping the home truths of ethology—the "weal and woe" of the whole human race depended upon it.

This might have been an undoctrinaire commendation of behavioral studies in general, but Lorenz had something more precise in mind. He saw authentic ethology as a vindication of the physiologically-triggered "spontaneity" of animals, a devastating refutation of environmentalist philosophies. All such philosophies were lumped together by Lorenz under the name of "behaviorism," defined by him as the doctrine that "Man is an infinitely modifiable product of his environment"—"the completely erroneous view that animal and human behavior is predominantly reactive and that, even if it contains any innate elements at all, it can be altered, to an unlimited extent, by learning." Lorenz attributed the general palatability of such views to "certain democratic principles" that forbade people to "admit that human beings are not born equal and that not all have equal chances of becoming ideal citizens." He, who had spoken kindly of Nazi racism during the Second World War, though he later repented it, sometimes preferred to say that his and ethology's quarrel was not with democracy but merely with the "pseudo-democratic," i.e., authoritarian, tendency toward the manipulation of mass man against his own interests in America, Russia, and Red China.

Lorenz himself proved to be extremely reactive to one factor in his own environment—the increasingly cosmic stream of pronouncements by Sigmund Freud in the 1920s and early 1930s, culminating in *Why War?* and *Civilization and Its Discontents*, in which he affirmed the existence of an instinctive death wish, temporarily deflected onto society in the form of aggression. This was a highly provocative foray into the central area of ethological concerns, and all the more provocative as a blatant example of pseudo-biological discourse, basically speculative, with no solid data to support it, but calculated to divert the educated public from what Lorenz regarded as the urgent teachings of true science. The differences between them should not, however, be allowed to obscure the fact that they were united in attaching supreme importance to aggression as a component in human nature.

As a long-standing irritant, Freud on aggression ultimately produced a direct rejoinder in Lorenz's most ambitious effort to apply the lessons of ethology to the analysis of human behavior, the book called in English *On Aggression*, but more revealingly in the original German (1963) *The So-Called Evil*. Here Lorenz incorporated Huxley's ritualization, Howard's territoriality, Schjelderup-Ebbe's dominance relations, Craig's appetitive and consummatory behavior, and the fruits of Heinroth's and his own researches into a general theory of aggression. Despite Freud, aggression was not an evil per se, rooted in forces inherently hostile to life, but the sanction among animals for enforcing territorial boundaries and hierarchically ordered social arrangements, by which, paradoxically, the peace was kept and the weak were spared the worst assaults of the strong by knowing their place. When territoriality took the form of an individual pair living separately with their unfledged offspring, inherent differences in strength or status were leveled or reversed by each animal's becoming more fiercely combative on home territory and potential intruders correspondingly less aggressive. In addition, in those "heavily armed" animals that were capable of killing members of their own species at a single stroke, there were ritual gestures of submission by which the one that was losing out in face-to-face combat, if it actually broke out, could compel the victor to drop the fight before dealing a death blow.

In some teleost (bony-skeletoned) fishes, birds, and mammals, aggressive impulses, reined in by stereotyped propitiatory behavior, had evolved into autonomous ritual displays between friends and particularly between male and female, deeply satisfying to both and the nucleus of the "personal bond" between individual animals—the ultimate source, in Lorenz's view, of all love and fidelity. He claimed that the personal bond was unknown except among animals with "highly developed intra-specific aggression" (i.e., within the same species) and was stronger the more aggressive the individual and the species. Apart from personal bonding, there could be "anonymous" companionship within an animal troop or flock. Here too the cohesiveness of the group was dependent upon aggressive instincts, vented upon other groups in collective attack and defense. Everywhere that Lorenz looked, he found aggression to be inseparably linked with the life-affirming and life-enhancing values.

All the evolutionary benefits from aggressive instincts envisioned by Lorenz could be and had been obtained without waging war to the death upon one's own kind. But pragmatic definitions of "kind" differed widely. Some animals scarcely ever killed a member of the same species as themselves. Others, notably rats, lived amicably within their own communities but slaughtered all "alien," though biologically identical, rats that they encountered.

Man was at one with the rats—able to live *fairly* peacefully within his own clan or nation but frequently murderous toward outsiders. He had preserved the aggressive instincts intact but the equally instinctive brakes upon them in many animals were either defective or inoperative in him.

Lorenz's explanation was that man belonged to the species that were lightly armed by nature, seldom able to inflict instant death upon their fellows, and fleet of foot if seriously endangered. In such animals, the inhibitions upon killing within the species did not have to act as infallibly as in the species that could kill their own with a single bite or blow. Apart from this, man had uniquely evolved into a prolific inventor of weapons for killing at a distance, with no opportunity for the victim to make the ritual propitiations that frequently do achieve their inhibitory purpose in face-to-face encounters even among human beings. He had acquired new organs, from arrows to hydrogen bombs, which were and, at the same time, were not extensions of himself. They did not connect organically with any remotely commensurate restraints upon their use.

For Lorenz, the development of technology had another supremely important bearing upon human aggression. With weapons and other tools, man had established enough mastery over the rest of nature, animate and inanimate, to escape from the most urgent pressures formerly exerted upon him from that source. But Lorenz held it to be axiomatic that a species would evolve in unadaptive directions if the selection pressures from the extra-specific environment let up. By becoming increasingly confined to intra-specific selection, man was doomed to raise up leaders who were the most unbalanced specimens of the warrior mentality, outbidding each other in ferocity, with aggressive impulses *toward other human beings* permeating the entire society.

Given the circumstances in which it now manifested itself, should the goal be to diminish aggression or even to breed it out of the human race entirely by some form of eugenics? Lorenz's answer was that if this were possible, which he doubted, it would be undesirable. He saw the "militant enthusiasm" generated by aggressive instincts as the driving force in all constructive, as well as destructive, human endeavors. It was "indispensable for the achievement of the highest human goals," which would otherwise be slackly pursued. As the aggressive component in human nature should not and probably could not be liquidated, the only recourse for Lorenz was to fortify its good results and mitigate the bad. Maximum personal acquaintance should be fostered between people of different nations and ideologies; psychoanalysts should be encouraged to expound the possibilities of sublimation; and, above all, there should be "intelligent and responsible channeling of militant enthusiasm" away from killing other people toward substitute objects of aggression.

Though Lorenz nowhere gave any indication of being aware of the fact, he was echoing William James's famous essay of 1910 on "The Moral Equivalent of War," in the double sense of assigning a positive role to aggressive instincts and trying to deflect them toward goals that could be shared by the entire human race. One obvious possibility was the "conquest of nature." This had some attractions for Lorenz as well as for James. In one sense, Lorenz was prepared to argue that man's triumphs over external nature were the source of his present plight because they enabled him to concentrate on being aggressive toward his own species; but in another sense, the trouble was that the vast majority of mankind did not participate, either directly or vicariously, in a truly insatiable thirst for the conquest of nature by science. They had accepted the practical benefits of being shielded from the brute pressures of the environment without enlisting their militant enthusiasm in the permanent adventure of mastering it.

Identifying praiseworthy objects of aggression, as distinguished from commending them sufficiently to the bulk of mankind, did not seem particularly hard in 1910, or for that matter in 1963, when Lorenz published *On Aggression*. But in the decade that followed Lorenz's book, the task of defining acceptable outlets for aggression became infinitely more difficult with the spotlighting of ecological issues. Many ecologically minded people began to say that far too much of man's aggression had already been vented outward upon his environment, whether physical or biological. In their view, social peace would be too dearly purchased, and not for very long anyhow, by glorifying the still further conquest of nature as the proper business of mankind. For some ecologically inclined social critics, though by no means all, the conquest ideal, hopelessly tarnished in their eyes, definitely encompassed the exploration of space, which was one of Lorenz's best bets for getting mankind to pull together.

The ecologists' aversion to the conquest of nature would not rule out the short-term persistence of militant enthusiasm as commended by Lorenz, for ecology *was* the militant enthusiasm of the early 1970s and one might be aggressive in preaching the ecological gospel to a still largely unconverted world. But if it were ever enthroned as the modern religion, ecology would represent the triumph of inherently unaggressive values in man's relation to his environment. The logic of Lorenz's argument, though unexpounded by him, was that this development might then drive the undischarged aggressive instincts more violently back upon man himself.

Lorenz on aggression was widely read (and vehemently criticized) throughout the world, but that was only part of his impact upon social and political thought. He unwittingly and a bit ruefully spawned a semi-popular literature on man as an animal which had become by the mid-1970s the most prevalent form of political and social theory after Marxism and Freudianism. The principal popularizers of ethology in this vein were Robert Ardrey in *African Genesis: A Personal Investigation into the Animal Origins and Nature of Man* (1961), *The Territorial Imperative: A Personal Inquiry into the Animal Origins of Property and Nations* (1966; dedicated "To the memory of Henry Eliot Howard"), and *The Social Contract: A Personal Inquiry into the Evolutionary Sources of Order and Disorder* (1970); Desmond Morris in *The Naked Ape* (1967) and *The Human Zoo* (1969); and Lionel Tiger in *Men in Groups* (1969) and, with Robin Fox, *The Imperial Animal* (1971).

Among them, Ardrey, Morris, and Tiger were effecting a fusion between ethology and primate paleontology, particularly as elucidated by Robert Broom, Raymond Dart, and Louis and Mary Leakey on the basis of fossil remains and artifacts discovered in Southern Africa in the course of the twentieth century. The heart of the paleontologists' contribution lay in their discovery of the Australopithecine hominid, the nearest of the near-men to man himself. With this discovery was coupled, but more controversially, the alleged demonstration of the killer-instincts of *Australopithecus* as deduced from the remains of his weapons and some of his victims. Apart from the intrinsic interest of these findings and inferences, *Australopithecus* became for Ardrey, Morris, and Tiger a particularly convenient object on whom to project the behavioral patterns uncovered by ethologists, chiefly in birds and fishes. The ethological discourse that carried solid conviction as applied to geese and tropical fish tailed off at the other extreme into tantalizing but insecure analogies with human conduct. The gap could be bridged by evoking the transitional figure of *Australopithecus*, generously endowed with the behavior delineated by the ethologists and plausibly foreshadowing the traits of the man-to-come. In popular ethology, as in paleontology, *Australopithecus* became a crucial link between man and the other animals, the most persuasive exemplification of ethological man.

The upshot of blending ethology with paleontology was the creation, largely by Ardrey, Morris, and Tiger, of a new myth of early man or near-man—not a "myth" in the invidious sense of a deliberate tissue of falsehoods but rather in the sense of a clarifying vision of the origin of things. The prototype of such myths in modern times is the allegedly Rousseauistic vision of the natural goodness of primitive peoples and the debilitating effects of civilization—a grave distortion of Rousseau's own opinions but nonetheless potent for that. It is highly revealing that the popular ethologists, particularly Ardrey, are vehement in their denunciations of Rousseau, as if to demonstrate their consciousness of competing with him in constructing a myth of early history.

The new myth of early man is set in Africa (not Asia) and takes its departure from the supposed demonstration that *Australopithecus* and by extrapolation early man were predators—"killer apes" as the mythmakers preferred to put it. Where other primates were (and remained) fruit-pluckers effortlessly harvesting the jungle whenever the urge came upon them, *Australopithecus*-on-the-way-to-man came down from the trees and out of the jungle on to the broad African savannas, treeless and barren, in pursuit of game. Everything else in the early history and ineradicable behavior of man allegedly followed from this resort to a killer's way of life. Apart from the long-term biological implications of moving on to a protein-rich diet, the carnivorous hominids needed weapons, if only the humerus of the antelope, to bring down prey bigger than themselves. As their prey was elusive, they had to improve their cognitive powers by gradually acquiring bigger brains. The socially decisive aspect of the situation was that they needed to hunt in packs. The hunters formed bonds to one another for collective attack and collective defense. Thus the rudimentary beginnings of fidelity within the group were inextricably bound up with aggression toward their prey and toward rival hunters. The hunting pack required leaders, and this necessity fostered dominance relations and consolidated the community still further by assigning a fixed place to its members in an orderly social scheme. This was the germ of all political arrangements.

Pregnant females, or females trammeled by suckling infants, were a drag on the hunters. A fateful sexual division of labor, transcending sheer physiology, inexorably followed, by which females not only bore the offspring but were increasingly confined to tending them while the males were off hunting. The net effect was to orient the female away from the most exciting public concerns of the troop toward individual encounters with males and infants. As the females were left behind with the young, there had to be a "behind" for the males to return to, bearing trophies of the hunt, a home base to fall back upon for securing the perpetuation of the species. This was the genesis of human "territory" in the ethological sense. The collective territory was susceptible of subdivision into smaller areas where a male could install his mate, secure in the knowledge that she was *not* common property. The pair-bond in turn strengthened the solidarity of the hunting cohort by reducing sexual rivalry for possession of the females. Private property in territory and females alike was no modern invention but the nub of the social order from prehistoric times.

The tacit assumption animating the whole myth was that adaptive forms of behavior in a predatory style of life, extending over vast periods of time before the comparatively recent introduction of agriculture, had become indelibly incorporated in human instincts by evolutionary selection of those who were naturally inclined toward the appropriate conduct. The implication was that for good and ill, the instincts of the hunting apes had survived substantially intact in twentieth century man.

Every link in this construction was highly problematical, but this is inherent in the process of myth-making about early man. If the craving to possess such a myth is legitimate, as well as irrepressible, the only criteria for judging it will be its internal consistency and its compatibility with fossil and other physical remains, the behavior of the surviving primates, the life of primitive tribes in recent centuries, and, the newest ingredient, ethological observations. None of these sources, singly or combined, can *prove* the historicity of a myth of early man; but negatively they can drain away its plausibility. Many, though not all, ethologists would question whether territoriality as classically exemplified in birds and fishes can be attributed in any rigorous sense to human beings. In the view of these skeptics, if the hunting apes really were "territorial," that was one thing they did not bequeath to us in any recognizable form. At least one reputable field observer has also objected that primates do not live (as the new myth of early man requires) in closed groups, excluding outsiders; but this appears to be definitely a minority opinion.

It would be a caricature to say that Konrad Lorenz or any of his popularizers had set out to write a political tract of whatever persuasion; but among them they framed a broadly conservative position. Tiger and Fox defined social justice as "an equal chance to become unequal" in a world where social hierarchies were inevitable and indispensable. Ardrey repeatedly recurred to the ethological sanctions of private property. He spoke of nature's "prejudice in favor of order" wherever living things were concerned and said that in most species the "instincts of order" were assigned to the males. Tiger and Fox denied that men's universal dominance over women was the product of a conspiracy to keep the latter down. They maintained that the sexual division of labor was deeply rooted in the biological and ethological foundations of social life, and not to be equated with racial discrimination. They spoke of the true function of schooling as conservative, in the sense of teaching children how things are rather than how they ought to be. Small human animals, they said, were still "geared," as in the distant past, to learn by building upon the established continuities of their lives, particularly the example of the parents. The effort to use the schools as an agency of social reform could easily result in disorienting the young by alienating them from the values of the home at the very period when they were most in need of psychological security as the condition of learning anything at all. As a high-minded example of diverting the school from its natural function (in a cause that they themselves approved of), Tiger and Fox cited busing for racial integration, with its implied criticism of the parents for making their homes in segregated neighborhoods.

Over and above any topical concerns of the 1960s and 1970s, the popularizers of ethology insisted upon the extremely limited malleability of human nature and the virtual impossibility of transcending man's animal origins. Ardrey, Morris, Tiger, and Fox, with Lorenz looming in the background as a tutelary spirit, were engaged in an aggressive updating of hereditarianism, subverting the liberal strategy of environmental reform at the source by dwelling upon the most palpably inborn and stubbornly enduring component in human behavior—the instincts that did not have to be inculcated and could not be snuffed out.

Even in this group, Robert Ardrey stood out as a peculiarly exasperated critic of environmentalism as a philosophy of social amelioration. He said that since the 1930s a sense had been steadily growing in him of living in the "Age of the Alibi," when juvenile delinquency and all other social problems were blamed on hostile environments, and offenders were invariably described as "sick or deprived or rejected," from "a bad family background," pathetic victims of worse wrongs than they themselves could ever inflict. Ardrey regarded all such arguments as variations upon the ubiquitous "romantic fallacy" that man was "a product of his social environment," only awaiting the redesign of society to shine forth in his pristine nobility. The main propagator of the romantic fallacy and Ardrey's *bête noire* was Jean-Jacques Rousseau, banefully seconded in America by Thomas Jefferson; but "the most stunning and cataclysmic triumph" of naive environmentalism over the minds of men had been Marxism. Ardrey held that the principal task of those who had mastered the recent developments in ethology and paleontology was to bring home to the human race that they were killer apes who had risen in the world but remained predatory by nature. Basic hostility was in themselves rather than in the environment.

The other popularizers of ethology, and Lorenz himself, had no quarrel with this proposition; but they were certainly prepared to lay much greater emphasis than Ardrey upon the possibility of rechanneling the instincts by changes in the environment. As Lionel Tiger put the matter, instincts were "genetically programmed propensities." Like all other genetic propensities, they could only find expression within the terms afforded by the organism's environment. Yet, though Tiger and Fox were among the least doctrinaire expositors of the politics of ethology, they too brought the weight of their argument heavily down on the side of the inborn "postures, gestures, and movements" that constituted the basic vocabulary of human behavior. Moreover, Tiger and Fox clearly regarded the cultural, social, and political environment into which human beings were born as itself a highly elaborated product of the instincts that were native to that kind of animal. Even in its least tendentious forms, the politics of ethology envisioned severe restraints upon the efficacy of environmental reforms in countermanding man's long instinctual heritage.

The other principal expression of contemporary hereditarianism is the renewed emphasis by the psychologists H.J. Eysenck, Arthur Jensen, and Richard Herrnstein on the heritability of intelligence. Herrnstein saw himself professionally as the product of a long immersion in behaviorism, which he regarded as part of the "prevailing environmentalism" against which he had begun to rebel. When he referred skeptically to the promises that kept coming from the behaviorists to "remake man," Herrnstein was unmistakably aiming at B.F. Skinner.

Though hereditarian thought as applied to social problems is currently growing in importance, often under heavy fire, the tantalizing possibility now floats before us, in the wake of Watson and Crick's discovery of the structure of DNA, of achieving notable feats of "genetic engineering" and thereby dissolving the polarity between heredity and environment. The theoretical possibilities include the manipulation of DNA in the genome; enucleation of germ cells cultured in laboratories and substitution of entire tailor-made DNA molecules; and hybridization of cells to bring superior genes into play.

The detailed variants upon these general strategies are almost innumerable. They all have in common the fact that they cannot be accomplished at present except in viruses and bacteria or in cell cultures. Yet even if appropriate techniques for altering functional human germ cells were at hand, which they most emphatically are not, the correlation of *instincts* with the relevant genes would still remain one of the remotest conceivable prospects in biology. Genetic engineering for superior intelligence, though remote enough, would be simple by comparison. For as far ahead as one can see, instincts and intelligence are likely to remain the most intractably hereditary factors in human conduct, the most insistent reminders of the limits on man's capacity to make and remake himself. To inculcate this lesson in the culture at large is one of the principal offices of contemporary biology.

XII

246 Years of American Foreign Policy: Doric, Ionic—and Corinthian?

Bayless Manning

In no nation do issues of foreign policy create more moral and intellectual turbulence than in the United States. Other countries, of course, do have serious internal disagreements about foreign policy, but these disagreements usually occur within an accepted and traditional definition of the "national interest," and they involve conflicting estimates of the practical import of different policies. In the United States, however, differences over foreign policy are an aspect of the process of moral self-definition of the American character. Our attitudes toward foreign policy not only prescribe what we should do, they inform us as to the kind of nation we are and wish to be. Paradoxically, this "pragmatic" nation which has always prided itself on keeping its politics at arm's length from ideological passions, finds in foreign policy the focus for intense ideological controversy.

The ideologies, of course, change and evolve as the nation itself changes and evolves. As Bayless Manning points out, the growth of the United States from a small, isolated republic to a world power has meant radical changes in the agenda of foreign policy debate. Yet, as he also emphasizes, the fundamental fact does not change: Americans still see foreign policy as an area in which American ideals are either realized or subverted, and one cannot understand our foreign policy without taking this into account.

The New World became a subject of European diplomacy immediately upon its discovery, as the Pope was called upon to settle the competing jurisdictional claims of the kings of Spain and Portugal.

253

For the Americas, the 1500s were Spanish. But after the destruction of the Armada in 1588 by a combination of English sailors and provident gales, His Catholic Majesty was forced to concentrate upon preserving his gold sources in South America and could no longer monopolize the Northern area. The English settled Jamestown in 1607, the French founded Quebec in 1608, the Dutch discovered the Hudson River in 1609, and the Puritans arrived in Plymouth in 1620. Throughout the 1600s, permanent English settlements spread along the Atlantic coast, while French trappers and priests, in search of skins to sell and souls to save, worked their way down the St. Lawrence, across the Great Lakes and south down the Mississippi, reaching New Orleans in 1682. The Glorious Revolution of 1688 put England in a position to challenge Louis XIV's France, Europe's new dominant land power, and North America was to be one of the prizes in the struggle—not only a subject of European politics but an object of it.

For 127 years, from 1688 to 1815, England and France were more or less continuously in hostilities, though historians customarily identify six wars. In the first three, the inhabitants of the American colonies were primarily onlookers, and the object of attention of map drawers at diplomatic negotiations. But in 1754 the fourth of these titanic struggles for empire started in America as the French and Indian War and was exported to Europe as the Seven Years' War. The residents of the North American continent had entered upon the stage of world politics, no longer as subject or as object but as a significant actor, and the American foreign policy experience was begun.

In 1754 French-Canadians built Fort Duquesne at the strategic river intersection that is today Pittsburgh. The Virginia Colony, which claimed the area as its own, sent a force to guard the mouth of the river under the command of 22-year-old Lieutenant Colonel George Washington. He was defeated by a larger force of Canadians and Indians and capitulated. In 1755 both France and Great Britain sent regular troops to support their colonials, and in 1756 declared war.

After four years of warfare in North America and seven in Europe, France and her allies were forced to the peace table in defeat, where the Treaty of Paris stripped France of her worldwide empire. In North America she ceded to England all of Canada and all of North America east of the Mississippi; she also ceded to Spain all of her claims to land west of the Mississippi, in part to keep that area from going to the British, too. Great Britain also received eastern and western Florida from Spain (who had inadvisedly entered the war on the losing side in its final year) and limited but rich trade rights in the Spanish-American colonies, theretofore closed to non-Spanish ships. But the American colonies, viewed separately from Great Britain, were the biggest winners.[a]

For the Americans, the threat of French and Indian forts and raiding parties to the west of the coastal colonies was removed. The way was opened to

---

[a]In the longer view, the biggest losers were the Great Lakes Indians, whose mode of life was compatible with that of the French-Canadian trappers, but not with that of the British farmers.

migration across the Appalachians to the Mississippi. Trade to the Spanish West Indies was opened to colonial ships and merchants. Colonials of all economic classes had fought for years side by side with British regulars and against formidable French and Indian adversaries; the colonials had gained invaluable combat experience and even more invaluable self-confidence, amounting even to a sense of superiority, at least in the art of backwoods warfare. The authority and independence of the elected colonial assemblies had increased during the war as the British colonial governors had found it necessary to call upon them for soldiers and money, and the assemblies had made good use of their consequent bargaining power to frustrate enforcement of unpopular imperial policies and laws emanating from London.

There were 1.5 million inhabitants of the British-American colonies in 1750. As the 1760s became the 1770s, their temper was increasingly the self-assurance of experienced and independent men. The American colonials were well on their way toward their first, and still their most important, explicit foreign policy decision—to declare themselves an independent actor among the nation-states of the world. They would bring to their relationships with other nation-states special attitudes and perspectives born out of their special history.

Part I—Doric

Every nation's perspective on foreign relations is unique, because it is the product of a specifically unique national history. But the uniqueness of the foreign affairs history of the United States is generic. The United States never shared in the fundamental experiences that predominate in the foreign affairs history of other Western nations.

Forging the Nation-State

Beginning at least with Charlemagne, the major business in European political history was the replacement of the feudal order by the secular, centralized nation-state. The United States had no participation in that great change. Most of the period of nation-state building was over by 1492, and substantially all of it (excepting the special cases of Italy and Germany) was over before the American colonies began to stir independently in the mid-1700s.

American government did, of course, have to deal with that most intractable of all political governmental problems, the relationship between the collectivity and its components, between the aggregate and the parts. The effort of the Articles of Confederation to deal with that problem was a failure; the effort of the Constitution to deal with it was ultimately successful, but only through a civil war; and the struggle for accommodation between centralized and decentralized power in the American federal system remains active and intense today.

But the United States did not have to endure through the centuries of struggle revolving about the birth of the idea of nationhood, the dilution of Vatican temporal power, and the growth of urban political power. For most countries, nationhood was bought at the cost of fear and hatred of near neighbors and earlier social power groups that had to be smashed. The United States was born without either of these costs, and its foreign policy had never had to reckon with either. For the United States, nationhood brought conflict with Great Britain only, and even that conflict was special since the Revolution bore with it on both sides the ambivalences of the adolescent freeing himself from parental strings. Once released from British imperial control, the American colonies had available to them, and built in, the basic components of contemporary nationhood and a leadership that proved skillful enough to organize and administer it.[b]

Wars of Dynasty

Connected with the growth of the monarchical nation-state was the irrepressible impulse of Europe's crowns to reach out to extend their hegemony over neighboring sovereigns and to seek to install their own dynastic lines in other realms. Wars like those of the Austrian succession and the Spanish succession were the primary occupation of princes, and the stuff of which international relations in Europe were chiefly made. While in time the United States was to see its own period of expansion and global power conflict, it did not experience, except in the most passing way in the early 1700s, the phenomenon of dynastic conflict for the personal vainglory and aggrandizement of hereditary monarchs. And the founders of the United States were resolved that the nation would not experience it.

Their solutions were to be two. Dynastic wars were perceived as the by-products of monarchy; the New World was to be a republic, immune (by definition) from dynastic strife and inherently indisposed (as many believed) toward war of any kind. The other solution was voiced by Washington as, in his farewell address, he warned the nation not to become embroiled in European disputes through the entanglement of foreign alliances. Ideology, geography, experience, and practical tactics all produced the same answer. The new republic was to stand aside from and above the jealousies and balance of power contests of European kings. In a later day, the term "isolationism" was to be invented to describe this basic foreign relations posture of the United States.

[b]A relatively high degree of social homogeneity in the colonies (excluding black slaves and dispossessed Indians) and a common language of course contributed invaluably to the virtually instant emergence of the new nation.

Wars of Religion

When in history dynastic competition has seemed insufficient to fuel a war, one or another group can usually be counted upon to set out to compel other groups to accept its view on what and how to worship. One of the more depressing aspects of history is the constant reminder it provides of the alacrity with which men will lop off the heads of other men over so-called "religious issues" that are incomprehensible to practically all and unknowable to any. A major component of the history of international affairs of other nations had been made up of such material, but again a fortunate United States has been spared.

Though the American colonies were in a substantial degree born out of religious conflicts of Europe, they had the fortune to grow to adolescence on a mountainside away from the poisonous environment of their parents' home. By the time the colonies became an independent actor in international affairs, the European epidemic of religious wars had subsided. Within the colonies, too, the earlier repressions of the Massachusetts theocracy had given way to an atmosphere of sectarian tolerance, at least as among Christian sects. As early as 1649—an astonishingly early year, as one thinks of the Cromwell-Stuart spasm being visited upon England at the time—the Maryland Colony had enacted its famous Toleration Act, and by the time of the American Revolution, the issue of religious toleration was not sufficiently in doubt to engage serious political discussion.

Once again, the United States simply skipped one of the major elements of classical international experience—religious war. It would never be an objective in American foreign policy to seek to impose religious orthodoxy on others, or to have to resist such an effort by others. It would never be understandable to most American citizens that other societies could be so motivated.

Security Against Assault

Many American families lived in daily fear of Indian or outlaw raids upon their frontier cabins. But unlike almost every other nation of the world, the United States has not, until the twentieth century, had to live with the continuing fear of assault, subjugation, or destruction by an armed neighbor. The Atlantic and in time the Pacific interposed continental moats to protect the young republic; and neither Canada nor Mexico has ever posed a threat credible even to the most paranoid. Once independence had been won by the United States the nation was given the extraordinary indulgence of more than a century free from external threat—a century to expand its population, build its infrastructure, occupy the West, and fight out its internal problems, in part through the Civil War.

The War of 1812 was a desultory affair, pursued uninterestedly by a Great Britain locked in mortal combat with Napoleon; the White House burning was a raid, not a conquering march threatening national existence through occupation of a capital. During the Civil War, it is true, there were some nasty moments when a few European eyes brightened at the thought that the brash American republic might be helped along in its efforts to tear itself apart and that there might be larger political prizes to be won than those taken by the *Trent* and the *Alabama*. But only the inept Napoleon III persisted in the tragicomic adventure of Maximilian and Carlotta, who proved unable in the end to save themselves, much less to threaten the reunited republic to the north.

It is difficult to overestimate the significance of the unique American inexperience with insecurity. Much of our international behavior and set of mind has been attributable to it. Most important, of course, it has provided the underpinning for isolationism. Without feared and powerful foes, the nation has experienced no basic drive toward balance of power politics and alliance diplomacy. Our sense of national security has made standing armies and armaments unnecessary and unpopular. It has taught us to believe that when conflict comes, industrial might will win it and there will be plenty of time to bring that industrial might on line. It has infected our thinking with a certain disdain for other countries around the world, as they appear to Americans to be always caught up in silly wars with their neighbors and lacking in the good sense to live peacefully with them, as we do with Canada and Mexico (now). It has persuaded some Americans to believe that wars are ineradicable and endemic in some societies, and it has led other Americans to believe that wars are easily prevented or ended by means of a few simple arrangements and agreements to do things "like we do."

The American inexperience with insecurity has done much more. It conduces to a lack of sense of proportion. When a hawk does fly over, or is reported to fly over, the American hen house goes wild. A nation oversecure will banish to concentration camps thousands of its best citizens at the rumor of a Japanese submarine off the California coast. Europeans who have lived for millennia with a clear view of the armor glinting in the campfires of their enemy just across the border have never understood the American reaction to Russians in Cuba; Khrushchev also misestimated it and nearly precipitated World War III.

The Vietnam debacle is also relevant here, another instance of a historically-grounded national ineptitude for calibrating accurately what the nation's security interests really are, when they are being seriously threatened and when they are not. This distorted capacity can of course work in the opposite direction too, as it did in the nation's general insensitivity to the actuality of the German-Japanese threat at the time of the Neutrality Acts Debates of 1939. It is hard to set the sails right if one misreads the Beaufort.

The American inexperience with insecurity is associated with yet another aberrant aspect of American international behavior—this one a blessing. The

United States has no inheritance of hatreds, no nursed mandate for vengeance. Other factors, such as the open frontier, are often cited as sources of the American propensity for open dealing, informality, and personal generosity. But in international affairs, most Americans have been unable or unwilling to give serious content to the word "enemy" or to pass along from generation to generation the idea of ethnic or cultural enmity. The Axis powers vanquished in World War II were particular beneficiaries of this tendency. While the sources for this attitude may also lie in part in our history as a country of immigrants, it is not likely that the United States would have been able to escape the bequest of hatreds if, like other countries, it had undergone periodic depredations by its neighbors.

Republicanism, Messianism, and
the Humanitarian Impulse

In their republicanism, the people of the United States uniquely inherited what the people of other countries have had to fight for or have never gotten. By the middle of the eighteenth century, the American colonies were self-governing mini-republics to an astonishing degree. The colonies emerged to political consciousness in the warm environment following the Glorious Revolution rather than in the authoritarian tradition of Louis XIV and Philip II and their successors, and the colonies thus managed to skip the whole ideological battle of king versus parliament as they had almost wholly skipped the battle of established religion. There never seemed to have been significant doubt that the colonies should have a say in making rules for themselves and that this power should be exercised by an elected governmental body, such as a House of Burgesses. The free election process that would become a battlecry for other peoples was a given assumption for the American colonies, in practice if not always in words.

The schism between the colonies and England came over the issue, not of king versus colonial assembly, but of mother-country parliament versus colonial assembly. "No taxation without representation" in the English context was an appeal for participation in London's parliament, or an appeal for more home rule by the colonial assembly. Underlying the issue was the resistance of local colonial economic interests to being subordinated to the broader interests of the empire as perceived by London. A wiser English king and government could probably have retained the colonial loyalty to the crown itself if the question of regional legislative autonomy or colonial parliamentary representation had been dealt with more creatively.

It has always been an anomaly of American history that there is such a contrast between the cool demeanor of the country's founders and the white-hot radicalism of their republican doctrine. There were a few strident voices, such as those of Tom Paine and Sam Adams. But the predominant tone of the men who made the American Revolution was that of accomplished persons of practical affairs, who were without flights of poetic oratory or theatrics, calmly confident of a whole series of radical propositions—that the new nation should be governed by public elections, that press and speech should be open to all (at a time when cost levels were such that newspapers could sprout like dandelions), that every man could worship as he would, that men were innocent until proven guilty, that they may be indicted and judged only by their peers, that they should be protected from government intrusion in their homes and their papers, and the like.

Is it not remarkable that there should have been such widespread acceptance of these tenets in the weak, new country at a time when no one had ever tried to run a country on these principles since 404 B.C.—and not even then. It is of course true that in its colonial form, the voting privileges of republicanism were, as in Athens, basically limited to the educated, propertied classes. But step by step, for 200 years, the ambit of political participation has been opened to include lower income groups, the less educated, the former slaves, the women, and most recently the young. The republic and its structured forms have absorbed each of these democratizing steps with equanimity and have stayed steady on course with relatively little rhetoric or chest-thumping.

Two observations may be made about the impact of this phenomenon upon the international policy of the newly independent country. The first is that it was then, and has ever since been, assumed comfortably and unquestioningly by Americans that its governmental forms are the forms of progress, of freedom, of liberation, of tomorrow—and that in time all countries will work their way forward to the same achievement. That is the radical, revolutionary aspect of the matter. But the cool, reasoned side had its repercussions, too. While it was clear to early Americans that they were in the ideological vanguard (hardly a colonial phrase), there was virtually no impulse in the new republic to export its revolution. There was no analogue to the European explosion of a decade later as the French marched forth under the revolutionary tricolor to liberate their neighbors. There was no rush to drive the Spanish king out of South America, or even the enemy parent British out of Canada.

A little later, the United States would be visibly sympathetic to the remarkable exploits of Bolívar and San Martin, as one Latin American community after another set itself free, but the United States firmly declined to enter into alliances with them. In 1823, Monroe would announce that the United States would look with displeasure upon the entry into the Western Hemisphere of powers from outside the hemisphere, but even the Monroe Doctrine contained a grandfather clause for powers already on the ground.

Akin to, but separate from, the nation's ideological leadership in republican government has been its receptivity toward a generalized humanitarian impulse. Historians link this feature of American life to church evangelism and to the special camaraderie and sense of brotherhood engendered by lonely life on the frontier. There is nothing in the literature of foreign relations, or the foreign affairs history of other countries, of this kind—a generalized nonsectarian universalist sympathy for the unfortunate and a traditional sense of the moral "oughtness" of helping others. This impulse, together with the tradition of voluntarism in American life, has, over the course of time, poured billions of dollars and the energies of hundreds of thousands of Americans into every imaginable form of relief work to the benefit of peoples in the remotest parts of the world. Money, manpower, and support can be raised in large amounts in the United States for virtually any cause that claims to be addressed to the needs of the dispossessed, the hungry, and those seen as having been unfairly treated.

Elements of deep tension can be readily seen in the mix of American foreign policy attitudes so far described. On one hand is the calm assurance that the American way is the advanced and progressive way, an impulse to reform, and a humanitarian desire to reach out to be helpful; on the other is a basic inclination to stay within our continental walls, to avoid the endless and pointless brawls in which others engage, to stay aloof and isolated. At different times in our history and under different pressures, one or more of these basic instincts has been successfully invoked by political leaders and the nation has responded. A war fought with ardor to end all wars was followed in turn by rejection of the League of Nations and the later adoption of a Neutrality Act designed to prevent our entering into another such war. World War II was followed by a policy of worldwide presence and unprecedented levels of aid and assistance to friends, strangers, and former foes; today in the aftermath of Vietnam, the course of history has once more swung back toward United States contraction.

One who fails to take into account the revolutionary tradition and the moral impulse of the United States, and the relevance of that tradition and that impulse to its foreign policy, will frequently guess wrong about where the country is going. This factor, unique in degree in the United States, has significant implications for the future course and management of the nation's foreign relations.

Anticolonialism

As in the case of republicanism, the general mind set of Americans toward colonialism was fashioned by its revolutionary experience. Its consistent bias has been to sympathize with the colony struggling with its metropolitan master. United States attitudes have uniformly favored the dismantling of the colonial structure of the world since World War II, with its role occasionally becoming quite active as in the case of Indonesia or opposition to the British-French Suez adventure in 1956.

Setting a unique example, the United States voluntarily predeclared that it would provide independence to the Philippines, and it did so. Closely linked to anticolonial attitudes is the Wilsonian prescription of irredentism as the key to peace after World War I; the principles of ethnic self-determination and independence for socially self-identified groups have powerful appeal to the American people.[c]

Even when the external behavior of the United States has in particular cases taken other than an anticolonial course, such action invariably triggers hot debate and criticism within the United States between those who see the question as one of "the need for moral leadership" and are outraged, and those who reluctantly approve the step as one of "realism," dictated by tactical necessities for the larger needs of the country and perhaps of the world. That debate is endemic to the conduct of American foreign policy, recurs periodically as issues change, is invariably conducted in the same vocabulary (but with proponents and challengers often changing sides), and the winning edge swings back and forth. That debate and ambivalence will continue to affect, inhibit, and occasionally determine American foreign policy in the future.

Pursuit of Economic Advantage

The nation's founders never had any doubt about the importance of economics to foreign policy. Until World War I, that part of American foreign policy that did not deal directly with the question of national borders was primarily concerned with the development and maintenance of American commerce and shipping. It is precisely because America's foreign affairs history has contained so few of the major components of other countries' international relationships that commerce assumed so central a position in American foreign policy.

Today, when the United States must contend with matters larger than its narrow mercantile interests, Americans often find it difficult to clothe with reality the issues that made up the nation's foreign policy history in the last century—its persistent emphasis on matters, such as prize courts, most favored nations treatment, rights of neutrals, contraband and the like. But to the earlier nation, these matters were central.

It never was quite "trade or starve" for the young republic, for a subsistence living could be wrung from the ground, but it was shipping and trade that made the difference between subsistence and civilization. British mercantilism perceived the colonies as trading partners—sources of raw materials and markets for finished goods. The American colonials, bunched together in port cities along the eastern seaboard, were primarily sailors, merchants or, in the South, producers of agricultural goods for foreign markets. One of the prizes of international politics, pusued for generations and finally won by England in the

---

[c]This has not applied within the United States itself, where the melting pot concept has been, and probably still is, the prevailing viewpoint.

Treaty of Paris at the end of the Seven Years' War was the *asiento* to permit British ships (which of course included American colonial ships) to participate in the highly profitable trade of the Spanish West Indies.

The American Revolution was fought in part on the issues of the Navigation Act, designed to curb colonial trade and commerce to the advantage of empire-wide and London interests. Despite the immeasurable debt owed to France for its indispensable help against Great Britain during the Revolution, the United States was by 1798 engaged in active naval warfare with the French in protest over French restrictions on American ships. The importance to the United States of freedom of shipping passage was remarkably underscored in 1803 when Congress equipped a fighting squadron and dispatched it to the remote Mediterranean to put down piracy on the Barbary Coast; piracy was a problem for all nations, but, for the United States, piracy—even 5,000 nautical miles away—was cause to build a war fleet.

The nation was on very bad terms with both England and France during the Napoleonic period as each competed with its available tools to deny to the other the trade and shipping of neutral powers. Search of American ships at sea, impressment into British naval service of sailors on American ships (some of them doubtless British deserters), controversies over contraband, privateers, prize courts, rules of effective blockage, smuggling and the like, led to Mr. Madison's war, to the embargo on trade, and to such economic devastation for New England that there was serious talk of secession from the Union. By the time of the high days of the great sailing clippers before the Civil War, the United States had developed the largest merchant marine in the world.

It was always well and fully understood that *the* foundation of United States diplomacy was to ensure that American ships and American commerce could go anywhere in the world unmolested and trade anywhere on terms as favorable as those given to others.

America's foreign policy was simple, functional, square, forthright, solid, consistent, and strong. Its design was Doric. No alliances, neutrality, freedom of the seas, and equal trading privileges. As Great Britain in the nineteenth century came to see its interests as lying more with free trade than with the mercantilist structure of the preceding century, British naval power, and the long relative peace following the Congress of Vienna, provided an underpinning and general environment for successful pursuit of these American policies.

Continental Expansionism

The period of the republic's continental expansionism, and expansion, is an interesting chapter of American foreign policy history. But it has little continuing significance upon national perspectives or attitudes toward the nation's foreign policy and no significance as a factor in its future policy.

The most fascinating aspect of the westward movement, in retrospect, was its essential automaticity. One cannot improve upon the vocabulary of the time; it did indeed seem quite manifest that it was the destiny of the nation to span the continent—and span it, it did. By the mid-nineteenth century, expansion westward gave rise to terrible convulsions as the slavery issue poisoned every aspect of political life and debate. But apart from the slavery issue, there was no debate about expansion west and there was little or no doubt on the part of any American, of whatever party, that it was the destiny of the United States to fill up the West.

Another odd feature of the movement westward was its linearity. With only the most modest adjustments for natural terrain features, the United States unrolled itself westward like a hall carpet, so that the limits of its Pacific latitudes are almost exactly those of its Atlantic latitudes. A few hotheaded war hawks would have had the country surge northward, and doubtless some few would have wished to seize Mexico; in either case the military task would have been easy enough in the early 1800s. But there was no significant popular impulse to pick up those options, or, as was more often proposed and equally accomplishable, to annex Cuba. For some reason, it seemed manifest to grow westward but not manifest to grow to the north and south.[d]

Governmental treatment of aboriginal Indian tribes is today one of the nation's bad dreams. It is interesting to note how insensitive nineteenth century American society was to the issue; how obvious it seemed, as it had seemed obvious from the days of Jamestown, that men of Stone Age culture must step aside for cultures of higher technology, or if they resist, be eliminated.

Considerably less dark than the Indian question, but uncomfortable nonetheless, is the complex history of the Texas republic, the annexation of Texas in 1845, and the Mexican War in 1848. Whatever the extenuating circumstances and the balance of outcomes, there is no doubt that in these episodes the United States took advantage of a weaker neighbor. Given the energy of the American westward thrust of the day, the disorganization of Mexican society, and the thin hold of the Mexican government on the northern portions of Spain's original empire, the result, however unedifying, was probably inevitable.

The aftermath of these two continental events remains with the conscience of the United States, and their moderating impact may be seen as a factor in the nation's total modern foreign policy perspective. In today's environment, and in the light of history, the nation is at last embarked on a degree of belated recompense, economic, political and psychological, to the American Indian. And contemporary United States attitudes toward Mexico are increasingly ones of respect, cooperation, and a predisposition toward accommodation that tends to go beyond mere cooperation.

---

[d]Alaska, purchased from Russia in 1867 for $7,200,000, was not an exception. Only the accident of an unexpected offer of purchase at a cheap price brought about this acquisition, and there was widespread condemnation in the country of the folly of buying Seward's "icebox."

Expansion Beyond the Continent—Misadventure
in Imperialism

The United States came late to the banquet table of empire, did not like most of the fare, and left early. Seen in retrospect, it should not have come to the table at all.

For the United States in the Pacific, the flag followed economics—except in Japan, where the sequence was initiated by Perry's frigates. Open Door in China was a simple and consistent application of the main line of America's century-old policy of free trade, designed, as always, to keep European imperial power from denying American ships access to trading areas. Seen in one perspective, Open Door toward China was actively anti-imperialist and helped prevent a mercantilist carving up of a weakened China by European powers. What the policy did not reckon on—what the West as a whole did not reckon on anywhere, and would take the whole twentieth century to learn—was that the local natives, in this case Chinese, might also wish to be significant actors in the determination of their future. The Boxer Rebellion, in which the United States suddenly and unhappily found itself committing Marines to combat in Peking against Chinese revolutionaries, was fraught with long-range warning for Western imperialism. The United States read the signals better than the others and got out.

Hawaii's metamorphosis to territorial status took place at the peak of imperialist fervor, 1898; but the outcome had probably been sealed generations before when American whalers and American missionaries entered upon the newly discovered Sandwich Islands (unaccountably missed by Spanish ships for 200 years, and hit upon by Captain Cook in 1778) and soon became the dominant cultural and economic force in the Hawaiian kingdom. Hawaii came close to being a true settlement colony, though the Americans left in place the native government that Kamehameha had unified in 1810. When in 1854 the native monarch made a move to cede the islands to Great Britain, a United States warship promptly appeared in protest and the British gave way.

Forty years later, the islands were still independent and the royal family still in authority, but the native social structure had fallen away and the American business and missionary interests had become concerned both about the government's stability and about the question of tariff-free entry of Hawaiian sugar into the United States market.

In 1893 revolution looking toward annexation occurred under the leadership of resident Europeans and (mainly) Americans, and Queen Liliuokalani was displaced. During a long delay the islands became an independent republic, as Democrat Grover Cleveland was opposed to the annexation; when Republican expansionist William McKinley succeeded Cleveland, the islands were formally annexed as a territory in 1898. Even then, the forces of expansion did not have easy sailing, as the two-thirds Senate vote required for the treaty was not to be found, and the annexation was effected by joint resolution of the two Houses of Congress, precedent for which procedure lay in the earlier annexation of Texas. Today a fully integrated state of the Union, Hawaii is no longer a subtopic of American foreign policy.

Those of populist leanings have long believed that war is the work of kings, aristocrats and dictators and have cherished the faith that the greatest bulwarks of peace are democracy and a free press.[1] The Spanish-American War must be seen as a challenge to, if not a refutation of, the universality of that argument. Street agitation for hostilities had been known at other times in American history, with the public more bellicose than the leadership, but the Spanish-American War is the only case in which public opinion, whipped by deliberate commercial tabloidism, actually brought the nation into a war. It must also be recalled that this occurred against a background of years of bloody attempts by Spain to suppress a revolutionary independence movement in Cuba, a movement toward which United States public opinion was strongly sympathetic.

The Spanish-American War coincided with the apogee of imperial impulses in American life. These enthusiasms were short-lived, as, fortunately, was the war. Even at this peak of expansionist fervor, however, the imperial concept did not sit well with many Americans and the country's efforts at imperial behavior at the end of the war were half-hearted. A century before, Jefferson had thought that Cuba should be acquired by the United States, and many had argued the same thereafter; but with the easy opportunity for annexation afforded by the unconditional surrender of Spain, the idea was rejected by the United States as it was content with its initial war goal, the liberation of the island and its establishment as an independent republic, coupled with a protectorate relationship under the Platt Amendment.

The "great aberration"[2] was the acquisition of the Philippines, an adventitious by-product of the war. While the most aggressive public figures in American life, Theodore Roosevelt and Henry Cabot Lodge, drew upon the naval power theories of Mahan to see the Philippines as some sort of entry foyer to an American imperium in the Far East, the United States would never have acquired the Philippines if it had not been faced with the question of what else to do with them. The Kaiser was then making evident his intention to take advantage of the collapse of Spain's military strength and incorporate the Philippines into the late, but growing, German Empire. Even so, the Senate ratified the Philippines Treaty by only two votes, and a concomitant resolution committing the United States to grant Philippine independence produced a tie vote in the Senate, defeated only by the vote cast by McKinley's vice president.

Theodore Roosevelt had been a young assistant secretary of the Navy when he prepared and sent Commodore George Dewey to the Pacific. Though hostilities in the Spanish-American War lasted only from April till the beginning of July, Roosevelt had time to resign his position, become a lieutenant colonel and lead the Rough Riders in the attack on Santiago. While this was not the only style of this unusual and talented man, who, after two years as governor of New York and one as vice president, suddenly became president on McKinley's assassination in 1901, it was the style that again emerged in 1903. Theodore Roosevelt "took Panama," to use his own words. Quickly recognizing the legitimacy of an insurrection in Panama against Colombia (this time a sister republic of the United States, not a European power), he used the power of the United States to warn the Colombians not to use their troops to suppress the insurrection, then signed a treaty with the newly independent Panama giving the United States full rights to complete, fortify, and maintain the canal left unfinished by an earlier French company.

With the acquisition of the Canal Zone, the territorial expansionist phase of American history had passed. A fundamental distinction must be drawn between the filling up of the contiguous continental areas west of the Atlantic colonies and the acquisitions made at the turn of the century. To most Americans it was manifest destiny that the nation should grow horizontally to the Pacific; there was nothing destined about additions made through the Spanish-American War, and the only thing manifest was that eventually Spain would have to leave Cuba as she had been forced to leave the rest of Latin America. These continental acquisitions, together with those of Alaska and Hawaii, early became integral parts of the core of the United States.

However, the accessions made in the Spanish-American War were out of line with the long-term life pattern of the nation, as their subsequent history illustrates. In 1934 the United States committed itself voluntarily to the independence of the Philippines and in 1946 made good its word. In the case of Cuba, the vexatious protectorate provisions of the Platt Amendment were voluntarily scrapped in 1934. In recent years, though with more difficulty for obvious reasons relating to security anxieties, the United States has been moving sporadically toward a reworking of its relationship vis-à-vis the Panama Canal (with, it must be said, more concern evinced for the Panamanians than for the original Colombian holders). Only Puerto Rico, with its special associated commonwealth status, has in effect been built into the body politic, and that story may not yet have fully run its course.

The United States has throughout the twentieth century continued to have problems in dealing with the Caribbean area because of the latter's political instability and because of its importance to the economic lifeline of the Canal. Several times, both directly and indirectly, the United States has used its military power to intervene in that area; these interventions have not been territory grabbing exercises, however, and there is reason to be optimistic that the United States government is learning that despite the temptations to step into volatile Caribbean situations, the long-term effect of intervention is likely to be more destabilizing than the reverse.

The United States entered World War I and World War II without territorial ambitions, and, except for limited military base rights, made no territorial claims in the peace treaties, though it would have been an easy thing to do at the time. Foreign ministries around the world assume, and are safe in assuming, that United States foreign policy does not carry with it a hidden agenda of territorial expansion. When the United States has intervened in local situations about the world since World War II, its intervention has been caused by cold war concerns. Once more, the element that has made up such a large component of the foreign policy history of other countries—the desire to add square miles of territory— makes up no significant portion of United States foreign policy.

There are voices today that seek to apply to the position of the United States in the post-World War II era the term "neo-colonialism" or "neo-imperialism." In this sense, "neo-colonialism," or "neo-imperialism," is seen as a systematic effort to use economic and technological power, in part through the vehicle of American-based multinational corporations, to make economic vassals out of less industrialized nations. The economic relations between the industrialized and nonindustrialized portions of the world are indeed a problem of the utmost significance, and will be discussed later in this chapter. Examination of that problem is not, however, advanced by seeking to misapply to it the term "colonialism," a term which, like "feudalism," describes a particular political system that has disappeared from the world. Particularly is the term misleading as applied to the special history and basic foreign policy attitudes of the United States.

Some Idiosyncrasies of American
Foreign Policy Attitudes

It seems useful to refer in passing to three other disparate but traditional aspects of American attitudes toward foreign policy.

The first special feature is the relationship among the American executive, the Congress as a whole, and the Senate. The country has had recent occasion to learn of the special primacy of the executive branch in the conduct of foreign affairs, and there is a well-elaborated thesis afoot that holds that the central explanation for the increasingly centralized (usurped?) power of the White House today has been built upon the executive's special authority in the field of foreign relations.[3] However, despite the fractional persuasiveness of this thesis and despite the growth of the executive agreement mechanism, in the longer view, and from time to time, the Congress of the United States must be seriously reckoned with in matters of foreign relations. The Senate's power to advise and consent with regard to treaties may be quiescent (as during World War II and immediately thereafter) or determinative (as in the rejection of the League of Nations at the end of World War I) or something in between (as when it forced John Hay to renegotiate the Hay-Pauncefote Treaty with the British in 1900). But the power is always there, ready to be given new life and vigor whenever a chief executive gets in trouble or substantially diverges from the prevailing senatorial attitude. In contemporary foreign affairs, the power of the House is hardly less whenever it chooses to assert it; defense budgets, trade and tariff laws, assistance programs for developing countries, funding of participation in international organizations, must all make their way not only through the Senate but through the House as well. And both Houses of the Congress have recently made visible, in new war powers legislation, the reassertion of their constitutional powers in that critical field.

However one may assess the value and the practicality of conducting foreign policy through such a split arrangement, and the realistic possibility of informing and involving the electorate in foreign policy matters, that effort is decreed in the American Constitution. It conditions, even when it does not determine, the way in which American foreign affairs are conducted.

Second, and this point is related to the preceding one, the American people have a profound historical distrust for ambassadors, foreign ministers, secretaries of state, and other such types who make up the working cadres of international relations. It is a commonplace observation that of all the components of the United States government, only the State Department is without a constituency and without political bargaining clout. The extraordinary talents of the present secretary of state have acquired for him not only a professional reputation but a public following; but it is far more normal in American life for the secretary and his department to be unknown or as often distrusted and disregarded.

Among other things, the basic regionalism that has characterized American history, and the necessarily local or regional commitment of an elected senator or representative, make the role of the Department of State extremely difficult, since its assignment requires that it take an integrated view of the interests of the whole country in its dealings with nations abroad. No nation in history has built into its machinery for the conduct of foreign affairs as many hobbles, vetoes, and fractionations of perspective.

Finally, there is the open press to be contended with, with its indefatigable competitive obsession to bring all matters, even the most delicate negotiations, to public light. As recent negotiations in the Middle East demonstrate, it is possible to do diplomacy under these conditions, but it is very difficult indeed.

Third, and here one can make little pretense of having systematic, supporting evidence, the conduct of foreign affairs by any United States government is further made difficult by a certain traditional American predisposition to accept a challenge (almost any challenge), coupled with a grim determination to win, once a challenge is accepted. "Don't tread on me," says the flag of the Commonwealth of Pennsylvania. "Not a damned cent for tribute," announces the fledgling republic to Tripolitan pirates. The War of 1812, a hopeless war for the United States if England had been free to fight it, was fought over a challenge of principle in the handling of American sailors. Every American child knows the inevitable and necessary scenario following Tom Sawyer's drawing the line on the ground with his toe; every horse opera has its duel arising out of a challenge and its acceptance. The nation's reaction to Sputnik was a political analogue.

Perhaps there is less of this value tenet at large in the country today than there was two generations ago. In today's environment it is not likely that the president, the Congress, and the country would support shelling and occupying a port city of a country at peace with the United States in order to compel a salute to the United States flag in reparation for the improper brief arrest of American sailors—as Wilson did in Mexico in 1914. In our international dealings in the last twenty years, we have become more willing to weigh the consequences in a longer time frame, less impelled to leap to defend honor against every slight. But it is a question how much change there has been in that direction. Any other country dealing with the United States must estimate the depth and the closeness to the surface of this national proclivity—the readiness to accept a challenge and the determination to win it completely. President Truman had to deal with this phenomenon in a particularly difficult form in the replacement of General MacArthur. And a significant factor in the stubborn continuation of our Vietnam involvement was traceable to this attitude inherited out of our past.

Summary: American Foreign
Relations—Doric

The foreign relations of the United States have gone through two major stages and are entering upon a third. It is time to recapitulate the basic components of the first of these stages—metaphorized here for its solidity, economy, simplicity, and primitiveness as Doric.

The policy lines were clear. Get out of the European dynastic balance of power game and stay out. Profit from the benefits of neutrality. As a neutral, insist upon the rights of neutrals, neutral ships, and neutral cargoes to go where they will, with recognized exceptions for limited categories of contraband and effectively enforced blockades. As a trader and shipper, insist upon most favored nation treatment for the United States and upon port access for American ships. Fight, if necessary, to preserve these rights of the neutral trader.

Do not be afraid of war. War will come from time to time and must be met frontally. Fight it with attack and vigor even when the odds seem very bad. Do not tolerate insult to national honor, and fight to win.

Fill up the western lands between the latitudes of Maine and Florida. As occasion makes possible, take advantage of special situations in the movement westward, as in Alaska and Hawaii.

Favor the cause of colonies striving for national independence and be quick to recognize their de facto success, but do not engage directly in their battles for self-determination. Protect the Western Hemisphere from attack or intervention by any outside power not already in place.

Be confident of tomorrow; progress is real and inevitable. Each individual man deserves to be his own master, have his own views, express his own thoughts and pursue his own talents in competition with others. The future lies with this philosophy and with democracy. In time all nations will model themselves on the successful radical experiment of the American republic. It is not necessary to export ideological revolution to this end since it will occur anyway.

Help the sick and the unfortunate with humanitarian compassion and with direct charity.

Keep an eye on the secretary of state and his ambassadorial entourage. They are symbols of, maybe agents of, aristocracy and foreignism, not to be trusted as wholly American and more likely to be representing the interests of fancy foreigners than of yeomen Americans.

In foreign policy matters, do what can be done to keep the president on the leash of the people's representatives, the Congress.

As time went by, these policies were pursued in an increasingly distinctive psychological environment. Success after success attended America's efforts. Though the historian can often see that early American successes were often attributable in large measure to outside actors or circumstances, it was inevitable that Americans of the day should assume and believe that the credit should go to them and to American institutions.

Americans can never be accused of viewing their fellow man with malice or envy or vindictiveness. But they did develop an air of patronizing superiority, and a propensity to preach to those parts of the world that had not yet overridden religious differences and dynastic squabbles, that have not yet given their citizens the luxury of free individual life, that have not learned to organize themselves for industrialization. In time there emerged a vague sense of cultural superiority and charitable pity, born out of a conviction that only Anglo-Saxon peoples are yet ready to experience these higher social achievements—though in time all men will come to them.

These Doric policies and attitudes were hardly designed to enable a rich and powerful United States to win first prize in an international popularity contest. But they were not designed to do so and, in earlier America, the question itself was hardly a conceivable one.

Part II—Ionic

A world ended in 1914. It is still too early to understand fully what happened and why. It is clear, however, that during the short thirty-year period between the beginning of World War I and the end of World War II at least three tidal changes of the utmost significance occurred in the international relations of the United States.

Security Against Assault: Revisited

It is perhaps debatable, and will long be debated, whether in fact the basic security interests of the United States were ever seriously jeopardized by the Central Powers in World War I. But the technology of the U-boat destroyed the lives and property of Americans and, so long as American ships, cargoes, and citizens claimed a right to travel the seas, they were placed in peril by the German campaign. The emerging concept of total national war provided new legitimation (or, more accurately, repealed old illegitimations) for all-out sea warfare in which the earlier more civilized standards of blockade, shots across the bow, boarding, and the like could not be used. Much of the shift was attributable to the new naval technology. As in the long period of French-English wars from 1688 to 1815, the struggle in World War I, once more, was between the strongest continental land power and Britain's naval power. One wonders whether Napoleon's U-boats, if he had had any, would have behaved any differently from the Kaiser's.

By the Doric precepts of United States foreign policy, the nation's response to unlimited submarine warfare was clear and predetermined. It is almost unbelievable that the Germans could have read so little United States history as to have mispredicted that response. For 125 years the United States had consistently declared itself willing to fight to protect its "rights" as a neutral and to guarantee safe passage for its ships goods and citizens. It responded in the same way in 1917, unaware that neutrality in the nineteenth century sense had ceased to be a serious policy alternative for the nation.

When World War II came after a brief ceasefire of only twenty-one years, there was no question about the reality of the threat to United States security. Once more, in 1939, an effort was made to ensure the nation's "neutrality," but this time, in an effort to learn from the World War I experience, the United States retreated from the nineteenth century concept of neutrality and instead imposed restrictions and embargoes upon its own ships' shipments and travel by United States citizens. But even this penned-up neutrality failed. Adolf Hitler and the Japanese military leaders made clear the fate that would lie ahead for a United States if the Axis powers should be successful in their openly avowed campaign to conquer all Europe, the USSR and Asia.

Once more the technology had changed. Long-distance aircraft and submarines were now realities, and military rockets would come soon. Strong Axis naval units were a threat in the Atlantic and a punishing reality in the Pacific, where America's jewel, Pearl Harbor, was attacked and virtually destroyed. For the first time since the days of Indian attack on frontier settlements, the United States knew the fear of assault and the pain of loss of security. The oceans would never be moats again. And "national security," standing armies, peacetime draft, military alliances, and astronomical defense budgets—all previously unknown in American history—would become a normal (some would say dominant) aspect of American life.

Secular Ideology: Republicanism
Revisited

Pessimists would say of man that he has always pursued and will always pursue organized homicide against groups other than his own; it is only his excuse for doing this that he changes from time to time. Understandably enough, he will kill out of fear of being killed. He will also kill for control of a well and grazing land; or for desirable women; for salable ivory, slaves, gold, spices or trade monopoly; for dynastic pretension and self-glory; out of fear and vengeance; or to impose his superstitions and religious theories upon others.

But the end of the nineteenth century and the beginning of the twentieth century have introduced a new level of sophistication. As religious and dynastic wars finally faded away, man has invented new categories of "principles" for which he will kill—variations of secular ideologies on how the social economy of the nation-state should be administered and how political decisions in the nation-state should be made and legitimated.

It was noted earlier that the young United States made no serious effort to export its radical republicanism in the eighteenth century. The French Revolution gave rise to a series of expansive efforts to spread the revolutionary principle, but within a very short time the movement had become Bonapartism instead. The Holy Alliance made a half-hearted, never applied, attempt to take a stand for the principle of royal legitimacy. And then suddenly in the twentieth century there came a burst of secular theory building and political "faiths" to provide the issues which men declare war on one another. There may come a day when wars about these eco-political ideologies will seem as remote and incomprehensible as the religious wars of the sixteenth century seem to us today. But for now, these are very serious matters and it is clear that the twentieth century is the century of the secular "isms"—socialism, national socialism, communism, Fabianism, Peronism, fascism, Fidelism, cooperativism, Maoism, etc.

However World War I was caused, it was not grounded in such secular ideological conflict. The contestants were all appropriately private property oriented and all but France monarchical. To the shattering dismay of the Rosa Luxemburgs, the supposed adherents of international social democracy in Europe rallied to their kings and national flags and marched against each other. However it was that the United States became involved, and for whatever reasons, it was the American president who introduced into the war an ideological element going beyond nationalism, land-grabbing, and commercial interests. Wilson saw it (once in the war) as a war to end all war, to give all men the right to national self-determination, to extend the Bill of Rights to all men, to create global machinery that would peacefully resolve differences among nations with justice. The Allied leaders were appalled by such naïveté and heresy but had no choice but to listen to it. The American people were inspired by this vision to fight the war; but in the cooler aftermath of the Armistice they broke the president's heart and health by rejecting the League of Nations and returning to "normalcy."

In the meantime, the world had suddenly set itself in earnest upon the ideological spree that was to dominate political attention for at least the next fifty years, and who knows how much longer. Every "ism" offered a theory on the right way to organize and manage a nation's social, political, and economic life. Since each "system" was declared to be unique, and had to be accepted in its entirety (the hallmark of dogma), each was committed to incompatibility with all others and each set itself to the necessity of total destruction of the others. The psychological spirit of the religious wars of the sixteenth century had returned, but in far more dangerous and destructive form as the new concepts of statism and total war conscripted the efforts, body, and mind of every man, woman, and child.

In the war that inevitably and quickly followed, Hitlerian totalitarianism attacked a temporary alliance of capitalist liberal democracy and Stalinist totalitarianism, and in time almost every nation was sucked into the maelstrom. Over a six-year period, more than fifteen million military personnel were killed or lost in action; more than twice as many were severely wounded; the numbers of tens of millions of civilians killed and wounded can only be guessed at. The Axis powers defeated, the survivors then squared off against each other in another ideological war that was, at least, kept "cold."

The introduction of secular ideology into the center of world politics was an event of critical importance to the United States and to American perspectives on foreign policy. Woodrow Wilson will always remain a fascinating puzzle in this respect. As a domestic politician, he sensed, accurately, both a missionary strain in the American people and the extraordinary achievements to which they can be inspired by moral impulse. Himself of missionary instinct, he seems to have experienced something close to a prophet's revelation of a future of world peace and world government. But he was also an historian, a student of American government, and as such he was familiar with the simple precepts of traditional American policy (they were indeed his until the United States was at war). It is difficult to account for his surprise that Americans should prove unable to leap in three years from isolationism and neutrality to leadership of a system of collective security. It is equally difficult to account for his surprise that old hands Lloyd George, Clemenceau, and Orlando should be carrying in their attache case the weight of centuries of balance-of-power European politics.

In any case, Wilson set at large in the American community the thesis of moral uplift in America's foreign relations. Since then, the circle of Americans who regularly think and talk about foreign policy has tended to be drawn toward one of two polar views, ever in debate with each other. The first is that the United States has a special role to play in world history—to hitch itself and its political power to universal moral ends, to stand forth against injustice wherever it occurs around the world, and to set as the goal of its national policy the enhancement of man's freedom and the improvement of his lot.

The other view sees itself as more realistic, believes that self-interest in international politics is unavoidable, believes that the United States had best take care of itself (in the long run as well as the short) since no one else will do it, and profoundly skeptical if not actively negative about the amount of good that is done—and the substantial amount of evil that is unintentionally done—by the zealotry of reformers, do-gooders, and idealogues.

The debate is disorderly, in part because most participants are themselves drawn simultaneously to both views, and in part because they sometimes switch sides, depending on the issue involved. That the debate often makes for peculiar bedfellows is well illustrated by the current controversy over expanded trade with the Soviet Union, where the opposition is a mix of intellectual civil liberties enthusiasts, United Nations internationalists, 1950s cold warriors, isolationists, high-tariff protectionists, United States nationalists, anti-Communist ideologues, minority ethnic groups, and a number of specific economic interest groups. Much of the intellectual confusion surrounding United States participation in Vietnam was born out of debate about the role of "morality" in United States foreign policy, and differences of view as to where that morality lay.

For present purposes, however, the central point is simply that just as the United States entered upon the world scene as a major power, the secular ideological volcano erupted. In World War II the United States saw before it the demonic face of evil and saw it attack the elemental decencies of civilized life wherever it could. The United States had not theretofore sought vigorously to sell or install its brand of liberal democracy in other parts of the world—once more, the Philippines were a special exception—or declare ideological war. But it happened that when the time finally came in its history when the national security of the United States was directly assaulted, the attack on the United States came from the exponents of one of the new secular "isms," bent upon destroying not only all nations who resisted them, but also the founding principles of the republic.

Whether or not World War I was fought to make the world safe for democracy, World War II certainly was. And a lesson of a sort was taught to the American people, or at least a lesson was learned by them: Evil is at large in the world; appeasement of evil will not work; better to take your stand earlier rather than later; battles may have to be fought in remote places over unfamiliar issues to prevent the battening of the forces of evil. It was that lesson that was applied, or misapplied, later in Vietnam.

In the long run, however, a more important aspect of the introduction of ideology into foreign relations is the realization it slowly brought about that, contrary to traditional expectation, the course of history does not run steadily in the direction of Jeffersonianism and the American liberal ideal. Each of the "isms" claims itself to be the wave of the future, claims to offer a better and brighter prospect for mankind than the liberal visions of the eighteenth century.

It had never occurred to America—accustomed to viewing itself as the standardbearer of progress, liberty, and freedom, as a symbol of the aspirations of the poor and of the colonial peoples of the world—that new political models and visions would not only compete for that role, but would actively attack American ideology and vilify the United States as the ultimate source of worldwide villainy and reaction. One result of this assault has been to force America's thinkers and commentators to reexamine in a basic way the role and mission of United States foreign policy and the traditional assumptions that have been made about what men want in their lives, how they are moved, and what elements of truth there may be, if any, in the notion of the United States as a force for reaction. Understandably, the reaction of the average American who encounters these charges is a kind of bristling irritation, dismissal, a sense of hurt, and a conviction that men in the end are all ingrates—especially foreigners.

World Position and Involvement

The third major change to come to the United States out of the thirty years from 1914 to 1945 was the transformation of the country's position among the nations of the world—a transformation that took place not by design, not even by accident, but almost contrary to design.

The economic bases of the empires of Europe were severely undermined in World War I. In World War II they were wholly spent. Germany underwent two devastating defeats, economic collapse and partition. Japan's empire, new and old, was stripped from her. The United States in 1914 was a debtor state of insignificant military strength. It emerged in 1945 with a monopoly of nuclear armament, dominance in conventional air, sea, and land forces, and undamaged physical plant, and an economic preeminence and creditor position defying measure.

The United States in 1945 was not only the paramount power in the world, it was now firmly and irretrievably in the world. There was no debate this time about returning to "normalcy" and isolation, or about the essentiality of United States participation in multinational institutions. A wholly new concept had arisen, and this time had been accepted by the American people, the concept of America's "responsibility" in world affairs—to help rebuild Europe, to advance the process of decolonialization, to maintain peace around the world, to defend the West against Soviet aggression, to be the guardian of liberal democratic institutions against totalitarianism, to maintain a stable international monetary system based on the United States dollar, and to assist the industrialization and modernization of developing countries.

This was quite an assignment. If Woodrow Wilson was watching, he could only have been proud of the way in which the American public responded this time. The United Nations, the GATT, the IMF, NATO, and dozens of other international institutions came rapidly into being, with the United States as the lead actor or a major actor in every one. In one step, the country abandoned its

Doric traditions in the field of foreign policy and adopted both alliance diplomacy and a commitment to collective multinational institutions.

Summary: American Foreign
Policy—Ionic

The Doric era was gone. United States policy after World War II became Ionic. The new design, though still simple, was one of grandeur, its graceful curves showing more sophistication than its Doric predecessor—almost imperial. But the Ionic design was also inherently bipolar and inflexible in its orientation, inherently unable to present itself with the same success and effect to all angles of approach.

The years are so close at hand that it is hard to say what new dimension this Ionic period may have provided Americans in their assessment of other human beings. Probably the long cold war impeded Americans in the development of viewpoints more sophisticated than the traditional ones. The bitter confrontations with the Soviet Union reinforced the tendency to see the world in Manichaean terms—to transfer to Stalin (with a large assist from him) the devil role formerly Hitler's, and to view all persons and nations who were not in the Stalinist camp as members of the "free world," who, naturally, would share all the classical standards and aspirations of the American liberal dream.

As much as anything else, that erroneous simplistic perception of the non-Communist world, and a corresponding monolithic perception of the Communist world, contributed in the post-World War II era to policy error by the United States, and to our embroilment in Vietnam, and would ultimately lead to disillusionment and disenchantment with American foreign policy generally among large segments of public opinion.

In any case, after World War II, for the first time in its history, the United States found itself concerned about its own security, engaged in a new kind of ideological competition, and committed to an activist alliance-based multilateral foreign policy. And in almost all matters the United States was the paramount nation of the world.

And so matters continued for two decades until, little by little, the postwar era faded away, and something new formed to take its place.

Part III—Corinthian?

Men generally do a poor job of detecting and assessing the major historical currents of their own time. Nonetheless, it is the thesis of this essay that as the first 220 years of American foreign policy draw to a close, the United States and the world are just now, in 1974, passing over a major divide in their international relationships. In the past, a major historic epoch could be expected to move sedately in a cadence of a hundred years or more duration. But in the modern world everything is speeded up. The post-World War II era held for barely a generation. Called upon only thirty years ago to see the world with new eyes and to respond in unaccustomed ways, the United States now faces the prospect of having to do it again.

Where did the postwar era go? What evidence is there to indicate that a new era is immediately at hand? There is quite a lot, some of it to be found in the disappearance of circumstances that characterized the postwar period, and the rest to be found in the emergence of circumstances which have never before been seen.

A key feature of the postwar era was United States nuclear monopoly, then nuclear paramountcy. In 1972 SALT I formally acknowledged a substantial nuclear standoff with the USSR; and over the past decade France, China, and most recently India, have joined the nuclear club.

At the peak of the cold war, the conventional military forces of the United States had a commanding predominance. The country may still be the most powerful military force in the world, but this assertion is at least debatable; Soviet military strength has continued to grow rapidly, while that of the United States has stood still or grown more slowly, and as, in the unmeasurable realms of psychology and prestige, the United States military has suffered acutely, both domestically and abroad, from its frustrating, inconclusive, muscle-bound performance in Vietnam.

In the postwar era, the entire economy of the world was based on the Bretton Woods Agreement and the American dollar. In August of 1971 the United States shut its gold window, scrapped what was left of the IMF, and has since in effect gone through two and one-half devaluations. The nation's economy remains by far the largest and most productive in the world, and its industrial technology still leads all the rest. But the gap between the United States and other industrialized societies is narrowing; it is no longer a matter of Gulliver surrounded by Lilliputians.

The world's nation-state structure changed radically during the postwar era, as the old empires were dismantled. That process is now complete, as even Portugal has now given up the fight to hang on to her colonies. As new nation-states have been born, the numerical balance between industrialized and unindustrialized countries has shifted radically toward the latter. Fifty-one nations signed the original United Nations Charter, of which nearly one-half could be said to have been industrialized; there are today 135 members of the United Nations, of which not more than one-quarter would be so classified.

It would be an exaggeration to say that NATO, the backbone of United States security policy, is in disarray or collapse. But as detente has advanced, the unity of the NATO allies, already deliberately disrupted by a de Gaulle and his successor, has been gradually weakened.

Not so far undermined as the Bretton Woods Agreement, the General Agreement on Tariffs and Trade (the GATT)—the postwar era monument to the classic American doctrine of equal access in trade and to liberalized if not free trade—is today undergoing erosion and circumvention. The specters of protectionism and neo-mercantilism are reappearing around the world and within the United States itself.

The postwar era of cold war has passed and its leaders with it. Detente and peaceful coexistence are the watchwords for United States-USSR relations, as the Soviet Union has found itself forced by the cost of the arms race and by pressures within the USSR and the socialist countries of Central Europe to try to raise consumer standards and to modernize its consumer technology. Detente is not alliance—nor even amity—and, as the Russians regularly remind us, peaceful coexistence means only the continuation of the ideological struggle against capitalist liberalism by peaceful means. The wellsprings of Russian nationalism may also be expected to inspire world power plays by the secretaries and commissars just as it inspired czars. Nonetheless, an era of detente is something quite different from an era of recurrent eyeball confrontation and rocket rattling between the two superpowers.

After a strange twenty years, which historians may never be able to explain fully, during which the United States followed a policy of simply averting its eyes from the reality of 800 million Chinese, avenues of trade and diplomacy are again opening between these two countries. In turn, another new basic world condition has emerged as relations between the USSR and China have sunk to such levels of hostility that outbreaks of fighting, or even all-out warfare along the 4,000 mile joint border are an ever-present possibility.

In the eyes of most of the world—developed and developing; Communist and non-Communist—and in the eyes of at least a large proportion of younger Americans, the United States has, through its appalling misadventure in Vietnam, thrown away its position of moral world leadership, and at the same time suffered a severe loss of prestige by the demonstration that its political, economic, and military power could be fought to a standstill by a small unindustrialized society.

The United States has also largely lost its reputation as the progressive liberating force in the world. As viewed by most of the developing world, and by the younger generation in much of the rest of the world, the United States, and particularly United States companies, are today perceived as villains intent upon extracting resources from poor countries to be consumed by rich Americans to the profit of the companies, and committed to preventing the fair and just development of the poorer countries.

In part, of course, this depiction is classical Marxist-Leninist propaganda, given credence by the Vietnam-born image of the United States as the enemy of social revolution. But more important, this indictment is mainly a cry of political desperation from two-thirds of the world's population which now knows from modern communication technology that it is falling further and further behind the living standards of the industrialized countries led by the United States. The American people have not yet absorbed the political significance of the fact that the United States, with 6 percent of the world's population, still consumes 30 percent of the total energy and raw materials consumed each year by the entire world, despite recent percentage declines.

Though the list could be extended, one may conclude by noting that, while the economy of the United States remains the world's largest and strongest, while its military power maintains its position as one of the two superpowers, and while its technological lead, though reduced, remains, the nation no longer stands in a position of such paramountcy that it can expect its wishes and preferences to be acceded to, even by its best friends and neighbors. The countries of Western Europe, Japan, good neighbors Canada and Mexico, the nations of South America—all today show a capacity for independent action, and an inclination to make use of that capacity, that would have been unthinkable only a few years ago.

Thus, even if one surveys only the main topographic features of the international world that we became accustomed to in the postwar period but that have now disappeared, it may be seen that an era in the history of the world's international relations has passed, and with it the base for America's Ionic foreign policy.

The point becomes all the more evident if one turns next to observe the new terrain features that have come seismically into being, bringing with them new problems of a kind that traditional international relations have never before had to contend with.

As an opening observation, it is interesting to note that every one of the new problem areas listed below is directly attributable to, or acutely aggravated by, the unprecedented leap in science and technology and the diffusion of scientific and technological knowledge that have occurred in this century. The basic stuff of traditional foreign relations continues as before—problems of boundaries, insecurity and aggression, commercial access, power, ambition, and the like. But to these there have quite suddenly been added whole new categories of problems and issues for which there are no precedents and no experience in the foreign ministries of the world's nation-states. Yet, it is equally apparent that the only solution to some of these problems lies in the development and use of still newer technology—doubtless bearing with its own unforeseen social repercussions.

Nuclear Control

If the world, or a significant part of it, is to be incinerated by nuclear weapons, none of the other issues make any difference. So far, in an essentially bipolar world, the balance of terror has worked, however perilously and erratically. But proliferation of nuclear capability is now at hand, and tomorrow bears the fearsome prospect of cheap, relatively simple nuclear devices that might—eventually, probably will—come into the hands of irresponsible political elements or even simple extortionists. Will the nations be able to see that their stake in nuclear control requires some form of agreed upon restraints?

Population

The general dimension of the world's population problem is finally becoming generally known to educated persons. In 1900 the world's population stood at 1.65 billion; by the 1970s, application of medical knowledge, simple standards of hygiene, and increases in education and caloric intake had combined to increase the population to 3.6 billion; by the year 2000, twenty-six years from the present, the projected population will be 6.5 billion.[4]

The distribution of this projected population is as important as the aggregates. At the present time, only about 30 percent of the world's population is in countries that are industrially developed, and the balance is in underdeveloped countries. The population of the industrially developed parts of the world in general approximate a zero-growth level. Eighty-five percent of the three to four billion person increase expected in the next twenty-six years will occur in the countries that are poorest and least developed.

Food

Closely tied to the population problem is the problem of food. The world's total supply of food, and particularly protein, has at last come to be seen as a massive problem and one that will grow much worse in the years ahead. World food prices have soared and, with the disappearance of reserve stocks, widespread shortages of important food commodities have begun to crop up sporadically—in soybeans and wheat, in rice and, of great importance, in fertilizer. There are indications that feasible ceilings in the annual fish catch have now been reached, as the total tripled from 21 million tons in 1950 to 70 million in 1970 and has since declined to 62 million tons.

As population has been increasing at almost exactly the aggregate rate of food production, increase per capita food consumption has remained fairly constant. If, as is projected, the world's population is to double again in the next twenty-six years, the aggregate food supply will also have to be doubled to feed the population at the same average levels as today.

Of people in the developing countries, it is estimated that 60 percent, or over one billion people, are malnourished, and that 20 percent are actually starving. Total famine conditions have begun to occur and are expected to occur with increasing frequency in various parts of the world. These developing countries are fundamentally dependent upon imports from developed countries to meet minimum food and fertilizer demands.

Raw Materials and Energy

It no longer needs to be argued that the world's fossil fuels and minerals have finite limits and that their random distribution can lead to severe economic and political dislocations. During the period from 1940-1970, more energy was consumed than in all prior history. Over the next thirteen years energy consumption is expected to double. The world's consumption of aluminum is doubling every nine years, the use of iron every ten to fifteen years, and of copper every twelve to fifteen years. During the period from 1950-1970 the world consumed almost half of the zinc that had been produced until that time.

Projections of increasing industrialization, increasing population and increasing diffusion of technology have recently led to the emergence of a computer-based neo-Malthusian school of thought that sees nothing ahead but dismal human misery and exhaustion of natural resources. Other observers believe that the effect of rising prices for scarce commodities will lead to new solutions through conservation and recycling techniques, extractions from lower-yield ores, and whole new technologies, particularly energy technologies that will supplant current reliance on fossil fuels.

Environmental Pollution

In the last few years the world has begun to become aware of the impact of industrialization upon the global ecological system. Industrial activity in Britain has led to higher levels of sulphur dioxide in rain falling on Sweden. Deforestation in Nepal has caused soil erosion in India. Coastal shellfish grounds have had to be closed because of pollution. Fresh water supplies, as in the case of the Great Lakes and the Rhine, have been curtailed through heavy industrial pollution. There is increasing recognition of the impact of urbanization and industrialization upon weather patterns and climate systems. The technology for deliberately inducing weather change is also advancing rapidly, with corresponding possibilities for good or ill.

Communications

The speed, ease and range of modern communication systems is giving rise to its own problems, such as the appropriate regulation of stationary satellites and of direct transmission from such satellites to the end user's receiving set. But the communications revolution of recent decades has had two far more important side effects. Virtually every village in the world, however poor, has a radio, and many have television. The disparity between poor nations and rich is increasing, not decreasing, and modern communications see to it that everyone knows it. The peoples of economically backward societies are forced to be aware of the comparison between the grinding poverty of their lives and the relative affluence of industrialized societies. As modern secular ideologies make glowing promises of improved standards of living, political frustration grows and becomes explosive.

A second impact of modern communications technology is that it immeasurably compounds leadership problems in international relations and diplomacy, particularly in an open society. As the Vietnam experience illustrated, international affairs can never again be set apart from the public eye as a special preserve for diplomats, generals and putative statesmen.

Economic Interdependency

There is nothing new about trade among nations. Phoenicians were trading for British tin in 1000 B.C., and Bahrain seems to have been a commercial entrepot 3,000 years before that. But the world has never been nearly as economically interlinked as it is today. Except for handfuls of isolated primitive peoples, every part of the world is fundamentally dependent upon other parts of the world to provide supplies and to provide markets. At large and growing cost (and with substantial self-denial), the United States and the USSR might still be able to approximate self-sufficiency; the Chinese are approximating it by rigidly suppressing their living standard; no other part of the world can even contemplate such a policy. Interdependency has been further increased by the elaboration of modern technological methods.

As the whole world has had occasion to be reminded in recent months, one consequence of that interdependency is that some national powers that would in classical terms have been viewed as weak and insignificant are increasingly able, through control of production or pricing, to disrupt the intricate interrelated multilateral pattern of the entire world economy. In the same way, the world outside the Communist bloc countries has become a common capital market with massive amounts of capital flowing in all directions in response to price changes, inflation, monetary pressures, and investment opportunity.

Increasingly it appears that the primary consequences of the recent oil embargo and the raising of oil prices will not lie in the unavailability of oil supplies to industrialized countries but in further handicapping the developing countries and in massive dislocations—or worse—of the world monetary and banking system, unable to develop techniques for funding the payments required or to recycle those payments into usable investment form.

Transnationalization of Politics

An implicit assumption of the classical nation-state was that all political activity was organized within the ambit of the state and was ultimately under the authority of the supreme governmental organs of the state. International relations, like public international law, dealt with relationships among chiefs of state, and their regular business was conducted through their foreign ministries and ambassadors through the process called diplomacy. In today's world there are still strong elements of validity in this model. It continues to describe satisfactorily, for example, dealings between the United States and the USSR with regard to strategic nuclear weapons. But as a description of the reality of the modern world, this model has become increasingly incomplete.

It is incomplete, first, in that an increasing number of actors at work in the world today are transnational rather than national in character. The most obvious example is the multinational corporation. The transnational labor union is less conspicuous, but in some instances, such as the union of the automobile workers in United States and Canadian factories, the transnational character of their operations can be seen. Transnational collegial relations are assuming importance in areas of professional expertise, as among the world's physicists. Some observers believe they see transnational generational alliances, with young people around the world relating more to each other than to the older persons in their own countries. Joint commitment to a universalist secular ideology works in some degree to create common interests among citizens of different countries; the earlier hope of the world's Communists for a worldwide Internationale has faded, but Communists in different countries can still be expected to act with a certain degree of sympathetic cooperation. Arab political action in the Mid-East is in part supranational as well as multinational. Meanwhile, the Palestinians, not a nation-state at all at this time, are major political and military actors in the Near East situation and are on the verge of becoming negotiating parties.

The inter-nation-state model is also incomplete, because many of the world's new problems are inherently and endemically problems calling for multinational arrangement rather than for binational relations. Pollution goes where the wind and current listeth. Management of an international monetary system is a multilateral undertaking. Interdependency penetrates the world economy at every level and calls correspondingly for multilateral management and the development of ground rules agreed to by many countries and many interest groups within those countries. Increasingly, the subject matters of international relations are growing in complexity, and increasingly they are less structured in the unitary format of the nation-state or amenable to bilateral management.

Rampant Nationalism

Probably the single most discouraging fact about the contemporary scene in world affairs is that while there are increasing instances of collaborative approaches to joint problems, there is also at large at this time a virulent impulse toward nationalist and ethnic self-identification. This surge of small-group "we-they" thinking is occurring exactly simultaneously with the increasing need to find multilateral ways to manage the world's emerging interdependency.

In this respect, as in many others, the worldwide political theater is simply a larger version of the politics of smaller units. In the United States, and in its urban areas in particular, the paradox is visible that there is an increasing political impetus toward decentralization and toward small group identification on geographic, ethnic or other grounds at the very time when we are encountering deep-seated problems of urban transportation, maldistribution of tax bases, and inequities of social services that can only be solved on a regional basis. To be effective, a political forum must be congruent with the scope of the political problems it is charged to deal with. Throughout the world, it seems that the scope of the problems is widening just at the time when in the postcolonial era, the number of discrete, intensely nationalistic units is increasing.

It took Western Europe a thousand years to develop the nation-state out of the chaos of the fallen Roman Empire, and it has taken another five hundred years for the nation-state to arrive at the rudimentary patterns of cooperative action that now exist. There is no chance that the political problems now confronting the world can await the emergence of new political institutions if their development proceeds at such a glacial rate.

Tomorrow's American Foreign Policy–Corinthian?

The United States in its Doric foreign policy period had very limited resources. But it also had, by circumstance and by policy, only the most limited involvement in international affairs. As a result, its foreign policy problems, while not easy, were manageable.

In the nation's post-World War II era, its Ionic foreign policy period, the nation's commitments and involvements were worldwide and almost without limit. But so were its power and its resources, as compared with other international actors. Its foreign policy problems, while not easy, were manageable.

In tomorrow's world, which has already begun today, the United States will for the first time find itself unavoidably heavily involved in international relations, but without a power paramountcy with which to assure that its wishes will be determinative. From now on, the conduct of foreign policy for the United States will, at best, be the conduct of endless negotiations and endless consultations.

A short list of foreign affairs problems of 1973-74 offers a good indicator of what the balance of the century will be like—at best.[e] Soaring price jumps in oil,

---

[e]Worst case scenarios, particularly nuclear warfare, would make all discussion of the future irrelevant.

with shortages aided by political embargo. Outbreak of hostilities in the Mideast, an area of dangerous sensitivity to the nuclear superpowers. A military alert, with the situation eventually localized and to some extent crisis managed by classical big power diplomacy. General instability of the world monetary system and continuous negotiations of the Committee of Twenty. Continuous negotiations on strategic arms limitations and domestic debate on expenditures to increase the accuracy of MIRV warheads. Twenty-five-nation conference in Geneva on security and cooperation in Europe. NATO-Warsaw Bloc negotiations in Vienna on troop reductions. Special session of the United Nations called by the Algerians to declare a "new economic order" as between rich nations and poor. Trade legislation blocked in the Congress by protectionist elements plus groups sympathetic to civil liberties claims of Soviet Jewry. Law of the Sea conference to attack fundamental problems of establishing a world regime for fishing rights, rights of maritime passage, access to and ownership of minerals on the seabeds, etc. Political terrorism and kidnapping of executives of multinational corporations. Starvation in the advancing south Sahara Desert. Impending major fertilizer and wheat shortages in India. Massive trade deficits in favor of oil producing countries. Sudden restriction by the United States of soybean exports in response to domestic pressures, with consequent sharp dislocation of Japanese food stock base. Portugal gives up.

The USSR grudgingly finally signs the International Copyright Agreement. Complete turnover in European political leadership, reopening negotiations on intra-EEC relations and EEC-United States relations. Post-Stockholm conference follow-up on international ecological safeguards proceeding in Nairobi. Atomic device "for peaceful progress" set off by India. Serious economic trouble in Europe and import restrictions reappear within the Common Market smacking of classical beggar-thy-neighbor tactics. U.S. military alert declared vis-à-vis USSR. United States and USSR jointly undertake space flight venture. Greece and Turkey, NATO allies, on near-war footing over Cyprus. The United States evinces interest in renegotiations regarding Panama Canal. Glacial cadence of normalization of relations with China begins to register. Opening moves toward dialogue with Cuba undertaken.

Long though this list is, it is far from a complete inventory of international subjects and areas that heated up to great activity in 1973-1974. It does not even mention the heavy ongoing agenda of the dozens of standing bodies of the United Nations and other international organizations. The list is nonetheless instructive. It demonstrates the almost unlimited and uncontrollable involvement of the United States. We are engaged in these matters, not because we have made some policy commitment to be involved, but because the issues themselves directly concern our national trade, security, resources, access, or basic sense of humanitarian decency.

The list also shows something of the kinds of diplomatic activities in which the United States will be almost continuously engaged, from the grim bilateral bargaining of SALT II, through different kinds of negotiating groups of ten, twenty, fifty, or all nations of the world, and including special functions such as the extraordinary mediating operation now being carried on by the secretary of state in the Near East.

Third, the list illustrates clearly how true it has become that, while the United States is *primus inter pares* in many of these situations, it has not the power to dictate the outcomes. Increasingly, the United States must negotiate for what it wants, increasingly it must do so in full consultation with groups of others, and increasingly it will not get what it wants.

Finally, the list hints at, though does not fully exemplify, the range and variety of issues that make up the agenda of modern international affairs. This essay has several times referred to the traditional "stuff" of which foreign relations has been made up, noting that the United States has, fortunately, missed a good bit of it. But the world's interdependency and the flow of currents across national lines are so far advanced that the "stuff" of foreign affairs has expanded a thousandfold.

Today, virtually any issue hitherto thought of as domestic can well have major impact upon international relations, and virtually any international relations issue will stir up domestic interests to react in diverse ways. As a result, and inevitably, what used to be the field of "diplomacy," separated from the domestic activity known as "politics," has itself increasingly become a part of an undifferentiated field of politics. The point is not simply that foreign policy is an extension of domestic policy, though that is true. It is rather that old issues that in an earlier era were negotiated out and resolved entirely domestically must today often be negotiated out and resolved in international fora. And at the same time, many of the new issues arising can only be dealt with internationally.

One way in which these phenomena can be observed and gauged is to note the increasing, indeed overwhelming, difficulty encountered by the Department of State as it seeks to organize and staff itself with the multiplicity of expertises, and the constituency pipelines, that are needed to deal simultaneously with the exploding agenda of foreign affairs. Correspondingly, other government agencies and departments increasingly find it necessary to build into their bureaucracy some kind of international division—a kind of in-house State Department. Not surprisingly, this process produces bitter struggles for bureaucratic supremacy, and new ways are constantly being sought to try to turn the hundred players into an orchestra. It is only a matter of time until a substantial reorganizing effort will be required to enhance the capacity of the United States government to handle its multiplicity of international relations and to provide steady and useful political inputs from the whole of the domestic society.

The demands imposed by negotiatory problems of foreign affairs on modern scale and in modern variety are staggering. American foreign policy, under the demands and pressures of the modern world, must move past its Ionic stage and develop a much more sophisticated form, as the Corinthian capital was more sophisticated than the Ionic, more delicately executed, with many separate parts but centrally unified, and, unlike its predecessor, subtle, flexible, capable of rotation, and equally successful as a design regardless of the angle of approach.

The Nixon administration, and the working team of the president and the secretary of state, made major progress in closing down one era of American foreign policy and turning toward the next. Accommodating to the comparative reduction in United States power, they have succeeded in lowering the nation's aggregate profile in international affairs, without withdrawing from the world. Former Secretary Rogers repeatedly projected the central theme that the world is moving from a period of confrontation to one of negotiation. In an astonishing whirling-dervish performance, Secretary Kissinger has managed to negotiate on many different fronts at once.

Every observer, of course, will have his complaints and differences with the administration regarding the way in which it has handled one issue or another—whether Vietnam could have been wound down earlier, whether Japan was unnecessarily affronted by the handling of the negotiations with China, whether insufficient attention has been given to consultation with Europe, whether MIRV was essential to SALT negotiations, whether there is insufficient attention given to problems of developing countries, whether the United Nations and its affiliates have been given too low a priority, whether an effort is being made to resuscitate old-fashioned balance of power theories and if so whether those theories are obsolete today, whether the administration has been hardnosed when it should have been conciliatory and conciliatory when it should have been hardnosed, whether the president and the secretary commit arrogant error by insisting on their own personal diplomacy and by failing to institutionalize the future capacity of the government to conduct its complex foreign relations through a strengthened and modernized Department of State, etc.

Nonetheless, it can be predicted with confidence that historians will see in the events of recent years a transition of United States foreign policy of the character that has been described here. And it is predictable that the course of events for the balance of this century will increasingly call for an active American participation, but participation in the new complex, negotiatory Corinthian form.

Which brings one at last to the central question. Can the United States do it? Does it have the sense of history, the manpower, the governmental structure, the domestic public understanding to conduct so sophisticated, and subtle a role? Can it live with the frustrations, the half victories, the periodic setbacks and the sheer fatigue of conducting such a foreign policy?

I think it is difficult to be optimistic. Neither the nation's small-power history in the last century nor its superpower history in the post-World War II era prepares it for this new role. A number of recurrent behavior patterns in American political life, described earlier, are certain to prove troublesome—particularly our propensity toward public impatience and a traditional demand for definitive clean answers. The only orchestrating power we have in international affairs is the presidency, and that office will inevitably emerge from the current Watergate debacle in some degree weakened and undermined in authority, credibility, and self-confidence. In matters of international affairs authority is constitutionally divided between the executive and the Congress, and even more fractionated within the executive branch; the structural suitability of the United States government for the new style it must adopt must be recognized as low.

Many will also contend that American democracy and the American press require foreign policy to be carried on in full public view—that this pressure will be all the greater as a result of Watergate—and that there is simply no way in which long, complex multi-interest negotiations of the kind required can be carried on effectively in the glare of publicity.

Finally, though many other grounds of doubt exist, the increasingly political character of international negotiations, and the inevitable diversity of interest among domestic elements that have a stake in particular issues under international negotiation, will make it almost impossible for any United States government to achieve a national position and negotiate for it successfully.

That is a gloomy picture and it would seem to compel a gloomy prognosis. But I am inclined to believe that such a prognosis will prove to be incorrect. The first 220 years of the nation's foreign policy have in fact proved to be remarkably successful. Again and again, the American Republic has exhibited the most remarkable political resiliency, the most astonishing capacity for adjusting itself pragmatically to deal with the demands of the time. In the shift in character of our foreign policy the most dangerous stage is already past; the nation has already successfully executed the sharp turn that was required as we left the Ionic era and entered upon the last part of this century.

Those observers who would demand a neatness, a symmetry, and a sense of well-ordered management in foreign affairs will undoubtedly continue to be disappointed in the performance of the United States government in the years ahead. But nothing in the history or institutional structure of other nations, or in their manner of conducting foreign policy, suggests that they are any better equipped to wrestle with today's and tomorrow's problems than is the United States. And the assets of the United States are very many as it enters upon this period. Its economic, technological, and physical resources, and the energy and skills of its people, will continue to rank it as the world's most powerful society, though no longer by so wide a margin as in the recent past. The international problems of today and tomorrow will call for pragmatic flexibility of a kind that has been the strongest aspect of America's political process. The nation's awareness and educational level in matters of foreign policy, and its intellectual resources committed to work on international relations, are far more advanced than in the past.

The United States has largely rid itself of the simplistic notion of an earlier day that the world should be made over into our image; increasingly there is a recognition and tolerance of diversity and difference. The record is that most people in the United States have in recent years ignored simplistic demagogues and come to accept the necessitous reality of limited successes and half-a-loaf results in international affairs, as everyone has always done in the negotiatory process of our domestic politics. The American private economic sector has moved, and is moving, to an entirely new level of appreciation of the social and political consequences of its own conduct at home and abroad.

Most important of all, the fundamental attitudes of the American people, inherited from its foreign relations history, provide a solid and unique foundation for an address to the foreign relations problems of the modern world. The United States remains unencumbered by the parochialism and scars of past grievances that other nations must carry from their foreign relations history, and is more free to turn to basic principles.

The fundamental tenets of the traditional American view of man were, and remain, that progress is possible, that reasonable men can arrive at reasonable solutions, that pragmatic results are more to be sought than doctrinal dogma, that government is for the many and not the few, that the future lies with difference rather than with conformity, and that the basic worth of every man is to be appreciated. It happens that those are precisely the fundamental tenets that will be most needed to deal successfully with the international problems that lie ahead.

As is so often the case, the real question is one of leadership. If America's leadership in the years ahead is of the wrong kind, it will play upon that part of our history and of our psyche that tends to be isolationist, suspicious of foreigners, reactive to skin coloration, devoted to a narrow and short-term definition of American interests, and uncomprehending of the social and political forces that impel many other societies to choose economic and political models different from our own.

Such a leadership would assign to our foreign policy three missions: (1) to use our military power to preserve our national security—at which we would probably succeed; (2) to preserve singlemindedly the interests of American investors abroad and of American users of imported raw materials—at which we can succeed only partially and for a time; and (3) to impede or prevent social change in societies abroad—at which we shall surely not succeed. We would also, with such a policy, be a pariah in the eyes of the rest of the world, and in the eyes of many Americans as well.

If, on the other hand, the nation is fortunate enough to develop and recognize the right national leadership, that leadership will, while hardheadedly conscious of the nation's security problems in an anarchic and dangerous world, call upon the American people to use its substantial strength to play a leading role in the long, difficult, and frustrating business of building a functioning world order. If our leaders make that effort, they will find that they can once more draw successfully upon the storehouse of the nation's great philosophic inheritance, to the immeasurable future advantage of the country and of the world as a whole.

Notes

1. The thesis, its background and its weaknesses are closely analyzed in Kenneth Neal Waltz, *Man, the State, and War* (New York: Columbia University Press, 1959), Chapter IV.

2. Bemis's term. See Samuel Bemis, *A Diplomatic History of the United States* (New York: Holt, Rinehart and Winston, 1965), 5th edition, Chapter XXVI.

3. Arthur Meier Schlesinger, *The Imperial Presidency* (Boston: Houghton Mifflin, 1973).

4. United Nations Population Studies #49, *The World Population Situation in 1970.*

XIII

American Pluralism: The Old Order Passeth

Wilson Carey McWilliams

As Wilson Carey McWilliams observes, e pluribus unum—*from the many, one—has been as much a mystery as a motto throughout this nation's two centuries, and it raises a profound question about America and Americans today. Who are we, culturally and spiritually? And since we have been and still remain so different from one another, in what sense are we a single coherent nation?*

In a society that is committed to the proposition that it should be individualistic and pluralistic, the ancient problem of the one and the many assumes a peculiar intellectual complexity and an extraordinary practical importance. In this essay, Professor McWilliams explores American conceptions of community and diversity, and the ideas of human nature upon which they have been built.

E pluribus unum is as much a mystery as a motto. Plato would recognize it: the Many and the One, a perennial question for philosophy and a paradoxical watchword for a country that has often prided itself on being prosaic. But there is nothing ordinary about the American attempt to unite politically different races, religions, and ethnic cultures—"the idea," Chesterton called it, "of making a new nation literally out of any old nation that comes along"—especially a people of many millions spread over a vast territory. Political philosophy, ancient and modern, counsels against it. Classical Greek philosophy argued for the small polity and modern political thought is predominantly on the side of the nation-state, but both regard cultural unity as a political necessity. Headlines echo the warning: bombings and terror in eternal Ireland, conflict between

Fleming and Walloon, war in Cyprus. Multi-nationality is *en vogue* for corporations, but not for states.

An assemblage of localities and peoples, America could not begin by relying
on the sense of immemorality, the deep-seated emotions and common customs
that were the unthought foundation of solidarity in older nations. Political
commitments had to be understood as the results of decision, covenant, or
contract, and so we still see them: Allegiance is not automatic, and children have
to be "sworn in" by pledges. Whimsically, Chesterton likened liberal America to
the Spanish Inquisition because both were founded on a creed, and there is
validity in the comparison. Thought is more changeable than feeling, and the
conviction that our political unity rested on ideas made Americans prefer to
leave those ideas unexamined. Danger, however, will not be banished by refusing
to look at it, and the existence of more conflict within our "civil religion" than
we have liked to admit has only added to our anxiety. Americans have not been
indifferent to political philosophy; they have feared it and what it might reveal.

Today, philosophy is forced on us. It is evident that the apparent stability of
our recent political past only concealed injustices and resentments. For a decade
conflict among races, generations, and ethnic groups—to name only a few
participants—has been the rule. The One is endangered by the Many; the
philosophic and moral bases of American political life are undeniably insecure
and the age of "self-evidence" is over. And whether we wish to pull down or
shore up our divided house, political necessity compels us to examine its
foundations.

We are tempted to think of eighteenth century America as arcadian and uniform,
a land inhabited by Protestant whites (and, if our memories are not too selective,
by slaves), pre-industrial and largely pre-urban, middle-class and Anglo-Saxon.
To those who lived in it, however, that old America seemed so diverse as to
make common government and political action, let alone common feeling, all
but impossible.

The country was overwhelmingly Protestant, but sectarian and religious wars
and persecutions were vivid in political memories; the majority of states had
established churches and people took their denominational differences seriously.
Most were North Europeans, but that was less salient than it would be now:
Contemporary German, Norse, and Celtic Protestants are "WASP" and hence
Anglo-Saxon by social conventions which were not applied to their ancestors.
Economic interests divided regions and groups within regions; class differences,
embryonic by our standards, were very real; slavery was politically offensive and
economically threatening to many who felt no moral qualms. Above all, America
was composed of localities, comparatively close-knit, small communities and
kin-groups, relatively autonomous and often distinctive in faith, nationality, and
patterns of production.

Those centrifugal tendencies in American life had persuaded Edmund Burke that a policy of "salutary neglect" would maximize the differences among and within colonies and, consequently, their dependence on the Empire. If the Framers exaggerated the dangers of disunity and faction, it was because they had learned Burke's lesson too well, but plurality was the fact and unity only an aspiration.

The Federalist distrusted the excessively democratic spirit which its authors discerned in American governments because it left unity too much to the conscious reasoning and virtue of individuals. The Framers preferred to rely on the yet-untested "new science of politics," convinced that the "artificial reason" of scientifically designed institutions could compensate for the frailties of unaided reason and the perils of plurality. Political mechanics could lessen, if not dispense with, the need for public-spirited citizens and enlightened statesmen, creating a union proof against the accidents of human character.

Human beings, as the Framers' science defined them, were by nature in want, endlessly struggling to master nature. Power was the fundamental interest of humankind. However, individuals were prone to mistake their true interests, partly from simple ignorance, more problematically out of the defects of affection. Appropriately self-centered—for man was individualistic by nature and concerned with his own preservation—affection was consequently parochial in time and space, over-valuing local loyalties and short-term goods. Moreover, it was backward-looking; groups which had once served an individual's interest or which were simply familiar acquired an emotional connection with his security and a hold on his affection even when such loyalties conflicted with present and future interest. To the Framers, Marx's similar argument that the "social relationships of production" acted to brake the dynamics of the "modes of production" would have seemed too limited. All concrete human bonds were at least potentially dangerous to the long-term interests of the individual and of humanity.

The familiar argument of *The Federalist* 10 follows naturally. Groups and communities within a political society are "factions" which seek to advance their own interests, indifferent or adverse to the public good. Yet, Madison argued, it was neither practical, given America's diversity, nor desirable to suppress faction, since to do so would destroy liberty. Fortunately, the size and diversity of America made factions so numerous that no one of them could prevail; a majority (or even a significant minority) could only be a complex coalition, unlikely to agree about much or for very long. Their individual weakness would dissuade factions from disorder or the hope of tyranny, but, equally important, it would shake the hold of factions on the affections of their adherents. No single group could greatly advance or safely protect the individual's interests, however he defined them. Whole-hearted loyalty would be imprudent, and the citizen would be likely to lessen his commitment to any one group in favor of good relations with many.

Nor did the Framers leave it at that: The grand design of the Constitution aims at accentuating the fragmentation of allegiance and the consequent liberation (or isolation, in a more critical view) of the individual. The federal government, Hamilton wrote, must be able to speak directly to the citizen without the mediation of state governments so that it may appeal to "the passions closest to the human heart." Directly allegiant to both federal and state governments, the individual became a dual citizen with divided loyalties. Conflicts over the "division of powers" would amount to conflict claims on the citizen and, in the last analysis, could only be settled in the tribunal of individual conscience. Before that bar, the Framers were confident; their theory of human nature assured them that the greater appeals to interest available to the federal regime would gradually wean affection away from the states and from localities generally.

None of this, the Framers would have noted, requires any *direct* infringement of individual liberty. Control is indirect, exerted by shaping the alternatives available to the individual, but that control did not disturb them. The Framers were convinced that they spoke with the same voice as human nature. The confusions of affection aside, man's group loyalties were instrumental only, justified no further than to the extent they served his interest in self-preservation and power. And while compelling men to follow their interests would inspire resistance, the subtler path of indirect control allowed "free choice" in a system whose dynamics worked toward more centralized, national allegiance.

Nevertheless, the Framers were aware that affection felt for large groups was bound to be diffuse, lacking the strength and intensity of more intimate bonds. The comparative bloodlessness of prospective national sentiment meant, for the Framers, that lesser groups and affections (the family is the obvious example) would never disappear. Such groups would, however, be forced to be orderly and to abandon excessive or exclusive claims on the individual's loyalty. Over time, autonomy and community would decline, and the lesser affiliations of the individual would either be harmless centers of warmth or would come to resemble modern "interest groups"—parts of the whole rather than contenders for moral primacy. Groups and individuals alike would adjust and conform to the political order as a whole, which would achieve the political miracle of being at the same time orderly, protective of individual liberty, and strong.

It would be unfair to call the theory developed in *The Federalist* "assimilationistic" for the Framers sought to create a nation, not to induce identity with an old one, and their doctrine is best termed "integrationism." But despite that qualification they laid down what became, for future generations, the outline of the assimilationist model—suspicion of cultural communities and groups with autonomous values; distrust of strong political sentiments and of affections generally; a policy of fragmenting loyalty by preventing exclusivity with one hand and appealing to the individual's private interests with the other—in the hope that one nation could be built from the ruins of many. And in our formal institutions of government, designed for a purpose at least analogous, assimilationism has always found allies.

The doctrines of *The Federalist* were not the only "science of politics" in America. Opposing them was an older political science, rooted in classical political philosophy and partly reaffirmed by later thinkers like "the celebrated Montesquieu," whose arguments in favor of small states and confederations *The Federalist* was so concerned to refute. More deeply embedded still in American thought were the social and ethical teachings of religion and the more communal customs and beliefs brought to America from the Old Country.

Politically, these views were at a disadvantage. As Madison had known, their adherents were divided and often hostile. The past gave traditional teachings the patina of authority, but it added the tarnish of ancient conflict: Puritan and Catholic were not inclined to submerge old rivalries in order to fight modern common enemies. More modern thinkers, part of the complex stream which would become liberalism, spoke with greater unity. But traditional thought, relatively weak in the "public" world, was at home in the "private" world of family, church, and community. It shaped many of the customs which Tocqueville thought more important than the laws in explaining American democracy.

There was, moreover, a common core to traditional thought. It saw human beings as naturally dependent, social, and political animals who required strong bonds to family, church, and community, not only for security but for moral education and the very development of personal identity. Isolated man was not "natural man": He was a beast or, as the ancient Greeks termed him, an "idiot." Individualism was itself unnatural, at best a kind of *hubris*, and the power-seeking which *The Federalist* took as the central dynamic of human life was a flight both from the realities of life and from the self. "What doth it profit a man to gain the whole world and lose his own soul?" The common life, and implicitly or explicitly political life, had educational and moral ends; freedom was less important than virtue; the procedure by which a law was made or a judgment arrived at mattered less than its substantive merit; the best guard against tyranny was public spirit and the small state—"limited, like man, to a little space"—where the citizen could know and watch his rulers even as he was watched and known.

That current in American thought was too powerful not to make an impact in practical politics and in the unwritten, informal institutions of public life. In the early days of the Republic, as Hamilton became the spokesman for Federalism, Jefferson came to symbolize the diverse and divided voices of opposition. This was not entirely appropriate: Jefferson accepted much of the new creed, regarding man in the "state of nature" as an individual endowed with "natural rights." (Traditional teachings would have preferred to say, "subject to Natural Law.") But Jefferson was too close to traditional religious and moral teachings to accept the notion that competitiveness and struggle were also "natural." Reason alone, Jefferson conceded, might lead in that direction—a concession the exemplars of traditional philosophy would never have made—but it was feeling and not thinking, "Heart" and not "Head" that was sovereign in moral affairs. Whatever the risk in strong bonds and affections, without them there could be no genuine public virtue or republican spirit.

That conviction (along with a nationalistic desire to uphold things American) pervades Jefferson's guarded defense of the Indian. "Barbaric" society, typified in America by the Indian, was half-way between "nature" and "civilization" and was, above all else, characterized by strong bonds and emotions. Indians, Jefferson observed, were courageous, capable of great personal sacrifice and loyalty, and formed friendships which endured despite adversity. Here, surely, were the foundations of public virtue. But Jefferson also recognized the other side: Affectionate with children, the Indian degraded women and was fatally inclined toward cruelty, especially in his relations with outsiders. "Civilization," by developing human reason, expanded the sphere of human feelings, leading to gentleness, "sympathy," and a more inclusive identification with humanity.

Sympathy alone, however, was no basis for political virtue. It diffused affection, tending to weaken it to the point of impotence; like Rousseau, Jefferson saw that a love for mankind may mean no more than a lack of love for particular human beings. Without strong particular attachments, the moral emotions would be unable to compete with either self-centered passions or the self-interested calculations and counsels of reason. Sympathy could degenerate into "good manners," gentleness into gentility, until civility became only a mask for individualism.

Politically, this tendency of civilization fatally weakened the bonds between citizens and, perhaps more important still for Jefferson, between rulers and ruled. Without personal attachments, class differences became immoderate, characterized by arrogance on one side and resentful servility on the other. What else could be learned from Europe's cities, their upper classes effete and vice-ridden, their lower orders reduced to a rabble? Left to itself, civilization violated the natural order of human moral education, for strong attachments were the necessary foundation of true sympathy. Reason could educate barbarism; it could not dispense with it. Moral identity could develop only in a rightly ordered synthesis of civilization and barbarism, and it was that order which Jefferson hoped for in America.

Jefferson admired the unity of local communities even when, like the "phalanxes" of the New England towns, it was marshalled by his opponents. The small community was necessary both for personal attachments and for full democratic participation; at the same time, Jefferson was convinced that it was not inevitable that such communities be narrowly parochial. Local democratic participation would select as leaders "natural aristocrats" who would be aware of local needs and sentiments while recognizing the interests of a larger polity. Assembled in another small, participant body these local leaders would select the natural aristocracy from their own ranks, and so on: A chain of intermediate natural aristocracies would bind the local ward to the nation. At the same time that they spoke for and shared in the "barbaric" sentiments and interests of their constituents, the "natural aristocracies" at every level would also be magisterial, informing and helping develop the sympathetic faculties of local publics. Secure in their local rights, guaranteed that their feelings and interests would be consulted and related to their rulers by a series of reciprocal personal attachments, citizens would find it easier to respect and even feel for the rights and needs of others and of the political order as a whole.

Nor was Jefferson's image only a matter of theory. While the "ward system" never became part of the formal Constitution, it was reflected in the structure of American political parties, powerful if informal elements of the constitutional order. This is ironic, for Jefferson distrusted partisan spirit, but it testifies to his understanding of the necessities of practical democratic politics. The traditional party, with its articulated chain of committees and conventions leading from the precinct to the nation has been accused of many things, but neglect of local prerogatives is not one of them. (Even today, parties are state organizations more than national ones and a major buttress of constitutional pluralism, though that is largely due to the electoral system.) Recently, traditional party structure has been rediscovered by the liberal Left as a vehicle for maximum democratic participation—another irony since liberal America spent so much energy in helping to dismantle it. Moreover, there was more than parochiality in the traditional party. George Washington Plunkitt boasted, with some truth, that the parties had been the schools of patriotism ("agencies of political socialization," social scientists would say with less eloquence and clarity). Plunkitt of Tammany Hall was hardly the sort of "natural aristocrat" Jefferson envisioned, but the Plunkitts remind us that there was a limited alliance, at least, between Jeffersonian structure and cultural pluralism.

The limitations of that alliance, however, were very severe. A *structural* pluralist, Jefferson insisted on a broad area of *cultural* unity. Less confident than the authors of *The Federalist* in the science of political mechanics, he was more concerned with political culture—education, social life, custom, and civic values—as it influenced the development of public virtue. If Jefferson was more willing to trust the American people, it was because their political culture, the diversities of American life aside, was uniquely republican.

Geographically halfway between European civilization and frontier barbarism, the American people were socially still agrarian, relatively equal, and free from the corruptions of massification and hierarchy. The Protestant heritage and the British political tradition, as Jefferson understood them, had provided Americans with a deep-seated belief in liberty of conscience, fundamental rights, and representative institutions. Americans, Jefferson asserted in his First Inaugural, are "brethren of the same principle." It was an inheritance to be reinculcated (a major value of the Bill of Rights, for Jefferson, was educational), but the existence of cultural unity made it possible to tolerate diversity. Different mores, sentiments, and beliefs, necessarily those of small minorities, would be unable to change the character of public life and would, under the impact of free institutions, gradually disappear.

Where cultural assimilation seemed difficult, Jefferson was anxious if not despairing. He came to regret his earlier aspersions on blacks and he always opposed slavery on principle. Seeing no way to assimilate the black population, however—the habits resulting from slavery, white arrogance, and black resentment seemed to make it impossible without more force than republican government could survive—Jefferson concluded that we could not let go the tiger's tail and abandoned the issue to more enlightened future generations. It was even more indicative that Jefferson distrusted unrestricted immigration, fearing that republican America would be unable to assimilate in any numbers the "canaille" of European cities, schooled in the habits of despotism. Education and free institutions took time to create new habits and feelings; immigrants might change the country before they were changed by it. The republicanism of Jefferson's ideal was exalted; it was also fragile, likely to be shattered by irreverent hands.

Moreover, Jefferson seemed almost unaware that his "ward system" logically required *stable* communities with a high level of interaction over time. Only where citizens knew one another's character and personality well could it be assumed that the public could distinguish the "natural aristocrat" from his demagogic counterfeit. Possibly Jefferson took stability for granted, but even that would be revealing. In any case, Jefferson would have found it difficult to support stability. Believing that the universal humanitarianism of civilization was morally superior to narrower and more exclusive creeds, he would have found closed communities unacceptable. He agreed with the Lockean argument by which naturally free individuals "gave up" some of their rights to the state and retained others, and hence would protect the private sphere—"society"—from interference by the public—"the state"—wherever those rights had not been explicitly surrendered. But "society" was made up of individuals still naturally free: Groups and communities had value only if they were voluntary and "social" institutions would have to survive without governmental support. (Private property was an individual right, not a social institution, and even there Jefferson was ambiguous; "The earth," ran his famous saying, "belongs in usufruct to the living.")

Favoring policies to preserve agrarian society, for example, Jefferson did not favor parallel policies to protect or create stable agrarian communities. Quite the contrary: Jefferson's agrarianism presumed abundant land available to succeeding generations, and consequently the new settlements of frontier society. That, at least, was one justification for his doubtfully constitutional purchase of Louisiana which, as Henry Adams observed, undermined local loyalties and transformed the Union. The federal government, originally the creation of the states, became a creator of states, the architect of the Union. Adams went to the heart of Jeffersonianism: "The Federalist theory was one of empire; the Republican was one of assimilation. . . ."

Essential to the democratic citizenry Jefferson hoped for, community was always subordinate in his thought and practice to individual freedom, progress, and the separation of state and society. His tolerance for different creeds presumed the political supremacy of the "self-evident" truths of liberal orthodoxy. Churches, localities, and cultural community, in Jefferson's doctrine no less than *The Federalist*'s, were forced to act within liberal premises or to eschew politics altogether. In either case, they would have to compete with the seductions of individualism and the promise of abundance, and the logic of that competition required that practices and values change toward conformity with the liberal creed that ruled "public" life.

Jeffersonianism presumed assimilation, but it favored structural diversity and had sympathy, at least, for minority cultural communities. To the unassimilated within America or newcomers from abroad, these were significant considerations in practical politics. It was a marriage of convenience, but one which made Jeffersonianism a part of the case for pluralism in America.

For a century and a decade after Jefferson left office, newcomers crowded the ports of entry. It was an erratic stream, starting slowly, reaching flood stage in the aftermath of the Famine and the revolutions of '48, receding during the Civil War years, rising and falling in the seasons of boom and bust, but it never ran dry. New peoples, new diversity: In the cities especially, language, costume and custom became riotous, and Catholics, Jews, and Orthodox Christians came to outnumber Protestants (many of whom were also foreign-born).

The Civil War tormented America, official corruption sometimes brought indignation, and the periodic collapse of the economy brought great hardship, but the country seemed—most of the time—optimistic, expanding, and energetic. The universe, William James remarked, was "buzzing." In flush times native and settled Americans were inclined to boast of the diverse origins of the people. Immigrants were proof of America's virtues and the Old World's bankruptcy. In darker hours, too, they were an assurance of the American promise. With few exceptions, however, assimilated Americans did not *value* cultural diversity; they boasted of *overcoming* it. The "melting pot," as Chesterton was to observe, was not formless. It was cast in the shape of the American creed, and in holding its shape when ancient cultures became molten, it proved that American beliefs were tougher, able to "take the heat."

The voice of patriotism, however, had a strident, over-aggressive tone, less confident than in need of reassurance. The ebullience of the age was superficial, concealing the dark turbulence Melville had detected at "the little lower level." Cultural diversity touched feelings of dread which only its defeat could assuage.

This uneasiness had its rational side. Increasingly, Americans saw grounds for Tocqueville's comment that custom was more important than law. American democracy, shining ideal or soiled practice, depended on a political culture that included deep feelings of respect for law, a belief in equality, and a sense of public obligation. The underlying "romance" of America, Chesterton was to remark, was "the pure classic conception that no man must aspire to be anything more than a citizen, and no man should endure to be anything less."

As ideals, those norms might have appeal to immigrants, but such beliefs were only in rare cases rooted in history, experience, or emotion. Immigrants brought a political culture that was not often republican; Jefferson had feared the city-bred, but peasants had studied in the school of feudalism. Southern and Eastern Europeans, especially, had lived for centuries in lands where government was alien and oppressive. The state was to be suspected, evaded, and resisted; ideal government left one alone. For many, the world outside the family was amoral, ruled by force and cunning alone; even Jews, who brought a collective tradition and communal institutions, suspected formal politics, and with reason. The Irish swam naturally in the political sea, but their own habits and history made them cavalier about the niceties of law and procedure. Every group had its potential liabilities, and the privation and discrimination which immigrants encountered made matters worse.

Well-founded doubt, however, was only a short episode in a very long story. The most powerful anxieties felt by native and long-settled Americans grew out of changes this side of the water; the most important movements were within America itself. Canals, steam transportation, and the telegraph facilitated the development of a commercial economy. At the same time, they made it easier to move—West to the new lands, East to the cities where industry was establishing its dominion. Even those who "stayed home" found their social world more affected by national and international economic fluctuations, less autonomous and less insular, more open to new ideas and products coming in and to restless migrants moving out. Already fragile, social bonds in America became even less secure; social sanctions weakened; at what seemed an alarming pace, old landmarks were obliterated and dynasties rose and fell. "No man's estate is sufficient to keep sail with his equals," John Winthrop had complained in the seventeenth century; two centuries later, his descendants had grounds for seeing themselves in worse straits.

Too rooted in older morals and manners to abandon them without guilt, most Americans were beguiled by progress, felt threatened into self-seeking and competitiveness by the risk of failure, and were tempted to ruthlessness by the opportunity they believed was over at hand. Moral tension was inevitable. The easiest path was to justify individualism and obedience to the laws of the market by reference to "necessity." Too weak to change conditions, the perennial argument goes, "I had no choice." In the nineteenth century, moreover, that negative defense could be given a moral gloss more easily than at most times. The idea of progress was compelling during the (rather misnamed) "century of peace," and the major currents in philosophy and science supported the belief that the plurality of self-interested actions, however mischievous in detail, was guided by Nature, the Oversoul, or the Invisible Hand toward some greater good. Also, the claim that individuals were too weak to do more than defend themselves was not simply rationalization. Hawthorne, regretting the decline of local communities, observed that America was too vast to be taken into "one small human heart." Only "one twenty-millionth of a sovereign," the citizen could not be expected to see himself as important in the decisions of the whole.

Tocqueville had described the process. Democratization moved toward individualism and social insecurity: Making "every man forget his ancestors ... it hides his descendants and separates him from his contemporaries; it throws him back upon himself alone and threatens in the end to confine him within the solitude of his own heart." Equality became less a public faith than a general but privately felt sense of weakness. Safety lay only in numbers and the majority became a tyrannical force of nature. Individualism and mass conformity, born out of the decline of community, were twins.

The unity and similarity created by the "tyranny of the majority," however, resulted from felt impotence and was deeply resented, especially since the new standards of "public" life—individualism, competitiveness, and materialism— warred with strong needs and old beliefs. The public world of the market was at odds with the "private" order in the family, the churches, and "society" generally, which was still ruled by traditional standards. In the family, for example, mutual dependence, devotion, and obligation were still first principles. Citizens of two worlds, men could feel a dignity too often lacking in public life by shielding women and children from the anxieties of the outer world. The duty to provide and the demands of success, however, inspired insecurity, frustration, resentment, and guilt, and these days it goes without saying that those who were passively provided for felt a similar if inverted ambivalence. Half-suspecting that the price was too high, assimilated Americans who had paid for respectability were not prepared to let anyone—especially a foreigner—evade the social cost of admission.

Immigrants bore an additional burden. They were most obvious in cities, where social decay and demoralization were also most evident. The association of the two was seductive, especially since most Americans were devoted to existing institutions and were disinclined to seek the internal causes of the malaise. If "foreigners" brought economic trouble and moral decay, exclusion or restricted immigration seemed to follow as logical cures.

Early exclusionism tended to follow Jefferson in basing its case on cultural arguments. Disturbed by the Jacksonian era, George Perkins Marsh theorized that only "Goths" were suited to freedom, but Marsh's fundamental antipathy was against Catholics rather than a race, and the case was similar with the Know-Nothings whose arguments paralleled Marsh's. Appropriately, Marsh later became a founder of the Conservationist movement out of a concern to preserve the physical basis of older American culture, but he never lost his hatred of "Romanism."

As biology grew in prestige, however, racial "science" came into vogue, especially since Darwinism waxed in the post-Civil War years when the ardors born in the anti-slavery movement waned. It became widely agreed that some "races" were clearly inferior and "unassimilable" except at too great a biological and political price. Blacks were here to stay (the reasons, especially economic, were not often examined), but even if kept rigidly separate were, by their mere presence—a thousand stump-orators declaimed—a standing danger. New races, however, could still be excluded. Labor organizations, for their own reasons, often supported such arguments and, in the case of the anti-Orientalists in California, had the eventual satisfaction of seeing the "yellow peril" fended off by an exclusion law. Anti-Orientalism also contributed to the opposition to imperialism through a desire to exclude the "unassimilable" Filipino. Temporarily, however, the movement for restricted immigration could go no further. Despite the urging of anti-Catholics, anti-Semites, and anti-foreignists generally, the heritage of free immigration, the needs of an expanding economy, and the belief (whatever its origins) in America's absorptive capabilities formed too strong a coalition to permit excluding foreign whites. America was not yet ready for counsels of despair.

Assimilationism still suited the country's mood, but it was more uncertain than in the early days of the republic. Cast in familiar molds, assimilationist theories in the nineteenth century showed the marks of new doubt. Backed by the authority of science, Social Darwinism came to be intellectual orthodoxy, a "steel chain of ideas" in Eric Goldman's phrase. In many ways, Social Darwinism resembled the teaching of *The Federalist*—suspecting untutored democracy and demanding that private property be protected, supporting federal supremacy (especially in the courts) as a protection against state experiments with social legislation and economic regulation, and regarding communities and cultural communities as too likely to be reflections of atavistic "folkways." Individualism, disciplined by the competitive necessities of the "struggle for survival" in the marketplace, was the true guide to progress. Minorities (like everyone else) would be forced to conform their habits of thought and action to that struggle or perish with the "unfit." The ruthless rhetoric of Social Darwinists, however, reflected a new concern to control the world of "society" which *The Federalist* had been content to leave to its own devices in the short term. Darwinism was unwilling to trust political mechanics and institutions. Claims to biological certitude could not allay the political anxieties of Darwinism, and theorists like William Graham Sumner worried lest the "unfit" and their sympathizers, through the "absurd attempt to make the world over," should cast it back into barbarism.

This sense of political vulnerability was well-founded. Darwinism warred too evidently, despite moralizing propagandists like Henry Drummond and Winwood Reade, with religious morality, humane sentiments, and traditional ethical codes. Survival too often went to the devious and amoral, and it hardly helped to define these, circularly, as "the fit." Darwinist doctrine also did not square with experience: There were too many depressions, productivity and reward seemed little related, and the "free market" was obviously a euphemism for an economy controlled by trusts and concentrated wealth. Far from assimilating the "unfit," moreover, Darwinism seemed likely to drive them into embittered radicalism.

There had always been social critics and movements of protest, of course, but discontent in the late nineteenth century took on a new and violent tone. Or at least, so it seemed to more conservative Americans, made sensitive by their own anxieties. Marxism and anarchism had their highly publicized (and much feared) adherents, but during its lifetime populism, part of the agrarian tradition, was more serious. Jeffersonians had shuddered when the free land ran out; Frederick Jackson Turner's eulogy of the frontier as the source of American democracy raised grave doubts about the future. Populism hoped to transform that problem into a new promise by making industrialists conform to traditional values. Whatever the merits of their platform, however, Populists suffered from a fatal political weakness. Not xenophobic in any strict sense, Populists did not admire social pluralism or cultural diversity. Distrusting separateness as likely to dissipate the people's strength, Populists were assimilationists with a vengeance in relation to their own values. In the cities, the ethnic minorities knew as much, and populism did badly; economic sympathy was not enough.

Populism, however, helped edge mainstream Americans—beset by their own ambivalence, harried by trusts from above and radicals from below—into the "reform Darwinism" of the Progressive movement. Progressive spokesmen saw the contradiction in orthodox Darwinism between its relativistic theory and its defense of immutable political and economic institutions. Institutions could not be exempted from the laws of evolution; Progressives lionized Holmes for his thesis that "the life of the law" had been "experience." But while logic was useful to discomfit conventional wisdom, it was only a secondary element in Progressive ideology. The belief in evolution, relativism, and a stress on adaptation could have led easily to a distrust of social engineering and government planning. (Holmes, for example, reached that conclusion.) Progressivism, by contrast, was activistic, convinced that institutions had a creative role and that "social science" could help to shape a more humane political order.

The failure of early "clean government" reformers only taught Progressives that throwing the rascals out was insufficient and that formal political institutions were comparatively superficial. Increasingly, Progressives revised the liberal distinction between "state" and "society." In historic liberalism, while only individuals had natural rights, "society" had been treated as second nature, the product of voluntary individual decisions. The right of society to be free from state control had a status practically equal to the similar right of individuals. (Hence, for example, the doctrine that corporations were "legal persons.") Progressivism recognized, however, that corporations, parties, and mass organizations generally had reached levels of scale, power, and permanence which made them supra-individual "governments over men." Society was becoming "unnatural," usurping the liberty of the individual, and now needed to be controlled. Rejecting the autonomous moral status that older liberalism had accorded "society," progressivism—still part of the "liberal tradition"—returned to the individual, always the fundamental datum of liberal thought.

Similarly, distrusting that other formalized abstraction, "the state," Progressives tended to refer to the "people." Organizations, law, and formal institutions generally were only instruments, and in a changing world their utility was tenuous and required redemonstration. *The Federalist*'s science of political mechanics was rigid, superficial, self-interested, and outdated. It was a time for debunking and innovation; Progressives used the word "new" so often that it became tiresome. But "new," in Progressive usage, was an adjective, suggesting modification and continuity rather than a break with the past. One science of politics was in ruins, a new one was needed; mechanics yielded to the science of management and administration.

Theodore Roosevelt's "New Nationalism," cribbed from Herbert Croly, was more enthusiastic about the possibilities of regulating trusts and mass associations, while Wilsonians spoke of breaking them up to usher in the "New Freedom," but the distinction was one of emphasis more than principle. Mr. Dooley, satirizing T.R. in his earlier, trust-busting phase caught the mood: "On the one hand, I would stamp them underfoot; on the other, not so fast." Both wings of Progressivism stood for centralized controls; Wilsonians only preferred that the control be indirect.

There were differences of degree, but Progressives agreed that the people could not be trusted to know their own interests. The ancient argument that the *demos* is a bad judge of means and measures seemed strengthened by the new complexity of the political world, and Progressives urged that the public limit itself to a choice of goals and "policies," leaving "administration" to experts. However, the great philosophers of progressivism—Dewey is the obvious example—knew that the distinction was fallacious; ends and means are inseparable, and by selecting means the scientific administrator would shape preferences as to policy. The whole argument was disingenuous, for progressivism doubted the ability of the public to formulate goals only slightly less than it suspected the people's choice of means.

Traditionally, moral training had been left to "society," and civic education generally had been a province of the private order. The Progressive critique of "society," however, meant that it could no longer be trusted; too many tyrannies and superstitions ruled the private order. At the same time, Progressive social science grew increasingly aware of the influence of "social control" in shaping and forming human character. True reform, then, would have to begin earlier and reach deeper into human life, changing the conditions of rearing, education, and socioeconomic existence.

There was an echo of Jefferson in this concern for political education. But while the social and affective side of human nature was a fact to be acknowledged, Progressives saw it chiefly as a barrier to be overcome or manipulated. (There were exceptions, but mainly in the last years of the movement.) Emotional bonds and group loyalties distorted reason; dependence and community restricted individual freedom. Ethnic and traditional communities were reflections of "cultural lag," surviving only because of the ignorance and lack of opportunity progressivism hoped to remedy. Race was a problem: Probably the greater number of Progressives accepted "scientific" racism and supported Jim Crow laws. But race was an exception and one about which Progressives disagreed; assimilation was the rule. Progressive social science, after all, helped make "deviation" into a euphemism for social pathology.

Gradually, restrained by the devotion of many Progressives to "competition" as a standard for policy, the movement discarded the "economic whip." "Cooperation" became the new norm of social control, and social service and public bureaucracy replaced laissez-faire. Honey instead of vinegar: The new, relatively humane social policies still aimed at assimilation to modernity and to liberal "civil religion." And, as their clients soon discovered, the new agencies could be as cold and as stern as the old market, though in different ways. Progressivism hoped to create a unified people which would support change, trust academically trained experts, and set acceptable policy goals because, as a part of modern, industrial culture and free from social tyrannies, it would define its interests in terms Progressives found rational. There was a brave new world a-coming, and pluralism could only be an interference.

This is not an entirely fair picture. Progressivism was a complex movement, made up of many schools and tendencies, and while disillusioning experience led many Progressives, like Hiram Johnson, into embittered rigidity, others admitted their mistakes and tried to learn from them. (Frederic Howe's *Confessions of a Reformer* is typical of the genre.)

In the cities, disappointment came early. The machines showed great reserves of loyalty, even when defeat temporarily deprived them of patronage, resources which reformers ("mornin' glories," Plunkitt mocked) could not equal. Victorious, reform was too often condescending, almost invariably impersonal, part of an alien world which acted on ethnic and poor neighborhoods but remained outside the network of feelings and personal relationships.

In an early and brilliant essay, Mary Kingsley Simkhovitch noted that reformers, unwilling to respect traditional culture, could not understand that desperate need and social instability made small, intense, utterly reliable groups mandatory in the great cities and placed a moral premium on personal loyalty. The "urban village" was not an atavism; it was an intelligent response to conditions of social demoralization.

Brand Whitlock, in his novels, drew a similar moral: The Boss, with his group and personal loyalties, had a moral strength and humanity which an isolated individual, insecure and self-centered, could not equal. A successful reform mayor, Whitlock presumably spoke from experience. But Simkhovitch also detected the weakness of the machine. Politicians lived in a world of divided allegiance, part of the neighborhood on one side and the larger society on the other; loyalty to party was the synthesis which held both worlds together. The party, however, lacked any positive vision of society; it adapted to the great currents of change and led its followers to do likewise. The machine, then, betrayed the neighborhood, drifting in the direction of assimilation, making no serious effort to shape events or to preserve old cultures. The patriotism Tammany taught, Plunkitt's vaunt, was contentless, lacking an ideal of civic virtue. To Simkhovitch, the defect was accidental; the structure of the political party was essential, and worthwhile reform was possible only within it. Hers was a sophisticated vision; most Progressives, however disenchanted, were yet unwilling to go so far in the direction of cultural pluralism—until 1914.

The "guns of August" changed a world. Before the war, philosophers had begun to fear the "omnicompetent state," and the war gave their arguments teeth. The belief that moral and material progress marched together was discredited, and Freud's musings on the ambiguity of civilization—echoing Jefferson's earlier warnings—rang all too truly. The malleability of human beings, grounds for hope to progressivism, became a terrible portent, especially where the public was reduced to a mass of isolated individuals subjected to insecurity, impotence, and indignity and filled with a volatile combination of anger and despair.

Progressives had hoped for a public "freed" from group control, united by mass education and communication, and able to pursue great purposes. The vision had turned nightmarish, and solidarity seemed of less moment than safeguarding moral autonomy and the ability to resist the claims of the state to speak for "the whole." War-born sensitivity discerned that the public was a "phantom," a vague abstraction for the individuals who theoretically composed it, a matter of symbols and stereotypes meaningful only to the extent that individuals identified them with more immediate emotions and interests.

There had always been theorists who detested mass society, convinced that there were limits beyond which human social affections and capacities for effective action would be fatally weakened. Josiah Royce had advocated a "New Provincialism," accepting the Jeffersonian premise that small communities were more likely to give citizens a sense of security, personal significance, and moral meaning. Royce also followed Jefferson in denying any necessary contradiction between local commitments and broader obligations. The small community built the human foundations of the greater. Moreover, Royce argued, to value community truly as an *ideal*, we must value the communities of others; the new ethical imperative was "Be loyal to loyalty."

Ideas like Royce's became appealing in the new uncertainty. Harold Laski's wartime celebration of resistance to the state by cultural communities was much admired (not many noticed that most of the communities Laski cited had eventually been defeated). Randolph Bourne was appalled by the new, social scientific technicians who lacked any moral standard for policy except increasing mastery, prisoners of historical drift and (like "the best and the brightest" of later times) fatally attracted by the challenge of war. Like Lippmann, who agreed with much of his argument, Bourne developed new respect for older cultures with a greater sense of human limitations, and his call for a "Trans-

National America" reflected a new conviction that plural ethnicity and nationality might have positive *value*. Americans should accept "dual citizenship" in
place of "narrow 'Americanism' or forced chauvinism."

> What we emphatically do not want is that these distinctive qualities should be
> washed out into a tasteless, colorless fluid of uniformity. . . . Just so surely as we
> tend to disintegrate these nuclei of nationalistic culture do we tend to create
> hordes of men and women without a spiritual country, cultural outlaws, without
> taste, without standards but those of the mob.

Bourne had his own variety of chauvinism—"America is already the world-feder-
ation in miniature"—and he was lamentably vague about the means by which his
ideal might be realized, but coming from a man of the Left, his argument was
striking and a sign of the times.

In practical politics, during the years after World War I, it was quite another
matter. The social changes associated with the war had further destabilized
localities, and the automobile soon made migration into a mass industry. The
war had also undermined the emotional foundations of the theory of progress;
waiting for the long-term seemed unacceptable and excess, desperation, and
installment buying went hand-in-hand. It was all rather tame by our contemporary standards, but to traditional Americans of the day it was terrifying—especially since so many were ambivalent in their feelings about the new order of
things. Prohibition was only the forerunner of a series of crusades—anti-Bolshe-
vism, suspicion of "aliens," racism and religious bigotry alarmingly reflected in
the expansion of the Klan—aimed at preserving an America that would be
Protestant, white, and devoted to the "American Way." The new stridency and
brutality, however, indicated that the Old America was on the defensive, feeling
that the gentler mechanisms of assimilation were unreliable. Restricted immigration revealed a conviction that opportunity had become a scarce resource, and
the National Origins Quota reflected the parallel belief that American political
culture, no longer all-conquering, needed protection from the contamination of
too-foreign peoples and "alien ideologies."

It was not only Yahoos who worried. War, social disorder, the new
intolerance at home and totalitarianism abroad, while confirming the warnings
of pluralist theory, raised fears that its prescriptions would only compound the
malaise. New to intellectual fashionability, pluralism never lacked articulate
critics.

First, there were those who argued that pluralism encouraged moral fragmentation at a time when new or restored unity was needed. Pluralism trusted
existing social groups to provide the base for its moral pyramid and relied on
political education to supply the capstone. Peril and change made political
education seem slow and chancy, however, and many intellectuals—disenchanted
with the liberal tradition that had informed public life—saw in the aggressive
banality of mainstream society a proof that the religious and communal

moralities of the private order had broken under the strain of new times, surviving only as cant. H.L. Mencken's vulgarized Nietzscheanism, Paul Elmer More's Neo-Federalism, and Walter Lippmann's emerging hope for statesmen guided by "the public philosophy" were among a myriad of schools which agreed, their distaste for one another aside, that American society needed an elite to guide it to a richer culture and a more humane existence. Even liberals, beset and troubled, sought for ways of indoctrinating a hostile and disillusioned public, and felt little enthusiasm for more diversity.

Second, critics observed that even structural pluralism—cultural and moral issues aside—demanded a decentralized polity limited to the snail's pace and half-measures of political give-and-take. Accelerating technological change and an interdependent, complex world made a pluralistic order amateurish, indecisive, and forever forced to react to events that had outrun its understanding. Moreover, pluralism would mean the loss of opportunities for new abundance which, the critics thought, might assuage old resentments and frustrations. Social thinkers like Veblen continued to urge the case for social engineering, tracing the causes of the war and the subsequent disorders to societies (and those aspects of all societies) in which the scientific and industrial revolutions had been incomplete. Even in the boom years, prosperity was uneven and there were areas—especially in rural America—where depression was semi-permanent. The Great Depression gave a powerful moral force to the technocratic critique, for widespread poverty and general desperation created a compassionate imperative for rapid and effective aid that reduced opposition to centralization to obstruction, and distaste for cultural uniformity seemed little more than aesthetic snobbery. Federal planning (and executive power) became a new "gospel of efficiency" which, obviously, the demands of the Second World War and the age of crisis which followed did little to dispel.

The appeal of Leninism to intellectuals in the thirties was based, in part, on its synthesis of the two critiques. There were reasons for discontent, of course: Hard times lingered and it was easy to accept the analysis that the New Deal was at best directionless (and possibly proto-fascist), too prone to compromise and too enmeshed with the existing system, creating only an elitist bureaucracy alien to those it governed and unable to resolve the economic crisis without war. Leninism—Stalinist or Trotskyite—promised both an efficient use of planning and a vanguard capable of remoralizing society, and was given added attraction by the democratic vision of an eventual proletarian fraternity.

Pluralist theory, however, outlasted its opponents in the race for intellectual dominance. Political facts, as much as intellectual merits, were responsible. Totalitarianism, especially as nazism and Stalinism became palpably gruesome, made elitism and technocracy into potential horrors quite capable, in the "novel" government of totalitarian polities, of combining their potential for manipulation and terror. Conservative elitism lost credibility in the Crash, as the graceful lords of finance deteriorated into baffled "money-changers." Leninism, saddled with the Bolshevik experiment, was also unable to explain how individuals could feel other than insignificant in a public of many millions organized in the mass associations that the Party favored. References to "new consciousness" did not help, for they suggested mass propaganda more than Marx's mystic notion of "species-being." Totalitarianism also helped pluralism against older enemies: Assimilation sounded suspiciously like *Gleichschaltung* in newly sensitive ears.

Pluralism, moreover, had advantages in practical politics. Communist theory regarded ethnic, local, and craft loyalties as atavistic; tactically, Communists recognized and sought to use such group differences. Marx had taught, however, that theory and practice were inseparable, and so it proved. Ethnic and racial minorities generally detected the Party's theoretical disdain, and its efforts to compensate were often excessive and evidently insincere. "The brother *does not sing*," insists the "Brotherhood's" spokesman in Ellison's *Invisible Man*, and like the New Left in its later years, the Communist party passed from integrationism to a stubborn advocacy of a black state with few intermediate steps, creating an inevitable impression of opportunism. Ironically, it was not so opportune; separatist through the integrationist decades, the Party abandoned its position just when nationalism was coming into fashion.

Pluralists, however, had their own ambivalences. The political dangers which increased the attractions of pluralism were also threats which demanded unity. That tension, difficult as it was and is, also calls attention to the fact that the most potent appeals of pluralism were negative. The theories which established a dominant position in political thought were "pluralistic" only instrumentally, conceding a point to a demanding reality. Their positive values were drawn from the liberal tradition.

John Dewey, for example, retained the individualistic *moral* premises of historic liberalism despite his rejection of individualism as a guide to policy. Dewey argued that man was a "social animal," but he also insisted that groups be defined in terms of the problems he presumed they existed to solve—a utilitarian (and implicitly contractarian) position. His quarrel with older liberalism lay not with its moral aims but with its legalistic, formal definition of associations which ignored historical change. Voluntary cooperation, Dewey argued, could be relied on only where problems were simple and the consequences and benefits of common action were immediately apparent. When most of human life had concerned such problems, individualism had made sense and the state had been a mere "shadow" on society. As problems had become complex and indirect consequences more vital, the public and the state—which existed to deal with such issues—necessarily took on an expanded role. Industrialism relegated society to a subordinate role.

It was a typically Progressive, historicistic case, and Dewey also contended that "cultural lag," emotional and socially based resistance to change, had to be overcome to permit the full use of technological and organizational resources for enriching life. Certainly, he had no desire to preserve older communities, although he conceded some "sentimental" regret at their passing. Influenced by World War I and the years that followed, however, Dewey observed that leaving the individual helpless and alone, facing problems he could neither solve nor understand and subject to a massive public order, only *heightened* resistance to change, encouraging a desperate clinging to old familiarities of thought and feeling. Interest groups like the corporations and mass associations were of no help. They were a kind of bastard—logically part of the public sphere as Dewey defined it, but conceived and governed as part of private society. They combined the parochial interests and vision of society with the mass organization and coercive powers of the state; weaker than the state, they lacked the warmth of face-to-face society, and constituted the worst of all social worlds.

Dewey advocated new, local communities, but chiefly as a kind of therapy, designed to give the individual an emotional warmth and security that would lessen his resistance to change and make him more open to a "common faith" in the scientific method, inculcated by a new "art of communication" which would provide the ideational basis of an "inclusive and fraternally associated public." Some of this would have appealed to Jefferson, and Dewey's argument shares many of the problems of Jeffersonian theory, but where Jefferson hoped to connect local communities to the public by a political structure of articulated "natural aristocracies," Dewey substituted the "art of communication" based fundamentally on the mass media. Whatever the other merits (or defects) of his case, "pluralism" in Dewey's theory was only part of the social technology of assimilation to mass society.

New Dealers admired Dewey, but programs to create neighborhoods and similar designs for returning government to the "grass roots" were sacrificed to the demand for restored prosperity and, later, to the requirements of military victory. Pragmatic, inclined to use the tools at hand, the New Deal found it easiest to work through federally-engineered compromises between organized interests. However spotty its record, success in war and postwar prosperity seemed to justify the political order created by the New Deal. Political and social scientists, taught by totalitarianism to distrust mass movements and ideological state planning, were disinclined to find fault with humane muddling-through, and out of their interpretation of the New Deal era, "interest group liberalism," as Theodore Lowi calls it, became established as the "new public philosophy."

The conventional definition of this theory as "pluralism," however, is at best misleading. Its origins go back to the Reform Darwinism of Arthur Bentley's thesis (advanced, hyperbolically, against both Social Darwinists and neo-Hegelians) that both "the individual" and "the state" were fictitious abstractions and only "the group" was real. But Bentley and later "group theorists" preserved individualism as a moral norm, just as Dewey had. Groups, Bentley contended, were justified by their "utility to the individual," and later theorists agreed with him in an up-dated phrase, referring to "filling the needs" of group members.

Group theory also sees politics in liberal terms, as a "struggle for power" in which a dynamic balance is the chief desideratum. It departs from older liberalism in a concern for the distribution of economic and social power made necessary by the imperfectly competitive market created by mass associations and great corporations. However, the child of Bentley's distrust of the state, schooled in the totalitarian era, group theory rejects Progressive and Deweyite notions of restructuring society, following the old liberal star of limited government. Toning up the science of *The Federalist*, group theorists have argued that competition between organized groups—what Galbraith called "countervailing power"—provides a new "self-regulating mechanism" to replace the market and supplement the Constitution. But it is not a perfect one: In oligopolistic society, the "night-watchman state" is inadequate, and government is required to act as a "broker" on the New Deal model. Nevertheless, the free market in *group* life becomes the new hallmark of free society.

The Framers, however, sought to give the state a moral mantle and to attract public affection to its support. Group theory, certain that the state will be tempted to expand beyond traditional liberal bounds and fearing that the people may encourage it to do so, has sought to debunk the moral claims of the state. Terms like "the public interest," David Truman argued, are only a guise for the interests of particular groups and coalitions. (In the era of Watergate, it is tempting to call this a wise precaution, but in denying that the state may appeal to morality, group theorists also imply that it is not *subject* to it.)

In fact, group theory has a notion of the public interest—maintaining the formal and informal "rules of the game," keeping power ordered and balanced, expanding the power of the system as a whole. Denying the state the right to speak of this as the public interest, group theorists are permissive in allowing groups to speak of a "group interest." A major element in this distinction is moral: The "empirical" argument that we never see "the public," but only groups competing for power, could be applied with equal force to mass associations and corporations. The more fundamental difference, for group theorists, is that membership in "the state" is *exclusive*, while membership in groups is "overlapping." The Framers would have approved: Potentially, if not actually, a member of many, sometimes competing groups, the individual limits his loyalty to any of them; group leaders, subject to competition and aware of limited allegiance, are forced to restrict themselves to the unambiguous core of the group's "interests." Should they not do so, members will withdraw their support or look elsewhere.

There are many criticisms of this set of ideas. Limiting groups to parochial interests and restricting the government's role, group theory leaves widely shared values to take care of themselves; it has radical defects, moreover, as a description of American political life. It is more to the point, however, that group theory lacks pluralism's commitment to preserving or creating *communities*.

Interest groups with power enough to play the role assigned to them in group theory are almost always too large to be meaningful to the individual. In them, as Dewey had argued, the member is insignificant, unable to shape alternatives, governed by personally distant leaders, restricted to a reactive role. Pursuing narrowly-defined interests, such groups have no legitimate moral claim on the individual (though they often try to manufacture one), nor does group theory contend that they should; overlapping membership, to the extent that it exists, weakens commitment and collective devotion.

For Dewey, and an ancient tradition, interest groups are "secondary" associations, supported to the extent that they support individual interests but hardly trusted to *define* the individual's values, interests, or personal identity. That prior shaping of emotional life and moral personality belongs to the "primary group"—the family and the small community. Group theorists recognize the distinction and accept it, but like classical liberals, they deny that molding the personality is a matter for *political* concern. Forced to extend politics to *gesellschaft*, they hope that *gemeinschaft* may be preserved as a "private" sphere. But group theorists draw the distinction between primary and secondary groups only to obscure it, using "group" as a near-universal. That blurring is understandable, since group theorists, intelligent men of the times, know or suspect that primary groups, the core of the private order, are themselves in disarray.

The Big Change, Frederick Lewis Allen called the years between the Crash and contemporary America, and so it has been—though much of what has happened only amplified what was going on before. Pluralism won its ambiguous dominance in political thought at a time when, in the polity, cultural pluralism went into accelerated decline.

Economic concentration and centralization continue to weaken localities, compelling individuals to seek protection in alliance or affiliation with national organizations or from the federal government. The mass anonymity of the cities encourages privatization, weakening social control as it increases temptation. Neighborhoods hold out, but the urban villages are permeable, defined by "the street" which leads through them, open to strangers and more and more dependent on a web of services which neighbors cannot provide and which "aliens" can interrupt.

The automobile has made mass migration easy; even within regions it has led to suburban expansion and to that weakening of social control manifested, over the years, by road houses, incurious motels, and easy riders. Moving has become an accepted aspect of life, supported by tax deductions and justified by many rationalizations. Bell Telephone reminds us that we can at least call our families and old friends; another advertiser urges that wiping a child's tears with super-soft tissue lessens the pain of leaving home. Strong ties to place and people are more than unnecessary; they are economically limiting, even socially dysfunctional. Even those communities which survive sense a loss of "naturalness" and a new insecurity, for their hold is increasingly only moral and emotional, and even those bonds are endangered.

Not so long ago, the mass media required literacy and gained access to us only after schooling. Our formative years were exclusively the concern of family and community. Obviously, as the media have claimed more of our senses, that province is invaded earlier and with more powerful effect. Radio left us visual autonomy and movies were a social activity; television has no such limits and has become a major factor in child-rearing. The media do treat ethnic and local culture, but they do so based on the decision by *central* authorities that such portrayals meet at least the minimum standards of *mass* appeal.

These days, in fact, many Americans learn their "own" ethnic culture through the media. Certainly, the media have diffused the social symbols of sharing and communality so far that they have lost meaning and significance. Cuisine, dress, and argot are purveyed to millions, losing depth, exclusivity, and cultural context ("You don't have to be Jewish . . . ") and becoming no more than "image." The media keep up with changes, too, with often astonishing speed; there is little time to build up new mores and vocabularies before they are shared with a mass audience. "Ways" of life yield to "styles," things of surface and fashion, and in the attempt to fend off intruders, the language and symbols of personal meaning become incoherent, even inarticulate. (In the same process, we become less willing to be moved by public speech, which is reduced to bare factuality and routinized sloganeering.) "Publicity" is conquering the private order; the *social* privacy of pluralism has been violated, even interpersonal intimacy is hard pressed, and more and more Americans flee into the deepest dungeons of Tocqueville's prison of the self.

Politically, it is obvious that local institutions have been dwarfed by centralization and bureaucracy. This is not only in response to economic and social change: Distinctly political elements are involved, war and permanent international crisis being preeminent. Their technology has reduced even national boundaries to legalisms; psychologically, they have helped fix attention on the present to the exclusion of past and future; socially, they have moved millions around the country and overseas and compelled and allowed women to lead more autonomous lives and to take up once tabooed jobs. And so on. Even the kindest face of war, the military necessity that encouraged a muting of ethnic prejudice, helped weaken the negative bases of ethnic solidarity—space, time, social relations. War and cold war have shaken the foundations of all social groups, leaving them as uneasy as the peace.

I do not mean to adopt the thesis that the "melting pot" has finally reduced us to a uniform metal. Pluralism persists in America, and not only in our innumerable formal associations and shifting social circles. Regional and local patterns, though weakened, still survive. If more sectarian restrictions have lapsed, Protestants, Catholics, and Jews are each largely endogamous; national distinctions matter less than they once did, but powerful norms still command marriage to "our kind"; racial intermarriage remains rare. Every city has its ghettos, its neighborhoods described as "Italian" or "Appalachian"; and patterns of urban and suburban residence encourage highly specialized, though superficial, communities of class and style. Race, region, and nationality say a good deal about the schools Americans are likely to attend, the jobs they will hold, and the associations they will form.

A good part of this, however, is simply structural and external, not a matter of deeply-felt identity and culture, and far too much is due to segregation and deprivation. Though less severely than blacks, "ethnic whites" suffer from serious economic disadvantage and social prejudice. (In academic circles, so often self-congratulatory, anti-Catholicism is ubiquitous and as blithely unconscious as sexism and racism once were.) The "communities" so created may be valued by their members, but they are inevitably resented to some degree as "marks of oppression" and exclusion, and loyalty to the group sits in a delicate balance with the desire to escape from it.

This dilemma is old and familiar in America, as is the attempt to resolve the problem by militant patriotism, a persuasion which permits attacks on the enemies of one's community—"disloyal" elites and disadvantaged groups which threaten the status and self-esteem of one's own—without being *confined* to it. Father Coughlin and Joe McCarthy had thousands of Protestants and townspeople among their followers, just as George Wallace numbers his Catholic and urban admirers. Allowing the individual to defend his community, xenophobia does not insist that he identify with it, and permits him to define himself as "white" rather than "hillbilly" or "anti-Communist" rather than Catholic, and is assimilative in intention if not in fact. In recent decades, however, the tone of super-patriotism has changed. Plunkitt praised America and Irishry quite as much as he denounced their foes; in our times, celebration has waned while denunciation has waxed. It is a lonelier time, and the positive bonds to country and community are weaker—for all Americans, not merely a racial or ethnic few.

The recent internal violence in America, however, has a hopeful side. In their own struggle for racial equality, pride, and power, blacks have helped others to see and express the ethnic and social dimension of their discontents. Experiencing exclusion and the pressure for self-hatred in extreme forms, blacks have also been acutely sensitive to the political nature of humankind. Racism made assimilation all but impossible and individualism nearly as futile; in religion, blacks preserved a knowledge of human dependence and the need for brotherhood which made community a passionate aspiration, whatever the possibilities in fact. And by demanding a dignified community for themselves, it is undeniable that blacks have sparked similar demands by others—ethnic groups and "new" groups like women, students, and the old.

The fear and resentment of blacks often expressed by ethnic movements is nothing new. Racism, after all, is implicit in the notion that "whatever blacks can do legitimately is certainly appropriate for us," which is evident at the origin of all such emulatory movements. What is new is the demand for community, the articulate awareness of the individual's need for and dependence on group security, warmth, and cultural pride. Recent movements have, in fact, changed the language of resentment: Anger is increasingly expressed on *behalf* of a community rather than simply *against* another, and potentially that tendency is a resource for a new pluralism and a more genuine unity alike.

The new movements, however, have not formed new institutions to develop, preserve, or carry forward a way of life. They have spoken, for the most part, in sporadic mass protest or small "consciousness-raising" groups, and at best have only checked the process of cultural and social decay. At worst, they have accentuated it. The "liberal tradition" encourages Americans to see every problem as due to a lack of "individual freedom," and reinforced by the media (the mass audience finds individualistic ideas familiar and their bizarre expressions pruriently fascinating), the theme of "liberation" becomes a diversion from the more difficult problem of reconstruction and a facile rationalization for loneliness, social impotence, and demoralization.

There is evident and deeply-felt opposition to the individualism and materialism of the "secular city" and American industrial culture. The values and feelings which inspire that opposition, however, although rooted in religious and ethnic tradition, are increasingly perceived as internal, individual convictions without a social or cultural context. Conflicts of culture and value which once took place *between* social groups and communities are more and more felt and fought *within* the self. In the psyche, traditional values speak as the lonely voice of "conscience," without the support of a secure, social world; modern culture, in addition to material rewards, offers at least the weak warmth of mass society. Traditional culture easily erodes into romances and regrets; protest, when it occurs, is likely to be brittle and bitter, reflecting an internal struggle against the temptations of material and social comfort. Tradition seems part of a trap laid by society; the exotic—Satanism, Maoism, Eastern religion, and a whole garden of political and religious *fleurs de mal*—appeals because it protects one's estrangement.

It does not weaken the point that discussions of "ethnic identity" are everywhere these days. Often perceptive and moving—Daniel Bell's essay on Jews comes to mind—such treatments urge that community identity, which once grew naturally out of social and cultural life, be reaffirmed as a matter of conscious *decision.* Feelings and habits, even where they persist, are too feeble; intellect must make good the deficit. Seeking to rekindle awareness of the ethnic dimension of "personal" values, such writings are revivalistic in the best sense of the word, engaged in only because an old culture is being lost or forgotten or preserved in fragments which lose their meaning when isolated from the whole.

Calling ethnic culture "unmeltable," as Michael Novak does, expresses a hope, not a fact. Ethnic and community revivalism may succeed, for ideas and eloquence are not without power, but words alone are underdogs, unlikely to prevail without support in the institutions of economic, social, and political life.

Watergate, impeachment, an appointed executive and all the attendant shocks and revelations are only symptoms of a deeper crisis in the republic. Luck favored the Constitution: It is doubtful if the "self-corrective" mechanisms of the system would have prevailed against less maladroit opponents. The more important lesson of the episode is that American political life is losing its moral foundation.

Our "moral center" survived, over the years, not because of the theory of the Framers but in spite of it. Federalists and Jeffersonians agreed that human beings were "naturally"—by which they meant originally—free, and that this individual liberty should be the regulating moral norm of political and social life. Jefferson valued local community, but even he thought it no task of government to create or even to preserve church, community, or any of the great institutions of "society." At best, the early leaders of the republic took it for granted that "voluntary" decisions would preserve the structure of the private order. And when anxious successors thought of reconstructing society, most were guided by the moral premises of the "liberal tradition."

This is to say that the formal institutions of the republic have been premised on a fallacy. Whatever the potential of our nature, we are not born free. Human beings need nurturance, security, friendship, and civic education. Where the emotional and social bases are neglected, reason is sophistry at best and freedom is little more than a synonym for bleak loneliness. Rousseau understood this: Human beings fear pain, limitation, and death, and often must be "forced to be free" by love, loyalty, and law.

Public virtue germinates in "private" life. Authority concerns parents and teachers as well as presidents and kings; justice, before it is sought in courts and law books, is taught or mistaught in homes, workplaces, and playing fields. The art of politics is learned in the practice of daily life; private and public orders are parts of an inseparable whole.

For most of our history, the private order sustained us, transfused by immigrants from abroad and migrants from "shadow-America" at home. With all its plurality—which protected us against the worst features of a "closed society"—society agreed on a core of traditional beliefs and virtues: family; loyalty to and sacrifice for one's own; a knowledge that human beings are limited, parts of the order of nature, yet hallowed with all their limitations by God Who made them. Defeated time and again by an army of enemies, those ideas—and the communities which upheld them—restrained and guided Americans. Our established political wisdom and institutions, however, when it did not ridicule or assail such faiths and communities, set out to dissolve them.

All of us feel the change. The old order has retreated to a few enclaves. The conjugal family, the last bastion for most, is itself under attack and, in any case, is too weak to provide more than a drifting retreat from the overpowering mass and bewildering change of society as a whole. Irresponsible because they sense their own social insignificance and lack of responsibility, more and more Americans engage in pilferings more or less petty; white collar crime and industrial sabotage are part of the expected order of things. The Watergate conspirators were simply cut to the pathetic, evolving pattern: isolated and weak for much of their lives, resentfully cherishing dreams of omnipotence, anxious even in moments of security and fearful of confrontation, schooled to a preference for concealment, and hopeful of reducing all problems to questions of technique. The "order" which so many Americans insist we uphold is at best a thing of surfaces; even the calm years in the recent past were only the eye of the storm.

And yet, there are great political resources in the movements which have grown up in our times. Protest among racial minorities, white ethnic groups, and the "new" ethnicities like women, students, and homosexuals is likely, if left to itself, to be incoherent and bitterly divisive, with each group limited by weakness to parochial concerns, exaggerated rhetoric, and self-defense, neglecting the needs of America as a whole. But for all their staggering diversity, such movements have common and creative themes.

There is a passionate concern for community, a search for meaningful social groups free from the insecurity of the dyad, expressed not only in the rather romantic "communes" but also in a desire for stable neighborhoods and "community control." This interest in the communal organization of political space has its reflection in the ecologist's concern for the land—which might be profitably expanded to include agriculture and rural America as well as the wilderness—and the neighborhood renewer's devotion to landmarks. The fact that the movements have undertaken to write "their own" history—however bizarre the results—suggests an attempt by Americans who have learned to distrust the "idea of progress" to rediscover a political time which has continuity and tradition, a past as well as a present and future. The vogue of oral history is only one additional example.

The effort to rediscover a collective space and time is paralleled by the longing for *substantive* moral values—not merely procedural norms defined as "functional" in terms of a "system." Part of the mass appeal of Puzo's *Godfather* lies in the introductory dialogue which poses Don Carleone's substantive justice against the procedural rules and spotty results of the courts of law. Of course, that is a dangerous teaching, especially since few Americans have been trained to deal with morality in serious ways. That students ended by equating substantive morality with slogans and self-interest is less surprising— since that is becoming a national pattern—than that they tried to do otherwise. But the yearning for authority which can be respected and for justice which is real speaks with the voice of human need. If we do not fulfill that need well, we can be prepared for worse.

Finally, the movements have repeatedly affirmed the ancient wisdom that we are *political* animals who need to participate in deliberation, in shaping the alternatives which limit our choices, in ruling and being ruled. Our political and representative institutions have evolved in ways unsuited to that civic ideal; the demand for reformed campaign laws is only a beginning. And we would be wise to heed the classical teaching that the education of political life and experience can help in developing values beyond politics.

Even to address such demands and possibilities requires a major rethinking of the bases of American political, economic, and social life. To attempt to realize them would demand a supreme statecraft, able to weave a fabric from many-colored yarn. In this newly articulated concern for community, tradition, value, and civility, however, there is at least a grain of hope for the restoration of the tension between unity and plurality, public and private orders, which was the historic strength of American politics. It would be dangerous to wait for more; this may be the last muster of the armies of the republic.

XIV

Beyond the Dream of Success: Notes on "The American Character" Today

Benjamin DeMott

It used to be thought that people led lives—whether of quiet desperation, quiet satisfaction, or of whatever description. It is now taken more and more for granted that people experiment with "life styles," putting one on and off as suits the mood and the moment. But what kind of life is a life style?

It is to this question that Benjamin DeMott addresses himself—and especially to the implications of this question for American society as a whole. This has always been, after all, and to a fair degree still is a "bourgeois" society—i.e., a society with certain fixed notions as to how a "decent" life should be lived, and with certain fixed assumptions as to what represented success or failure in life. At the same time, however, this has always been a rather "open" society, receptive to innovation and experimentation, and, in principle, at least, willing to recognize that "the pursuit of happiness" can take many legitimate forms. In the 1970s, these two traditions confront one another in the actuality of intergenerational conflict, hostility, and suspicion. Our ability to cope with the cultural tensions we are all now experiencing will to a large degree shape the future destiny of this nation.

I'd like to run a combination bookstore and tavern. (Laughs.) I would like to have a place where college kids came and a steelworker could sit down and talk. Where a workingman could not be ashamed of Walt Whitman and where a college professor could not be ashamed that he painted his house over the weekend.

—Studs Terkel, *Working* ("Steelworker")

321

In the widest sense of the term, culture change is a permanent factor of human civilization; it goes on everywhere and at all times.

—Bronislaw Malinowski

For longer than a century, as every schoolboy knows, the charged wire between American character and American culture has been the dream of success. The timbre of one's voice, the content of one's feeling, the very quality of one's inner reconciliation to the conditions of human life—all could be understood in light of one's self-casting as winner, loser, average Joe. Out there, a culture of opportunity; in here, a creature who either has or hasn't seized the lucky chance.

Claims that a major modification of this sensibility is at hand rouse skepticism among many. Polls of middle-class undergraduate attitudes, together with samplings of other opinion, confirm that success measured in earnings survives as a primal value; further confirmation comes with scrutiny of one's own middle-aged response to strangers. (Has he made it? Does he *believe* he's made it? Death alone seems likely to quiet these thoughts.) But while the old hot line between character and culture, the dream of success, remains hot, the wire has begun carrying some static. In some minority cultures, separatists scorn "Whitey's Rainbow" as a vision alien (and alienating) to "The Community." In the majority culture itself, a new breed of "life-experimentalist" lures folk away from the pastures of ambition, piping seductive, vaguely related, occasionally interactive tunes—mid-life career change, self-transformation sex-role variousness, lateral or downward mobility, anti-enclaveism, sequential polygamy, Plimptonism. And while dissent from success-religion varies, periodically, in intensity, the power of its signals is, arguably, increasing.

One reason for this is that some of the dissenting behaviors have proved exceptionally easy to fit out with a moral decor. From the beginning, success hunters enjoyed the Protestant blessing—the invaluable privilege, that is, of not being obliged to fret about virtue. Jeb Stuart Magruder's recent memoir, *An American Life*, is acute about the dangerously false moral security engendered by ambition. But they are no longer alone in this exemption. Ghetto blacks who repudiate upward mobility as a value are taught that this repudiation betokens moral superiority. Post-women's-liberation mates who repudiate "careerist monomania" in favor of full self-expression for each party understand themselves to be engaged in moral self-improvement. The same holds even for educated dropouts and their sympathizers. When a few years ago, a portion of the country's most favored youth played dropout roles, rejecting the fellowships and internships that precede top jobs, preferring service as cabdrivers, letter carriers, or barmen (the downward mobility theme), it was quickly proposed, and by many accepted, that such behavior possessed hopeful ethical substance. The dropouts were perceived as renunciators, purifying themselves by refusing to compete for the honors of a System discovered by them to be corrupt. More recently, as certain persons of prominence have undertaken fresh experiments in breakout—college presidents dropping down for a stint as garbagemen or busboys—the revisionist moral calculus has been further refined. Privileged people, it is proposed, lose touch not only with the common life but with the inner contours of guilt; attempting to reestablish links with "real life" is therefore a deed of conscience.

Theories of self-transformation and critiques of success dogmas aren't, to be sure, always reverently treated. The moral pretensions of black separatism have been effectively criticized by, among other black writers, Professor Martin Kilson of Harvard. Comparable extravagances in the women's movement have been mocked by Midge Decter. Popular culture has not hesitated to tease assorted life-experimentalists, or to celebrate them simply as *Playboy*-style happy hedonists rather than as new saints. A 1964 movie called *Seconds* savaged some characters who confused thoroughgoing self-transformation with whoring after lost youth; a current book called *The Life Swap*, a report on Greenwich Village types who, arranging logistics through classified ads, actually exchange lives, is zealously amoral. In the world of responsible affairs, moreover, discussions of mechanisms of schooling designed to foster "life flexibility" usually are conducted in non-evangelical tones. A recent Danforth Foundation paper announcing the institution's embrace of a new wisdom concerning life-long educational and career intermittency, and offering "positive" redefinitions of "dropping out," related the commitment to rates of technological change rather than to ethical or spiritual aspirations.

And in any event it surely would be mistaken to imply that the static in the success system has no other sources than our gift for moralizing new appetites. The phenomenon of technological obsolescence among highly trained professionals, the advance of automation, high unemployment rates, intuitions that the pace of change is now beyond anyone's power to master through personal "drive"—all these trouble faith in The Rise. So too does the emergence of a cause, Species Survival, that is plainly inimical to the cause of unchecked individual ambition. When right-minded columnists or TV documentaries chastise 210 million Americans for wasting the world's resources, for eating as much annually as would suffice to feed 1.5 billion Third Worlders, the reverberations of the challenge to the "bitch-Goddess" (William James's name for the success deity) resound at their loudest and clearest.

For present purposes, though, a precise etiology of the challenge is not essential; it matters only that the field of forces in which orthodox success region maintains itself is increasingly intricate and in certain respects under-examined. Efforts at understanding change in the success culture have suffered from numerous defects—beamishness, narrowness of perspective (the change in question is understood to affect only the children of the liberal elites), absence of critical concern for long-term psychocultural consequences. Where in the American mainstream, as distinguished from the Berkeley-Aspen-Madison-

Harvard Square-West 8th Street axis, are signs now found of gropings toward a new Good Life? Who in authority responds to these signs and how? What ideas, if any, figure in the equation? What ideas ought to figure? Hanging back from such questions preserves dignity, but leaves the present unmapped and possibilities for the future unexplored.

Predictably, all contemporary schools of anti-success have been affected by the traditional complaints stressing the success-hunter's selfish, calculating nature, and his inability to experience other human beings except as means to his end, objects to be manipulated. But separatists and life-experimenters alike have added unique thrusts to this critique. The separatist mentality (its history antedates Marcus Garvey by a century) posits a recoverable ethnic or racial *Ur*-identity and power stolen by the cruelly emasculating American majority. The stress falls sometimes—as with "native Americans"—on tribal values corrupted on this ground, sometimes on a vision of a remote culture of origin such as Jordan, the Muslim world or the lost cities of Africa.

Great minds or master texts unfamiliar to the majority culture figure in the effort to define qualities desiderated for recovery—the name of Ibn Khaldum, the rites of the Oglala Sioux. The central moral themes—tribal or racial solidarity, self-control, and self-purification—echo and re-echo in speech and in writing, not always as passionately as in *The Autobiography of Malcolm X*, rarely as coolly as in James Baldwin's *The Fire Next Time*. Emerging racial and ethnic pride toughens the will to look upon "integration" and "ascent" as opiates. Stokely Carmichael puts the point plainly:

According to the advocates of integration, social justice will be accomplished by "integrating the Negro into the mainstream institutions of the society from which he has been traditionally excluded." . . . This concept of integration had to be based on the assumption that there was nothing of value in the Negro community and that little of value could be created among Negroes, so the thing to do was to siphon off the "acceptable" Negroes into the surrounding middle-class white community. Thus the goal of the movement for integration was simply to loosen up the restrictions barring the entry of Negroes into the white community. Goals around which the struggle took place, such as public accommodation, open housing, job opportunity on the executive level . . . are quite simply middle-class goals, articulated by a tiny group of Negroes who had middleclass aspirations . . . Now, black people must look beyond these goals . . .

The life-experimentalist intellectual, for his part, occasionally invokes celebrated European thinkers—Marx on the nonalienated man, pleased to hunt in the morning and to perform as music critic at night; Hegel on the tendency of the social classes to go dead to the human particularity underlying such labels as *worker*; and certain critical theorists of the Frankfurt School (Marcuse, Habermas). But the chief absorption is with the concepts of *experience* and *ways of experiencing*—which is to say, there's a distinctly American cast to this mode of thought. It is well represented by that most American of philosophers, John Dewey, in *Democracy and Education* (1913):

A democracy is more than a form of government, it is a mode of associated living, of conjoint communicated experience. The extension in space of the number of individuals who participate in an interest so that each has to refer his own action to that of others, and to consider the action of others to give point and direction to his own, is equivalent to the breaking down of those barriers of class, race, and national territory [we should now add the barriers of sex] which kept men from perceiving the full import of their activity.

The overt argument holds that if the classes and races communicate with one another, work to make themselves privy to one another's motives and interests, ordinary life in every level and sector will achieve a more democratic tone. If, on the other hand, we fail to raise questions to ourselves about the manner in which the action and interest of—for example—the excluded minorities give point and direction to the action and interest of the elites, or vice versa, we shall never achieve clarity about the ultimate significance of our own work and, worse, we shall cut ourselves and others off from access to the democratic way of experiencing.

It is the way, the process of experiencing, that Dewey—like many present-day life-experimenters in and out of the elites—regards as all important. Democracy in its letter is a matter of laws governing the franchise. But in its spirit it is a mode of experiencing life, a multiplicity of languages, a continuous imaginative mobility; the good democrat, whatever his station, is someone whose experience is new, whose path diverges from habitual ways fenced and tended by enclave, class, profession, congregation or sex. Dewey's belief in the sanctity of experience and experiential variegation has a past; it turns up everywhere in American thought from Winthrop and Edwards to Emerson, Whitman, and William James. Professor John McDermott has remarked that, "For the most part, that tradition of American *thought* which we now regard as seminal and even patriarchal, clearly sides with experience over reflection as the primary resource in formulating beliefs."

The implicit related theme in Dewey's writing—that the "lower levels" have much to teach the "upper"—is also a life-experimentalist commonplace. On this subject Dewey is but one of several dozen relevant voices. In *America's Coming of Age* (1912) Van Wyck Brooks insisted that the best hope for the creation of a worthy middle life in this country lay in bringing together, in effective adjacency, the "highbrow" and "lowbrow"—in terms Brooks invented—hothouse bureaucrat-diplomat-litterateur and roughhewn man-of-business. Brooks argued that neither the top nor the bottom can afford ignorance of what the other knows:

Twenty, even ten years, ago, it would have been universally assumed that the only hope for American society lay in somehow lifting the "Lowbrow" elements in it to the level of the "Highbrow" elements. But that quickening realism which belongs to contemporary thought makes it plain on the one hand that the mere idealism of university ethics, the mere loftiness of what is called culture, the mere purity of so-called Good Government, left to themselves, not only produce a glassy inflexible priggishness on the upper levels which paralyzes life; but that the lower levels have a certain humanity, flexibility, tangibility which are indispensable in any programme: that Tammany has quite as much to teach Good Government as Good Government has to teach Tammany, that slang has quite as much in store for so-called culture as culture has for slang—that the universities, while emphatically not becoming more "practical," must base their disinterestedness on human, moral, social, artistic, and personal needs, impulses, and experience.

Countless other observers, from Randolph Bourne to Richard Sennett, have underlined this theme. Bourne, who went so far as to announce himself terrified of "a shrinkage of ... environment, a running dry of experience," believed profoundly in the worth of access to the mind of the down and out. The right style of mind, he declared in *Youth and Life* (1913), is that which "tests ideals ... by their general interchangeability among all sorts of people and the world. ..." The wrong style is that which fails to move its beliefs and ideas out of class and other sequestration:

The little tabooed regions of well-bred people, the "things we never mention," the basic biases and assumptions that underlie the lives and thinking of every class and profession, our second-hand dogmas and phrases—all these live and thrive because they have never been transplanted, or heard from the lips of another. The dictum that "the only requisites for success are honesty and merit," which we applaud so frantically from the lips of the successful, becomes a ghastly irony in the mouth of an unemployed workingman. There would be a frightful morality of points of view, could we have a perfectly free exchange such as this. ... Many of our cherished ideals would lose half their validity were they put bodily into the mouths of the less fortunate.

Subtler versions of the idea of imaginative and experiential mobility as a mode of salvation are found in the writings of the sociologist Charles Horton Cooley, a proponent of the notion that the true end of democratic man lies in the perfection of an aptitude for "imagining the imaginations" of those whose condition in life isn't one's own. Gloomier views about the likelihood of anyone's achieving this kind of mobility have appeared in several more recent American social thinkers—Riesman, Keniston, Friedenberg. And, as will appear, justification for their doubts can be found in the short histories of various contemporary projects for developing cross-cultural and cross-class communication.

But the gloom of a few sixties' intellectuals has had small effect on the rhetoric *or* the behavior of the new mobilitarians. One or another of the latter band regularly steps forth, at political gatherings, planning board meetings, conferences, to remind the group that "our mission is not only to teach from above but to learn from below"—often to strong murmurs of assent. The endorsements of this piety in American letters over the last half-century are remarkable in their range—from James Agee's discovery of a great tragic poem on the interior bedroom wall of a sharecropper's cabin to Norman Mailer's homage to the "faith of graffiti." And youth-cult heroes seem increasingly inventive in producing "evidence" that the wit at the bottom can compete, however perversely and self-destructively, with the wit at the top—witness this tribute to the drug culture by Kurt Vonnegut:

The drug thing . . . shows that, damn it, people are wonderfully resourceful. . . . Thousands of people in our society found out they were too stupid or too unattractive or too ignorant to rise. They realized they couldn't get a nice car or a nice house or a good job. Not everybody can do that, you know. . . . And they realized that if you lose, if you don't rise in our society, you're going to live in the midst of great ugliness. . . . So what can you do? You can change your *mind*. You can change your insides. The drug thing was a perfectly marvelous, resourceful, brave experiment. . . .

It is without interest—or irony—that rationalizations of dissent to success-religion rest on opposed views of the bitch-Goddess, the separatist often reviling her for sanctifying a self-indulgently greedy racism, the experimentalist reviling her for sanctifying puritanical self-denial. When scrutinized in light of the pertinent backgrounds and sources—huge deprivation on one side, a nearly maddening sense of possibility on the other—these divergencies don't mystify. But the presence of contradictory rationales does not obscure the ultimate harmonies of interest—the shared fascination, that is, with differences and alternatives, the concern for "quality of relationship," and the taste for perspectives beyond the proferred or denied middle-class slot.

To state that mainstream America has for some time been permeable to these tastes and concerns is not to claim that life-experiment is the talk of every rowhouse stoop. It is only to say that behavior related to those tastes has long been discernible. In the business and manufacturing mainstream, hostility to "slot culture" surfaces as absenteeism, employee turnover rate, declines in management prestige and authority. Among minorities it surfaces as the higher intransigence—forms of "mau-mauing" and other militancy erupting in cross-cultural negotiations initiated "for their own benefit," and giving rise to doubt that "they" are negotiating in good faith and actually desire the "better chance" that's being offered. In civic life the hostility surfaces as a demand for "rights of participation"—programs permitting ordinary citizens to move from the periphery to the center in shaping local goals, and to perceive life, for intervals, from points of view different from that of "the ruled."

In responding to these behaviors authority has not followed a single line or strategy; even uniformities of tone are lacking. Naturally, management seldom regards, say, absenteeism as a cause or ideal; it is usually addressed as a problem, an item susceptible to encapsulated problem-solving approaches. The latter perspective cannot always be sustained, to be sure. A life-insurance group executive speaking at an Insurance Institute session last spring at Princeton brought the classic difficulty freshly into view, in the course of reporting on a counter-offensive against worker alienation. In the old days, he recalled, "before the psychologists," and before a recent revamping of processing areas:

Susie or whoever never got to follow through on a claim, but now it's a different ball of wax. Susie takes a couple of dozen a month straight through from the top, cradle to grave, opens the agency envelope, checks the coverage, the premium status, calls the S/A if she has to . . . starts the checks. It's beautiful and Susie was happy for six weeks. Until the next problem came along. There was this new problem that most of the claims are sort of boring—I mean, when you follow them through only a few really amount to much. So why can't she just work fulltime on the interesting ones?—Gentlemen, Susie has bit of the apple and she's full of desires she never knew, and I welcome your thoughts.

The bemusement was real; momentarily the System had run out of magic. Yet the manager's tone made evident, subsequently, that he hadn't by any means jettisoned the problem-solution approach. Here and there groups join together convinced that the "problem" is rather more than a problem, and that coping with the new appetites may require, at the minimum, reorganization of relationships among businesses, cultural agencies, schools, and professional organizations on a community-wide basis, "without limit of time." (The so-called "Greater Hartford Process," in Hartford, Connecticut, is an attempt at such a reorganization.) But the more common assumption is that revisions on the line can "lick the thing" and one result is that concepts of the nature of "the thing" remain reductive.

A second response to the surfacing on nonintellectual turf of anti-work-ethic behavior places the behavior as a feature of the "decline of culture." Not long ago a major telephone company arranged a career conference for executives, teachers, and university seniors during which the moment of near-excitement for the students occurred when several phone company people happened in to chat about the nonmanagement jobs they had performed during the '69 strike. The undergraduates would not let the subject go, and the managers humored them, running on about the joy of the interruption—"everybody getting out from behind the desk after all those years . . . in the soup together . . . going down and handling calls, learning the operator's jobs . . . bumping elbows . . . a $65,000 line v.p. counting beeps with headsets, doing a $7800 job." Protracting the talk, pressing questions, seeming to take the facetious joy and nostalgia straight, the undergraduates had finally to be shaken off the subject—and became eligible, as a result of the interlude, for treatment as symptoms of cultural decline. Several executives opined that the seniors' attitude reflected "basic frivolity," dislike of responsibility, "reverse snobbism," and total absence of feeling for the "service obligation." They dismissed out of hand the notion that the students' enthusiasm for an unplanned field experience might also reveal fear that management roles enforce experiential restriction (office, secretary, executive washroom) and immersion in the habitual—in experience whose meaning never needs to be invented, in life bare of the kind of learning that, in Peirce's phrase, "takes place by surprise."

A third response to the "aberrant" behaviors is flat denial: Alternative desires to upward mobility *cannot* exist; minorities and the disadvantaged, whatever their antics and provocativeness, have nowhere to turn for models, realistically speaking, except to the white middle class. It is scarcely astonishing that the majority culture's obsession with upward mobility dominates negotiators in current interracial conflicts—busing and housing in particular. "Equal opportunity" is the announced foundation of court decisions holding that federal housing subsidies to cities must be cut off unless substantial portions are used to bring low-income minorities into white enclaves. And hence it is natural for observers and participants in the ensuing battles to return ceaselessly to the issue of whether or not scatter-site housing or an integrated classroom can actually grade up a black's chances of ascent.

"What is the greater good," a mayoral negotiator writes in his diary, following a day of exhausting inquiry into the possibility of detente at Forest Hills, "the breaking up of the ghettos at the risk of deteriorating middle income areas or the insulation of the middle income areas at the risk of exacerbating the cycle of poverty?" He goes on as follows:

Should the moral obligation require the Forest Hills people to embrace their low-income brethren even at the risk of deterioration? Yes, if it can be said that the project is good for its potential tenants, and so the question becomes: Is it good? And the answer is "yes" if the Forest Hills residents can supply for their brethren an "upward mobility." Then the question becomes: Will the proximity supply this kind of example and inspiration? And to this, there is no clear answer. . . . The Forest Hills area would undoubtedly be particularly vulnerable to the kind of crime that would be generated by large numbers of low-income people. The pre-determined "example" may be the example that they provide for one another, instead of the example that the external community provides for each of them.[1]

Meanwhile, in the ghetto itself, black leaders in storefront academies and poolhalls, following the example of Charles Hurst, Baraka, and others, are teaching the young that hatred of white values like upward mobility is the beginning of integrity; Muslims carefully distinguish their "code of respectability" from that of the white bourgeois; ambivalence and/or apathy toward liberal white "solutions" to social problems is unquestionably increasing. Yet many capable negotiators in the field persist in obliviousness to the possibility that blacks are defining other aspirations for themselves besides that of tapping into white careerism.

Still another response—characteristic of educational and cultural bureaucracies—can properly be described as sensitive but timid. Aware of the desire for "participation," and for more cross-cultural communication and for the forging of links between noncommunicating sectors, program directors work up proposals enabling groups to step forth from their compounds—but then fail to provide either suggestions about purpose, designs for exchanges, or ideas about new subject matter bases that might inspire pointed talk. A federal agency creates fellowships to bring community college teachers to university campuses for a summer or longer, to enable them to work with established scholars, providing the latter with an interruption from their own careerism and with access to a world beyond the immediate enclave, while enabling the former to seek fresh counsel on problems of "remediation" and "introduction." But after two summers the selection processes wash out to blandness. The research professors hunt through piles of applications for people resembling themselves, youngsters who are at "bad" places only accidentally—i.e., because of the job squeeze—and who are perfectly capable in another market of becoming graduate professors themselves. The original goal, to create adjacencies and supportive relationships between significantly different academic perspectives, recedes from view; the opportunity for "conjoint communicated experience" is not seized.

Or again: Responding to the "participatorial ethos," the Office of Education invents a school program designed to shape working relationships in selected urban communities among groups of teacher-trainers in education schools, graduate research faculty, line high school teachers, and parents from the minority community. Congress appropriates several hundred million dollars, sites and people are chosen, programs are launched with much talk of "Relevance"— but thereafter waste and gloom. Access to alternative life roles is one goal of the enterprise, as is the development of a body of experience at referring differing interests and actions to one another. But these "quality-of-experience" goals lack articulation—and the mystique of "grading-up" succeeds in suppressing them. Graduate research faculty use the monies received to fund new fellowships for orthodox graduate study. Recipients of these fellowships obliged to "do something" for the local schools, but lacking guidelines about how to function in the new setting, offer seminars in advanced research fields, like those in which they themselves are enrolled, to black, ghetto-based, seventh-grade teachers. Befuddled teachers end by intimidating community parents. Bureaucrats fume, grants bleed away, the programs shut down after five years amidst feelings of frustration and failure.

Each of the foregoing responses to disaffection with stereotyped life-models of upward ascent, and to the growing appetite for variegated experience, is unique unto itself, bound into a separate set of assumptions and values. The phone company critics of undergraduate frivolity are not to be confused with the bureaucrats who, to their credit, think up a scheme calling for cooperative shaping of school curricula by professors of academic subjects, professors of education, high school teachers, teachers in training, and parents of the children to be taught. Yet when all this is said, it would be evasive not to acknowledge that, implicit in each response—implicit wherever and whenever so-called new values come under discussion—is a measure of conscious or unconscious doubt about the fundamental moral worth of the emergent desires.

The Good News of Life-Experimentalism, appetites for experience in a new key, alternatives to Working Your Way Up—these do not really cause rejoicing in the corridors of power. The links between highbrow and lowbrow behavior, between the greening at Yale and the greening at Lordstown, do not clamor for attention. It is altogether possible not to perceive the remotest tie between Susie's failure to show up on Monday and the decision by a novelist to cry up the spraycan artistry of some dropped-out Puerto Rican teenager. It is possible, in other words, to miss the extraordinarily interesting cultural drama—the amending of a national faith in salvation-through-ascent—that may now be in progress.

But it is not possible, seemingly, to calm the undefined sense of disquiet noticeable wherever authority undertakes to examine itself and its surroundings. Wariness, unease, the feelings that weird and unpredictable forces are at work—these are already pervasive enough to qualify as evidence in themselves that the cultural changes spoken of here are ultimately capable of redirecting the mainstream. What if it should happen? Is fear appropriate? On what terms can a sound moral assessment of the prospect begin to be framed?

Arriving even at a provisional assessment in the absence of a case is impossible; so too is finding a case sufficiently representative to be suggestive. The best that can be done is to sketch out a passage or two in a fictional experimentalist life-story, attending carefully to the entanglements, hoping to gain from the story an inkling of states of mind ahead, and the attendant possibilities and dangers.

Toward this end, consider some recent days in the life of William Robinson, associate professor of humanities at a well-regarded engineering college in the Midwest, an imaginary character who has been at odds in recent years with a number of his colleagues. The original differences had to do with (1) admissions policy and (2) a phase of curriculum called "experiential education." Robinson advocated more aggressive recruitment of minority students, and broader institutional commitments to off-campus, discipline-related work-study projects. A Harvard Ph.D. "Americanist" with solid though minor research achievement behind him, he has lately been teaching a course in the Humanities Department wherein "Students Go Forth Unto The World" (as the ironists describe the enterprise to themselves) with tape recorders, interview local working people on war, inflation, environmental changes, and such, and then return, transcribe this material—raw data?—and reshape it into finished papers. Robinson took his last leave of absence as a visiting professor at an impoverished Southern black college, leaving his family behind when they refused to go, and doing nothing to advance himself professionally in the period. On his return he began agitating, as indicated, for more concerted effort at recruiting minority students and securing scholarship funds; in addition, as faculty enemies saw it, he "curried favor" among the minority community, "befriended" black faculty members, provided rooms in his own home for transfer students from the black college at which he taught, attended reunions of black alumni, and otherwise puzzled his colleagues.

Many of the latter remembered that in the years before the civil rights movement and the fashion for field study, Robinson had espoused a fundamentally anti-intellectual cause. He and a second humanities professor were active in what was called "humanistic ed"—encounter groups, sensitivity training, etc. And the memory, together with Robinson's subsequent deeds, led to his being placed, by a faculty majority, as a sentimentalist and a self-deceiver, a person who flattered himself for moral probity and concern for the weak, even as he stimulated impossible-to-satisfy longings among those for whose happiness he purported to care. Was it not a fact—so went a faculty club question—that Bill Robinson believed teaching had less to do with communicating bodies of knowledge than with altering political power balances? Was he not a mere promoter, advocating precisely those institutional changes that were likely to render the best defender of probity and sensitivity—the academy—incapable of honoring either?

Robinson and his friends, for their part, were not much troubled by the adversary relationships developing between themselves and the majority. Enamored of the word "open," Robinson himself argued confidently that significant human learning cannot take place except where the unpredictable is admissable, and declared his membership in the school-reformist party whose slogan was that the single subject taught or learned in most schools is "school." Hostility to his meditative and T-group phases reflected, as he saw it, the ignorance of people who knew nothing about themselves and were terrified of learning. Hostility to his admissions proposals looked to him like "unconscious racism," and he believed he had evidence that some of his bitterest opponents, colleagues in economics and mathematics in particular, were themselves overtly racist in behavior. He had heard it reported that one economist-enemy, finding an unusual number of students in class at the first meeting of a course, remarked aloud that "this place looks like an Afro-Am class." And he took no little satisfaction when minority students forced a joint faculty-student-administration inquiry into "discrimination against blacks" by the math department.

Although Robinson regarded himself for no little while as a "reformer from within the system," a critical spirit refreshing himself with new experience, preparing for new battles, he conscientiously sought not to turn his "opposition" into monsters. Was it their "fault" that they were locked in cultural "slots" subservient to amoral professional codes and prejudices? Their notion of triumph was to achieve a national departmental reputation for the quality of their Ph.D.'s; a characteristic boast was that "even" their below average bachelor was farther along toward the completion of a doctorate in the field than were grads in other places at the end of a full year of graduate school. They were blind to the possibility that "opening up the system" would be of intellectual benefit to all, blind also to the moral claims of those sectors of the general society bidding for a fair share of the cultural riches formerly denied them, and improperly dismissive of students who spurned the riches because they were "turned off" by a pedagogy remote from the real world. But the causes of this benightedness were not to be sought, Robinson told himself, in personal failings. His colleagues were what they are, believed what they believed, because a thousand appurtenances and accidents to "The System" allowed them to live the life of the enclave.

Yet for all his effort at even-handedness, Robinson *felt* embattled, and his embattlement served his cause poorly. In the past the Tory Caucus—the "Hardnoses," as Robinson called them—had been composed of believers in "bootstrapism"; the reviled math department itself divided introductory courses into fast and slow groups, teachers doubling their teaching loads, voluntarily and without pay, to permit head-to-head tutorial sessions with less well-prepared students, many of whom were black. But as exacerbation increased about "compensatory" admissions policies, math tutorials for poorly prepared students became less common.

There were other troubling turns. Robinson was made aware that blacks at the college were suffering peculiar kinds of inner impactment, checking their own ambitions in order to dissociate themselves from whiteness, and simultaneously failing to turn out for calls for help from black tutorial projects in the nearest city—calls issued in the name of black solidarity.

Black college students . . . get so hung up about "soul loss" that they cannot study . . . [They] hide their ambivalence about low-income blacks by busying themselves with "black talk" on the predominantly white campus, while they make no effort to help the black children around the block who cannot read.[2]

Among the majority of the whites, furthermore, impatience mounted toward black students—resentment at separatist behavior in the dining hall and elsewhere and at ceaseless demands for "favored treatment." Even those white activist students who had anticipated genuine interaction gave up on that hope, dwindling into unproductive wistfulness and whimsy about the future of communication.

. . . [O]n every hand one comes up against puzzling difficulties in thoughts about the blacks. How enviable the accessibility of their emotions! What fun they have, how loud they laugh, how easily they weep! They really seem to love each other. Their phrase "brothers and sisters" is so meaningful that we (white youth) take it over, but we have a harder time *feeling* like members of an extended family, a tribe, a folk. And—wow—how they hate us!

Perhaps one way to find the family feeling is through rebellion. Brothers and sisters in the revolution. Perhaps even the blacks will extend their family of rebellion to include us. That may be one road to richness of feeling.[3]

And then at length came the turn that induced, for Robinson, genuine pain and loss: He himself was ordered out of the Afro-American house. The "minister of information" who passed the word to him, a senior, was "one of his own"—a transfer student recruited by Robinson when he was in the South. The lad had lived in Robinson's apartment as a sophomore, and Robinson had tutored him in Great Books. Robinson did not grasp what was being said to him at first. He had been in attendance at the meeting to report on local ABC finances and was sitting down after delivering the report, the only white in the room, when the blow fell: He was told to leave. Afterward he had a moment of severe disorientation. Self-pity, never entirely unreliable, informed him that, as of this moment of iron rejection, he who earlier had shed a career was about to lose what he had seen as his virtue *and* as his distinction *and* as his fun. Yet amidst the depression another voice spoke, telling him that he was richer no matter what happened, better off somehow "for the experience" than he would have been without it.

Nothing obscure here, obviously. A middle-class professor turns away from a conventional academic career to seek, in social terms, access from above to below—to an impoverished black society, and to the local non-college community. He seeks also to "import" this experience—perceiving it as a value—into the previously "pure" college world. Minority students, brought to campus as a gesture toward cultural pluralism, arrive in thrall to the dream of success but, once within the enclave, discover that many intellectual doors are not really open to them, protest, and gradually close in upon themselves. White students withdraw, in their own style, from interaction. Academicians, once eager to lend their energies to the upwardly mobile, but now troubled by faculty promoters of inferior preparation as a "Valuable Cultural Resource," forego their own good works, claiming that weak-willed enthusiasts of exotica are in the process of destroying standards. Suspicion, moral purpose, *noblesse oblige*, traditional American experientialism, intransigence, democratic faith, loyalty to excellence—all coil and uncoil in this scene in a manner peculiar to academies (though the pressures and counter-pressures have parallels in certain other work worlds).

To contemplate all this is to see beyond abstract competitions of ideology, symbol, and myth into new kinds of tension within persons—feelings traceable to ambivalence about values once unquestioned. It is also to discover anew the difficulty of moral assessment. "Self" erupted in Robinson: An honorable "professorial slot" struck him as not "good enough" (unique enough) just as mere alignment on a success track struck black and white students as not good enough for them. He sought an original relation to his experience; but in pursuing his goal he positioned himself—not wholly by intention and never entirely without satisfaction—as the best (most beleaguered) local friend of the poor, and in the process helped to polarize the interracial situation. Yet it would be wrong to focus only upon egotism: Concern for social equity, a longing to know other human beings for themselves, altruism—as shapers of this narrative, they were at least as potent as self.

What matters most, perhaps, is not finally the moral rating; it is the state of mind of the character at his exit point from the experience. That state of mind may be described as "historicistically reconciled." Robinson copes with his regrets and frustration by historicizing them. A particular "period," he tells himself, the sixties, created an opportunity toward which he moved; the cycle carried him for a space, offered him growth, variousness . . . at length cut him off. The period having "ended," Robinson sees no prospect either for alteration in his adversary relationships with the faculty majority, or for a step forward in efforts at communication with the blacks. In his own mind he has already begun sealing off "that time" from the present: He "learned a lot," he tells people, but now there is nothing for it except to move on. Did not T.S. Eliot himself remark that "a man capable of experience finds himself living in a new age every decade of his life?"

At one level Robinson's story confirms that good will and the desire to discharge the obligations of the strong to the weak are impotent without thought-through modes of interaction—steady awareness of the separate realities perceived by the newly communicant groups, patient probing of fields of interest in search of buried points of commonality; readiness to seize on marginal, even trivial possibilities for common endeavor as a means of enlarging areas of pointed talk, avoidance of the good-guy-bad-guy syndrome, avoidance of the notion that "conjoint communicated experience" is a problem to be solved once-and-for-all (whether by admissions policy, fellowships, field study or whatever) rather than a frame for the living through of an entire professional life, a project for a century. Yet the most interesting levels of meaning are more general, and have to do with the deepest psychocultural continuities.

Chief among those continuities is the human power to sustain intention, to postpone gratification. We have learned to speak with respect of the new tendencies in our social character, advising ourselves that it is a mark of cultural advance that the simplicities and manipulativeness of Horatio Algerism no longer stand unchallenged; that among the more privileged a desire for experiential variegation—for life outside the enclave—has begun to breathe; and that those among us hitherto denied full participation in the dream of success are, at this hour when wider access is offered, skeptical of its promises, too proud to fall into the role of snappers-up of considered trifles. Subtleized, complicated, "open to experience," human beings in numbers neither vast nor negligible appear disposed to shed the rung-to-rung, perch-to-perch, upward-ever-upward metaphor of life; their imaginations are loosened from power lust; their preoccupation is with "between," with the quality of moment-to-moment experience, with their own newness, their own curiosity, their decent liking and interest in people different from themselves. And these subtle "new people" are cried up by others, not alone by themselves.

Yet the chances of self-deception about their worth are extremely high. Openness means, just at the moment, proceeding without task definitions or effective guidance—despite a sort of nimbus of "goodness"—concerning honorable moral directions, and there is no rudder of projective intentionality within the life-experientialist sensibility. Consider, by way of amplification, the kind of figures who, at present, stand as embodiments of contemporary "un-driven" role-variousness. Judged for geniality, courtesy, capacity for bodying forth uncondescending effort by privilege and power to go to school to an underclass, more than one such figure deserves better than a chuckle. But who would deny that the marks of these figures are invariably aestheticism, fascination with the semi-genuine, the complaisance of the dabbler?

Success-religion was morally productive in its resistance to drift and in its nourishment of faith in destination: God died but intentionality survived—a purposefulness stern enough, when upright, to bear burdens of social responsibility without absurdist camp or mugging. Whether equal burdens can be borne by life-experimenters as connoisseurs, as motherhusbands, as wifefathers, as picaresque adventurers is unclear. The latter are key performers in the emergent cultural drama that has been described, but—like the slumming novelist and the absentee clerk—they do not know its theme; they do not know what they could make of themselves. And they cannot be taught by privileged Harvardians who perform as exercise boy or sparring partner, who wonder aloud (charmingly) at the rough diamonds discovered on every side, who hail the world briefly on camera and thereafter cut and run, self and scene unchanged.

The choice that matters, in sum, is a choice of theme, and the best advice concerning it remains that given by Dewey. This great man and his successors proposed that *work* must continue to be our theme—but that the task should be redefined as that of imagining and creating situations in which democratic experience, mobile, allusive, ceaselessly communicative, ceaselessly skill-sharing, becomes possible; the struggle before us becomes that of achieving democracy by bringing into being a genuinely democratic mind. Can we be aided by the culture heroes of the present hour, those who give themselves forth as "Serious" and "Committed," in defining and clarifying this theme?

Judged for independence, boldness, resolution and devotion to the interests of the weak, Ralph Nader places high; yet his characteristic posture is that of the crusader against evil; the situations the Raiders bend themselves to construct are invariably polarized: We against them, death or victory. Nor can the ranks of contemporary specialists in arbitration and negotiation produce a "model." The social conflicts of the past two decades have produced many new roles, brokers, facilitators, ombudsmen; the roles have been filled by men and women of outstanding quality, from Marian Wright to Mario Cuomo. But these are figures of crisis, managing sometimes to escape the morally neutral stance of the fixer, but seldom suggesting, through personality or strategy, a role continuity beyond "troubleshooting," or an awareness of the need for permanent bases—again, the "project for a century"—from which to extend consciousness of the ways in which the action of others gives point and direction to one's own.

We are at liberty to fantasize; we may tease ourselves with models of nobility to come. Grown from the American past, he or she must be a doer, naturally, a relisher of experience at every level, proof against the temptation to aestheticize experience (to strip it, that is, of moral-political dimensions), unaristocratic to the core (yet conscious that many senses of grace, familiar once only to the few at the bottom and the top, would not corrupt the polity if moved closer to the center of the general mind), skeptical of win-lose negotiations, an inventor and contriver, a tripper with a feeling for the continuity and long-term end of the human journeying, a patient, ingenious soul, product-conscious but in love—far gone in love!—with process. This he or she is to serve as spokesperson for the moral-political *uses* of variousness, is to appear to his fellows as "Doer of Molecular Democratic Deeds," is to—. . . But should we not cease defining and begin at once calling the new hero forth from the deep, promoting him, organizing his lobby?

Worse could be done—and better. The soundest labor will aim at this point, not at propagating fantasy, but at heightening understanding of the success-culture as itself a process, as a system of beliefs simultaneously struggling toward and repressing critical self-consciousness, inventing new possibilities and imperatives as it goes, exciting itself with orgies of vicariousness and with ideals of exalted aesthetico-moral sensitivity free of political involvements—that is, dreaming dreams that hide from it the human need for the directing coherence of the fully moralized project, the concrete long-term social goal. Sinning through sobriety, all self-containment and calculation, the success pilgrim whose skin will perhaps shortly be thrown lacked humor and sympathy, could not bear connection, could neither teach difference nor learn from it. But he was a pilgrim, and it could be fatal to neglect that truth; the man energized himself, kept up *quest* as a value long beyond its time.

And it must be kept up still longer. Our obligation is to step within the theater, carnival, circus of the present and gather it toward a meaning. First the recovery of belief that it can have meaning, that a line can be tossed to the lady in ripped jeans with the tiara—or to the Federal Reserve chairman digging a ditch, or the ghettoist romanticizing rats, or the pro-abortion nun running for Congress—that will save all from heady aimlessness or self-destructive despair. Next, hard labor at "process design," means of translating the ideal of "conjoint communicated experience" into deeds do-able day to day. And before and after, unceasingly, prayer that the smiling easy riders to come may themselves one day rise to be seekers.

Notes

1. Mario Cuomo, *Forest Hills: The Crisis of Low-Income Housing* (New York: Random House, 1974), pp. 98-99.

2. James Comer, *Beyond Black and White* (New York: Quadrangle, 1974), pp. 199-200.

3. John Hersey, *Letter to the Alumni* (New York: Knopf, 1971), p. 32.

# XV Ideologies, Myths, Moralities

Peter L. Berger

It may have been thought by many, at least until recently, that we were all born either little citizens of the Left or of the Right, and that this was a perfectly natural way for humanity to assort itself politically. That was before we entered the Age of Confusion, the Age of Anxiety, the Age of Discontinuity, the Postindustrial Age, the Age of Aquarius—in short, that was before today, when a great many people find it quite difficult to decide whether they wish to categorize themselves as liberal or conservative or radical, and when the categories of Left and Right keep changing political complexion, chameleon-like.

Nevertheless, as Professor Peter Berger points out, beyond such problematic dichotomies of Left and Right there is a real and permanent substance to these ideologies—if one views them as secular religions expressing certain fundamental "myths" of modern technological, mass civilization, and as defining political attitudes which derive from these "myths." But as modernity becomes disenchanted with its own "myths," and as ideologies fail to satisfy the impulses out of which they were born, the modern world finds itself having to learn to look at its own political reality in a new way.

The contemporary spectacle of political ideologies, in America as elsewhere, is bewildering indeed. It becomes even more bewildering if one attempts to relate the political programs and sympathies of the various ideological camps to the broad philosophies that supposedly inspire them. Thus, people who identify themselves as conservatives seem to owe ultimate allegiance to classically liberal views on economic and social matters. On the other hand, self-designated liberals habitually espouse socialist or semi-socialist programs that are in direct contradiction to the fundamental assumptions of classical liberalism. As to those who consider themselves socialists, much of their emotional if not intellectual energies seem to be invested in the admiration of exotic despotisms whose social systems are most adequately described in terms reminiscent of feudalism. What today is "on the left," what "on the right"? And what is the proper ideological designation of that "vital center" on which, reputedly, the political health of American society depends?

An observer trying to make sense of this spectacle has several options. He can try to bring order to the scene by imposing on it a "correct" ideological viewpoint. Efforts along these lines usually become arid scholastic exercises on just who is a "true conservative" or a "true socialist." The end result is often a set of reciprocal excommunications. Alternatively, the observer can simply discount the ideologies that people mouth and look instead at their "real interests." After all, as Marx pointed out long ago, every corner grocer is superior to most philosophers in knowing the difference between what people are and what they pretend to be. This procedure is more promising than the first. It is also more fun (especially if one enjoys baiting intellectuals). But it suffers from excessive cynicism. To be sure, there are "real interests" behind most ideological movements. But people are not motivated by such interests alone. At the very least they are *also* motivated by ideas, beliefs, values.

The course taken here is different from either of the preceding two. In what follows there will be no attempt to formulate a "correct" ideology, nor will ideologies be debunked as irrelevant. Rather, different ideological positions will be related to certain deeper impulses that underlie them—that is, they will be related to the level of *myth.* More specifically, different ideologies will be interpreted in terms of their relationship to the central *myths of modernity.* This course is chosen because of the belief that such a "mythological" perspective makes sense of the bewildering ideological scene in a way that is not only intellectually but also practically useful.

A word about the term "myth." It is not used in a pejorative way, but rather in the way that has been common in the social sciences since George Sorel. A "myth" in this sense is a deeply held set of beliefs that inspires people to social or political actions. The phrase "deeply held" in this definition should be stressed. It implies that what is involved here is not just intellectual persuasion. Myths have powerful emotional and even religious components. Myths, in the end, always seek to answer the old questions of how man is to live and how he may be redeemed. To relate ideologies to myths is not to brush aside the intellectual pretensions of the former. It is only to say that most people in the world are not terribly interested in intellectual questions, which means that politically successful ideologies (as against those that are discussed by small groups of intellectuals) must have more to offer. For example, Marx provided very interesting and highly sophisticated analyses of the world. Intellectuals have debated these for over a century. But the success of Marxism in inspiring large numbers of nonintellectuals in different places and at different times has very little to do with these analyses or these debates. Very, very few individuals have become Marxists as a result of studying *Das Kapital.* On the contrary, converts to Marxism have studied that thoroughly uninspiring book to give intellectual cohesion to the Marxist position they had already espoused. If one is to understand the conversion, therefore, one will be ill-advised to turn to a study of *Das Kapital.*

Modernity may be defined as a complex of social patterns based on the application of thoroughly rational methods to the solution of human problems. Max Weber, the classical German sociologist, has called "rationalization" the prime moving force of the recent era in world history. Its pervasive spirit marks all the new social constructions of this period, especially the major ones—the capitalist economy, the bureaucratic state, and the system of industrial production. Each of these represents a revolutionary "rationalization" in its particular sphere of influence. Each has brought forth types of men—entrepreneurs, administrators, engineers—who share an ethos of emphatic rationality. The application of this rationality to every conceivable area of human concern largely accounts, no doubt, for the historically unprecedented successes of modern institutions in transforming the world. Yet there are powerful myths inspiring even the most rationalist modernizers. Central among these is the *myth of progress.*

The key beliefs of this myth can be formulated as follows. Man is, above all, a rational animal. To the extent that he is not, he is to be made into one, by whatever educational programs appear plausible. There are, at least in principle, no individual or collective problems that cannot be solved by rational means. Indeed, where such problems seem to exist (as, for example, the ancient problems of death and of evil), rational analysis will show them to be spurious problems. The proper attitude toward all real problems, of the individual or of society, is rational understanding coupled with rational planning. This attitude had been nicely summarized by Auguste Comte, a prophet of the myth of progress if there ever was one, in the formula "to know in order to predict in order to control." Rationality of this kind is redeeming. The more men arrange their lives in its terms, the better and the freer they will be. Human history is given meaning by this drama of redemptive liberation from unreason. Human history, therefore, is a forward and upward movement. The culmination, up ahead somewhere, will be a truly reasonable and free human order. The moral imperative for each generation is to push further toward that goal.

This is obviously not the place to trace the historical sources of these beliefs. They were formed in an historically unique coming-together of two modes of human consciousness—the consciousness shaped by the Greco-Roman faith in reason, and the consciousness shaped by the Biblical faith in the purposiveness of temporal events and human history. Both faiths had to be transformed before they achieved their peculiar modern potency—the first "baptized" by the Christian Middle Ages, the second secularized in the Renaissance and the Enlightenment. Thus the myth of progress linked the faith in reason to highly optimistic expectations regarding human history which would have appeared very irrational indeed to a Greco-Roman mind. It derived these expectations from the Biblical faith in the God of history who will bring all things to their final culmination. This marriage between the faith in reason and the faith in history, however, was only accomplished by secularizing the second—that is, by elminating the God of history from the expectation of historical redemption. Since the myth of progress has found itself in a culture still heavily saturated with Christianity—and with Christians (albeit some very half-hearted ones)—its relation to the religious tradition of western culture has been uneasy.

Seen in the perspective of traditional Christianity—Latin or Greek, Catholic or Protestant (and, indeed, in the perspective of traditional Judaism)—the modern myth of progress is a heresy. At best, it could link up with some heterodox, partially subterranean doctrines of Christian provenance, such as those of medieval millenarianism or of the so-called left wing of the Reformation. The mainstream of Christian tradition could accept neither the belief in man's rationality nor the belief that this rationality is capable of achieving any sort of redemption. Christianity has always been pessimistic both about man and about his ability to construct his own history, and the (literally) godless optimism of the myth of progress clashed directly with the root proclamations of the Christian tradition.

It is perfectly understandable, therefore, that when the myth of progress was first propounded loudly and clearly—sometime between the late seventeenth and early eighteenth centuries—it was perceived as a dangerous enemy by the official guardians of the Christian tradition, which in turn, was so perceived by the major apostles of progress. Both groups, in terms of their respective universes of discourse, were correct in their perceptions. Voltaire was quite right in seeing the church as a major obstacle to the rational salvation he was preaching; he could only recommend to his contemporaries that they "destroy the infamous thing." The church was equally right in placing Voltaire's works on its Index of Prohibited Books. As Napoleon's armies carried the myth of progress on their bayonets across Europe, a rabbinical writer put the matter rather well: He opined that while Napoleon might be good for the Jews (the Napoleonic laws gave them full civil rights), he was very probably bad for Judaism.

This antagonism between the myth of progress and the religious tradition, however, was not everywhere as sharp. Broadly speaking, it was sharpest in France, erupting cataclysmically in the revolution of 1789 and continuing wherever that revolution was reenacted in one version or another both in Europe and in Latin America. The antagonism was generally much more muted in the Anglo-Saxon world. In the latter, the myth of progress emerged in a more moderate form—less radical, less violent, and less inimical to the religious tradition. The American revolution, unlike the French, was not anticlerical and was at least vaguely religious in its own rhetoric.

Still, the myth of progress was everywhere non-Christian, if not anti-Christian. Even with vague religious trappings, its basic inspiration was secular—a fact which makes for some serious difficulties. Every myth promises something. As long as a myth is based on a religious worldview, it can locate its promises in a realm beyond empirical verification. This is seen readily when the promises refer to another life, in another world. A secular myth, one that locates its promises in this life, in this world, is under inconvenient pressure to produce results. In light of this difficulty, it is remarkable to what degree the myth of progress has continued to be believable to large numbers of people.

The best explanation of this phenomenon is that the myth has, indeed, produced results and kept promises. Modernity, in other words, is anything but a record of disappointed expectations. At least some of its achievements are truly stupendous. The application of rational methods to human problems has, in fact, transformed the world, and to many people that transformation continues to seem benign. The prolongation of individual life spans, the long series of victories over disease and hunger, the astronomical increase in the capacity to satisfy material needs, the increase in the safety and comfort of everyday living, the extension of educational and cultural participation to the great majority and in some countries to virtually the entire population—all of these achievements constitute a record of promises made and kept. Nor is there much doubt that modernity has brought to the individual a vast increase in his range of options, and thus, in this sense at any rate, an increase in his freedom. From the beginning, modernity has meant the promise of a better life, if not for the individual then for his children. The myth of progress has been built around this promise. To a high degree, therefore, the continuing credibility of the myth has been due to its having been empirically verified in many individual biographies.

But, alas, nothing in history is achieved without costs. The costs of modernity have been great. The most important cost, on the level of individual experience, has been the condition which, since Marx, has come to be called "alienation." The imposition of rational methods upon every conceivable area of social life has dismantled many of the old structures within which men found collective solidarity and meaning. Pre-modern men everywhere lived in strong and comprehensive communities—of family, clan, tribe, village, guild. Modernization everywhere has meant the weakening if not destruction of these communities and their replacement by highly abstract, often remote and incomprehensible institutions. Modernizing ideologies—that is, ideologies emerging from the central myth of progress—have quite logically interpreted these transformations as liberations: The individual was freed, for instance, from the constraints of the family by modern education, and from the constraints of clan or village by the avenues of social mobility opened up by modern society. *But in becoming more free, he also became more solitary.* Increasingly, social experience came to be characterized by a very disturbing constellation—high individuation and a high degree of freedom from immediate constraints, and with this the overwhelming presence of vast, abstract institutions, which by their very nature are unsuited to provide a sense of community and of meaning.

Modernity has provided (not by design, needless to say) a kind of solution to this problem: It might be called *the invention of private life.* The social experience of the individual has been dichotomized as between two social spheres. There is the public sphere, in which he must come to terms with the abstractness and the anonymity of the great modern institutions—technology, the technologized economy, the bureaucratic state, and a network of subsidiary bureaucracies. This sphere provides little community and few satisfying meanings. But there is also the private sphere—the world of family, friends, voluntary associations, local affiliations, and personal hobbies. In this sphere, the individual is granted a very high degree of freedom—including the freedom to construct his own communities and his own meanings. For large numbers of people this solution has worked, and it continues to work. The trouble with it is that the abstract institutions of the public sphere are quite imperialistic: They keep pushing against the fragile boundaries of private life. Thus the educational system pushes against the family, voluntary associations grow and are bureaucratized, and corporations take over the pursuit of personal hobbies.

What is perhaps even more serious is that most people find it difficult to construct community and meaning without strong institutional supports. As a result, many families are greatly relieved if the school takes over their children, and many individuals are grateful if their hobbies come prepackaged by this or that branch of the "leisure-time industry." The solution to the problem of alienation offered by private life, therefore, has been precarious even where it has continued to work. It has generated psychological tensions, which in turn have led to political consequences: Ideological platforms and political programs have promised relief from these tensions—and some of them have been promised salvation from all forms of alienation.

To sum up the argument thus far: Different contemporary ideologies may be understood in terms of their relation to the myth of progress and to the discontents of modernity. Insofar as one of the chief sources for these discontents has been the lack of community and of integrative meanings for social life, different ideologies may be investigated in terms of the solutions they purport to offer to this problem. Some have tried to solve the problem within the framework of the myth of progress. Others have been ideologies of counter-modernization. Others yet, of course, have attempted various kinds of synthesis between modern and counter-modern themes.

Liberalism is the most direct ideological embodiment of the myth of progress and, by the same token, the closest to the spirit of modernity. Despite its miscellaneous transmutations, liberalism as a political creed still comes closer than any of its major rivals to the beliefs outlined previously as central to the myth of progress. Rationality, faith in the perfectability of man, faith in a sort of engineering attitude to both individual and collective problems, optimism about the course of history, and a strong moral sense about one's obligations to history—this "package" of beliefs, with their concomitant attitudes and even emotions, continues to be recognizably liberal. Very commonly there is among those who hold this creed a definite consciousness of being part of a tradition that goes back to the Enlightenment. In view of the period of time that has elapsed since then, it might be surprising that this is also a consciousness of being in the vanguard; a 250-year-old *avant-garde* somehow seems odd. If, however, one relates this consciousness to the socio-cultural complex of modernity as a whole, it becomes much more plausible. When modernity first emerged, liberalism was that political ideology that was "with it"; it is still "with it"—that is, with modernity. Logically enough, then, the crisis of modernity is felt most sharply in that ideological camp.

Ever since the eighteenth century, liberalism has been an international ideology. Even today, a village liberal from, say, Sweden can recognize his Latin American counterpart with a wink of shared conspiracy against their respective "rearguard" opponents. This sense of shared beliefs and attitudes cuts across the differences between what was previously designated as the French and Anglo-Saxon versions of the myth of progress. In other words, a visiting campus liberal from the Midwest could join the little recognition scene without too much trouble. The case of the United States, however, is unique in its relation to the liberal creed. While all the republics of the Western Hemisphere were created under the banner of liberalism, the United States is the only large society in the world in which there has been a pervasive and generally successful institutionalization of liberal ideology in every major societal sector. The "American creed," as political ideology and, beyond that, as a kind of civil religion, is not only the foundation of the political order: It permeates the class system, the educational system, the web of voluntary associations, and, to an amazing degree, ordinary everyday life. The phrase "it's a free country," tossed out in some casual encounter, is very often a genuine appeal to the liberal creed that should not be dismissed as just a manner of speaking.

American liberalism has gone through some very interesting changes in this century, including some paradoxical ones. The greatest paradox dates from the New Deal and lies in the increasingly "statist" orientation of the liberal camp. Classical liberalism sought the liberation of social life from the constraining embrace of what was then called the absolute state; twentieth century liberalism has increasingly sought to impose state controls on every conceivable area of social life in order to foster its notions about a better society. This particular permutation cannot be pursued here. But there is another change that is important to look at here, and this is the increasing failure of liberalism to inspire. In the context of the present argument, this could be called the *mythological deprivation* of liberalism. It means, quite simply, that liberalism's programs increasingly fail to activate the deeper levels of human motivation.

This phenomenon makes better sense if it is related to the affinity between liberalism and modernity. In its basic thrust, liberalism is committed to the great modern institutions of the public sphere—the market, the state, the educational system, and so forth. In other words, it is committed precisely to those vast abstract entities that are the root cause of the contemporary sense of alienation. *Liberalism has no real message for private life.* Its attitude toward private life is, essentially, that it should be left alone, for the individual to manage as best he can. While this attitude has of late been in some tension with the "statist" trend, it is still quite vital. Liberals continue to have a serious commitment to the protection of private freedoms against encroachment by large public institutions. Now, this laissez-faire attitude works well as long as private life is given structure and meaning from other sources—religion, the family, folk or ethnic subcultures, and the like. The crisis of modernity, however, is precisely the fact that these other sources are in danger of drying up. *The liberal political order itself depends upon the continuing viability of these other structures—yet these are structures that liberalism has tended to be uninterested in and, in some instances, has even tended to oppose as narrow or "backward."*

A prime example of this peculiar dilemma of liberalism—and of its peculiar blindess vis-à-vis this dilemma—is in the area of educational policy. The public school, a prime symbol of liberal ideology, was probably a marvelous instrument as long as it was grounded in other, less abstract, indeed less modern social realities. Today, when these other realities have greatly weakened, the public school is above all an instrumentality of alienation. Yet liberals, in their unshaking devotion to abstract institutions, continue to push for ever more comprehensive, vast, and communally detached public school systems. The abstract schemes of racial integration worked out by a liberal judiciary are only one of many such policies (and, incidentally, one of the more salutary shocks to liberals has been the increasing reluctance of the alleged beneficiaries in the black community to be enthusiastic about these schemes). The debate over prayer in the public schools illustrates even more sharply the failure of liberals to understand the relation between an abstract institutional order and its concrete, communal substratum. In all likelihood, the future of liberalism as a political ideology depends upon its ability to grasp this point. It is also likely that liberal politicians will do so much earlier than liberal intellectuals.

Classical conservatism in Europe was, above all, a counter-modernizing ideology. Both on the level of intellectual theories (by authors like Bossuet or Burke) and of political action, conservatism meant upholding the old banners of communal solidarity against the onslaught of modern institutions—certainly the modern state, and, just as much, the modern market economy. Thus, classical conservatism was as much anti-capitalist as it was anti-"statist." It correctly perceived the capitalist economy and the centralized state (in whatever degree of democratization) as inimical to the communal traditions that it held dear. By the same token, classical conservatism was antibourgeois, culturally as well as politically. Again correctly, it perceived the bourgeoisie as the modernizing class *par excellence*—and it detested all its works. Thus, old European conservatism was rooted in all those classes that were least affiliated with the modernizing processes set loose by the bourgeoisie, and was most importantly rooted in aristocratic and in peasant settings. Everywhere conservatism was counter-modern in holding concrete loyalties against abstract ones—loyalties, that is, to the "small platoons" (a phrase of Burke's) of local community, region, church, and family against the vast institutional formations of modern society. It would be misleading to say that this conservatism defended the private against the public, because the very dichotomy of the two spheres is a specifically modern invention. Rather, conservatism intuitively defended every social form that maintained or promised to restore the premodern unity of public and private life. The enormous strength of the forces of modernity made conservatism lose most of these battles.

It is helpful to become attentive to a simple historical fact: This type of conservatism, at least since the defeat of the South in the Civil War, has been marginal in America. Nor is there any great mystery as to the reasons for this. American society was a bourgeois affair from the beginning, and thus a modernizing one. Seymour Lipset's description of the United States as the "first new nation" is singularly appropriate in pointing to this fact. There were simply no indigenous aristocracies or peasantries against which the bourgeois order had to be set up. Premodern social and cultural patterns were transplanted from Europe, but they lost much of their strength in the process. A "Little Italy," for instance, is much less resistant to modernization than a Sicilian village. The efforts to create indigenous aristocracies, with the possible exception of parts of the Old South, were short-lived and not very convincing. To this day, what passes as aristocracy in America is really a plutocracy—that is, it is wealthy bourgeois playing at being aristocrats. Needless to say, no one tried to create indigenous peasantries.

This historical fact has an important ideological corollary: Measured by the yardstick of classical European conservatism, *the contemporary American ideology of conservatism is deeply and unmistakably liberal in inspiration.* It adheres to all the classically liberal affirmations, very clearly so in the economic area. It is committed to bourgeois democracy, to capitalism, and to the nation-state; indeed, in the last commitment it tends to be vehemently nationalistic. What goes today under the heading of struggles between liberals and conservatives is, in an historical perspective, a family quarrel within the liberal camp. This also means that contemporary American conservatism has deep commitments to the myth of progress, as is becoming rather dramatically clear these days in the celebrations of the upcoming bicentennial of the

American revolution. The actual antagonism between liberals and conservatives today has its focus on the "statist" trend within liberalism, a trend to which conservatives are strongly opposed. In an historical perspective again, this antagonism could be accurately described as being between old-style and new-style liberals.

This commonality between American conservatives and liberals (a *liberal* commonality, that is) is brought into sharp focus when American conservatives are confronted by a representative of classical European conservatism. Since the latter species is fast dying out, such confrontations are rare events. But a few years ago such a confrontation did take place, when William Buckley invited Otto von Habsburg to his television program. Buckley seemed genuinely puzzled by his guest's attitude of detached tolerance toward socialism, for instance. From a classical conservative point of view, of course, socialism is in the same bag with such other modern concoctions as capitalism, liberal democracy, and nationalism—all basically deplorable phenomena, with which an intelligent man must make a regretful accommodation.

This is not said in order to depreciate the contemporary conservative critique of liberal programs, which is very real in many instances. But it is important to see the wide range of assumptions held in common by both sides in this family quarrel. There is no comparison at all, for example, between current conservative/liberal issues in America and the issues that divided the two camps during the Third Republic in France, or even that divide some Latin American countries today. The American political and ideological scene continues to be dominated by a far-reaching family consensus. Recent challenges to this consensus have mainly come from the Left rather than the Right. One result of these challenges has been that, in the last decade, many old-style and new-style liberals (if these terms may be used now) have become more conscious of their commonality. By the same token, however, American conservatism has participated in the credibility crisis of the myth of progress and has been less than helpful in clarifying the underlying crisis of modernity. At best, American conservatives have shown greater sensitivity than liberals to communal and subcultural resistances to the abstract structures of modernity.

A brief comment on fascism: The use of the generic term with a small "f" (as against Fascism in Mussolini's Italy) has become so confused that it might be best to abandon it. The Marxist theory of fascism as an organic outgrowth of bourgeois capitalism is hopelessly at odds with the historical facts (the movements designated "fascist" in this theory were everywhere anti-capitalist in ideology, even though they frequently made accommodations with capitalists). But the common liberal perception of fascism as being a "right-wing" phenomenon is almost as misleading. One may question the usefulness of subsuming under one category such discrepant phenomena as the Nazi revolution in Germany (it *was* a revolution, social as well as political) and the counterrevolutionary Falange in Spain. If one allows this usage, however, it is clear that fascism generically was certainly not a conservative ideology and can only precariously be located "on the right." Indeed, the Falange is probably the only important case where this description has a good deal of plausibility. Mussolini was vociferous in his denunciations of bourgeois capitalism along with bourgeois democracy, but he was also self-consciously modern, antitraditional, and more than a little anticlerical. And Hitler was not just engaged in verbal camouflage when he called his movement the German National *Socialist Workers'* Party.

If the generic term "fascism" means anything at all beyond a term of abuse, then fascism as an ideology is the elevation of nationalism to the level of a quasi-religion. The nation, typically through the mediation of the authoritarian nation-state as managed by the ideologically inspired movement or party, becomes a redemptive community. In this salvific formula, fascism is very similar to the salvation doctrines of ideological socialism. The similarity is rooted in the way in which the crisis of modernity is to be overcome: *An overarching community, organized by the state, is posited in order to overcome the dichotomy of public and private spheres.* This national and political community is to allow the individual to overcome his alienations and to find the meanings necessary for social life. In view of the marginality of anything that could be called fascism in contemporary America, however, it would seem more profitable to look at this formula in its "left" rather than "right" version.

There exist socialist ideologies, of course, which can best be understood as amplifications of liberalism. This type of "liberal socialism" (represented by the bulk of Social Democracy in Europe) only deepens the egalitarian component of the liberal creed and adds the belief that the public ownership of the basic means of production is desirable or necessary for the attainment of liberal goals. "Mythologically" speaking, this type of socialism relates to the myth of progress and to the spirit of modernity very much in the way liberalism does—and it has similar problems of credibility. Indeed, if the term "mythological deprivation" fits anyone today, it fits European Social Democrats.

It is the more radical types of socialism, especially those emanating from the Marxist tradition, which are more interesting from a "mythological" point of view. For what these are, at bottom, is *an ingenious synthesis between the myth of progress and its counter-myths, between modernity and the very impulses that resist modernity.* It is in this synthesis that the peculiar appeal of radical socialism, and especially of Marxism, should be sought. It is the appeal of having one's cake and eating it too.

On the one hand, Marxism is identified completely with the myth of progress. Even more than liberalism, it has faith in history moving toward a great culmination and it inspires people with a moral sense of participation in this process. Even more than liberalism, Marxism has faith in the perfectibility of man and in the possibility of bringing this about by the application of rationality to human affairs. In Marx's own work one finds hymns of praise to modern industry. One also finds, over and over again, the insistence that the ideology being propounded is a *scientific* socialism, as against the unscientific ("utopian") socialisms of an earlier period. Marxist theory is supposed to be a science, Marxist practice a kind of political technology.

On the other hand, however, Marxism also appeals precisely to the mythic themes that are opposed to progress and modernity. Those are the themes of community, of collective solidarity, of meanings that can overcome and reintegrate the fragmented parts of modern social existence. The Marxist vision holds up a future society in which all alienation will be overcome, in which even the division of labor and the coercive power of the state will be overcome. Precisely because modernity (which Marx identified with capitalism) stresses individuality, Marxism stresses the collective. Man is a collective being, Marx insisted, and modern individuation is one of the symptoms of alienation. In all these themes, there are unmistakably counter-modern tonalities, which bear a striking resemblance to the counter-modernizing ideologies of classical conservatism. In both cases, the counter-vision is one of an essentially bucolic harmony, pre-modern and virtually medieval in its imagery. It is instructive, for example, to compare the polemics against industrial capitalism of, respectively, Friedrich Engels, Marx's friend and collaborator, who wrote a very influential book on the English working class, and John Calhoun, who, in his defense of the Southern way of life, took pleasure in detailing the degradations of New England slums. Engels and Calhoun not only resemble each other in that they are both against the same things—namely, industrial capitalism and bourgeois society—but also in the pastoral idylls they evoke in contrast with the evils of the status quo.

The decisive difference between classical conservatism and Marxism, of course, is that the former seeks its counter-modern symbols in the past, while the latter projects them into the future. Marxism promises both progress and redemptive community. It promises to alleviate the discontents of modernity by very modern means. This is a great strength as long as Marxists are in an opposition movement; it becomes a great weakness the moment they obtain positions of power, for the simple reason that the promise cannot be kept under modern conditions.

A revolutionary movement, especially if it is engaged in heroic struggles against a powerful enemy, can very often provide its members with a strong sense of redemptive community. Individuals who become affiliated with such movements repeatedly testify to the experience of having their lives suffused with new meaning, of being freed from the alienation and anxiety of their earlier existence. A very important feature of this experience is overcoming the typically modern breach between public and private roles. In the revolutionary community this breach is healed and individuals suddenly experience themselves as *whole* in an exhilarating way. If and when a revolutionary movement succeeds, however, it is compelled to run a society by mechanisms that, at least under modern conditions, restore the very conditions from which redemption was sought. Marxism prophesies the disappearance of alienating division of labor and of coercive state power in the truly socialist society (in Marxist terms, after the "transition from socialism to communism"). "In the meantime," alas, people have to put up with very different kinds of conditions.

A history of Marxism in terms of the way in which different branches of the movement have dealt with this dilemma between modern imperatives and counter-modern promises remains to be written. In the central Marxist stream, as embodied in Soviet Marxism and in the Communist parties oriented toward it, the "scientific" component has tended to outweigh the "redemptive" component—with the result that in these groups there has taken place rather massive "mythological deprivations." Very few people who are at a safe distance from Soviet bayonets are much inspired today by the ideological proclamations coming out of Moscow. The Marxisms that are popular in the American Left today are of a different kind. The three major types are, probably in descending order of importance, the New Left, Maoism, and Trotskyism. There are important differences among them, particularly between the first and the other two, but they have one important characteristic in common: They are efforts to revivify the old Marxist synthesis between progress and community by stressing redemption rather than "science." Prophecy, once more, takes precedence over engineering.

The counter-modernizing themes are particularly visible in the New Left, which has discovered strong ideological affinities with youth-culture and counter-cultural groups vehemently hostile to modernity. It is by no means accidental that one of these affinities has been the wish to overcome the dichotomy between public and private life, a wish at least partially realized in some contemporary communes. Individualism and privacy, it is proclaimed (and the perception is quite correct), are "bourgeois hangups." By contrast, "liberation" is the collectivization of both social existence and self. The opposition to the liberal creed is crystal-clear at this point: Liberalism understood liberation as a delivery *from collective bonds to individual autonomy*. The new liberation of socialist and counter-cultural ideologies is understood as a delivery *from individual autonomy to collective solidarity*. In other words, what is freedom on one side of this ideological divide is bondage on the other, and vice versa.

To sum up the above argument: Different ideologies relate differently to modernity and its central myth of progress. Liberalism is related most directly to both. Ideologies of the "right" and of the "left" embody counter-modernizing impulses in various ways, all designed to cope somehow with the discontents of modern society. But modern and counter-modern themes cut across the ideological divides. The main contention of the present argument is this: While the contemporary ideological scene can be analyzed in a number of ways, one very useful way is to do so in terms of the modern/counter-modern alignments. In many instances such a procedure brings more light to the scene than an analysis in terms of conventional categories, e.g., "right"/"left," capitalist/socialist, democratic/totalitarian. Some contemporary examples may help to make this point.

The black upsurge in America over the last decade has been perceived, by different observers, as belonging to just about every segment of the "right"/ "left" ideological spectrum. Liberals first perceived it as the noblest expression of their own ideals, but were subsequently puzzled and disturbed by tonalities that sounded anything but liberal. In the late 1960s, American radicals pinned their major revolutionary hopes on the black movement and neo-Marxist theorists went to some trouble trying to show that blacks constituted the true proletariat (as against the white working class that had consistently rejected their overtures). More recently, both liberals and Marxists, disillusioned with their black allies *manqués*, have sometimes concluded that American black national-ism is but another variety of fascism. And blacks seem to have had comparable difficulties in defining their own position along the ideological spectrum.

When a group has grievances as real as those of American blacks, any ideology that promises relief is likely to have a measure of success. Thus, no theory about the discontents of modernity or of "mythological deprivation" is required to explain why American blacks have come to rebel against their situation: Their discontents have a very concrete basis and their deprivations have been harshly realistic. All the same, the choice of ideologies is instructive. And as the black movement has developed in recent years, an instructive change may be observed in terms of the modern/counter-modern dilemma. The early civil rights move-ment was clearly and unambiguously liberal in inspiration, *ipso facto* moderniz-ing in intent. The desired "integration" of the black was not just into white society, but into the structures of progress and modernity from which he had been previously excluded. Once more, liberation was from collective constraints to individual autonomy. The rights sought were rights of the liberated *individ-ual*—"irrespective of race, color or creed." In other words, this liberation was based on the specifically modern doctrine of man as essentially an abstract entity—abstracted, that is, from any collective identifications. Real humanity is neither white nor black—nor does it have any other collective identification.

What emerged subsequently as the new black nationalism was animated by altogether different notions. Individualism, far from being a value, was now put down as a white pathology. Liberation could only be collective—and, increas-ingly, it included liberation *from* a white-inspired individualism *to* a collective black solidarity. The wholeness of social experience and self was again defined in essentially pre-modern terms. Seen in this way, it is hardly surprising that recent black nationalism has identified with Third World symbols. It is not just because American blacks feel oppressed in the way that Third World peoples are believed to be oppressed. It is also because the Third World stands for alternatives, however vaguely defined, to the structures of modern society. It is precisely for these reasons that the counter-culture has identified with the Third World as well. The paradox that this same Third World is, on the whole, trying desperately to modernize, need not arrest us here.

This modern/counter-modern dilemma continues to divide the American black community and its political expressions. *Everyone* today talks about "liberation." It is, therefore, very useful to know *which of the two liberations* any particular spokesman is talking about. By and large, they are diametrically opposed to each other. A number of policy issues will remain hopelessly confused unless this particular dilemma is clarified, put on the table.

The same dilemma has reappeared in the feminist movement. Again, everyone talks about the liberation of women, but this means contradictory things to different people. There is a large segment of the feminist movement that is liberal and modernizing in exactly the manner in which this could be said of the civil rights movement. Women are to be liberated from the collective constraints imposed on them by their "sex roles." Women's rights are the rights of individuals—"irrespective of race, color, creed, *or sex.*" Again, there is the specifically modern doctrine of abstract humanity: What an individual truly is cannot be defined in terms of any concrete social categorization—which is now extended to include biological categories as well. Put differently, all collective identities are fictitious and alienating; only the individual is real.

And, once again, another branch of the feminist movement has emerged, comparable to black nationalism, which is marked by a very different spirit. Feminity is celebrated instead of being declared irrelevant. "Integration" is rejected: Female is "beautiful." The solidarity of sisterhood replaces the quest for individual rights; indeed, as in the black case, the latter is perceived as a betrayal of the collective cause. The autonomy of the individual against the group is understood as male pathology—just as, in other contexts, it has been defined as white or bourgeois pathology. Individual autonomy, equated with alienation, is precisely that *from which* liberation is sought. However confused the formulations in this branch of the movement sometimes are, it is this understanding of liberation that comes out very clearly. It is very definitely a counter-modernizing understanding—if one wills, a new form of "tribalism." Moreover, it is on the basis of this neo-"tribalism" that otherwise discrepant ideological groups have recognized each other as kindred souls—New Left radicals, counter-culturists, black nationalists, feminists, and others (such as many of those finding redemptive meaning in the ecology movement and in various oriental sects). It is important to understand that this sense of underlying kinship is essentially based on a correct perception. By the same token, it is to be taken seriously.

It is a commonplace that policy options involve moral options. Different ideologies, however, lead to different moralities. There is no ideology that does not claim for itself the moral dignity of promoting human freedom and justice. What these values mean, though, depends to a large extent on the aforementioned alignment in terms of modern and counter-modern positions.

Should the moral intention of policy be to promote the liberty of the individual *against* collective groupings, or should it be to define liberty *in terms of* such groupings?

Is justice to be accorded to the individual "irrespective of race, color . . . " or any other collective identification, or should justice be accorded to collectivities?

Is policy to protect the modern dividing lines between public order and private life, or should it seek to integrate the two spheres in some overarching unity?

Obviously, these questions can ultimately be dealt with only in philosophical terms. Equally obviously, this cannot be done here. Only one word of caution on this: Wherever one may wish to place oneself with regard to these questions, one will be well-advised not to dismiss the other side too easily.

Thus those who, in the end, wish to affirm the values and the morality of modernity should be aware of the great costs that such a decision will entail. And those who identify with this or that version of the counter-modernizing impulse will be wise to remember that even moderate modifications of modernity will exact costs as well. There is no easy solution to this dilemma.

For practical purposes, in any case, the ideological options in America are limited. Barring vast and (happily) unlikely cataclysms, American society will continue to be modern, capitalist, bourgeois—and essentially liberal in its political creed. Counter-modernizing movements are likely to be encapsulated in sectarian subcultures or to become greatly moderated as they are socially accepted. Ideologies of redemptive revolution, "left" or "right," are likely to remain marginal in the political spectrum for the foreseeable future. Conservatism of the classical European type, as against the "old liberalism" of what commonly passes for conservatism in America, is unlikely to develop beyond small coteries of intellectuals.

All this adds up to a simple political fact: *The politically practical options will all be within the ideological ambience of the liberal "family."* This is not necessarily said in a partisan fashion. Whatever reservations one may have about the beliefs and assumptions of liberal ideology, there is no viable alternative to it in contemporary America. Even the skeptic should be capable of recognizing the considerable humane values represented by the liberal tradition, especially when they are compared with the ideological monstrosities that dominate much of the world beyond the American borders. Even the skeptic may, at the point of this comparison, develop a good measure of enthusiasm concerning the protection of this liberal heritage. He may also, of course, want to modify it at certain points, within the limits of what is realistically possible.

Politically viable ideologies, therefore, are likely to be reformulations and reapplications of the old "American creed." One major test of such reconstructions will be their capacity to deal with the central paradox of modernity—the confrontation of highly "rationalized" social structures and highly individuated persons. The old liberal formulas and programs are increasingly unable to deal with the alienation brought on by this confrontation. If individual freedom is to survive in modern society, the old formulas will have to be modified and some very new programs will have to be conceived.

In principle, there is reason to be optimistic about this possibility within the framework of the "American creed," which has shown itself to be, very probably, the most flexible ideological framework in recent human history. A renewal of respect for the concrete structures that give meaning (including mythical meaning) to the life of the individual—structures of family, church, neighborhood, ethnic group—will have to be an ingredient of all such new programs. In other words, the liberal ideology will have to cure itself of its penchant for abstraction and cultivate a new understanding of all the "small platoons" on which a liberal political order depends for its very survival.

Index

Index

About the Authors

Irving Kristol is the Henry Luce Professor of Urban Values at New York University and co-editor of *The Public Interest* magazine. In the past, he has been editor of such magazines as *Commentary, Encounter* (which he co-founded) and *The Reporter*. A prolific author, Professor Kristol published a collection of his essays, entitled *On the Democratic Idea in America*, in 1972.

Paul H. Weaver is associate editor of *Fortune* magazine. His writings cover American politics, government, the press and business. He is a former Assistant Professor of Government at Harvard University and was associate editor of *The Public Interest* magazine.

Martin Diamond is now Professor of Political Science at Northern Illinois University. He has recently held fellowships at the Woodrow Wilson International Center for Scholars and the National Humanities Institute at Yale University. In addition to many articles on the political thought of America's Founding Fathers, his publications include *The Democratic Republic* (with Winston M. Fisk and Herbert Garfinkel) and *The 1930's: A Reconsideration* (with Morton J. Frisch).

Daniel Patrick Moynihan is the United States Permanent Representative to the United Nations. He served as Assistant Secretary of Labor from 1963 to 1965, Counselor to the President from 1969 to 1971, and Ambassador to India from 1973 to 1975. He is Professor of Government at Harvard University. He is co-author of *Beyond the Melting Pot* and author of *The Politics of a Guaranteed Income* and *Coping: Essays in the Practice of Government*.

Sheila M. Rothman is Research Associate at the Center for Policy Research in New York City. She has edited, with David J. Rothman, *On Their Own: The Poor in Modern America* and *Sources of the American Social Tradition*. She is currently completing a book, *Social Policy and Social History: The Case of Women, Children and the Family* and is at work with David J. Rothman on a history of incarceration and its alternatives in twentieth century America.

James Q. Wilson is the Henry Lee Shattuck Professor of Government at Harvard University, where he has taught since 1961. He has served as chairman of the National Advisory Commission for Drug Abuse Prevention and chairman of a White House Task Force on Crime; he is currently vice chairman of the board of directors of the Police Foundation. His most recent book, *Thinking About Crime*, was published in 1975.

Marcus Cunliffe is Professor of American Studies at the University of Sussex. He was a visiting professor of American History at Harvard University and a fellow at the Center for Advanced Study in Behavioral Sciences at Stanford. Among his books are *Soldiers and Civilians: The Martial Spirit in America 1775-1865, American Presidents and the Presidency*, and *George Washington, Man and Monument*.

Mortimer J. Adler is director of the Institute for Philosophical Research, which he founded in 1952. He is associate editor of Encyclopaedia Britannica's *Great Books of the Western World* and co-editor of *Great Ideas Today* and *Gateway to the Great Books*. He invented and edited the *Syntopicon*, to which he contributed 102 essays on the great ideas of Western civilization. He is now chairman of the Board of Editors of Encyclopaedia Britannica and honorary trustee of the Aspen Institute for Humanistic Studies, where he conducts executive seminars during the summer months.

Robert Coles is a research psychiatrist to the Harvard University Health Services. His multivolume *Children of Crises*, a study of the effect of social stress on children, won a 1973 Pulitzer Prize for nonfiction, as well as the Four Freedoms award and the Phi Beta Kappa Ralph Waldo Emerson award. His other books include: *Dead End School, Still Hungry in America, The Image Is You, Uprooted Children, Drugs and Youth*, and *Erik H. Erikson: The Growth of His Work*.

Nathan Glazer is Professor of Education and Social Structure at Harvard University and co-editor of *The Public Interest* magazine. He is the author of *American Judiasm*, and co-author of *The Lonely Crowd* and *Beyond the Melting Pot*. His newest book, *Affirmative Discrimination*, was published in January.

Thomas Sowell is Professor of Economics at the University of California at Los Angeles, and a fellow of the Hoover Institution and the American Enterprise Institute. He is the author of *Economics: Analysis and Issues, Black Education: Myths and Tragedies, Say's Law: An Historical Analysis, Classical Economics Reconsidered,* and *Race and Economics.*

Philip Selznick is a Professor of Sociology at the University of California at Berkeley. In 1961, he founded and for many years was chairman of the Center for the Study of Law and Society. Among his many writings on law and sociology are *Law, Society and Industrial Justice, Leadership in Administration, TVA and the Grass Roots, The Organizational Weapon*, and *Sociology: A Text with Adapted Readings* (with L. Broom).

Donald Fleming is the Jonathan Trumbull Professor of American History at Harvard University. Since 1973, he has been director of the Charles Warren Center for Studies in American History. He is the author of *John William Draper and the Religion of Science* and *William H. Welch and the Rise of Modern Medicine.*

Bayless Manning is president of the Council on Foreign Relations. Formerly dean of the Stanford Law School, law professor, special assistant to former Under Secretary of State George Ball, and practicing lawyer, he has specialized in problems of legal education, corporate law, and international trade and investment. He has been a consultant and task force member for a variety of federal, state, and local governmental agencies and is the author of books and articles on law, foreign policy, and other public affairs issues.

Wilson Carey McWilliams is Professor of Political Science at Livingston College, Rutgers University. He received his Ph.D. at the University of California at Berkeley and has previously taught at Oberlin College and Brooklyn College. He is the author of *The Idea of Fraternity in America.*

Benjamin DeMott is Professor of English at Amherst College. A columnist for the *Atlantic Monthly* magazine, Dr. DeMott is the author of *Scholarship for Society*, published in 1974, and *Surviving the '70's*, published in 1971, several volumes of essays, and the novel *The Married Man* (1968).

Peter L. Berger is a Professor of Sociology at Rutgers University. He is the author of *Pyramids of Sacrifice: Political Ethics and Social Change*, and co-author (with Brigitte Berger and Hansfried Kellner) of *The Homeless Mind—Modernization and Consciousness.*

101313

DATE DUE